Religion and Social in Africa

Religion has played a major role in both the division and unification of peoples and countries within Africa. Its capacity to cause, and to heal, societal rifts has been well documented. This book addresses this powerful societal force and explores the implications of a theology of reconstruction, most notably articulated by Jesse N. K. Mugambi. This way of thinking seeks to build on liberation theology, aiming to encourage the rebuilding of African society on its own terms.

An international panel of contributors brings an interdisciplinary perspective to the issues around reconstructing the religious elements of African society. Looking at issues of reconciliation, postcolonialism, and indigenous spirituality, among others, they show that Mugambi's cultural and theological insight has the potential to revolutionize the way people in Africa address this issue.

This is a fascinating exploration of the religious facets of African life. As such, it will be of great interest to scholars of religious studies, theology, and African studies.

Elias Kifon Bongmba is Harry and Hazel Chavanne Chair in Christian Theology and Professor of Religion at Rice University. He is author of *The Dialectics of Transformation in Africa*. He is Managing Editor of *Religious Studies Review*, and President of the African Association for the Study of Religion.

Studies in World Christianity and Interreligious Relations
Series Editor: Frans Wijsen, Radboud University, The Netherlands

The aim of this series is to publish scholarly works of high merit on relations between believers of various streams of Christianity, as well as relations between believers of Christianity and other religions. We welcome studies from all disciplines, including multi- and interdisciplinary studies, which focus on intra- and inter-religious relations and are non-denominational.

The Decline of Established Christianity in the Western World
Interpretations and Responses
Edited by Paul Silas Peterson

Religion and Social Reconstruction in Africa
Edited by Elias Kifon Bongmba

For more information about this series, please visit: www.routledge.com/religion/series/WCIR

Religion and Social Reconstruction in Africa

Edited by Elias Kifon Bongmba

Routledge
Taylor & Francis Group
LONDON AND NEW YORK

First published 2018 by Routledge

2 Park Square, Milton Park, Abingdon, Oxfordshire OX14 4RN
52 Vanderbilt Avenue, New York, NY 10017

Routledge is an imprint of the Taylor & Francis Group, an informa business

First issued in paperback 2020

British Library Cataloguing-in-Publication Data
A catalogue record for this book is available from the British Library

Library of Congress Cataloging-in-Publication Data
Names: Bongmba, Elias Kifon, 1953– editor.
Title: Religion and social reconstruction in Africa / edited by Elias Kifon Bongmba.
Other titles: Studies in world Christianity and interreligious relations.
Description: New York, NY : Routledge, 2018. | Series: Studies in world Christianity and interreligious relations | Includes bibliographical references and index.
Identifiers: LCCN 2018011014 | ISBN 9780815348283 (hardback : alk. paper) | ISBN 9781351167406 (ebook)
Subjects: LCSH: Christianity—Africa. | Church and social problems—Africa. | Christianity and other religions—Africa. | Mugambi, J. N. Kanyua.
Classification: LCC BR1360 .R46 2018 | DDC 261.096—dc23
LC record available at https://lccn.loc.gov/2018011014

ISBN: 978-0-8153-4828-3 (hbk)
ISBN: 978-0-367-58993-6 (pbk)

Typeset in Sabon
by Apex CoVantage, LLC

Essays in honor of
Professor Jesse Ndwiga Kanyua Mugambi
Ph.D., FKNAS, EBS
University of Nairobi,
Department of Philosophy and Religious Studies
In recognition of your Scholarship and Leadership in
African Theology and Religious Studies

Contents

Notes on contributors

Rev. Prof. David Tuesday Adamo, author of several publications, is Professor of Biblical Studies and the Hebrew Bible in the Department of Religious Studies, Kogi State University, Anyigba, Nigeria. He is a Research Fellow at University of South Africa and The University of Stellenbosch, South Africa.

Elias Kifon Bongmba is Harry and Hazel Chavanne Chair in Christian Theology and Professor of Religion at Rice University. He is author of *The Dialectics of Transformation in Africa*. He is Managing Editor of *Religious Studies Review*, and President of the African Association for the Study of Religion.

Jonathan Bonk is Mission Research Professor at Boston University, and Founding Director of the Dictionary of African Christian Biography.

Ntozakhe Simon Cezula is Lecturer of Old Testament in the Faculty of Theology, Stellenbosch University, South Africa, with a research focus on Theology of Reconstruction. His latest publication is "Waiting for the Lord: The Fulfilment of the Promise of Land in the Old Testament as a Source of Hope" in *Scriptura*, 2017.

James R. Cochrane, PhD, DDiv h.c., Emeritus Professor Religious Studies and Senior Research Associate, Public Health and Family Medicine, University of Cape Town, co-directs the International/African Religious Health Assets Programme and convenes the Leading Causes of Life Initiative. Cochrane has authored about 150 essays and articles. His most recent book is *The Human Spirit: Groundwork* (with Douglas McGaughey).

John Fischer, Ph.D, University of Western Cape, currently teaches at Vineyard School of Ministry Africa and serves a Vineyard Church in Cape Town. His goal in missions in Leadership Development. He is author of "Perceptions on Possessions: A Comparison of African and Western Views on Material Possessions."

Enoch Olujide Gbadegesin earned his Ph.D. in Religion from Rice University, Houston Texas in 2014. Gbadegesin has coedited a book with

Yunusa K. Salami and Kola Abimbola titled: *Ethics of Individualism and Communitarianism: Multidisciplinary Essays* published by Harvest Day Publisher, MD, US 2006.

Franz Gmainer-Pranzl, Dr. theol., Dr. phil., born 1966 in Steyr (Austria), Studies (Theology, Philosophy) in Linz, Innsbruck and Vienna, Professor and Director of the Center for Intercultural Theology and Study of Religions at the University of Salzburg.

Knut Holter is professor of Old Testament studies in Vid Specialized University, Stavanger (Norway). He has authored and edited a number of books on Old Testament interpretation and African biblical hermeneutics, and is currently directing a project on the Maasai and the Bible.

Laurenti Magesa is a priest of the Catholic Diocese of Musoma in Tanzania. He teaches African Theology at Hekima University College Jesuit School of Theology in Nairobi, Kenya. He is the author of many articles and several books, including *What Is Not Sacred? African Spirituality* (NY: Orbis 2013).

Loreen Maseno is a Senior Lecturer, Department of Religion, Theology and Philosophy, Maseno University, Kenya. Currently, she is a Humboldt Research Fellow, University of Bayreuth, Germany.

Madipoane Masenya (Ngwan'a Mphahlele) is Professor of Old Testament Studies in the Department of Biblical and Ancient Studies at the University of South Africa, Pretoria, South Africa. Her book, *How Worth is the Woman of Worth? Rereading Proverbs 31:10–31* has been published by Peter Lang in New York, US.

John S. Mbiti is a Theologian, writer, and Bible translator from original languages and has translated and published *Kiikamba translation of the Greek New Testament*, Nairobi 2014.

Harold Miller has served as Missionary Dar es Salaam, Tanzania and was seconded to the National Christian Councils in Tanzania, Sudan, Kenya, and the All African Council of Churches. Miller has served as representative of the Mennonite Central Committee in East Africa and in Sudan. Miller and his wife Annetta Wenger are retired and live in Nairobi, Kenya.

Kyama Mugambi, PhD, is a researcher with the Centre for World Christianity at Africa International University. His recent research work investigates leadership in African Urban Christianity.

Peter Mutuku Mumo is Senior Lecturer in the Department of Philosophy and Religious Studies University of Nairobi. His area of study and research is theological Education and African Culture.

Philomena Njeri Mwaura is Associate Professor of Religious Studies in the Department of Philosophy and Religious Studies and previously served as the Director of the Centre for Gender Equity and Empowerment at

Kenyatta University. Mwaura's research and teaching focus on Gender and theology, new religious movements and Pentecostal and charismatic Christianity in Africa. She has published numerous essays on Christianity, gender, and health in Africa.

Abraham Waigi Ng'ang'a is a Kenyan scholar and a Research Fellow at the Akrofi-Christaller Institute of Theology, Mission and Culture, in Akropong, Ghana. His PhD thesis, "African Theology and African Literature: A Theological Critique of Wole Soyinka's Aesthetic Framework for Reconstituting African Life and Thought," was completed in 2015.

Dickson Nkonge Kagema is Senior Lecturer in Religious Studies and Philosophy at Chuka University in Kenya and Research Associate in Practical Theology and Missiology at Stellenbosch University, South Africa. He is the Director of Theological Education and Extension and Education Secretary for the Anglican Diocese of Meru, Kenya. His research interest is Science of Religion, Theological Education and Leadership.

Diane Stinton is Associate Professor, Mission Studies and Dean of Students at Regent College. She previously taught at Daystar University and Nairobi Evangelical Graduate School of Theology and launched Master programs at both Universities. Stinton is the author of *Jesus of Africa: Voices of Contemporary Christology*.

Tite Tiéno, Research Professor and Dean Emeritus at Trinity Evangelical Divinity School, 2065 Half Day Road, Deerfield, Illinois.

Mika Vähäkangas is professor of mission studies and ecumenics at Lund University, Sweden. He is former lecturer of Tumaini University Makumira, Tanzania and president of the International Association for Mission Studies.

Prof. Dr. Frans Wijsen is the Chair of Empirical and Practical Religious Studies and Vice Dean of the Faculty of Philosophy, Theology and Religious Studies, Radboud University, Nijmegen, The Netherlands.

Preface

The conversations leading to this book started in Kenya in 2012 at the African Association for the Study of Religion Conference at Egerton University by Elias Kifon Bongmba and S. Kip Elolia. Two years later, a panel was organized at the Annual Meeting of the American Academy of Religion (AAR) and the Society for Biblical Literature (SBL) in San Diego November 23, 2014. Initial discussions and deliberations about the panel included extended conversations with Knut Hulter, Mika Vähäkangas, Diane Stinton, Professor Waruta of the University of Nairobi, and Dismas Masolo. At the AAR and SBL, the first was a general panel on the state of African theology today and participants on that panel included S. Kip Elolia, Teresia Mbari Hinga, Gwinyai Muzurewa, Emmanuel Lartey, Edward Phillip Antonio, and Jacob Olupona. A second panel specifically addressed the work of Mugambi and the presenters at that panel included Teresia Mbari Hinga, Mika Vähäkangas, Diane Stinton, Knut Holter, Ernst Conradie, and Elias Kifon Bongmba.

Following the AAR/SBL Annual meetings, an extended call for papers was sent around the world. Scholars were asked to write on a theme of their choice, and the result has been a dialogue with Mugambi on different themes that emerge from his scholarship, especially on one of his most widely received, discussed, and debated contribution religion and theology in Africa; his revolutionary call for a theology of reconstruction. Two years later, this project has coincided with the 70th birthday of Professor Mugambi, and we are delighted to dedicate this work to his honor.

I thank Harold Miller for taking the time to read the texts and provide very useful editorial suggestions. His many years of intellectual and ecclesial engagement in Africa was critical to some of the historical perspectives of the manuscript. I thank April De Connick, Chair of the Department of Religion at Rice University, for her enthusiastic support for this project from the beginning. I also thank Robert Pucket, the Director of the Annual Meeting of the AAR, for supporting the initiative and providing useful information and letters that made it possible for some participants to attend the Annual Meetings. I also thank the African Association for the Study of Religion for sponsoring the panels at the AAR and SBL. I also thank those who presented papers at the AAR and SBL, the many colleagues who did not attend those meetings but answered the call to submit essays that appear in this volume. I also thank Professor John Mbiti, Diane Stinton, Frans Wijsen, Madipoane Masenya (Ngwan'a Mphahlele), John S. Mbiti, and James R. Cochrane. At Rice University, I express my appreciation to Dean Nicholas Shumway for a financial support that supported my research and travels to Africa, April DeConick, Chair of the Department of Religion for financial support of the AAR panel at San Deigo, Jeff Kripal, Anthony Pinn, and Matthias Henze for their many suggestions. A work like this is not possible without the guidance and support of the press. I want to thank the commissioning editor at Routledge press, Josh Wells, editorial assistant, Jack Boothroyd, and project manager, Chris Matthews for their insights and suggestions. Finally I thank especially my partner, Odelia Yuh Ngala Bongmba for her suggestions and patience. A project like this grows on you and just when you think you have understood or checked everything, there may be some issues, and if there are, the errors are mine.

Elias Kifon Bongmba
Houston, TX
January 2018

Introduction

Engaging religion and reconstruction

Elias Kifon Bongmba

Religion, theology, and reconstruction offer critical essays on the public face of religion in Africa. A central theme in the work of Jesse N.K. Mugambi, one of Africa's foremost scholars of religion, theology, ethics, and an ecumenical leader, is his concern for the Christian Church in Africa to champion liberation and reconstruction. Mugambi has served with distinction as Professor of Religion, Philosophy, and Theology at the University of Nairobi; held university administrative positions; trained and mentored many post graduate students; and distinguished himself through his numerous publications. Mugambi was born in the Embu community in Eastern Kenya, and grew up during the Kenyan independence struggle against colonial domination when British colonial administrators in Kenya engaged in

> the confiscation of property and land, the imposition of special taxes, the issuance of special documentation and passes, the censorship and banning of publications, the disbanding of all African political organizations, the control and disposition of labor, the suspension of due process, and detention without trial.[1]

Kenyans were subjected to a huge loss of life, dislocation and forceful resettlement of families, loss of property, rapes, and beatings. Mugambi's family suffered under these circumstances. These challenges not withstanding Mugambi excelled as a student in the schools he attended and was also involved in theatre, youth work, cultural education, debate clubs, Christian Union activities, and poetry writing.[2] He studied at Machakos Teacher's College, Kenyatta College, Selly Oaks College in Birmingham and earned his doctorate from the University of Nairobi.

Mugambi developed a special interest in the humanities, religion, philosophy, and literature, and this led to an abiding concern for cultural and social justice. He has prioritized Africa, its religious and cultural realities, and championed a creative theological perspective which has invited the pursuit of justice, human rights, and economic development to promote liberation and reconstruction. He had an early start by serving as a member of the Church Panel of Educators, where, as one of only four Kenyans, Mugambi championed a contextual curriculum.[3] Mugambi is a lifelong member of the Anglican Church in Kenya and active promoter of ecumenical work in Africa with the All African Conference of Churches, where he served as a senior consultant for development, and later Deputy General Secretary. Mugambi has served the World Council of Churches in several capacities including being a member of the Faith and Order Commission, The Sub unit on Church and Society, and the Working Group on Climate Change. Early in his career he worked for the World Student Christian Federation, where he was responsible for promoting theology for the African Church. It is this opening that gave Mugambi an early start on formulating his theology.

Mugambi's engagement with the local and global Church and public and private education has shaped his teaching and critical interdisciplinary approaches to religion and ecclesial and social reconstruction. Mugambi has carried out a sustained dialogue with scholars around the world and stood at the front of a robust theological imagination, especially on the theology of reconstruction.[4] He has also been influenced by missionary teachers such as Stephen Neill, with whom he disagreed strongly on the existence and place of African religions.[5] His philosophical orientation has been shaped by an African world view which privileges community and relation, balancing critical questions from scholars like Kwasi Wiredu of Ghana and the ontology of Paul Tillich to underscore the importance of social relations in the African context.[6] Such groundings have worked largely because like Fabien Eboussi Boulaga of Cameroon, Mugambi has countered Rudolf Bultmann's demythologization with a remythologization which takes the African worldview seriously.[7]

Mugambi's theological imagination draws from the biblical tradition as well as the African social and cultural reality. We refer to Africa here broadly as a construct, but must emphasize that we mean the continent of Africa with all its diversity, cultures, symbols, and political arrangements, yet bound in many ways by world imperial powers, the liberation struggles, and postcolonial despoliations which have given food for thought and action in Mugambi's theology.[8] For Mugambi, studying African religions and theologies requires a clear methodological approach that includes an inductive approach which addresses the divine human encounter in context.[9] This itinerary requires a theological anthropology that focuses on the persons, society, the environment, and all forms of life. Methods of study for Mugambi are not monads, but diverse frameworks for pluralistic and collaborative theological thinking, debates, and reasonable positioning. Mugambi argues that Africans can no longer be content with theological anthropology, as important as it has been, but must move through theological reflection to develop a self-critical perspective that is grounded in African social and cultural realities.[10]

African theology for Mugambi begins with the Bible, early North African theology during the patristic era, development through the missionary and colonial encounter, but more specifically African theological imagination in the 20th century. African theology involves a critical engagement with African cultures, and Mugambi has emphasized the cultural heritage in the study of Christianity and theology as a constant theme in his research and publications.[11] Such a critical theology must reflect indigenous religious views, philosophical perspectives, and the ecclesial vision of African initiated Churches.

The essays in this book discuss the articulation of that African theology and demonstrate that Mugambi will always be associated with a theology of reconstruction. Mugambi called for a theology of reconstruction when he addressed the Central Committee of the All African Conference of Churches on March 30, 1990 on the future of the Church in Africa.[12] Mugambi later expanded reconstruction theology at the Rockwell Lectures delivered at Rice University in 1991. Those lectures were published under the title, *From Liberation to Reconstruction: African Christian Theology after the Cold War*.[13] South African theologian Charles Villa Vicencio began his journey to reconstruction in 1990 when he published his essay titled "Religion, Revolution, and Reconstruction: The Significance of the Cuban and Nicaraguan Revolutions for the Church in South Africa."[14] James Cochrane and Gerald West also discussed the theme of reconstruction in an essay in the *Journal of Theology in Southern Africa*, in 1993.[15] There is a rich reception history for the theology of reconstruction that includes several doctoral dissertations on Mugambi's theology.[16] Mugambi's extensive peer reviewed publications, editorials, opinions, and unpublished papers reveal a probing and critical mind, which has prioritized Africa and its religious traditions in his intellectual life and mission.

In the first part of the book, we offer selected perspectives on biblical and theological analyses of Mugambi's scholarship. In his chapter, Knut Holter argues that Mugambi has used biblical texts to affirm humanity. Holter points out that Mugambi has engaged in critical hermeneutical readings of both the Hebrew Bible and New Testament and called for a contextual approach that makes the Bible relevant to Africans because some biblical texts resonate with African indigenous religious cultures. In calling for a hermeneutical approach to the Hebrew Bible that would resonate with African readers today, Mugambi cited the notion of reconstruction. At a New Testament Society meeting in South Africa, Mugambi also appealed to the use of hermeneutic reconstruction to make the New Testament relevant to Africa. Holter argues that biblical texts play an important role in Mugambi's theology, and his use of biblical texts demonstrates a knowledge of the critical methodology and literature. This strategy allowed Mugambi to focus on things that are relevant to the readers of the Biblical texts today.

In his chapter David Adamo returns to the Hebrew Bible and argues that King David, one of the most popular persons in the Bible, engaged in reconstruction in the theological tradition Mugambi has shaped. Adamo begins the chapter with a critical analysis of the figure and place of David in the Biblical narratives from the Deutoronomistic texts, the prophetic texts, as well as the Psalms within the context of the critical studies done by Hebrew

Bible and Ancient Near Eastern scholars on the historicity of David. Adamo argues that as King of Israel, David was a model of reconstruction in the political realm as well as his personal life because David's repentance from the Bathsheba affair demonstrates his diligence to reconstruct his spiritual and personal life.

In Chapter 3 Madipoane Masenya (Ngwan'a Mphahlele) argues that in light of Mugambi's use of scriptures in his theology, it is important to examine the biblical text that discusses the meeting of Jesus, a Jewish rabbi, and a Samaritan woman, who was considered unclean by the social norms of the day, and offers an example of differences in contextual worship and liturgy. This story would have been problematic in an African context because that would have been similar to a meeting with an authority figure like the *dikgoshi* (traditional political leaders) and a woman. The meeting between Jesus and the woman reverses inequality.[17] In addition, the account demonstrates that true worship has an impact on how people relate to others because liturgy is a service to God. Worship is also contextual and should transcend barriers even as it provides an opportunity to address local needs, especially in the South African context where gender concerns remain high even after the end of apartheid.

In Chapter 4 Enoch Olujide Gbadegesin argues that the Olódùmarè, the Yoruba deity, is hidden because he is not visible but is revealed through different facets of the created order and life. Gbadegesin argues that Olódùmarè, who is of indeterminate origins, is a deity described in "superlatives" because of the power, presence, and activity of Olódùmarè through his divine messengers.[18] The belief system recognizes the presence and power of Olódùmarè, the Yoruba

> people do not claim to know what is beyond this ephemeral and earthly world of existence. So, it is very clear in their day-to-day interaction that the abode here has a more immediate and ontological meaning for the people than a place that is beyond their conceptual understanding.

Olódùmarè is hidden but present and the creation myth is indicative of a belief in the presence of Olódùmarè who delegated authority for his messengers to create the things that exist. Humans experience Olódùmarè in different ways, and therefore hiddenness is just a function of the divine nature.

John Fischer in Chapter 5 discusses the idea of destiny in the eschatology of Mugambi, beginning with an analysis of African cosmology which affirms one world and argues that time and destiny are tied to this view of the world. Fischer argues that Mugambi, who has linked his eschatology to African cosmology, demonstrates a mono-sectional view of the world in which everything is integrated. The Christian community gives witness to a future of the reign of God. Africans who have died continue to live in the next world with an immaterial soul. In the afterlife, people will be rewarded for what they have done on earth. All people who are born will someday return to the world of the ancestors.[19] Death and funeral ceremonies are meant to bid the dead farewell and prepare them to meet their ancestors. This is a communal and pragmatic view of humanity that recognizes the visible and invisible reality, and eschatological hope does not imply leaving one space for another. This view coheres with Mugambi's view that salvation refers to the overcoming of all domination imposed by the imperial and postcolonial orders. Therefore, members of the ecclesial community have a responsibility to engage in social justice rather than simply dream of a utopia in the next world.

In Chapter 6 Elias Kifon Bongmba reflects on the Church of the future in light of Mugambi's ecclesiology where the Church that serves as the witness of Christ on earth stands in need of renewal.[20] Mugambi's theology of reconstruction calls for a future-oriented Church, and Bongmba argues that such a Church must be an intersubjective community in which members of the ecclesial community assume responsibility for the other. The precondition for building that kind of community lies in the cultivation of the art and practice of listening. The Church should listen to several constituencies, including those who are not members of the Church, if the Church is going to serve the society in which it exists.

In Chapter 7 Harold Miller, who has an extensive background in relief services and ecumenical work in Africa, discusses Christian Councils, institutions that have been key to the ecumenical and social ministry of the Church in Africa. Christian Councils in Africa follow ecumenical developments traced to the beginning of the Edinburgh Missionary Conference and were formed during the independence era to assume responsibility, self-governance, self-propagation, and self-support. The work of the CCA grew from the 1970s to include ecclesial support for critical response to political developments and championing the work of liberation movements in Southern Africa where organizations like the South African Council of Churches worked to aid victims of apartheid. Church Councils in Rwanda worked on reconciliation following the genocide. Miller points out that there are 30 national councils and 24 of those councils are affiliated with the AACC.

The essays in Part 2 discuss Mugambi's signature theological subject, a theology of reconstruction. Mika Vähäkangas begins the dialogue in Chapter 8 by placing Mugambi's work within the postcolonial discourse which advocates Christian and social responsibility in the political sphere. The postcolonial struggle in Kenya led to the violent suppression of the Mau Mau liberation movement. Tens of thousands of Kenyans died in that struggle for *uhuru* (freedom). Vähäkangas argues that postcolonial Kenya faced enormous challenges, one of them being limitation of free critical discourses about the postcolony. A postcolonial theology addressed liberation but some theological perspectives did not check political excesses of the new era. Mugambi's call for critical solidarity through a theology of reconstruction takes the fallenness of humanity seriously and acknowledges the possibilities that humans can influence change when state and political institutions work well. Mugambi offers a critique of social praxis, proposes critical ideas for social change, and establishes solidarity with those who are oppressed.

In Chapter 9 John S. Mbiti, argues that the peace of African Religion must be part of the dialogue for liberation and reconstruction. Mbiti argues that Mugambi built on the legacy of liberation and initiated his signature theological project, a theology of reconstruction, in which he called for a Nehemiah type project of reconstruction of the African community.[21] As Nehemiah called his people to rise up and rebuild Jerusalem, the theology of reconstruction anticipates peace for a continent that has been ravaged by colonialism and postcolonial mismanagement. Mbiti argues that theologians must focus on the need for peace in the African context because reconstruction and peace are interrelated. Africa has been severely wounded by the "ugly struggles and conflicts in political, social, economic, and religious spheres" and needs peace. Peace from the perspective of indigenous religions in Africa is necessary for healing.[22]

Franz Gmainer-Pranzl in Chapter 10 discusses reconstruction and intercultural theology arguing it is a re-orientation of theology which takes into consideration individuals and their roles in social reconstruction, which Mugambi believes should be the ultimate outcome of evangelization. Such intercultural theology is grounded in its local context, and the root of such theology lies in its rejection of the mainly Eurocentric project of the past and offers its proposal for a new way of understanding mission, culture, and religion in a pluralistic context. Gmainer-Pranzl argues that intercultural theology draws theoretical perspectives from contextual theology, intercultural theological epistemology, comparative approaches such as a theology of religions, as scholarly approaches that allows scholars to explore the nature of salvation and truth claims of a particular religion. While there are no strict demarcations of these four areas of inquiry, inculturation responds also to the cultural turn in social studies, but in theology it signifies the importance of culture as the locus for theological activity. He cautions that cultural issues should not be emphasized above poverty and other aspects of social justice. A theology of reconstruction tackles social issues that must be addressed at a time Gmainer-Pranzl calls a *Kairos* which invites interdisciplinary theological analysis.

In Chapter 11 Diane Stinton examines Mugambi's theology through a case study of a Nairobi Pentecostal Church. Using an insider/outsider approach, she brings a critical *einfülung* in her analysis of the Church in light of the idea of reconstruction. The Mavuno Church was started the same year Mugambi launched his theology of reconstruction. Kyama Mugambi, Mugambi's first son, is a leader in the non-denominational Church which started as Nairobi Chapel. Following independence, the Church has grown under the leadership of Oscar Muriu and his wife Beatrice. Stinton discusses the structure, ministries, growth, and teachings of the Church and argues that the social outreach of the Church reflects a reconstruction theology that is grounded in African realities and avoids the false separation of salvation and liberation. The outreach and mission of the Nairobi Chapel/Mavuno Church mirrors themes of liberation and reconstruction.

Kyama Mugambi argues in Chapter 12 that the theology of reconstruction offers tools for constructing a new society but reconstruction overlaps with liberation and demands a critical understanding of life in postcolonial Africa and its cultures. It also requires a self-critical and holistic approach to life, a greater appreciation of the sciences, and an ecumenical vision of contemporary and future ecclesial imperatives. Mugambi examines these dimensions in the context of East Africa, analyzing the spiritual revitalization movements in the era of Pentecostal and New Pentecostal Charismatic Churches in Kenya which continue to foster a self-awareness using language and ritual practices. He argues a holistic approach is necessary to effectively promote the ideas of a theology of reconstruction. To make this possible some of the younger Churches are developing discipleship training materials to promote a practical theology that would advance the needs of reconstruction. These Churches promote a post denominational phase of Christianity in East Africa.

In Chaper 13 Ntozakhe Simon Cezula discusses the rebuilding of ruined societies in Mugambi's idea of reconstruction.[23] While affirming that real change has taken place in South Africa, Cezula argues that xenophobia is hampering reconstruction. He rejects Nehemiah as an example of reconstruction because of the rigorist legalism that Nehemiah espoused. While Cezula agrees with Mugambi on the imperative of reconstruction, Cezula contends that the Nehemiah-Ezra model contains seeds of discrimination and cannot serve South Africa because the specific ethnic nature of the Nehemiah-Ezra model focused on returnees from exile at the expense of those who remained in Israel.

In Chapter 14 Philomena Njeri Mwaura discusses the mission of the Church today and argue that the reconstructing mission of the Church in Africa ought to issue in service for justice, peace, and reconciliation.[24] Mugambi's multi-disciplinary concept of reconstruction emphasized the need to redesign, reconstruct, and reorganize the ecclesial and broader social community in the post-colonial state. Reconstruction calls for a shift in missions from *mission ad gentes* to what Magessa calls *mission intre gentes*. This eliminates the conceptualization of sending and receiving Churches. It promotes methodologies in missions that prioritize respect for all cultures in the African context where misery and political domination remains strong. Mwaura laments that the numerical growth in Christianity has not promoted a deeper spirituality and social cohesion as ethnicity has divided people and led to crises like The Rwandan Genocide, electoral violence in Kenya, and political struggles in several countries in Africa. Reconstruction offers a model to promote peace, reconciliation, justice, gender justice, and work with partners in the fight against HIV and AIDS and the Ebola Virus Disease.

The future of Christianity and theology in Africa calls for a rigorous "rethinking of missions."

The essays in Part 3 of the book address religion, theology, and future trajectories. In Chapter 15 Peter Mutuku Mumo discusses the African religio-cultural identity in a global context in the theology of Mugambi. Mumo argues that Ngugi Wa Thiongo's novel *The River Between* demonstrates that Africans have embraced Christianity and their cultures. Mugambi's theology offers resources to counter colonial ideology and imperial projects that have been taken over by global capitalism which is driven by advances in technology, media, and the popularization Euro-American values in Africa.[25] Despite this assault, many African scholars of religion and theology have emphasized the place of culture in African religious life as catalyst for the evolution of indigenous forms of Christianity as was the case in Kikuyu land in Kenya.[26]

In Chapter 16, Tite Tiéno, an African in the Diaspora, analyzes the topic from the perspective of the gospel, because if we think of the Church as African it must have implications for missions because of Africans' enormous challenges even with the phenomenal growth of Christianity on the continent. He underscores the importance of training Africans who must redefine missions and Africa's relationship to the rest of the world. Thinking and acting for Africa must exceed Afro-pessimism, and Tiéno doubts if the discourse of the African renaissance is as central to renewal as others think because Africans must solve their problems. In light of Christian missions, this calls for service with integrity that must promote nation building in light scriptures, prioritize freedom, check profiteering, and authoritarianism. The Church, which is called to be part of this change, must abandon "foolish worldliness" and serve as agents of hope.

In Chapter 17 James R. Cochrane addresses Africa's yearning for freedom. Cochrane discusses grounds for the possibility of a universal freedom and argues that the core of Kant's thought and writings center on the concept of freedom because freedom defines what it means to be human and that "causally effective capacity of creative freedom" is determinative of most of what we do. This non-material capacity enables humans to grasp the reality of world, make choices and control their impulses, and follow certain patterns and act in a teleological manner. Freedom endows individuals with the capacity to follow a moral law or respect moral impulses and then work with others and natural phenomena because humans can transcend their inclinations.

Cochrane argues that while Kant stated these ideas in the past, similar ideas about moral agency are found in the work of Frantz Fanon who rejected colonialism and its dehumanizing practices. Likewise, Steve Biko articulated black consciousness to foster a true humanity where freedom means the ability to define oneself. Judge Laurie Ackerman in South Africa defined human dignity as the lodestar of the new political community because it is an intrinsic worth. Cochrane argues that Mugambi has championed African liberation and also called for reconstruction grounded in African intellectual and cultural resources. In this sense Mugambi calls for a shift from negative freedom (freedom from) to positive freedom (freedom for) reconstruction.

In Chapter 18 Laurenti Magesa discusses challenges that face a new generation of theologians in Africa as he tracks the footprints left by Mugambi on the theological landscape of Africa in living, teaching, and publishing, and he calls on the next generation to follow in Mugambi's footsteps. Magesa argues that Christology and ecclesiology are contested theological issues because these two doctrines relate to inculturation of the gospel in light of the ministry of Jesus and the Church which is a witness of the reign of God. The task of African theologians is to explain the redemption of Christ in the language and symbols of their people. The Jesus question, though important, did not receive attention until the second half of the 20th century because the continent had to address liberation and set a new agenda.[27] To maintain convergence between African cultures and the Bible and a contextual theological understanding, African theologians should reimage Jesus for today and know the truth about Jesus for the times. Saul of Tarsus (Paul) transformed the message of Jesus from Palestinian issues into a global message, and Mugambi has articulated a Christ that speaks to African values, cultures, and issues.

In Chapter 19 Loreen Maseno discusses the theme of reconstruction as part of the narrative of the future arguing that liberation and reconstruction propose change and diversity. Mugambi's call in a post-cold era indicated that liberation as a theological construct had run its course, although it echoed the spirit of the Pan-Africanist Movement, which sought to liberate the entire African world at home and abroad and also offer a critique of the missionary era.[28] The subsequent formation of the Organization of African Unity did not substantially change the fate of Africa as violence, war, poverty, and all other forms of disparity continued to ravage Africa. Reconstruction had to proceed in a self-critical manner, drawing critical resources from religion, economics, culture, and ethics. Its main goal was not only institutional change but also the transformation of personal and social relations within Africa.[29] Reconstruction is a future movement which Maseno argues must involve African women who must use local symbols, metaphors, models, and theories to advance the cause of reconstruction, and such theology remains intermediary because it remains open to changes and innovation.

Abraham Waigi Ng'ang'a in Chapter 20 introduces readers to a relationship between theology and literature, a rich field that has not been tapped completely by scholars of religion and theologians but which Mugambi has argued should be studied by scholars of religion and theologians to understand other critical perspectives on Christianity in the African Christian vision. Mugambi offers a tripartite framework for an alternative ethical vision for Africa. First, Africans must reclaim their own religious heritage, develop an African vision for humanity grounded in justice, and reconstitute transcendence from an African perspective. This implies what Wole Soyinka has called the Ogun factor, a reference to the Yoruba God, who is the God of technology. Wa Nganga argues that although Soyinka rejects Christianity, theologians and Christian scholars must understand Soyinka's perspective in order to make a case for the relevance of Christ in the African context.

Dickson Nkonge Kagema in Chapter 21 maps Mugambi's contribution to theological education in Africa through the study of African religions, Christianity, Christian theology, global missions, ethics, social justice, ecumenism, and academic publishing. Central to Mugambi's intellectual journey is the view that theological scholarship must speak to Africans. In *The Biblical Basis for Evangelization: Theological Reflection Based on an Africa Experience*, Mugambi demonstrated a concern for theological education, and in his own research and publications, Mugambi has worked with Africans and African Church leaders to improve theological education.[30] Mugambi has expressed concerns regarding the sustainability of the Church in light of the critical lack of theological and intellectual leadership in a context where theological curriculum is not relevant to African needs. Mugambi has called for a contextualized curriculum that will train scholars to address the needs and hopes of Africa and championed the publishing of academic work in Africa.[31]

The future of the Church in Africa will continue to involve missions and that makes the question of money important, and Jonathan Bonk addresses it in Chapter 22. Bonk, who was raised in a missionary family in Ethiopia, returned to Ethiopia and worked on development and promoted financial equity among the mission and local staff. While working with Kale Heywet (Word of Life Church) Bonk went through tribulations under the Marxist Ethiopian government. The tensions about employment and accusations labeled by the state against Bonk led to his book *Missions and Money: Affluence as a Missionary Problem*.[32] Bonk returns to the core arguments about disparity in finances between western missionaries and locals and calls on missionaries to come out of the insular world in which they live and see the contrast in living standards between missionaries and locals. Theology today must address the issue of the righteous rich, a group which includes the mission agencies and missionaries who serve around the world.

In the final chapter Frans Wijsen discusses religious diversity in Tanzania within the context of Islamic revivalism and focuses on new governance in a country where Islam and Christianity have a nearly equal number of adherents. Wijsen highlights Muslim voices today because Muslims were part of the independence struggle in Tanzania and supported Julius Nyerere. But Nyerere soon marginalized Muslims on suspicions that the East African Muslim Welfare Society was scheming to have its members gain power. Nyerere further pushed for the Union of Mainland and Zanzibar for many reasons which might have included fear that Zanzibar would be a Muslim stronghold in the region.

Wijsen analyzes controversies surrounding the Muslim Party and also maps out the complicated and often conflicted relationship between the Nyerere regime and Muslims in which Muslims thought they were not given equal treatment in the republic. Muslims think that their leaders failed to represent them well, and they have continued to experience discrimination in Tanzania at many levels. Attempts to liberalize education and the court systems have not gone far enough for some Muslims. Constitutional reforms today must take the concerns of the Muslims seriously. Wijsen argues that the Zanzibar crisis caused the bloody election crises in 2000, and Muslims think that the government of the Republic has not listened to Muslims all along. Solutions to the problems must take the country's diversity seriously and recognize that the option of secularism proposed by others might not solve all the problems, especially if some state leaders cannot practice neutrality.

Notes

1 Caroline Elkins, *Imperial Reckoning: The Untold Story of Britain's Gulag in Kenya*. (New York: Henry Holt, 2005), 55. See also, David Anderson, *Histories of the Hanged: The Dirty War in Kenya and the End of Empire*. (New York: W.W. Norton, 2005); David Lovatt Smith, *Kenya, the Kikuyu and Mau Mau*. (Eastbourne: Anthony Rowe Ltd. 2005); E. S. Aieno Odhiambo and John Lonsdale, eds. *Mau Mau and Nationhood: Arms, Authority, and Narration*. (Oxford: James Currey, 2003).

2 Julius Mutugi Gathogo, 2007, 20 ff.

3 See Gathogo, 2007, I. M. T. Mwase, "A Critical Evaluation of J.N.K. Mugambi's Correlation of Christianity with the African Heritage: An Apologetic Perspective." PhD Dissertation, Southwestern Theological Seminary, 1993; See also Robert S. Heaney, *From Historical to Critical Post-Colonial Theology: The Contribution of John S. Mbiti and Jesse N.K. Mugambi* (Eugene Oregon: Pickwick Publications, 2015).

4 See for example; Andrea Karamaga, "A Theology of Reconstruction," in J. N. K. Mugarnbi, ed. *Democracy and Development in Africa: The Role of the Churches*. (Nairobi: All Africa Conference of Churches, 1997); Jose B. Chipenda, A. Karamaga, J.N.K. Mugambi and C. K. Omari, eds. *The Church of Africa: Towards a Theology of Reconstruction*. (Nairobi: All Africa Conference of Churches, 1991); Charles Villa-Vicencio, *A Theology of Reconstruction: Nation-Building and Human Rights*. (Cambridge: Cambridge University Press, 1992); Valentin Dedji and Ukachukwi Chis Manus, *Intercultural Hermeneutics in Africa: Methods and Approaches*. (Nairobi: Acton, 2003).

5 I am indebted for some of the information to Julius Gathogo. See Gathogo, 2007, 58.

6 Gathogo, 2007, 63.

7 J.N.K. Mugambi, *From Liberation to Reconstruction: African Christian Theology After the Cold War*. (Nairobi: East African Educational Publishers Ltd, 1995), 35–6; See Fabien Eboussi-Boulaga, *Christianity Without Fetishes: An African Critique and Recapture of Christianity*. (Maryknoll: Orbis Books, 1984).

8 J.N.K. Mugambi, "Christianity in Africa 1910–2010," in Todd M. Johnson and Kenneth R. Ross, eds. *Atlas of Global Christianity 1910–2010*, 110–1. (Edinburgh: Edinburgh University Press, 2009).

9 J.N.K. Mugambi, "Theological Method in African Christianity," in Mary Getui, ed. *Theological Method & Aspects of Worship in African Christianity*, 5–40. (Nairobi: Acton Publishers, 1998).

10 J.N.K. Mugambi, "Theological Method in African Christianity," 1998, 29 ff.
11 J.N.K. Mugambi, "Christianity and the African Cultural Heritage," in Ogbu Kalu, ed. *African Christianity: An African Story*, 516–42. (Pretoria: UNISA, 2005); J.N.K. Mugambi, *Christianity and African Culture*. (Nairobi: Acton, 2002).
12 J.N.K. Mugambi, "The Future of the Church and the Future of the Church in Africa," in J. B. Chipenda, A. Karamaga and C. K. Omafi, eds. *The Church of Africa: Towards a Theology of Reconstruction*, 29–50. (Nairobi: All Africa Conference of Churches, 1991).
13 Mugambi, 1995.
14 Charles Villa-Vicencio, "Religion, Revolution and Reconstruction: The Significance of the Cuban and Nicaraguan Revolutions for the Church in South Africa," *Journal of Theology for Southern Africa*, 73, (December 1990): 48–59.
15 Vicencio, "Religion, Revolution, and Reconstruction."; James Cochrane and Gerald West, "War, Remembrance and Reconstruction," *Journal of Theology for Southern Africa* (September 1993).
16 See critiques offered by Tinyiko Maluleke, 1994; Jospeh Wandera, *The Voice Magazine*, 2002, 23; Musa Dube; See for example, Julius Mutugi Gathogo, *Liberation and Reconstruction in Africa: A Critical Analysis in the Works of J.N.K. Mugambi*. (Saarbrüken: LAP Lambert Academic, 2011); Heaney, *From Historical to Critical Post-Colonial Theology*.
17 Daniel G. Groody, *Globalization, Spirituality, and Justice: Navigating the Path to Peace*. (Maryknoll: Orbis, 2008), 212–13.
18 E. Bolaji Idowu, *Olodumare: God in Yoruba Belief*. (New York: Wazobia, 1994).
19 1971, 158.
20 J. N. K. Mugambi, "The Ecumenical Movement and the Future of the Church in Africa," in J. N. K. Mugambi and Laurenti Magesa, eds. *The Church in African Christianity: Innovative Essays in Ecclesiology*. (Nairobi: Initiatives, 1990), 5–28.
21 See J.N.K. Mugambi, "God, Humanity and Nature in Relation to Justice and Peace," in *Christian Mission and Social Transformation*, Church and Society Documents, No. 2. (Geneva: WCC, 1989).
22 See John S. Mbiti, *Concepts of God in Africa*, Second Edition. (Nairobi: Acton Publishers 2012).
23 Charles Villa-Vicencio, 1992.
24 John S. Pobee, "Lord, Creator-Spirit, Renew and Sustain the Whole Creation," *International Review of Mission*, 29 (April 1990): 55.
25 M. M. Gecaga, "Globalization and Churches," in I. Mwase and E. Kamaara eds. *Theologies of Liberation and Reconstruction*. (Nairobi: Acton Publishers, 2012), 329.
26 N. W. Ndungu, J. M. Bahemuka and J. L. Brockington, eds. *East Africa in Transition Images Institutions and Identities*. (Nairobi: University of Nairobi Press, 2004), 240.
27 A. Abble, et al., *Des pretres noirs s'Interrogent*. (Paris: Editions du Cerf, 1956).
28 Cary D. Wintz and Paul Finkelman, *Encyclopedia of the Harlem Renaissance. Vol. 1 and 2. A–Z*. (NewYork: Routledge, 2004), 952.
29 Elelwani Farisani, "The Post-Exile Motif in Mugambi's Theology of Reconstruction," in I.M.T. Mwase and Eunice K. Kamaara, eds. *Theologies of Liberation and Reconstruction: Essays in Honour of Professor J.N.K. Mugambi*. (Nairobi, Kenya: Acton Press, 2012), 198–220.
30 J.N.K. Mugambi, *The Biblical Basis for Evangelization: Theological Reflections Based on an African Experience*. (Nairobi: Oxford University Press, 1989).

31 J.N.K. Mugambi, *The Future of Theological Education in Africa and the Challenges It Faces*, Op.cit, 117–25.

32 Jonathan J. Bonk, *Missions and Money: Affluence as a Missionary Problem . . . Revisited.* Revised and Expanded Edition. (Maryknoll: Orbis Books, 2006).

Bibliography

Abble, A. et al. *Des pretres noirs s'interrogent.* Paris: Editions du Cerf, 1956.

Anderson, David. *Histories of the Hanged: The Dirty War in Kenya and the End of Empire.* New York: W.W. Norton, 2005.

Bonk, Jonathan J. *Missions and Money: Affluence as a Missionary Problem . . . Revisited.* Revised and Expanded Edition. Maryknoll: Orbis Books, 2006.

Chipenda, J. B., A. Karamaga, J.N.K. Mugambi, and C. K. Omari, eds. *The Church of Africa: Towards a Theology of Reconstruction.* Nairobi: A.A.C.C, 1991.

Cochrane, James and Gerald West. "War, Remembrance and Reconstruction." *Journal of Theology for Southern Africa* (September 1993).

Dedji, Valentin Dedji and Ukachukwi Chis Manus. *Intercultural Hermeneutics in Africa: Methods and Approaches.* Nairobi: Acton, 2003.

Dube, Musa W., and Fabien Eboussi-Boulaga. *Christianity Without Fetishes: An African Critique and Recapture of Christianity.* Maryknoll: Orbis Books, 1984.

Elkins, Caroline. *Imperial Reckoning: The Untold Story of Britain's Gulag in Kenya.* New York: Henry Holt, 2005.

Farisani, Elelwani B. "The Post-Exile Motif in Mugambi's Theology of Reconstruction." In *Theologies of Liberation and Reconstruction: Essays in Honour of Professor J.N.K. Mugambi*, edited by I.M.T. Mwase and Eunice K. Kamaara, 198–220. Nairobi, Kenya: Acton Press, 2012.

Gathogo, Julius Mutugi. *Liberation and Reconstruction in Africa: A Critical Analysis in the Works of J.N.K. Mugambi.* Saarbrüken: LAP Lambert Academic, 2011.

Gecaga, M. M. "Globalization and Churches." In *Theologies of Liberation and Reconstruction*, edited by I. Mwase and E. Kamaara. Nairobi: Acton Publishers, 2012.

Groody, Daniel G. *Globalization, Spirituality, and Justice: Navigating the Path to Peace.* Maryknoll: Orbis, 2008.

Heaney, Robert S. *From Historical to Critical Post-Colonial Theology: The Contribution of John S. Mbiti and Jesse N.K. Mugambi.* Eugene Oregon: Pickwick Publications, 2015.

Iduwo, E. Bolaji. *Olodumare: God in Yoruba Belief.* New York: Wazobia, 1994.

Karamaga, Andrea. "A Theology of Reconstruction." In *Democracy and Development in Africa: The Role of the Churches*, edited by J.N.K. Mugarnbi Nairobi: All Africa Conference of Churches, 1997.

Mbiti, John S. *Concepts of God in Africa*, Second Edition. Nairobi: Acton Publishers 2012.

Mugambi, J.N.K. *The Biblical Basis for Evangelization: Theological Reflections Based on an African Experience.* Nairobi: Oxford University Press, 1989.

———. *God, Humanity and Nature in Relation to Justice and Peace*, WCC/Church and Society Documents, No. 2, Geneva, 1989.

———. "The Ecumenical Movement and the Future of the Church in Africa." In *The Church in African Christianity: Innovative Essays in Ecclesiology*, edited by J.N.K. Mugambi and Laurenti Magesa, 5–28. Nairobi: Initiatives, 1990.

———. "The Future of the Church and the Future of the Church in Africa." In *The Church of Africa: Towards a Theology of Reconstruction*, J. B. Chipenda, A. Karamaga, and C. K. Omafi, 29–50. Nairobi: All Africa Conference of Churches, 1991.

———. *From Liberation to Reconstruction: African Christian Theology After the Cold War*. Nairobi: East African Educational Publishers Ltd, 1995.

———. "Theological Method in African Christianity." In *Theological Method & Aspects of Worship in African Christianity*, edited by Mary Getui, 5–40. Nairobi: Acton Publishers, 1998.

———. Christian Mission and Social Transformation, ed. 1989. *Christianity and African Culture*. Nairobi: Acton, 2002.

———. "Christianity and the African Cultural Heritage." In *African Christianity: An African Story*, edited by Ogbu Kalu, 516–542. Pretoria: UNISA, 2005.

———. "Christianity in Africa 1910–2010." *Atlas of Global Christianity 1910–2010*, edited by Todd M. Johnson and Kenneth R. Ross, 110–111. Edinburgh: Edinburgh University Press, 2009.

Mwase, I. M. T. "A Critical Evaluation of J.N.K. Mugambi's Correlation of Christianity with the African Heritage: An Apologetic Perspective." PhD Dissertation, Southwestern Theological Seminary, 1993.

Ndungu, N. W., J. M. Bahemuka, and J. L. Brockington, eds. *East Africa in Transition Images Institutions and Identities*, 240. Nairobi: University of Nairobi Press, 2004.

Odhiambo, E. S., Aieno Odhiambo, and John Lonsdale, eds. *Mau Mau and Nationhood: Arms, Authority, and Narration*. Oxford: James Currey, 2003.

Pobee, John S. "Lord, Creator-Spirit, Renew and Sustain the Whole Creation." In *International Review of Mission* Volume 79 (April 1990): 151–158.

Smith, David Lovatt. *Kenya, the Kikuyu and Mau Mau*. Eastbourne: Anthony Rowe Ltd., 2005.

Villa-Vicencio, Charles. "Religion, Revolution and Reconstruction: TheSignificance of the Cuban and Nicaraguan Revolutions for the Church in South Africa." *Journal of Theology for Southern Africa* 73 (December 1990): 48–59.

———. *A Theology of Reconstruction: Nation-Building and Human Rights*. Cambridge: Cambridge University Press, 1992.

Wandera, Jospeh. *The Voice Magazine*. 2002.

Wintz, Cary D. and Paul Finkelman. *Encyclopedia of the Harlem Renaissance. Vol. 1 and 2. A–Z*. New York: Routledge, 2004.

Part I

Biblical and ecclesial perspectives

1 Texts of affirmation rather than negation

Jesse N. K. Mugambi and African biblical studies

Knut Holter

According to the official academic profile of Professor Jesse N. K. Mugambi in the webpages of the University of Nairobi, Mugambi is not only Professor of Philosophy and Religious Studies, he is also a resource person in the Commission for University Education on philosophy, theology, religious studies, and applied ethics; and he has professional training that includes education, communication policy and planning, publishing, and ecology (https://profiles.uonbi.ac.ke/jesse_ndwiga/). The list is impressive; still, something is actually lacking in this quite massive official portrayal, namely, Mugambi's interaction with the guilds and discourses of critical biblical studies in Africa and beyond. The following pages, therefore, will offer a few remarks on this particular segment of his scholarship.

Jesse Mugambi's interaction with the guilds and discourses of critical biblical studies can be illustrated by the role he played at two international conferences that took place in 1999, at the turn of the century, when we all wanted to call a halt for a while and reflect on past and future. There are some parallels between these two conferences. First, both attracted biblical scholars from various parts of the world onto African soil; one – in October 1999 in Nairobi, Kenya – assembled Old Testament scholars, whereas the other – in August 1999 in Hammanskraal, South Africa – brought together New Testament scholars. Second, both conferences explicitly intended to expose African and western guilds of biblical studies to each other, on hermeneutical levels, of course, but also on institutional and personal levels, deliberately facilitating interaction between African and Western scholars and their respective universities and seminaries. And third, both conferences asked Professor Mugambi to deliver the respective keynote addresses. In both cases, the conferences received what they had requested. Mugambi met the two scholarly communities, he drew some major lines in relation to ancient texts and contemporary interpretive contexts, and he challenged his audiences to participate in the developing of African biblical studies that would be characterized by contextual sensitivity as well as societal relevance.

Mugambi's participation in these two conferences was an expression of his outstanding position in African theology. One can hardly say that he is a biblical scholar, at least not in a traditional, exegetical sense of the term.

Rather, he is a kind of unusual plant in the garden of academia: a philosopher and theologian, who, if I may put it a bit bluntly, actually reads the Bible and finds it worthwhile to interact with guild members and discourses of critical biblical studies. This was precisely why he was invited to address African and western biblical scholars already in 1999. This is also why I will interrogate these two keynote addresses to illustrate and reflect on some of Mugambi's concerns vis-à-vis the biblical texts themselves and the academic discipline of critical biblical studies.

Mugambi visiting the guilds of Old and New Testament studies in 1999

Let me begin with the Old Testament conference in Nairobi, in October 1999. The conference was organized by Mary Getui (Kenyatta University, Nairobi), Victor Zinkuratire (Catholic University of East Africa, Nairobi), and myself (MHS School of Mission and Theology, Stavanger, Norway). The papers read at the conference were published in an anthology two years later.[1] When colleagues from various parts of Africa as well as from the Scandinavian countries were invited to come together in Nairobi, the purpose was to make a critical analysis of the methodological, hermeneutical, and institutional Africanization of the academic discipline of Old Testament studies that were seen to be emerging all around. The first generation of African Old Testament scholars – in 1999 around 100 African colleagues with doctorates in Old Testament studies had developed a comparative paradigm allowing Old Testament texts and African contexts to interact and mutually illuminate each other.[2] The conference, therefore, sought to reflect on the form and function of this comparative paradigm; Mugambi was invited to draw a kind of interpretive map of Africa and the Old Testament, that is, a map of the ancient texts and their contemporary African interpretations.

Mugambi began his Old Testament keynote address with reference to the assumed affinity between traditional African religion and culture and certain texts and motifs in the Old Testament: there is a puzzling but exciting affinity between the African religious heritage and the way of life which the Old Testament presupposes and takes for granted. This affinity is evident throughout the continent, from Cape Town to Cairo and from Somalia to Senegal, from Port Sudan to Luanda, and from Beira to Casablanca.[3]

The question is: how can this affinity be explained? On a textual level, Mugambi argues that Africa and Africans are present in the ancient texts of the Old Testament and play significant roles in the textual portrayal of the ancient Israelites. Cases here include the texts about the descendants of Abraham seeking refuge in Egypt, but also the texts regarding Cush, the African nation south of Egypt. Moreover, on a contextual level, Mugambi argues that African readers find their own experiences and concerns reflected in the lives and thoughts of the ancient Israelites. Here various parallels with regard to socio-political and socio-religious experiences could be cited. The obvious crucial question is: what consequences do these examples of an assumed affinity between Africa and the Old Testament have for African interpretive strategies vis-à-vis the Old Testament? Here Mugambi draws a sharp line between the implied biblical hermeneutics of the missionary heritage, and a more explicit biblical hermeneutics of contemporary African theology and biblical studies. The former, he argues, rejected key aspects of African cultural and religious experiences and concerns, and therefore also ignored their interpretive potential vis-à-vis the Bible, whereas the latter finds its interpretive potential vis-à-vis the Bible precisely within the interaction between the biblical texts, on the one hand, and African religio-cultural experiences and concerns, on the other.

Mugambi's key illustration, not surprisingly, is the Old Testament motif of "reconstruction." Throughout the 1990s, Mugambi argued increasingly that the liberation and black theologies of the 1960s through the 1980s – with their emphases on the Old Testament motifs of Moses and "exodus" – should now be replaced by a *theology of reconstruction*, with the books of Ezra and Nehemiah providing texts and interpretive models. The October 1999 context of Old Testament scholars coming together in Nairobi was obviously well suited for a presentation of this alternative hermeneutical paradigm; Mugambi contrasted the figure of Moses and the exodus motifs with texts related to the figure of Nehemiah and the idea of a post-exilic reconstruction of religion and society. Moses was then depicted in the image of the first generation of African leaders, as a political hero, who "led more by inspiration than through managerial training and skill. Whenever he was present, the people were orderly. In his absence there was anarchy."[4] Nehemiah was depicted in the image of the second generation of African leaders, as "a well-trained civil servant," who heard the cries of his people and responded by conducting a feasibility survey (Mugambi 2001a:17–18). In conclusion, therefore, Mugambi argued that a shift of paradigm from liberation to reconstruction in biblical hermeneutics made it possible to use the Bible constructively in the context of an African renaissance.[5]

Turning to the New Testament conference (in Hammanskraal, South Africa, in August 1999), there was a post-conference following the first meeting of the Society of New Testament Studies (SNTS) on African soil, a post-conference with a particular focus on African biblical hermeneutics. The papers presented at the conference were published in an anthology two years later.[6] Now, the SNTS is a rather elitist organization, dominated by traditional European academic structures (cf. its membership criteria) and concerns (cf. its *de facto* emphasizing of traditional critical approaches). In spite of this, however, SNTS representatives expressed quite inclusive attitudes vis-à-vis the younger guild of African New Testament scholars present at the Hammanskraal conference. One example took the form of a welcome by a past president of the SNTS in which he challenged his African colleagues to form an African society of biblical or New Testament studies:

When an African Society of Biblical or New Testament studies is organized, it should not, in my view, be seen as a subordinate satellite organization of the SNTS. The African scholars should meet the challenge and stand on their own feet, and its character should be defined by the African scholars themselves.[7] In spite of these inclusive words, however, it proved difficult to completely hide the paternalism of the western center and an African periphery of biblical studies: "The two societies [i.e., the SNTS and the suggested African counterpart] should be closely associated with each other, and step by step an increasing number of African New Testament scholars will become members of the global SNTS."[8]

In this context of global inclusiveness and western paternalism, Professor Mugambi was invited to present a keynote address. He immediately raised his flag, expressing concerns similar to those voiced at the Old Testament conference. He challenged western historical and political concepts of Africa, arguing that "only a reconstructive hermeneutic will help Africa to transcend this dark history and look to the future with hope," and he claimed that it is a responsibility of theologians – who are part of society's intellectual elite – to contribute towards achieving this.

Using the paradigm of *reconstruction*, it should be clear that the New Testament is a collection of reconstructive texts, with Jesus as the leader of a movement of social reconstruction. His 12 disciples are invited to form the vanguard of a reconstructive movement. The paradigm of reconstruction helps to provide a critique on Euro-American Church history, both within the North Atlantic region, and in the areas where the modern missionary enterprise has been operative.[9] More than in his discussion of the idea of reconstruction in relation to the Old Testament, Mugambi here included the whole collection of New Testament texts and their core message, seeing Jesus as a "leader of a movement of social reconstruction." Moreover, he also allowed this new hermeneutic of reconstruction to reveal the colonial paradigm of the North Atlantic interpretive tradition.

Some reflections on Mugambi's approach to biblical texts and studies

Three aspects of Mugambi's approach to biblical texts and critical biblical studies call for comment. First, it must be emphasized that biblical texts and motifs – as well as academia's critical discourses on these texts and motifs – actually play significant roles in Mugambi's thinking and publications, much more than is expected from other theologians and certainly other philosophers.

Re-reading Mugambi, I am struck repeatedly by the dialogue he is able to create between the ancient texts of the Bible, the discourses of critical biblical studies, and the contemporary interpretive experiences and concerns in Africa. On the textual side, Mugambi's presentation of the biblical texts is informed by critical biblical studies, not from detailed, exegetical perspectives, but from consciously theological perspectives. The texts are conceptualized as texts of affirmation rather than texts of negation with regard to Africa's culture and history. Whereas the missionary tradition tended to use the Bible to condemn African culture, African Christians "have found in the Bible an affirmation of their dignity as human beings created in the image of God."[10] This understanding of the texts presupposes a sensitive understanding of the interpretive contexts, and Mugambi meets this expectance with a form of Geertzian "thick" description of the context, allowing historical and sociological perspectives to form the overall picture.[11]

Second, this way of relating ancient texts and interpretive contexts enables Mugambi to highlight questions that are of relevance to the contemporary interpretive communities. Here, he concurs with a major characteristic of the comparative paradigm of African biblical studies, whether in its liberation or inculturation hermeneutical variants or for that matter in the variant of social criticism that in particular has characterized the most influential interpretive community of the Bible in Africa, namely the Nigerian one.[12] Whereas the major role of academia, generally speaking, is to be a critical servant of society, the more particular role of biblical studies is to facilitate a kind of interaction between ancient texts and contemporary interpretive communities that both challenges and supports these communities. In the words of Mugambi:

> The Bible as a beacon of hope in the wilderness of despair, should become an open library for everyone to read and appreciate. The challenge to African biblical scholars is to facilitate that process of making the Bible an open library.[13]

In language full of metaphors, Mugambi acknowledges that the Bible has a potential to improve life for its contemporary readers. The biblical texts are referred to with the expression, "a beacon of hope," which probably refers to their orientation function. The readers in need of orientation are described as being in a "wilderness of despair," an expression which does not refer to the colonial past but rather to the difficult post-colonial decades – in particular the 1970s through the 1990s – that followed the more euphoric first few years after liberation. In this situation, the role of biblical scholars is to facilitate the interaction between text and reader. The academic discipline of biblical studies – with its material, methods, theory, and hermeneutics – is expected to make the Bible "an open library," thereby contributing to the anticipated African renaissance.

Finally, a third aspect of Mugambi's approach to biblical texts and studies is informed by critical biblical studies, from detailed exegetical perspectives rather than from socio-historical and theological perspectives. Against this background, Mugambi has been criticized, not least by the South African biblical scholar Elelwani Farisani, for building his paradigm of reconstruction on a quite superficial reading of Ezra and Nehemiah. According to Farisani, Mugambi does not identify or critically examine the ideology behind the conflicts between the returned exiles and the non-returnees, the so-called *am haaretz*, "people of the land."

Mugambi, by using the reconstruction theme in Ezra-Nehemiah without isolating the ideological agenda of the text and identifying the group which is dominant in the text, has inadvertently identified reconstruction as that which is driven by the returned exiles at the exclusion of the *am haaretz*.[14]

Farisani's criticism would seem to be justified, in the sense that a deeper analysis of the texts in question, exegetically and ideologically informed, would strengthen the case and add new and important perspectives to the reconstruction discourse. However, the value of an interpretive paradigm lies primarily in its potential for further development and explication. A kind of parallel would be the relationship between Alan Boesak's and Itumeleng Mosala's respective uses of Genesis 4 in the struggle against apartheid in the 1980s. As Gerald O. West has shown, Boesak's surface reading of the text as well as Mosala's much deeper interpretation, explicitly making use of diachronically and ideologically informed tools, both have the function of encouraging the participants in the struggle.[15] Similarly, in Mugambi's case the point is not the text per se, rather it is about the text as an instrument for a contemporary purpose. When commenting on the transition from "exodus" to "reconstruction" as an interpretive grid, Mugambi (2001b, 25) accordingly argues:

> The figure of Nehemiah becomes paradigmatically more relevant than that of Moses. This is not to suggest that Nehemiah is an exemplary character. Rather, it is to propose that Nehemiah provides us with a mirror through which we can see our endeavours to rebuild Africa out of the ruins of the wars against racism, colonial domination and ideological branding.
>
> The focus, in other words, according to Mugambi, is the contemporary use of the text as a mirror through which we as an academic, interpretive community are challenged to participate in the building of a better society.

Conclusion

This essay began with a reference to Jesse Mugambi's multi-disciplinary focus and competence; philosophy, theology, religious studies, and applied ethics, but also education, communication policy and planning, publishing, and, not least, ecology. Let me then conclude with an anecdote illustrating these multi-disciplinary characteristics of his. One day, a decade or so ago, I had a telephone call from Jesse. After the usual "long time no see," he suddenly said, "I will actually come to your city in Norway on Friday this week, for an international conference." I had to admit that I was not aware of any philosophical or theological conference in Stavanger that week, to which Jesse just laughed and said, "It is a conference on water resources, and I am part of the Kenyan delegation." I should have remembered, of course, that conservation and distribution of fresh water is a key issue for Jesse Mugambi, the philosopher and theologian, a trustee of the Kenya Rainwater Association as well as other ecological and ecumenical groups and associations that are concerned about the current climate changes. Therefore, let this anecdote serve to illustrate Mugambi's firm conviction that we as members of academia – with its broad specter of disciplines, such as philosophy and theology, and I am sure he would allow me to include biblical studies – are to perform our scholarship not simply for sport's sake. Rather, as academics, with the tools and material provided to us by our respective academic disciplines and by the critical discourses in which we engage, are called to *serve* the community from which we come and to which we are accountable.

Notes

1 M. N. Getui, K. Holter and V. Zinkuratire, eds. *Interpreting the Old Testament in Africa.* (Nairobi: Acton, 2001).
2 K. Holter, *Yahweh in Africa: Essays on Africa and the Old Testament.* (New York: Peter Lang, Bible and Theology in Africa, 2000), 1; K. Holter, "The Current State of Old Testament Scholarship in Africa: Where Are We at the Turn of the Century?" 27–39, M. N. Getui, K. Holter and V. Zinkuratire, eds. *Interpreting the Old Testament in Africa.* (Nairobi: Acton, 2001); K. Holter *Old Testament Research for Africa: A Critical and Annotated Bibliography of African Old Testament Dissertations, 1967–2000.* (New York: Peter Lang, 2002), 3; E. Anum, "Comparative Readings of the Bible in Africa," 457–73, G. O. West and M. W. Dube, eds. *The Bible in Africa: Transactions, Trajectories and Trends.* (Leiden: Brill, 2000).
3 J.N.K. Mugambi, "Africa and the Old Testament," 7–25. M. N. Getui, K. Holter and V. Zinkuratire, *Interpreting the Old Testament in Africa.* (Nairobi: Acton, 2001), 7.
4 Mugambi, 2001, 17.
5 Mugambi, "Africa and the Old Testament," 2001, 22–3.
6 J.N.K. Mugambi, "Foundations for an African Approach to Bliblical Hermeneutics," in M. N. Getui, T. Maluleke and J. Ukpong, eds. 9.29, *Interpreting the New Testament in Africa.* (Nairobi: Acton, 2001), 9–29.
7 P. Borgen, "A Necessary and Important Step," 1–4. M. N. Getui, T. Maluleke and J. Ukpong, eds. *Interpreting the New Testament in Africa.* (Nairobi: Acton, 2001).
8 Borgen, 2001, 4.
9 Mugambi, "Foundations for an African Approch to Biblical Hemeneutics," 2001, 26.
10 Ibid., 16.
11 Clifford Geertz, *The Interpretation of Cultures: Selected Essays.* (New York: Basic Books, 1973), 3–36.
12 E. Martey, *Africn Theology: Inculturation and Liberation.* (Maryknoll: Orbis Books, 1993); K. Holter, *Yahweh in Africa: Essays on Africa and the Old Testament.* (New York: Peter Lang, 2000), 61076.

13 J.N.K. Mugambi, "Challenges to African Scholars in Biblical Hermeneutics," in J.N.K. Mugambi and J. A. Smith, eds. *Text and Context in New Testament Hermeneutics*. (Nairobi: Acton, 2004), 6–21, 20.

14 E. B. Farisani, "The Post-Exile Motif in Mugambi's Theology of Reconstruction," in I.M.T. Mwase and E. K. Kamaara, eds. *Theologies of Liberation and Reconstruction: Essays in Honour of Professor J.N.K. Mugambi, Ph.D.* (Nairobi: Acton, 2012), 199–223, 212.

15 Gerald O. West, *Biblical Hermeneutics of Liberation: Modes of Reading the Bible in the South African Context*, Second Edition. (Pietermaritzburg: Cluster Publications, 1995).

Bibliography

Anum, E. "Comparative Readings of the Bible in Africa." In *The Bible in Africa: Transactions, Trajectories and Trends*, edited by G. O. West and M. W. Dube, 457–73. Leiden: Brill.

Borgen, P. "A Necessary and Important Step." *Interpreting the New Testament in Africa*, edited by M. N. Getui, T. Maluleke, and J. Ukpong, 1–4. Nairobi: Acton, 2001.

Geertz, C. *The Interpretation of Cultures: Selected Essays*. New York: Basic Books, 1973.

Getui, M. N., T. Maluleke, and J. Ukpong, eds. *Interpreting the New Testament in Africa*. Nairobi: Acton, 2001.

Getui, M. N., K. Holter, and V. Zinkuratire, eds. *Interpreting the Old Testament in Africa*. Nairobi: Acton, 2001.

Farisani, E. B. "The Post-Exile Motif in Mugambi's Theology of Reconstruction." *Theologies of Liberation and Reconstruction: Essays in Honour of Professor J.N.K. Mugambi, Ph.D.*, edited by I. M. T. Mwase, and E. K. Kamaara, 199–223. Nairobi: Acton, 2012.

Holter, K. *Yahweh in Africa: Essays on Africa and the Old Testament*. New York: Peter Lang (Bible and Theology in Africa, 1), 2000.

———. "The Current State of Old Testament Scholarship in Africa: Where Are We at the Turn of the Century?" In *Interpreting the Old Testament in Africa*, edited by M. N. Getui, K. Holter, and V. Zinkuratire, 27–39. Nairobi: Acton, 2001.

———. *Old Testament Research for Africa: A Critical and Annotated Bibliography of African Old Testament Dissertations, 1967–2000*. New York: Peter Lang (Bible and Theology in Africa, 3), 2002.

———. *Contextualized Old Testament Scholarship in Africa*. Nairobi: Acton, 2008.

Martey, E. *African Theology: Inculturation and Liberation*. Maryknoll, New York: Orbis Books, 1993.

Mugambi, J.N.K. "Africa and the Old Testament." In *Interpreting the Old Testament in Africa*, edited by M. N. Getui, K. Holter, and V. Zinkuratire, 7–25. Nairobi: Acton, 2001a.

———."Foundations for an African Approach to Biblical Hermeneutics." In *Interpreting the New Testament in Africa*, edited by M. N. Getui, T. Maluleke, and J. Ukpong, 9–29. Nairobi: Acton, 2001b.

———. "Challenges to African Scholars in Biblical Hermeneutics." In *Text and Context in New Testament Hermeneutics*, edited by J.N.K. Mugambi, and J. A. Smith, 6–21. Nairobi: Acton, 2004.

West, G. O. *Biblical Hermeneutics of Liberation: Modes of Reading the Bible in the South African Context*, Second Edition. Pietermaritzburg: Cluster Publications, 1995.

2 The life of King David as a model of reconstruction

David Tuesday Adamo[1]

Introduction

Jesse N. K. Mugambi has taught religion and philosophy and has been a key voice in theology and religious studies in Africa. Although Mugambi is not a biblical scholar, the place of the Bible and its narratives have provided material for Mugambi's theology. Perhaps, the best usage of Biblical narratives in the theology of Mugambi is the fact that he grounded his theology of reconstruction on the biblical account of Ezra and Nehemiah, who promoted the reconstruction of Jerusalem. By returning to that account, Mugambi reaffirmed the place of biblical narratives and reinforced the idea that past narratives introduce characters that play a paradigmatic role which later generations could embrace in a critical manner. Mugambi's theology of reconstruction grounded on the work of Ezra and Nehemiah demonstrates that Biblical characters can be seen as models of different aspects of ministry.

In this chapter, I discuss the work of David, who along with Abraham and Moses, is an important figure in the Hebrew Bible because of his leadership role.[2] David was one most respected kings and writers of the Hebrew Bible who before Ezra and Nehemiah demonstrated that the political community can be reorganized.[3] David's mission was much broader, and he approached it with a complex and contradictory a personality.[4] Some traditional scholars consider David a pious individual who became King of Israel, some critical scholars see him as "a cunning usurper who murders and schemes his way to a throne not rightfully his."[5] Marti J. Steussy is also one of the critical scholars who believe that the Bible portrays David as "innocent and attractive hero" and another aspect of the narrative add human dimensions to David as "a shrewd political operator of suspect motives who is a mixed blessing to his people."[6] There is still a need for a well-balanced presentation of the personality of David as it appears in the Deuteronomistic, prophetic, Chronicler, and psalmic literature to demonstrate how David is a model of post-fallen humanity (without exception) yet offers different models of leadership necessary for the reconstruction of Africa today as Mugambi has argued. Although David did not build a wall or temple, his life mirrors a reconstructed life and kingdom. How David lived a life of reconstruction as Mugambi propounded for Ezra and Nehemiah is the task of this paper.

David in the Deuteronomistic History

The term Deuteronomistic History is an invention of biblical scholars.[7] Martin Noth was considered the father of the Deuteronomistic History-hypothesis even though he was not the first person to speak of the Deuteronomistic redactions.[8] Romer argues that before Noth, the idea of the Deuteronomistic hypothesis was already mentioned by John Calvin, Andreas Masius, Baruch Spinoza, Wilhelm De Wette, John William Colenso, Heinrich Ewald, Abraham Kuenen, Julius Wellhausen, and Bernhard Duhm.[9] The Deuteronomistic author indicates that the most memorable figures of ancient Israel are the kings of the united kingdom of Israel (Saul, David, and Solomon) whose stories are narrated in 1–2 Samuel and 1 Kings 1–11.[10] However, a very different version of their stories appears in 1 Chronicles 10–29 and 2 Chronicles 1–9. Many scholars depend on these biblical narratives to portray the situation in Palestine in the 10th century (900s) BCE, especially the so-called united monarchy of Israel.[11]

The first episode in David's rise to power is his anointing by Samuel as the future King of Israel (1 Sam. 16:10–13).[12] His first public appearance was his encounter with Goliath which leads to Goliath's death (1 Sam. 17). The books of 1 Samuel 16–1 Kings 2, describe David the reign as a central function in the Deuteronomistic history with literary and theological perspectives.[13] From the literary analysis, it has been divided into two: the description of Saul and David and a Succession History. Although there is no unanimous agreement as to the extent of the history of David's rise, the unity of the succession history has greater acceptance, and this includes 2 Samuel 9–20–1 Kings 2. A closer examination of Chapter 7 shows that the theme in it is in light of Deuteronomistic theology and reflection because the emphasis is on the inseparable connection between the house of David, the people of Israel, and the hereditary land.

God rejected David's proposal to build a temple, but gave David the mandate to finish the work of Joshua and fulfill the work of the fathers (2 Samuel 7:9–11). 2 Samuel 7:12 connects Abraham with David. David is seen as the second Joshua in 2 Samuel 7:10–14 who will defeat Israel's enemy and Israel will find rest in the promise land. Even though David was not allowed to build the temple, he would make "a great name" for Yahweh. This has to do with the powerful political office which David was to attain by his successful wars. The promise of David's dynasty is given forever in 2 Samuel 7:16. 2 Samuel 23:1–7 uses the expression *berith olam*, an everlasting covenant. The unbroken loyalty to Yahweh warrants this dynastic promise as the Deuteronomistic redactor characteristically emphasizes in 1 King 3:3, 6; 8:25; 9:4; 11:4, 6, 33, 38, and other passages agree with the consistent emphasis on the loyalty and righteousness of Yahweh's servant, David.[14] The religiosity of David is portrayed in the expression, "Yahweh was with him"(1 Samuel 16:18) and the claim that David sought the oracle of Yahweh at the beginning and the end of his life (1 Samuel 23:1–4; 2 Sam. 5:17–25).

The Deuteronomic historians give further positive details of the life David. He was reluctant to shed innocent blood and he punished those who committed the crime (I Sam. 25:28–31). However, David's kingdom fell because of apostasy and syncretism. Yet David's loyalty and the choice of the city of David sustained the mutilated kingdom until the fall. The Deuteronomistic conception expresses the greatness of Yahweh, the work of Yahweh and the people of God as markers of the Davidic dynasty which is portrayed as blessed by God and also criticized when things did not go right (2 Sam 10–24).[15] The Deuteronomistic redaction of the Bathsheba event made 2 Sam 10–12 a key section in the description of David under the curse. It is basic for the understanding of the episode to see that the punishment which David unknowingly pronounces upon himself is sevenfold. The Deuteronomistic presentation of the life of David certainly reflects human life, yet David demonstrated an ability to reconstruct Israel as a political community despite the fact that he had fallen so many times. David was an ordinary shepherd, but Yahweh and his prophets enabled him to live a life of reconstruction.

David in the Psalms

There are about 73 Psalms connected with David by the superscription *ledavid*. Very early it was said to mean David's authorship of those Psalms, particularly since in Psalms 34:1; 51:1; 52:1. However, this meaning has been called into question. Mowinckel thinks that *ledavid*a actually means "for David." In light of the comparison of *ledavid* with the discovery of the Ugaritic documents *lb'l* which means "belonging to the Baal Epic," and *lkrt*, belonging to the Keret Epic, many scholars interpreted *ledavid* to mean the same thing, "belonging to the David collection."[16] The tradition of David as a great poet and singer influences this superscription in the Psalms. Some of the Psalms present David as the founder of the dynasty and the reigning king. For example, Psalm 144:10 which is the Thanksgiving vow of the Royal Psalms says "who givest salvation to kings, who rescues David, his servant." David is reflected in the saving acts of Yahweh, and called the servant of Yahweh who has seen the "triumphs, saving acts" and "steadfast love of Yahweh" (Pslam 18:51).

Psalms 78, 89, and 132, mention the role of David and his significance for the reigning king extensively. It is noteworthy that the building of the temple is mentioned before the choice of David despite the fact that it does not correspond to the sequence of events in the Deuteronomistic account. However, the Davidic tradition and that of Zion are interwoven. David's life of reconstruction is seen in his choice of the city of God which became the common theme of a cultic celebration and became the actual setting of this Psalm even though Yahweh did not permit him to build the house of the Lord. However, no one can dispute the fact that he sincerely had the mind of reconstruction when he desired to build the temple.

Psalm 89 also talks about Nathan's prophecy (vv. 20–38) as a background for a petition on behalf of a king. David himself is the object of this oracle rather than Solomon or his descendants. Psalm 89:23 mentions the promise of victory over enemies without parallel in II Samuel 7. It is certain that the permanency of the dynasty of David is an important issue in Psalm 89 because of the divine choice of David which mentioned his desire to build a temple, the taking of the ark to Jerusalem, and an oath to preserve Davidic kingdom.

David in the prophets

Although there is no common prophetic attitude toward David, occasional references to ideological significance and influence of the Davidic tradition is perceptible even when his name is not specifically mentioned. The prophets are not unique among biblical writers when they chose figures from the past to express their ideas of morality and truth.[17] The book of Amos has only two allusions to David. Amos 6:5 says, "Like David, they invent for themselves instruments of music." Amos 9:11 mentions the restoration of the fallen booth of David.[18] Hosea mentions David only once in 3:5 when it says that "the children of Israel shall return and seek Yahweh their God, and David, their king." This expression is also found in Jeremiah 30:9.

In Isaiah, the Davidic and the Zion traditions are combined as in the Psalms,[19] Emmanuel prophecy is directed to the "house of David" in 7:13 just as the oracle of the Prince of Peace in 9:1–6 refers to the throne of David and his kingdom in 9:6. In 16:5 there is the promise of the messianic ruler who will "sit in the tent of David." In 37:35, Yahweh will defend Jerusalem from the king of Assyria and deliver it "for my sake and the sake of my servant David."

The book of Jeremiah designates the king as "the one who sits on the throne of David" in his direct address, "thus says Yahweh concerning. . . ." It appears more frequently in statements concerning the king and the people as in 13:13, 17:25; 22:4. Yahweh was to raise up for David a genuine Branch (23:5), an indication that Jeremiah expects a new king from the lineage of David to fulfill the ideal and righteous king. This promise was repeated in 33:15 with emphasis that the permanence of the dynasty will guarantee the continuation of the kingdom (33:17, 21). The book of Ezekiel also contains the hope of a new king who will rule over the reassembled and reunited people of God as one shepherd, that is "my servant David" (34:23), and the same thought is repeated in 37:24–25 where the new David is called king.

In Deutero-Isaiah the concept of David is remarkably reinterpreted. In 55:3 Yahweh promises to make an everlasting covenant with the whole people because of Yahweh's love for David. Zechariah speaks of the restoration of the Davidic dynasty, the "house of David." The eschatological kingdom of salvation, the citizens, will be like David and the dynasty like a divine being and "angel of Yahweh."

David in the Chroniclers

It is remarkable that 19 of the 65 chapters in the book of Chronicles are devoted to the history of David (I Chron. 11–29), indicating significance that the Chroniclers ascribe to David. The Chroniclers differ from the Deuteronomistic account. First, the Chroniclers omit all the unfavorable activities of David. For example, Uriah's story (II Sam.11) and the civil war with Absalom and Sheba (II Sam. 15–18 and 20), his war with Eshbaal, and all the events during David's youth are omitted. The Chroniclers made David an ideal figure who did not only found the dynasty but prepared all the necessary things for the building of the temple and planned for the organization of the cult by divine commission and authority (1 Chron. 28:19; 2Chron. 29:25). According to the Chroniclers, all the musical instruments are "the instruments of David" (2 Chronicles 29:27) in Nehemiah as "the musical instruments of David the man of God" (Neh. 12:36).

The Chroniclers in their reconstruction of the life of David made three changes to the account of the prophecy of Nathan in II Samuel 7. The first one is that they retain the promise of Yahweh who will be the king's father but omit the sin and punishment of the king and continues with the divine permanence of Yahweh's steadfast love (II Sam. 7:14–5; I Chron. 17:13). The second modification is that while 2 Samuel 7:12 speaks directly of Solomon, "who shall come forth from your (David's) body," 1 Chronicles 17:11 speaks of an offspring, "who will be from your sons."[20] The third modification is that, while 2 Samuel 7:16 says that "your house and your kingdom shall be made sure forever before me," 1 Chronicles says, "I will confirm him in my house and my kingdom." That means the Chroniclers tend to elevate the kingdom of David into a theocratic realm. The decisive new element in the Chroniclers' work is the Messianic tendency. Hope for the restoration/reconstruction of the royal house is connected with the very idea of the steadfast love of David which Yahweh promised and showed to him (II Chron. 6:42). The importance of the Davidic covenant to the Chronicler's interpretation of the kingdom is expressed emphatically and repeatedly.

David as a model for reconstruction

In ancient Israel, not many shepherds became kings. This shows that David as a shepherd rising to such a high position of eminence in King Saul's court would have acquired many talents. What impressed Saul in David that he brought him to his court possibly impressed the people because they soon began to sing David's praises on the streets that Saul has killed thousands but David tens of thousands (1 Sam. 18:7). The author of the book of Samuel concerns himself mainly about "David as a king" and "as a man."[21] God reconstructed David's life and made him a king and promised to safeguard his tenure in office and dynasty.[22]

David is a man of reconstruction with his strong desire to build a house for the Lord in the Deuteronomistic, Chroniclers, Psalms, and prophetic account of David.

In 1 King 8:25 and 9:4 the Deuteronomist narrated David's request to build a temple for Yahweh. Even though he was refused because the necessary condition of complete rest from Israel's enemies had not yet been fulfilled (1 Kgs 5:18–19), he was commended for his request (1 Kgs 8:18). David's commitment to the policy of centralized worship can be said to make David a person of true reconstruction. The Deuteronomist centers this section of this history on the prophecy of Nathan in 2 Samuel 7. The Deuteronomist presents David's willingness to consult and obey the Prophet Nathan's words for this, David was rewarded for his obedience and fidelity. As part of this reward, the division of the kingdom did not take place during his reign (I Kings 11:36).[23]

David as a military genius reconstructed his military personnel, rebuilt Jerusalem, and erected significant buildings and the Deuteronomistic calls David the greatest national hero that Israel ever had. Soon after he became king, the gifted warrior, and military tactician, he employed this military ability to defeat or contain his enemies who were his neighbors. Prior to becoming King, David was exiled by Saul, but David was able to organize a court in Adullam and supported himself and his troops by running a protection racket (1 Sam. 25). When the Amalekites raided Ziklag, David avenged the raid and brought back his people and took back all the Amalekites had taken (1 Sam. 30). When Saul died, he became the king of Judah in Hebron and later the whole of Israel.

After David defeated the Moabites, Ammonites, Edomites, Syrians, the Philistines, the Girshurites, and the Girzites, he incorporated them into his administration and secured their pledge of allegiance to him. The spoils and taxes from these conquered people were used to erect an important building, and he conscripted mercenaries into his private army. David used his military genius reconstruct his army, conquered Jerusalem and made the city his capital.

David was a reconstructionist in his political and administrative life. Perhaps the biblical portrait of David that comes close to the analysis Mugambi has done on Ezra and Nehemiah, and the returning exiles. In 1 Samuel, he was able to make both the Israelites and the Philistines believe that he was for both of them.[24] After the death of Saul, his adroitness led to his being crowned king of Judah and later king of the entire Israel. He requested that his wife who was Saul's daughter, come back and this action supported his claim to the throne. Through this move David found it relatively easy to overcome tribal suspicions and resistance to the monarchy and to unite the whole Israel into a remarkably powerful alliance that brought all of Israel together. To do this, David promoted social stability and external security to consolidate Israel as a dominant political force. David took control of Jerusalem a major administrative center and made it the capital city, and for that reason, it was made a neutral city that did not belong to the North or South, and with that David avoided petty jealousy between the North and South.

David's administrative genius which he used effectively for reconstruction was demonstrated by his establishment of royal administration with eminent officials. David moved the Ark of Covenant to Jerusalem to mark the reconstruction of the kingdom. The Ark of the Covenant was of iconic significance because it represented the story of Exodus and the covenant and symbolically the act of common worship of Yahweh which held them together (2 Sam.6). Jerusalem became the "city of David." It removed the powers from the tribes to the center of authority. David combined military prowess with inspirational leadership and that secured for him a successful ruler and a religious icon for future generations.

David as a skilled musician used his song and music to reconstruct Saul's life whenever an evil spirit possessed him. According to 1 Samuel 16:18, David was a skillful musician and a gifted poet. When Saul was looking for a musician to help him overcome his difficulties, one of his servants said,

> I have seen a son of Jesse the Bethlehemite who is skillful in playing, a man of valor, a warrior, prudent in speech, and a man of good presence; and the LORD was with him (1 Sam. 16:18).Saul loved him greatly, and he became his armor-bearer (I Sam 16:21). Moreover, whenever the evil spirit from God came upon Saul, David took the lyre and played it with his hand and Saul will be relieved and feel better and the evil spirit would depart from him (1 Sam.16:23).

David was a traditional composer of Israelite love-songs. Seventy-three psalms out of the 150 psalms are attributed to David.[25] A composition found in the Dead Sea Scrolls credited David with 3,600 Psalms and 450 songs.[26]

To say that David was chronically religious is not an exaggeration. One of the most significant stories that described how religious David was is his sexual affair with Bathsheba and the murder of her husband (2 Sam. 11). Normally, such affairs would not have been a surprise considering ancient culture but what is surprising is the courageous denunciation of David's behavior by the prophet, Nathan. What is more amazing that revealed David's religiosity is his sincere repentance (2 Sam 12:2–15) and his action to reconstruct himself through repentance. The inclusion of such a story by the Deuteronomistic Historian is probably to emphasize David's religiosity, humility, and to tell the readers that even the greatest of all kings was still accountable to Yahweh and his covenant. The episode also demonstrates that David's failure did not threaten his enduring dynasty, which was to last forever according to the Deuteronomistic account (2 Sam. 7:1–17).

According to 2 Samuel 23:2, David says, "The spirit of the Lord speaks through me." This appears to mean that David was a prophet and was regarded as such in antiquity. The composition from the Dead Sea Scrolls that listed the work of David says that David composed all his psalms and songs in the spirit of prophecy and that he was wise.[27] David's religiosity is also demonstrated in the fact that, he always consulted the ephod to obtain Yahweh's will in the battles he fought, especially with the Philistines. Realizing the pain, they went through; he dedicated that water to Yahweh instead of drinking it (11 Sam. 23:15–17). He "poured it out to Yahweh." Another way that King David demonstrated his religiosity was his ability to forgive Saul when he had every opportunity to kill him. Instead, he cut a piece of his cloth and showed it to him and then promised not to destroy the anointed person. Further, he made an oath not to destroy his descendants (1 Sam.24:1–24). No doubt David used his religiosity to reconstruct the life of ancient Israel into deep religious commitment than ever before.

Conclusion

Despite scholars' suspicion of the portrayal of David in the Deuteronomistic, prophetic, and Psalmic literature, David was an exceptional and well-rounded character in the Bible. He was a model of what a post-fallen person. Even though he was named "the beloved of Yahweh" he was not a saint by any standard. He established the Davidic monarchy and remains one of the outstanding leaders of Israel. David's life invites others to personally reconstruct their own lives and engage in activities that will reconstruct their political community as David did to the nation of Israel. The accomplishment of David makes his story "one of the finest pieces of literature to come down to us from antiquity" because he was a reconstructionist *par excellence*.[28]

Notes

1 Research Fellow, Unisa. The research for this paper is supported generously by the Department Biblical and Ancient Studies University of South Africa (UNISA).

2 David Pleins, "From the Stump of Jesse: The Image of King David as a Social Forcein the Writings of the Hebrew Prophets," *Proceedings*. (Grand Rapids: Eerdmans, 1986), 161–9.

3 Michael Coogan, *A Brief Introduction to the Old Testament*. (New York, Oxford: Oxford University Press, 2009).

4 J. M. P. Smith, "The Character of King David," *Journal of Biblical Literature*, 52, no. 1 (1933): 1–11.

5 J. M. P. Smith, "The Character of King David," 1–3; Bosworth David, "Evaluating King David: Old Problems and Recent Scholarship," *The Catholic Biblical Quarterly*, 68 (2006): 191–210.

6 Marti Steussy and Marti David. *Biblical Portraits of PowerStudies on Personalities of the Old Testament*. (Columbia: University of South Carolina Press, 1999), 8.

7 Thomas Romer, *The So-Called Deuteronomistic History*. (New York: T & T Clark, 2007), 13.

8 Thomas Romer, 13.

9 Ibid.

10 K. L. Noll, Canaan *and Israel in Antiquity*. (New York: London, Sidney: Bloomsbury, 2013), 215.
11 The Words United Monarchy never occurs in the Bible, but it is the term constructed by scholars in contemporary scholarship (Noll, 2013:2015).
12 Victor Matthews, *The Hebrew Prophets and Their Social World*. (Grand Rapids: Baker Academic, 2012), 88.
13 J. M. P. Smith, "The Character of King David," 11.
14 F. H. Cryer, "David's Rise to Power and the Death of Abner," *Vetus Testamentum*, XXXV (1985): 4, 385–94.
15 Ringgren, 1978, 16.
16 H. Ringgren, *Theological Dictionary of the Old Testament*. Edited by G. Johannes Botterweck, Helmer Ringgren,es. Translated by John T. Willis, Geoffrey W. Bromiley, David E. Green, and Vol III. (Grand Rapids: WB. Eerdmans Publishing Company,1978), 157–69.
17 Pleins, 169–79.
18 The passage is said to be spurious because it seems there is an assumption that Davidic dynasty is already fallen.
19 G. von Rad, *Theology of the Old Testament*, 1965, 169–75.
20 Ringgren, 168.
21 D. M. Gun, *The Story of King David*. (JSOTS 6 Sheffield, JSOT, 1978), 87–111; Cryer, 1985, 385–481.
22 Tremper Longman, III and Raymond B. Dillard, *An Introduction to the Old Testament*. (Grand Rapids: Zondervan Publishers, 2006), 159.
23 Bosworth, "Evaluating King David," 68, 191–210; Smith, 1–11.
24 Yael Shemesh, "David in the in the Service of King Achish of Gath: Renegade to His People or a Fifth Column in the Philistine Army?" *VetusTestamentum*, 57 (2007): 73–90.
25 Coogan, *A Brief Introduction to the Old Testament*, 20.
26 John Collins, *Introduction to the Hebrew Bible*. (Minneapolis: Fortress Press, 2004), 242–3.; John Collins, "The Historical Character of the Old Testament in Recent Biblical Theology," *The Catholic Biblical Quarterly*, 41 (1979): 185–204.
27 Collins, *Introduction*, 243.
28 Ibid., 209.

Bibliography

Berger, Yitzhak. "On Pattering in the Book of Samuel: News of Death and the Kingship of David." *Journal for the Study of Old Testament* 33, no. 4 (2011): 463–81.

Bosworth, David A. "Evaluating King David: Old Problems and Recent Scholarship." *The Catholic Biblical Quarterly* 68 (2006): 191–210.

Brueggeman, Walter. *Abiding Astonishment, Psalms, Modernity, and the Making of History*. Louisville, KY: Westminster/John Knox Press, 1991.

Childs, B. *Introduction to Old Testament as Scriptures*. Philadelphia: Fortress Press, 1979.

———. *Introduction to the Hebrew Bible*. Minneapolis: Fortress Press, 2004.

Coogan, Michael D. *Brief Introduction to the Old Testament*. New York, Oxford: Oxford University Press, 2009.

Cryer, F. H. "David's Rise to Power and the Death of Abner." *VetusTestamentum* XXXV, no. 4 (1985): 385–94.

Gun, D. M. "The Story of King David." *JSOTS 6 Sheffield, JSOT* (1978): 87–111.

Jones, Alfred. *Jone's Dictionary of Old Testament Proper Names*. Grand Rapids: Kregel Publications, 1990.

Kirkpatrick, P. G. *The Old Testament and Folklore Studies*, JSOTSup, 62. Sheffield: Sheffield Academic Press, 1988.

Longman, Tremper III, and Raymond B. Dillard. *An Introduction to the Old Testament*. Grand Rapids: Zondervan Publishers, 2006.

Mazar, A. "The Search for David and Solomon: An Archaeological Perspective." In *Quest for the Historical Israel: Debating Archeology and the History of Early Israel: Lectures Delivered at the Annual Colloquim of the Institute for Secular Humanistic Judaism, Detroit October 2005*, edited by Schmidt, 117–39. Leiden: Brill, 2007.

Noll, K. L. *The Faces of David*, JSOT Sup, 242. Sheffield: Sheffield Academic Press, 1997.

———. *Canaan and Israel in Antiquity*. New York, London, Sidney: Bloomsbury, 2013.

Noth, Martin. *The Deuteronomistic History*, JSOTSup 15. Sheffield: Academic Press, 1991.

O'Brien, Mark. "The 'Deuteronomistic History' as Story of Israel's Leaders." *Australian Biblical Review* (1989): 14–34.

Plains, I. David. "From the Stump of Jesse: The Image of King David as a Social Force in the Writings of the Hebrew Prophets." *Proceedings*, 161–9. Grand Rapids: Eerdmans, 1986.

Ringgren, H. *Theological Dictionary of the Old Testament*. Edited by G. Johannes Botterweck, Helmer Ringgren, Translated by John T. Willis, Geoffrey W. Bromiley, David E. Green, and Vol III, 157–169. Grand Rapids: WB. Eerdmans Publishing Company, 1978.

Romer, Thomas. *The So-called Deuteronomistic History*. New York: T & T Clark, 2007.

Seters J. Van. *The Biblical Saga of King David*. Winona Lake: Eisenbrauns, 2009.

Shemesh, Yael. "David in the in the Service of King Achish of Gath: Renegade to His People or a Fifth Column in the Philistine Army?" *Vetus Testamentum* 57 (2007): 73–90.

Smith, J.M.P. "The Character of King David." *Journal of Biblical Literature* 52, no. 1 (1933): 1–11.

Steussy, Marti. *David: Biblical Portraits of power studies on Personalities of the Old Testament*. Columbia: University of South Carolina Press, 1999.

3 Worshipping God the spirit "in spirit and truth" in Africa

One African woman's reflections on John 4:19–24

Madipoane Masenya (Ngwan'a Mphahlele)

Introduction

In some of his writings, Jesse N. K. Mugambi has highlighted the crucial role that the Bible plays in African Christianity irrespective of its emergence in alien cultural contexts. He links the preceding appeal to the belief by African Christians that the Bible has a message. In Mugambi's view, the power of the gospel message enables people to engage in the reconstruction business as they get encouraged to live up to their potential through God's help.[1] Due to the belief that the Bible has a Message, many African Christians, argues Mugambi, approach the Bible as a manual for life. Such an approach cannot do justice to both the Bible and the interpretive process as the Bible cannot address all of the challenges that are faced by present day African Christians.[2] A critical approach to the Bible will enable the readers to discern consistency in biblical teaching.[3] He thus recommends that cognisance should be taken of the contexts in which biblical books emerged and the different cultural and religious contexts of African Bible readers.

> Today, biblical literalism has reduced the Bible into an instruction manual that it was never meant to be. The Bible is, in my view an anthology of stories, told from a wide variety of perspectives, put together to convey the dynamics of a community of faith. In the same way, Biblical Studies can best be conducted with conscious attention to the cultural specificity of the scholars and the communities of faith they represent.[4]

Mugambi has proposed a theology of reconstruction in which certain biblical figures, especially the figure of Nehemiah in the Hebrew Bible are used as models for African Christians to all engage in the process of rebuilding and reconstruction. Even the figure of Jesus in the New Testament is cited as a model for reconstruction theology. People from all walks of life learned something from their interaction with Jesus.[5] What Mugambi argues in the preceding statement will hopefully become evident as we engage the text of the encounter between Jesus and the woman of Samaria here below. The text will be engaged within the framework of the theme of liturgy and worship in African contexts. The main question addressed in this essay is thus: how may we read the text of John 4:19–24 in an African Pentecostal liturgical context in South Africa?

Why the choice of John 4:19–24?

The text of John 4:19–24 records an unusual encounter between Jesus, a Jewish Rabbi, and a woman not only of "questionable" character but a woman from an "outside" ethnic group. The rabbis saw Samaritan women as monstrous from birth, that is perpetually unclean and as a result, a permanent source of uncleanness for their community.[6] The encounter was not only questionable within the social context of the first-century Mediterranean world (cf Jn4:27),[7] but also within a traditional African context. In the African hierarchical context, figures of authority like *dikgoshi* (traditional political leaders), could not be approached directly by subjects, let alone female ones. What is it that attracts me to a text which to my mind is the least preached about within African Pentecostal Sunday "worship" services here in South Africa?

First, one of the main reasons for my attraction to the episode of John 4:19–24 is the intriguing connection between Jesus and the situation of (African) women. For African Catholic theologian Tèrésa Souga, Jesus in his identity as God-man takes on the situation of weakness experienced by many an African woman. Hence,

> There can be no understanding of Jesus Christ outside of the situation in which we seek to understand ourselves. It is by way of these situations that Jesus bears on his person the condition of the weak, and hence that of women.[8]

Jesus' meaningful encounter with a questionable rural woman, one from a "problematic" race,[9] can thus only be affirming to the present author. She comes from a context which continues to grapple with the racial legacies left by both colonialism and the *apartheid* regime.

Second, the broader "liturgical" framework in which the encounter between Jesus and the Samaritan woman occurs, seems to buttress the notion that true worship cannot be like a pie in the spiritual sky. The impact of a believer's individual and corporeal encounter with God (the Sacred Other) within a specific liturgical setting, of necessity, should spill over into the everyday lives of the people. However, the caution by Kevin Seasoltz on the creation of a healthy balance between liturgical acts and our commitment to social advocacy should be welcomed:

> The temptation on the part of liturgists is to retreat from the world's problems into a safe, comfortable, aesthetically pleasing past and to

> convert liturgical worship into thematic celebrations of abstract universals that supposedly please God but have little to do with responsible life in the world. The temptation on the part of social activists is to reject the liturgy as totally irrelevant, as a distraction of valuable time and energy which should be spent solving the world's problems.[10]

In the same vein, Susan White reasons, "Unless the community is seeking to be a just community within itself and seeking justice for all people, then the worship of God in [the] church is to no avail."[11]

Liturgy is thus not the only service to God; it happens in the context of the believer's acknowledgment of the salvific acts of God in Christ, enabled by the Holy Spirit in the believer's life in the world through the acts performed to fellow human beings in the world. The Trinitarian God we worship created us in love. God redeems us through the unmerited power of the resurrection of Jesus. In God's Spirit, we are joined in the holy and eternal life of God.[12] The Bible thus plays a pivotal role in our theory and praxis of worship.

In line with the last section of the title of this essay, that is, "One African Woman's Reflections on John 4:19–24," in the following paragraphs, I offer reflections by asking the following questions: What does it mean to worship God neither in Samaria nor Jerusalem but in Africa? Is the worship of God gendered? What could it mean for an African Pentecostal woman to worship God who is Spirit, in spirit and truth? The experiences of African Pentecostal women in South Africa will serve as a hermeneutical lens through which to unlock the true nature of worship according to John 4:19–24. Factors such as culture, racial background, and gender among others, might in one way or other, affect one's way of worship. As already observed with Mugambi, there is thus a need to take seriously the situation of various Bible readers (read: worshippers) in their varied contexts. The place of true worship, maintained Jesus, could not be confined to Jerusalem or Samaria.[13] However, once a worshipper is in perfect harmony with the rhythm of the Spirit, she/he would be able to experience the thrill of what it means to worship God in spirit and truth.

One of the premises upon which this essay is based is that just as worship should not remain within the confines of sacred spaces and worshippers' lives, worship cannot be separated from the real lives of the worshippers themselves. James White is thus on target that "Christian worship has to be experienced to be understood, and this cannot be done in laboratory or library but only in church. Only by participating can we understand what it is Christians do worship."[14]

On the reader's context

Although one was fortunate to be exposed to the liturgical contexts of the following ecclesiastical traditions, Anglican, Roman Catholic, Dutch

Reformed, Lutheran as well as the mainstream Pentecostal ones, as already noted, our reading of the text of John 4:19–24 will be informed by an African Pentecostal context in South Africa. In the latter context, just like in the Ghanaian charismatic context, one of the significant hallmarks of spirituality is "the affirmation of worship as an authentic encounter with God."[15] Could this be the reason why the liturgical item, "Praise and Worship" occupies a special place within the Sunday "worship"[16] services in my context? The preceding liturgical item usually occurs just prior to the "message" to be delivered on a specific day, as if to give the believers an opportunity to approach God in humility and honour, and surrendering their hearts. As they do the latter, they would be able to receive from God as God's servant would stand in the gap between the believers and God through the delivery of the sermon. Public worship is thus a service to God. It is a duty performed by the children of God in thankful obedience to the One who is their life and their salvation.

For African female readers located in rural contexts wherein strong links exist between women and water resources, the setting depicted in John 4:19–24 will make perfect sense. In varying African contexts, many rural women still walk long distances to draw water for their households. Such strenuous but necessary trips might have been the lot of many a woman of Samaria. The Samaritan woman's desire to no longer come to draw water once she would have received the living water to be offered by Jesus might be pointing in the same direction. (Jn4:15).

Reflecting on the conversation between Jesus and the Samaritan woman

Within my rural setting, sacred mountains (like Modimolle and Thaba'a Mahlatjie) are believed to be inhabited by the ancestors, hence the various taboos around people's connections with such mountains. Also, in present day South Africa, it is not uncommon for some Pentecostal African Christians to visit certain mountains to pray. Thus Mt. Gerizim, on which a shrine was built to enable the Samaritans to worship, would make sense within the preceding African traditional context.

Although there was a racial rift between South African people of different races and ethnic groups, the harsh response from the Samaritan woman to Jesus would not make sense to an African Christian Bible reader. Informed by her context, she could ask the following questions: What had become of the Samaritan woman's *Ubuntu/botho* or humanness? How could she have been so harsh with a thirsty stranger? Did she not know that one hand washes the other according to an African proverb? As God, Jesus assured the Samaritan woman that he, in fact, had something better to offer than what she could offer. Jesus could offer heavenly water which had the capacity to quench the believer's thirst eternally: "If you knew the gift of God, and who is it who is saying to you, 'Give Me a drink,' you would have asked Him, and He would have given you living water." (Jn4:10NRSV).

Noteworthy is the tenacity and courage of the woman of Samaria as she continued to dialogue with Jesus. Perhaps the faith she had exercised to God through the years as she worshipped on the same mountain, was somehow being strengthened. Maybe she was coming to terms with the recognition of the possibility of the same God to manifest Godself even through unlikely persons like the strange Jewish man who was holding a conversation with her. In his commitment to include all, Jesus did not mind holding a conversation publicly with a woman, a Samaritan one at that. Such inclusivity is also acknowledged by Mugambi when he reasons, "In my view, Jesus was much more radical than a trade unionist or lobbyist. . . . He called for an entirely new social dispensation, transcending ethnicity, gender and social class."[17]The Jewish Rabbi was busy, slowly but surely revealing his true identity as the anointed one of God, to the lowly creature from the margins. As the woman became fascinated with Jesus' offer, thus requesting Jesus to provide her with living water, the Rabbi, to further reveal what his true identity was, asked her about her marital life. The woman had not only exceeded the number of husbands who, one could have had within their lifespan, even the man with whom she was living then, was not hers! As if to reveal the kind of faith that had begun to build and grow with the conversation, the woman of Samaria perceived that she was talking with someone special, a prophet! The linking of the stranger's prophetic capacities with the mountain of Gerizim rather than Jerusalem, as the true place of worship enables an African Christian reader of this episode to speculate that the Samaritan woman, had an amazing sense of spirituality:

> 19. The woman said to Him, "Sir, I perceive that you are a prophet.
> 20. Our fathers worshipped on this mountain, but you all say that in Jerusalem is the place where men ought to worship."
>
> (Jn4:19–20; MEV)

The preceding response also brings to light the underlying religious tensions about the true place (and nature) of worship between the Jews among themselves on the one hand, and the Jews and the Samaritans, on the other. The Samaritan woman's response led Jesus to proclaim the nature of true worship. True worship is neither geographically bound nor restricted to a specific gender. The worship that is due the Creator, who is Spirit, One who cannot be bound by time and space, can never be restricted to Jerusalem nor Samaria. It goes beyond ethnic as well as racially-charged prejudices. It belongs to those committed believers who approach God in all honesty. These are such creatures who empty themselves, allowing the gift of God, even Jesus, the Messiah, to manifest himself through the Holy Spirit, as they give God all the glory due to God.[18]

> One must come to God in complete sincerity and with a spirit that is directed by the life and activity of the Holy Spirit. 2) "Truth" (Gr *aletheia* is typical of God (Ps31:5; Ro1:25; 3:7; 15:8), incarnate in Christ (14:6; 2Co.11:10; Eph4:21), intrinsic to the Holy Spirit (14:17; 15:26; 16:13) and at the heart of the gospel (8:32; Gal2:5; Eph1:13).

Worship must thus, continues Stamps, "take place according to the truth of the Father that is revealed in the Son and received through the Spirit."[19]

At the revelation of what the nature of true worship is, the Samaritan woman's speculation about Jesus as the Messiah becomes revealed. It is at that point that this amazing Rabbi came to the climax of his theological discourse with the woman: "Jesus said to her, 'I who speak to you am He' " (Jn4:26). At the mention of such a profound statement of identity, the courageous woman, who chose not to be selfish ran to inform her community about her encounter with one who could be the expected Messiah. At the woman's testimony about Jesus as the Messiah, her neglected people, that is the Samaritans also came to eventually taste God's gift of salvation to them as well. We thus agree with Mugambi that

> In his public ministry, Jesus had viewed the Church as an entirely new community in which people of different backgrounds might together witness the love of God. People of all walks of life came to Jesus- Roman soldiers, *Samaritans*, tax collectors, wealthy Pharisees, poor peasants, cripples, the blind and deaf, men, *women*, [and] children-everyone had something to learn and gain from interacting with Jesus[20] (italics author's).

The dialogue between Jesus, the Messiah who could stoop so low to beg from a lowly creature, enables us, the later hearers of the story, to get a glimpse of what the true nature of worship is. Teresa Okure rightly observed,

> Through his dialogue with the woman, Jesus gradually leads her to transcend the barriers of prejudice and the stigmas of racism and sexism, and to know and accept God's free gift in himself who offers to all who believe in him salvation, "living water," and the Holy Spirit (4:7–10; 7:37–39). In the scheme of values portrayed in this pericope human traditions of worship cede place to God's action in the individual's life. It is no longer a question of worshippers seeking God, but of God seeking people who will worship him in the way God wants, "in spirit and in truth" (4:24). Such worshippers surrender their lives to God, making God the organizing principle of their lives and receiving the salvation that comes with the divinizing gift of the Holy Spirit freely given to all who follow Jesus (1:12–13). This worship, neither in Jerusalem nor on the Gerizim Mountain, transcends race, class and

gender (Gal3:28). Receiving this message, the woman is freed from the sociocultural shackles that bind her (see Gal5:1–2) and is able to lead her own townspeople to the same freedom.[21]

Concluding reflections

In a continent such as Africa, one that "has been divided by the same God," one in which religion, including Christianity continues to be commercialised, in a South Africa that continues to be haunted by the legacies of colonialism and *apartheid*, where racial and ethnic tensions manifest even within the context of the people of faith, one whose people claim worship as their lot, in a context where in the name of God, worshippers are persuaded to drink petrol, eat rats and snakes, in particular within some of the neo-Pentecostal and charismatic Churches, in a context where patriarchy and sexism continue to determine who the true worshippers really are, how may the narrative of the encounter between Jesus and the Samaritan woman be received? If only the reader would reflect on the conversation between Jesus and the Samaritan woman prayerfully, allowing God the Spirit to open her/his eyes, the reader will be enabled to truly perceive what true worship is. Such worshippers are those who willingly present their bodies as living sacrifices to God. Their lives impact even those whose lives must still be touched by the gift of God to the world, even Jesus, the lowly Rabbi.

Notes

1 Mugambi, Ibid., 27.
2 J.N.K. Mugambi, "The Bible and Ecumenism in African Christianity," in Hannah W. Kinoti and John M. Waliggo, eds. *The Bible in African Christianity: Essays in Biblical Theology*. (Nairobi: Acton, 1997), 79.
3 Mugambi, *The Bible and Ecumenism*, 80.
4 J.N.K. Mugambi, "Contextual Theology," in J.N.K. Mugambi and Michael R. Guy, eds. *Contextual Theology Across Cultures*. (Nairobi: Acton, 2009), 113.
5 Mugambi, *Contextua Theology*, 28.
6 Teresa S. C. Okure, "Jesus and the Samaritan Woman (Jn4:1–42) in Africa," *Theological Studies*, 70 (2009): 401–18/ cdn.theological studies.net.
7 Gail R. O'Day, "Gospel of John in Newsom," in Carol Newsom, Sharon H. Ringe and J. A. Lapsley, eds. *Women's Bible Commentary*, Twentieth Anniversary Edition, Revised and Updated. (Louisville: Westminster Jon Knox, 2012), 521(Author's brackets).
8 Teresa Souga, "The Christ Event from the Viewpoint of African Women: A Catholic Perspective," in Virginia Fabella and Mercy A. Oduyoye, eds. *With Passion and Compassion: Third Word Women Doing Theology*. (Maryknoll: Orbis, 1989), 176.
9 For a detailed discussion of the historical background to the rivalry, division, and hatred between the Jews and the Samaritans, See Okure, "Jesus and the Samaritan Woman (Jn4:1–42) in Africa," 401–18; cdn.theological studies.net. 2009, 407–8.
10 Kevin Seasoltz, "Justice and the Eucharist," *Worship*, 58, no. 6 (November 1984): 509.
11 White, Ibid., 16.

12 Ruth C. Duck and Patricia Wilson-Kastner. *Praising God: The Trinity in Christian Worship*. (Louisville: Westminster John Knox, 1999), 19.
13 Daniel G. Groody, *Globalization, Spirituality, and Justice: Navigating the Path to Peace*. (Maryknoll: Orbis, 2008), 212–13; White, Ibid., 162–3; Okure, Ibid., 415.
14 James F. White, *Documents of Christian Worship: Descriptive and Interpretive Sources*. (Westminster, John Knox: Louisville, Kentucky, 1992), 3.
15 J. Kwabena Asamoah-Gyadu, *African Charismatics: Current Developments within Independent Indigenous Pentecostalism in Ghana*. (Brill: Leiden, 2005), 240.
16 Worship is not synonymous with Sunday services. The word "kereke," an adoptive from the Afrikaans word "kerk," is used to refer to Sunday services. During colonial times African people who rejected Christianity were called bahedene (heathens) while converts were called majakane (Church goers).
17 Mugambi, *Feminism*, 59.
18 Argues White, "And today when we speak of our ordinary worship as a 'sacrifice,' we are suggesting that it functions in a similar way, as a sign that we offer to God all that we have and all that we are: heart and mind and possessions, body and soul. In our hymns and our prayers, in our preaching and in our creeds and affirmations, we discharge the debt we owe to God for all the blessings bestowed upon us." White, *Foundations of Christian Worship*, 16.
19 Donald C. Stamps, ed. *The Full Study Bible*, New International Version. (Grand Rapids: Zondervan Publishing House, 1984), 1591.
20 Mugambi, Ibid., 28.
21 Okure, Ibid., 409–10.

Bibliography

Asamoah-Gyadu, J. Kwabena. *African Charismatics: Current Developments within Independent Indigenous Pentecostalism in Ghana*. Brill: Leiden, 2005.

Duck, Ruth C., and Patricia Wilson-Kastner. *Praising God: The Trinity in Christian Worship*. Louisville, Kentucky: Westminster John Knox, 1999.

Groody, Daniel, G. *Globalization, Spirituality, and Justice: Navigating the Path to Peace*. Maryknoll: Orbis, 2008.

Mugambi, J.N.K. "The Bible and Ecumenism in African Christianity." In *The Bible in African Christianity: Essays in Biblical Theology*, edited by Hannah W. Kinoti, and John M. Waliggo, 58–85. Nairobi: Acton, 1997.

———. "Theology of Reconstruction." In *Theologies of Liberation and Reconstruction*, edited by Isaac M. T. Mwase, and Eunice K. Kamaara, 17–13. Nairobi: Acton, 2012.

Mugambi, J.N.K., and Michael R. Guy. "Contextual Theology." In *Contextual Theology Across Cultures*. Nairobi: Acton, 2009.

Groody, Daniel, G. *Globalization, Spirituality, and Justice: Navigating the Path to Peace*. Maryknoll: Orbis, 2008.

O' Day, Gail R. "Gospel of John." In *Women's Bible Commentary (Twentieth Anniversary Edition, Revised and Updated)*, edited by Carole A. Newsom, Sharon S. Ringe, and Jacqueline E. Lapsley, 517–30. Louisville: Westminster John Knox, 2012.

Oduyoye, Mercy A., and Kanyoro Musimbi R. A. *Talitha Qumi! 1989 Conference Proceedings*. Ibadan: Daystar, 1990.

Okure, Teresa S. C. "Jesus and the Samaritan Woman (Jn4:1–42) in Africa." *Theological Studies* 70 (2009): 401–18.

Schmit, Clayton J. *The Power of Preaching, Prayer, and Ritual in Worship: Too Deep for Words: A Theology of Liturgical Expression.* Louisville: Westminster John Knox, 2002.

Seasoltz, Kevin. "Justice and the Eucharist." *Worship* 58, no. 6 (November 1984): 509.

Stamps, Donald C. ed. *The Full Study Bible, New International Version.* Grand Rapids, Iowa: Zondervan Publishing House, 1984.

Souga, Teresa. "The Christ Event from the Viewpoint of African Women: A Catholic Perspective." In *With Passion and Compassion: Third Word Women Doing Theology*, edited by Virginia Fabella, and Mercy A. Oduyoye, 22–29. Maryknoll: Orbis, 1989.

White, James F. *Documents of Christian Worship: Descriptive and Interpretive Sources.* Louisville: Westminster John Knox, 1992.

White, Susan J. *Foundations of Christian Worship.* Louisville: WJK Westminster John Knox Press, 2006.

Wolfson, Harry Austrin. *The Philosophy of the Church Fathers.* Cambridge: Harvard University Press.

4 Olódùmarè

The hidden but relevant God in the Yoruba religious imagination

Enoch Olujide Gbadegesin

Introduction

Professor Jesse N. K. Mugambi's scholarship has in different ways highlighted African belief in a divine being. Belief in a divine being is one of the components of religious life in many African communities. Mugambi has also demonstrated through his theology of reconstruction that people appeal to divine vision or wisdom for ideas to rebuild their societies that have gone through hardship and ruin. Many Africans consider God to be a relevant presence in their lives.[1] Yet, it seems that a majority of Yoruba shift their responsibility to God, which makes life more complicated especially when they think God is hidden. In 2012, Mugambi was instrumental in the publication of a new edition of John Mbiti's *Concepts of God in Africa*, because it is a seminal text on God and offers insight into a theological perspective on God by Africans.

My premise for this paper is that Africans believe in God, but that God remains a mystery and is hidden. I argue in this chapter that the Yoruba deity, Olódùmarè, is hidden and as such hiddenness is part of his being. Hiddenness is not inactivity or passivity, but only means that Olódùmarè is constantly delegating activities to the Òrìsàs in the universe and the lives of the Yoruba people. This is a multidisciplinary investigation into the idea of hiddenness, the relationship of a hidden God to creation, and how that relationship has been maintained over time. What responsibility (or responsibilities) is (are) involved in this inter-subjective relationship? I will bring Mugambi's theological nuances to explore how he would have interpreted hiddenness vis-à-vis human responsibility. The paper concludes by showing that the idea of a "hidden but relevant God" seems to be part of the Yoruba cultural and religious belief systems.

The Yoruba belief systems

Mythic accounts provide a window through which the Yoruba cultural society is known, yet myths are themselves not only dynamic but they are also in fact, problematic. Hence, they defy rigid classifications. While one cannot talk of a consensus or see the Yoruba mythic accounts as some sort of closed canon, it is nevertheless clear that it is generally agreed that Olódùmarè[2] in the Yoruba religious belief is not only conceived metaphysically and anthropologically, but Olódùmarè is also assumed to be a male figure by all ethnic groups in the Yoruba society. This assumption is so because, comparatively, Yoruba people have a mostly patriarchal system.

Feminist scholars have argued that the assumption that God is male subdues and marginalizes women. The gender of God is complex because no Yoruba person has claimed that he or she has seen Olódùmarè, and we therefore have no description of how the figure looks. Second, the name Olódùmarè means "shrouded in mystery" or "the owner of mystery." Since the origin of the name is difficult to determine it demonstrates the challenges of making Olódùmarè a male figure. I have used the preposition *he* throughout this paper simply because most of the panegyrics the Yoruba use for Olódùmarè often make use of male symbols notwithstanding their occasional usage of female symbols such as: "a being with big breasts," and "a caring mother-figure with a very long swaddling cloth to pick-aback her children," and so on to describe his nature.

The concept of Olódùmarè among the Yoruba

The word Olódùmarè is not too easy to determine.[3] The Yoruba regard him as the Supreme Being whose other names further describe him. He is known as Olórun (the owner of heaven), so it is very common to hear Yoruba people combine the two names together either when saying their prayers or when expressing a concern. Thus, the Yoruba people are fond of saying *Olórun Olódùmarè* (Owner of heaven and *Olódùmarè*). According to Awolalu, the Yoruba elders say that Olódùmarè means "the one who has the fullness or superlative greatness; the everlasting majesty upon whom man can depend."[4] But Idowu who believes that the name Olódùmarè defies human interpretation,[5] explains that the name is made up of two words, with a prefix, *Ol* and an elision of the vowel "*i*" from *Oní*, which means "the owner of," "the lord of," and "one who deals in." He later indicates that the word *Odù* has various meanings ranging from the heading of a chapter as in Odù Ifá (Ifa corpus), or chief or fullness. But when Idowu gets to explain the last word *Marè*, he struggles without any success to give a sufficient explanation and some of his ideas seem objectionable. For instance, according to him *Marè* can mean *omo erè* (child of boa or python); or *òsùmàrè* (rainbow); or *odùkárí* (full cell of Ayo game).[6]

There are many problems connected with Idowu's interpretations. Accepting his interpretation could lead to the view that such a god is born of either created things such as rainbows or boa constrictors (pythons); or it even could be similar to a non-living object as Ayò game. In this essay I argue that Olódùmarè's name is one that is "shrouded in mystery" and all interpretations demonstrate a human quest to understand the divine personality and essence.

Hidden God: a brief historical background

The concept of a hidden God emerged in Enlightenment period and gained widespread popularity after World War I and World War II. This concept of hiddenness is also present in the Christian Bible. God told Moses that no man sees him (God) and lives (Exodus 33:20). In the Gospel, according to John, it says, "No one has ever seen God, but the one and only Son, who is himself God and is in closest relationship with the Father, has made him known" (John 1:18, NIV). In many medieval secular literatures, the idea of hidden God was present. Even in Judaism and Islam, the idea of unseen actor often comes up. In these religious books, we see a being that is unseen but constantly acting on the world. In recent times, C. Mathew McMahon speaking from the Evangelical Christian perspective observes, "There are aspects of God which remain hidden from our eyes because we are finite beings. God is infinite and we cannot possibly understand everything about Him."[7] In philosophical parlance, this is called *Deus Remotus*, or hidden due to distance, but one who controls the created order or delegated that responsibility to the competent divinities. Saint Thomas Aquinas used the terms *Deus Absconditus* to refer to the idea that the Supreme Being retreated because of the problems with the creation.[8]

Hidden god in the Yoruba religious imagination

In spite of *Òlàjú* (intellectual, cultural, and political changes that have taken place in Africa), the concept of Olódùmarè (God) has not lost its practical and veritable meaning in the religious language and practices of the Yorùbá people. In the religious imagination of the Yoruba people, Olódùmarè is *Oba àìkú* (Immortal king), *àìgbó* (can never grow old), àì*dibàjé* (can never grow stale), *Oba adàgbà má pààrò oyè* (the king who though is too old, yet does not change his throne), *arúgbó ojó* (the ancient of days), *Oba t'á npè lájò tí ó njé wa n'ílé* (the king we call in our journey and answer us in our homes), and various other panegyrics are used to express that Olódùmarè is ever alive. Yet Olódùmarè is O*ba àìrí* (the king that cannot be seen, hidden from view or invisible). That is why the Yoruba people say, whether God (Olódùmarè) is black or white, we do not know, but one thing is certain: the sky is sparkling white. A Yoruba proverb also implies this: *Èké Ìbídùn tí ó nkí ará Òrun kú àtijó, e bií níbo lóoti rí ará Òrun rí* (*Ibidun* who is a liar, is greeting a heaven dweller that it is quite a long time, let us ask her, where she has seen a heaven dweller before).

This proverb has at least two meanings: First, it is often used when a person claims to know a being behind a wearer of mask. A masker is a metaphor for an ancestor who had died, and now has his abode in the heavens. So, it could not be true that anybody can claim to know the type of ancestor that has just arrived to pay a visit to earth dwellers. In fact, Olódùmarè is called *Àrîırò àlá* (A being one dreams of, but has no word to describe such an experience) an experience William James calls *ineffable*.[9] Second, it also implies that the Yoruba people do not claim to know what is beyond this ephemeral and earthly world of existence. So, it is very clear in their day-to-day interaction that the abode here has a more immediate and ontological meaning for the people than a place that is beyond their conceptual understanding. Two sayings are also quite apposite here to buttress this assumption. First, *Ayé ni á o se kí á to se Òrun* (Before we think about heaven, it is good we first take care of this present earthly abode). Second, *Ónse bí pe ayé ó paré, ayé kò kú ní paré, ìta baba enìkòòkan ni yó di gbòòrò* [Some people (obviously reacting to Christian teachings of the end of time) think that the world will end, the world will not come to an end, each person's verandah will turn into bush obviously after death]. Olódùmarè's hiddenness is not equal to helplessness; it is only part of his almightiness to hide from people's view: though hidden, his impact is still constantly being felt.

Olódùmarè: hidden yet present

In Idowu's account, Olódùmarè is the Supreme Being; he is *behind* the creation of living and non-living things in the world. The word "behind" as it is used here means overseeing or supervising. The world was created systematically and this was done through the agency of Olódùmarè's principal divinities that were charged with the responsibilities of creation. So Olódùmarè is still very relevant, either as a supreme co-creator or supervisor of his creation (I hope to shed more light on this later). Since Olódùmarè is over and above all these divinities, they must *always* and *only* do Olódùmarè's bidding. Again, Olódùmarè is called Olorun or *Olu Òrun* (the owner of heaven), the divinities by implication are the owner of the earth or in charge of the earth (*Olu aye*). It is also part of this arrangement that kings in the Yoruba society are also called Olu aye (owner of the earth) because they are regarded as gods' vicegerents (*Èkejì Òrìsà*).[10] So it should be clear to us that an *Olú Òrun* (the controller of heaven) might not be physically seen in the aye (world or cosmos) occupied by human beings, but because of the power possessed by *Olú Òrun* as the supreme creator, it is possible that at least certain degrees of responsibility is expected of him to his creation. He remains invisible and people make imagery representations of the tutelary deities.

Yoruba myth of creation and God's hiddenness

Yoruba myths of creation demonstrate one of the ways of knowing the hidden God in the Yoruba tradition. Yoruba myths of creation claim that the earth was initially a watery and marshy waste.[11] The watery waste constituted, in a way, the sporting place for divinities who dwelled above. Upon it they used to descend by strands of spider's web which also formed bridges by which they walked over it. Some of them came down from time to time for hunting. Olódùmarè decided to create the earth, and then set in motion how he/she would have to go about it. He summoned Òrìsà-nlá (or Nlá),[12] the arch-divinity, to his/her presence and charged him (Nlá) with the duty:

for material, he/she gave him a leaf packet of loose earth (some say that the loose earth was contained in a snail's shell), and for tools a five-toed hen and a pigeon. Upon arrival into the world Òrìsà-nlá threw the loose earth on a suitable spot on the watery waste. Then he let loose the hen and the pigeon; and these immediately began the work of scattering and spreading the loose earth. These they did until a great portion of the waste was covered. When enough of it had been covered, Òrìsà-nlá went back to Olódùmarè to report that the work had been accomplished. Whereupon, Olódùmarè dispatched the chameleon to go down and inspect the work that had been done.

The choice of chameleon according to Idowu is because of its extraordinary carefulness and the delicacy with which it moves about. From the first visit, the chameleon told Olódùmarè that although the work had been accomplished and in fact, the land is wide and spread enough, it was not yet safe to have anybody dwell on it. It was upon the chameleon's return the second time that, it brought the good news of the solidity of the ground. The place where the work takes place was named *Ifè* (spread). Hence, the place called Ile-Ife in the Southern part of the Yoruba in Nigeria. It is not a coincidence therefore that the Yoruba claim Ile-Ife to be the sacred city – a place where the Yoruba world (or earth) was created. It was after the work had been found to be satisfactory that Olódùmarè commissioned Òrìsà-nlá to go and replenish the earth with fruit-bearing trees for human consumption. But the hen and pigeon that were used were left behind to reproduce for the purpose of providing meat for human beings that would soon populate the earth. It was after all the work had been finally accomplished, that Olódùmarè told *Orelúerè*, another divinity in heaven to lead the beings who had been living with Olódùmarè in the heaven to the earth. *Orelúerè* eventually became the first leader (or king as it is understood among the Yoruba) to rule over the people. There are other mythic accounts that this chapter may not be able to accommodate due to space constraint.

Myth of creation of human beings

One Yoruba account of the creation of persons holds that the human body (*Ara*) was molded by *Òrìsà-nlá* (one of the deities in Yoruba traditional religious system) out of clay. It is thereafter that the lifeless body is infused with èmi (life or breath of life) by Olódùmarè (Supreme deity). The body at this stage becomes activated with life and then goes to *Àjàlá* (deity responsible for making *Orí*) to select an *Orí*.[13] The act of selecting Ori in Àjàlá's house has three important aspects: First, it is supposed to be one of free choice. You are said to be free to choose any of the Ori available in Àjàlá's storehouse. Second, the Ori selected determines, finally and irreversibly, the life course and personality of its possessor on earth. Third, each individual is unaware of the content or quality of the chosen Ori, that is, the person making the choice does not know if the destiny embedded in an Ori is good or bad. Other terms used to symbolize *Ori* include *Àkúnlèyàn* (that which is chosen kneeling), *Ìpín-Orí* (allotment), *Àyànmó* (that which is chosen or affixed to oneself), and *Àkúnlègbà* (what is received kneeling). Apart from the above account of the determination of destiny through a choice of Ori in Àjàlá's house, there are other versions of the Yoruba belief on the determination of destiny.

One version has it that it is Olódùmarè who confers destiny on each human person, which is later doubly sealed by *Oníbodè* (the keeper of the gate between heaven and earth). However, all the available versions agree that destiny is determined by the *Orí*, either chosen or conferred upon a person. They also agree that by the time people arrive in the world, through birth, they are ignorant of the type of destiny awaiting them. This myth will help us to capture the import of my argument that it could easily be explained away that Olódùmarè is hidden by implication in the foregoing myths. Let us quickly see the analysis.

Relationship between Olódùmarè and divinities

Yoruba creation myths credit Olódùmarè as the origin of everything, yet he is invisible and does not deal directly with people. Divine presence is felt because Olódùmarè delegated divinities to oversee the earth and take care of the people's requests and concerns.[14] Each of these divinities plays a different role among human beings to the extent that Olódùmarè is almost already made irrelevant by implication. Òrìsà-nlá, for example, is vested with the power of procreation, so all the seekers of children go to Òrìsà-nlá for children; this also goes for *Òsun* – a female goddess;[15] *Òrúnmìlà* is the chief priest who helps to reveal the heart of the gods (divinities) to the various seekers. According to Wándé Abímbólá, *Òrúnmìlà* knows through Ifa oracular divination what each divinity will accept, and it becomes almost impossible to make a wrong sacrifice.[16] Other divinities, such as *Ògún, Èsù,* and *Odùduwà,* have their significant roles they play among the people. Èsù in particular is assigned a greater role with respect to the notion of *Ebo* (sacrifice); every sacrifice must take into consideration the portion that belongs to *Èsù* first. That is why, the Yoruba says, "*Bí a bá rú ebo, kí ámú ti Èsù kúrò*" (If we make a sacrifice, we must remember to set aside what belongs to Èsù).[17]

We must stress here again that Yoruba myths do not answer all questions. Gbadegesin points out that the account seems to suggest that Olódùmarè is not All-Knowing as indicated in the Yoruba account of creation, where Olódùmarè had to send someone to see what happened to *Òrìsà-nlá*. We also note that Olódùmarè is not All-perfect and All-Powerful. In that case Olódùmarè needed the help of equally imperfect and less powerful divinities as he was to co-create, a clear example we see in the case of Òrìsà-nlá and Àjàlá's creation of both human bodies and Ori.

This argument, it seems, is compelling evidence that Olódùmarè is either hidden or not directly involved as far as the creation of human is concerned.

If he were directly involved, Olódùmarè could have had his input in the making of choice in heaven. Whereas certain scholars have explained this kind of choice scenario to mean that God was allowing for "free willing agency" as argued above; however, it does not distract from the fact that if I am free to make my choice, then Olódùmarè is not duty bound to be involved in my fortune or misfortune in life. Although it is expected that Olódùmarè would sympathetically struggle with me in my life aspiration or life pain to achieve a desirable end. That is why in the Yoruba conceptual belief, the bad lot I chose could still be changed if I can placate Olódùmarè through sacrifice to the *Òrìsàs* (divinities). The inference could then be drawn here that Olódùmarè once in a while comes to the aid of his unfortunate creation. This means that all responsibilities for the functioning of the world, especially human community cannot be put on Olódùmarè. Mugambi has challenged assumptions that God must be held accountable for all things and stressed that human beings also have their own responsibilities to the created order. For Mugambi, human agency is needed in all areas such as economic, social, political, scientific, and ethical reconstructions of the world. He contends convincingly that religion and theology have great roles to play in all these areas.

Yoruba and their response to Olódùmarè's hiddenness

The Yoruba people have pragmatic ways of dealing with their life situations. While they acknowledge the importance of Olódùmarè as a creative deity, they nevertheless apply practical approaches to issues of life. Such are reflected in songs, sayings, and naming, among the Yoruba people which express their dealings with the Òrìsàs who are Olódùmarè's messengers. For example, the Òrìsà-nlá was given the position that ought to be occupied by Olódùmarè. When people meet a pregnant woman, the customary prayer is: *Ki Òrìsà ya ònà ire ko ni ò* – "May the Òrìsà (not Olódùmarè) fashion for us a good work of art." In this case, pregnancy is seen as the work of art fashioned by Òrìsà-nlá. Again, because Òrìsà-nlá keeps a continued eye on human beings he had already fashioned make the worshippers sing to him:

Eni s'ojú, se'mu
Òrìsà ni maa sin;
A-aa-'ni b'o ti ri;
Òrìsà ni maa sin;
Eni ran mi wa;
Òrìsà ni maa sin.

He who makes eyes, makes nose;
It is Òrìsà I will serve;
He who creates as he chooses;

> It is Òrìsà I will serve;
> He who sends me here;
> It is Òrìsà I will serve.

Èsù also enjoys a predominant status with the Yoruba and people tend to fear Èsù more than Olódùmarè and placate Èsù with offerings. Were Olódùmarè to be visible in the religious sensibility of the Yoruba people, they would not have such a dreadful relationship with Èsù. It may also interest us to note that Èsù and not Olódùmarè is equally feared by Òrìsàs; thus, people say *Èsù òtá Òrìsà – Èsù* the enemy of Òrìsà. Sill Olódùmarè appears to enjoy the pride of place in the mind of the Yoruba as the ultimate foundation of everything.

Hiddenness expressed through diverse human experiences

In this section, I show how the Yorùbá people express the hiddenness of Olódùmarè especially in their diverse experiences such as personal, social, economic, ecological, and even spiritual life. I will link this to Mugambi's thoughts on the connection between religion and technology as his response to hiddenness of God in the next section.[18] For example, when an individual is faced with a challenge and have no solutions, such individual may claim that he or she has been neglected or abandoned by God. Hence an individual might ask, Olódùmarè, where is your face or where are you?

At the time of collective disaster such as earthquake, tornado, flood, and epidemics, one could imagine that quite a number of Yorùbá people must have asked where Olódùmarè was. At a time when Nigeria is going through economic hardships, many Yoruba people have suggested that Olódùmarè has ceased to answer prayers; meaning that God has hidden his face away from the plight of Nigerians as a result of sins, avarice, corruptions, and wickedness of the Nigerian people. In another cultural context people have expressed the similar yet, familiar statement, where is God? Elie Wiesel, who survived the unspeakable suffering of the death camps in which his family perished, tells of a Polish rabbi who, in the dark, hopeless world of the prison camps was driven to despair, to a loss of faith. The rabbi asked, "Where is the divine Mercy? Where is God? How can I believe; how could anyone believe, in this merciful God?"[19]

Hidden god and Mugambi's theological response

Mugambi's theological and religious writings have brought God, who is assumed to be hidden, much closer. He challenges Africans and their leaders to be agents of the change in the world. He has argued that African leaders should act as "indispensable agents of social legitimation like Archbishop Desmond Tutu of South Africa who became the 'conscience of the society' in the struggle against apartheid."[20] Africans would move beyond my argument of seeing God as hidden but demonstrating the presence of God in their own actions as they embrace social change. Reading Mugambi's theological thought one has the impression that God's hiddenness results in human silence on issues of social justice and human development.

For Mugambi, religion and cultural values of any people should serve as social engineering or "it is at the social level that religion becomes pivotal in influencing the direction of institutional change. From this social perspective, religion is technology – a tool and a method of social organization."[21] Mugambi suggests that "part of the strategy for a new Technological revolution in Africa is for the scientific and technological communities to 'rationalize, modernize, and put on stream the continent's indigenous technologies for wider and more sustained production.'"[22] This is a crucial important step since the African has been told so many times that he has no indigenous science or technology that he has almost come to believe it. Mugambi thinks, "The Third World as a whole need to exploit its own areas of leverage and influence – such areas as producer power, consumer power, debtor power and the newly emerging skill power."[23] In another context, Mugambi suggests that we should be able to go back to the basic ways of doing things, which were working in Africa before the advent of the colonials. For example, Mugambi argues that Africans used organic storage before the coming of colonials, balanced nomadic and agrarian modes of production, ensured stable food production by growing food traded with each other, and ensured food security by cultivating perennial root, fruit and grain and legume crops. The nomadic communities used the culling of livestock as a means of organic food storage. The disruption and destruction of these social systems led to chronic famines in tropical Africa, and imported technology has failed ever since to solve Africa's problems of food security.[24]

Conclusion

I have argued that, in spite of the fact that the Yoruba people believe in the existence of Olódùmarè, there seems to be some distance between God and people so much so that God is thought of as a hidden God. The Yorùbá people know Olódùmarè or Supreme Being is also a hidden God, but is manifested in different ways. The devotees (of Olódùmarè) use rites and private or collective prayers, private or public sacrifices and rituals to the intermediaries (the divinities) to bring Olódùmarè closer. While the Yorùbá people know through their religious orientation that Olódùmarè cannot be seen physically they also believe that he is concerned about their daily welfare. Even if per chance, he seems to be too far when prayers are not answered they still hold this kind of belief that, the hiddenness is just for a moment. Therefore, while it is true that through Olódùmarè's mystery and hiddenness, Olódùmarè is a distant or hidden God, it is also clear that the systems and structures of Yoruba belief is open to the presence of the very One who has been conceived as hidden.

Notes

1 E. Bolaji Idowu, *Olódùmarè: God in Yoruba Belief*. (London: Longman Press, 1962), 8.
2 Olódùmarè (a being shrouded in mystery) is also called Olorun (the owner of heaven).
3 Awólàlú also shows this very clearly see J. O. Awólàlú, *Yoruba Beliefs and Sacrificial Rites*. (New York: Athelia Henrietta Press, Inc., 2001), 11.
4 Awólàlú, 2001, 11.
5 E. Bolaji Idowu, *Olódùmarè: God in Yorùbá Belief*. (London: Longman, 1990), 31.
6 Idowu, 1990, 31–4.
7 C. Mathew McMahon, *The Hidden God* in www.scribd.com/document/95149019/The-Hidden-God downloaded 19/9/2016.
8 Max Weber, *Selections in Translation*. Edited by Walter Garrison Runciman. (Cambridge: Cambridge University Press, 1978), 220.
9 See William James, *The Varieties of Religious Experience*. (New York: Penguin Classics, 1985, original work published 1902).
10 See Pemberton and Afolayan, *Yoruba Sacred Kingship: A Power Like That of the Gods*. (Washington, DC: Smithsonian Institution Press, 1996).
11 This myth is adapted from Idowu, 1990, 18–27.
12 Òrìsà-nlá is also known as Obàtálá in all the Yoruba societies.
13 On Ori and personality, see Gbadegesin, 194; Olusegun Gbadegesin, "Destiny, Personality and the Ultimate Reality of Human Existence: A Yoruba Perspective," *Ultimate Reality and Meaning*, 7, no. 3 (1984): 173–88; M. Akin Makinde, An African Concept of Human Personality: The Yoruba Example," *Ultimate Reality and Meaning*, 7, no. 3 (1984): 197–8 and Adebola Babatunde Ekanola, "A Naturalistic Interpretation of the Yoruba Concepts of Ori," *Philosophia Africana*, March, 2006, http://findarticles.com/p/articles/mi_7050/is_1_9/ai_n28451612/pg_10/?tag=content.
14 Idowu, 1990, Chapter 7; Awólàlú, 2001, Chapter 2.
15 See Joseph Murphy and Mei-Mei Sanford, eds. *Osun in Osun across the Waters: A Yoruba Goddess in Africa and the Americas*. (Bloomington: Indiana University Press, 2001).
16 Wande Abímbólá, *Ifa: An Exposition of Ifa Literary Corpus*. (Ibadan: Oxford University Press, 1976), 26.
17 Idowu, 1990, 80.
18 J.N.K. Mugambi, "Religion and Science in Social Reconstruction," in Ariane Hentsch Cisneros and Shanta Premawardhana, eds. *Sharing Values: A Hermeneutics for Global Ethics*. (Geneva: Globaethics.Net, 4, 2011), 324–44.
19 See Schmidt, *Exploring Religion*, 341; see also Elie Wiesel, *Night*. (New York: Avon Books, 1969), 87.
20 Mugambi, 2011, 327.
21 Ibid., 330.
22 Ibid., 332.
23 Ibid., 333.
24 Ibid., 338.

Bibliography

Abímbólá, Wándé. *Ifa: An Exposition of Ifa Literary Corpus*. Ibadan: Oxford University Press, 1976.

Auden, W. H. *The Living Thoughts of Kierkegaard*. New York: New York Review Books Classics, 1999.

Awolalu, J. O. *Yoruba Beliefs and Sacrificial Rites*. New York: Athelia Henrietta Press, Inc, 2001.

Babatunde, Lawal. "Ori: The Significance of the Head in Yoruba Culture." *Journal of Anthropological Research* 41, no. 1 (1985): 91–103.

Barber, Karin. "How Man Makes God in West Africa: Yoruba Attitudes towards the Òrìsà." *Africa*, 51, no. 3 (1981): 724–45.

Gbadegesin, Olusegun. "Destiny, Personality and the Ultimate Reality of Human Existence: A Yoruba Perspective." *Ultimate Reality and Meaning* 7, no. 3, (1984): 173–88.

———. *African Philosophy: Traditional Yoruba Philosophy and Contemporary African Realities*. New York: Peter Lang, 1991.

Idowu, E. Bolaji. *Olódùmarè: God in Yoruba Belief*. London: Longmans Publishers, 1990 edition.

James, William. *The Varieties of Religious Experience*. New York: Penguin Classics, 1985. (Original work published 1902).

Magesa, Laurenti. "A Portrait of Professor J.N.K. Mugambi's Theological Project of Reconstruction": A Review Article of *Theologies of Liberation and Reconstruction: Essays in Honour of Professor J.N.K. Mugambi, Ph.D.*, edited by Isaac M. T. Nwase, and Eunice K. Kamaara in *Studies in World Christianity*, 19, no. 2: 187–97, ISSN 1354–9901 Available Online Jul 2013, https://doi.org/10.3366/swc.2013.0051.

Makinde, M. Akin. "An African Concept of Human Personality: The Yoruba Example." *Ultimate Reality and Meaning* 7, no. 3 (1984): 197–8.

Mugambi, J.N.K. "Religion and Science in Social Reconstruction." In *Sharing Values: A Hermeneutics for Global Ethics*, edited by Ariane Hentsch Cisneros, and Shanta Premawardhana, 324–44. Geneva: Globaethics.Net, 4, 2011.

Murphy, Joseph M., and M. M. Sanford, eds. *Osun Across the Waters: A Yoruba Goddess in Africa and America*. Bloomington: Indiana University Press, 2001.

p'Biket, O., ed. *African Religions in Western Scholarship*. Nairobi, EALB, 1970.

Pemberton III, John, and Funso Afolayan. *Yoruba Sacred Kingship: A Power Like That of the Gods*. Smithsonian Institution Press, 1996.

Phiri, Isabel Apawo, and Sarojini Nadar, eds. *African Women, Religion and Health: Essays in Honor of Mercy Amba Oduyoye*. South Africa: Cluster Publisher, 2006.

Rodney, Walter. *How Europe Underdeveloped Africa*. London: Bogle-L'Ouverture Publications, 1983.

Schmidt, Roger. *Exploring Religion*. Belmont: Wadsworth Inc., 1980.

Wiesel, Elie. *Night*. New York: Avon Books, 1969.

Internet Resources

Ekanola, Adebola Babatunde. "A Naturalistic Interpretation of the Yoruba Concepts of Ori." In *Philosophia Africana*, March 2006, http://findarticles.com/p/articles/mi_7050/is_1_9/ai_n28451612/pg_10/?tag=content.

Gbadegesin, Segun. "Using History." in *The Nation Newspaper*, Nigeria of July 17, 2009. http://thenationonlineng.net/web2/articles/10635/1/Using-history/Page1.html.

McMahon, C. Mathew. "The Hidden God." in www.scribd.com/document/95149019/The-Hidden-God downloaded 19/9/2016.

Other Useful Internet Resources that could be consulted

Dictionary of the History of Ideas http://web.archive.org/web/20080401021657/etext.lib.virgnia.edu/cgu-local/DHI/dhi.cgi . . . downloaded 12/18/2009.

"Toward a Hidden God." published in April 08, 1966 in Time in Partnership with CNN, www.time.com/time/printout/0,8816,835309,00.html, downloaded on 2/23/2010.

5 Destiny and eschatology in Jesse N. K. Mugambi's writings

John Fischer

The state of the dead is dominant in the thought of African peoples, particularly about the dead's relationship with the living. John Mbiti argues that in African societies a person is made up of body and spirit.[1] In death the spirit leaves the body. The spirit is related to breath, and so when a person stops breathing the spirit has left the body. Christian theology addresses the afterlife in the doctrine of eschatology, an area of study that requires investigation and analysis in African theology. Mugambi is an interesting conversation partner on this topic because he has written and commented much on death and afterlife. In this chapter, I discuss his thoughts on this topic to place it in the larger debate on the future of African Christian Theology. I begin with African approaches to destiny. Then I discuss Mugambi's understanding of destiny, followed by a discussion of Eschatology and Africa, Mugambi's Mugambi's eschatology, and a concluding reflection.

African approaches to destiny

African cosmology (the understanding of the universe) differs from Western cosmology in that in traditional African cosmology there is one world comprised of two parts. Mugambi refers to the traditional African worldview as "mono-sectional."[2] He argues that in traditional African understanding, there is no spatial heaven and hell. There is only one world.[3] Typically, a Western worldview carries over from the early Church fathers a three-sectional worldview: heaven above, the earth in the middle, and hell below.[4] A scientific worldview, on the other hand, leaves no place for the invisible world which people believe is real in traditional African thought system as they believe the visible material world is real. Turaki[5] shows how this African worldview allows for no clear boundaries between the physical and spiritual dimensions of life. One further quote[6] serves,

> Man [sic] lives in a sacramental universe where there is no sharp dichotomy between the physical and the spiritual. The physical acts as a vehicle for spiritual power while the physical realm is held to be patterned on the model of the spiritual world beyond.[7]

In African Traditional Religion (ATR) the concepts of time and destiny are related.[8] According to Mbiti, African concepts of time emphasize the past and present than on the future; making belief in an indefinite future almost non-existent except in the case of the next few years.[9] Mbiti argues, "All our myths (of creation, the first persons, the coming of death, the birth of our nations, etc.) look towards the 'past,' and no myths talk about or look to the indefinite 'future.'"[10] Mugambi does not agree with such a position.[11]

Other scholars have argued that the problem here lie in the difference between African thought and western dualism. For example, Turaki argues that Western dualism creates serious theological problems for traditional Africans who have an organic or holistic view of life.[12] Thus, the African worldview sees all of the reality within one circle, that comprise the living, the living dead and the whole spirit world as well as the cosmos. In Turaki's view, there are clear elements of pantheism in African holism.[13] E. Orji and Kwame Bediako[14] agree with Turaki. For traditional Africans, life is part of a whole governed by a law of harmony which seeks to maintain an atmosphere of cooperation and peace.

African Independent Churches (AIC) have a view of destiny that is closely related to those held by ATR. The cosmology of AICs also follows that of ATR. Life is cyclical: people are born, live, and die. When they die they join the spirit realm. The movement is from visible existence to invisible existence. The conclusion may be drawn that ATR has had a significant impact on AICs. John Pobee refers to AICs as an indigenizing movement in Christianity offering a celebrative religion making considerable use of symbols, music, and dance, often expressing cultural beliefs that line up with ATR.[15] P. Makhubu, a leader in the AIC movement, has argued, "It is clear that apart from the Christian teaching of immortality, black people have all along believed that there is life beyond the grave."[16] Makhubu's comment is significant in the light of Mbiti's view that Africans have almost no concept of the future and Mugambi's strong assertion that they do.[17]

The evidence of the belief in a future seems justified by African practices that venerate ancestors and also by Biblical texts such as Genesis 35:29.[18] I have discussed with a colleague in another denomination who was adamant that black people do not worship ancestors, but venerate them, thereby continuing the African custom of showing respect for the elderly and departed. Makhubu however, refers to the practice of even "born again" evangelical Christians who in a crisis secretly turn to ancestral diviners. He also points to the way Christians in elite black townships bring goats and sheep which are secretly brought home in the boots of cars for sacrifices to be made to the ancestors, sometimes camouflaging the get together as a party or social gathering.[19] Pobee mentions how these Churches tend to mix Christian beliefs with traditional African beliefs and ethos, highlighting the mixture of Christian beliefs and particularly traditional African cosmology.[20]

Established (historic) African Churches such as Methodist, Anglican, etc. are mainly the same as their Western counterparts. There is however, a difference in that many of the traditional African practices is followed such as the use of salt to keep evil spirits away; use of sea water for healing; reversion to traditional healers when pressure comes on. Adam Ashforth says, "The commonly cited figure for consultation with a traditional healer is 80% of black South Africans."[21] The point I am seeking to make is that many African people, even when Westernised and Christianised, still revert to their traditional beliefs from time to time. Bediako refers to six features of the African worldview which still influence "modern" Africans.[22] They all emphasize supernatural spiritual power in one form or another. The last of the six is helpful: "Humans live in a sacramental universe where there is no dichotomy between the physical and spiritual and the physical can act as a vehicle for the spiritual."

Mugambi and the notion of destiny

Before discussing Mugambi's concept of destiny, I will examine his cosmology. Within the ambit of Mugambi's theology, the standard usage of the Greek term *kosmos* may be accepted. The term was used of "ordering" and could be applied to the earth as well as to the broader cosmos, including the heavenly bodies. TeSelle describes cosmology as "God's good ordering, as the field of Providence, and as the basis of natural theology that discovers not only God's existence but also God's goodness."[23] From the perspective of eschatology, the early Church answered to the negative aspects of the world around them by anticipating that a new age would soon supersede the present evil age.[24]

In *Christianity and African Culture* Mugambi examines various cosmologies and contrasts especially African cosmology with Western and Scientific cosmology. As an introduction to the chapter Mugambi states the following: "It is true that the traditional beliefs of people form the basis on which new ideas or innovations are accepted or rejected."[25] Although this chapter is devoted to the influence of cosmology on mission work, Mugambi nevertheless describes contrasts different worldviews. He points out that prospective converts to Christianity take for granted traditional African worldview.

Mugambi's eschatology is affected by his worldview (cosmology), and it has a significant bearing on the way he views creation and God. Mugambi is critical of the worldview of Western Christians because their view has moved from the two-tier view of the Old Testament to the three-sectional worldview of the Greek philosophers. In his view, the mono-sectional view of traditional African thought is closer to what he considers to be a biblical worldview.[26] Mugambi argues that western empirical science is different from African worldviews and can be confusing to Africans who have to juggle different worldviews in their thinking.

> At home, they presuppose the traditional African view, in the Church they are expected to believe in the biblical view, in geography and physics they are taught the Copernican worldview, and in biology, they have to accept Darwin's theory of evolution.[27]

The mono-sectional worldview clashes with Christian notions of the afterlife because of the African view holds that a person continues to live in this present life after death, albeit in an invisible form; the person maintains their life, and visits their friends. Additionally, the person relates to people according to the relationship they had enjoyed with them before they died. From this mono-sectional perspective, there is no cessation of life. This view is very different to the "heavenly expectation" of Western Christians, although I will have more to say on this later.

The interesting conclusion Mugambi comes to is that this mono-sectional worldview is not supplanted by the worldview introduced and taught by the missionaries, nor by empirical science. Moore and Sanders support Mugambi's contention that African people (even Christian converts)[28] will revert to the traditional African worldview in times of crisis.[29] This worldview stresses that the universe is one and that all reality consists of only two parts: the visible and the invisible and all things are integrated. Life continues almost "as usual" after the person has died. "Duration, in this worldview, is continuous, with no break in actual events here and now."[30] Mugambi is correct when he states that Christian eschatology would be meaningless and irrelevant from the perspective of such a worldview. It's hard to decipher whether these are Mugambi's original views or if he has adopted a Christian worldview, or whether he holds to a combination of the two views. When Mugambi states that the introduction of a Western Christian worldview has created an epistemological crisis among Africans, one must ask how far he thinks like an African or to what extent he has left the African worldview and accepted a Western worldview (or a biblical one; if there is such a thing). This is a rather difficult exercise, but Mugambi states his position most clearly in the reply he offers to Michael Guy in a letter concerning poverty in Africa. In his reply[31] he states that there is only one God and denies the existence of a different "Christian" or "Muslim" God. His view is that we all worship the same God[32] and that the differences arise out of interpretation and responses. Reasoning from an African perspective, Mugambi takes this insight for granted.

In this letter to Guy, Mugambi refers to the African notion of a single reality as an approach he would take. One may, therefore, conclude that, to an extent, Mugambi accepts there is only one underlying worldview, the traditional one. In fairness to Mugambi I refer to a conversation I had with him on March 3, 2013 where he once more emphasized that the Western approach that derived from a Greek philosophical approach to reality is further from the biblical view than was an African view. He stressed the importance of recognizing the difference between the Hebraic and the Greco-Roman worldview. He pointed out that the Chalcedonian formula was formulated from a political perspective and has since formed the core statement on a Christian worldview and that this view is what is expressed in Western notions of reality. My perspective would be that both Western and African worldviews need to be examined and corrected from a biblical perspective and changes made where necessary. In further discussions with

Mugambi during a visit to Nairobi, he pointed to himself and made the statement, "This is not the real me, when I die the real me will continue, only invisibly." Mugambi's views on cosmology are related to his ontology and destiny.

In this section, I take up the disagreement between Mugambi and Mbiti about African notions of the future. Mbiti has described what he considers a typical African view of reality. He argues that Africans have a two-dimensional view of time, with a long past, a present, and virtually no future. The linear concept of time in Western thought, with an indefinite past, present, and infinite future, is practically foreign to African thinking. The future is virtually absent because events have not taken place, thus not realized and cannot, therefore, constitute time.[33]

Mugambi has stated that, in his opinion, Mbiti is wrong in maintaining that there is no concept of future in African thinking[34] and offers the following notion: "In the context of their own cosmological assumptions, African peoples do have notions of past, present, and future. Eternity is also understood, though it is not viewed metaphysically regarding an infinite time scale."[35] Mugambi argues that in African[36] ontology, the past is "present that has already been experienced," and the future is "present waiting to be experienced." This means that the reference point is always the present. In Mugambi's view, where Christianity is in tension between the past (creation) and the future (consummation), in African thought the past and the future both point to the present, not the future! As he says, "This is why there is so much dynamism in African Christian worship: prayer is a celebration of the blessings we enjoy, not complain about what God has not yet bestowed on us."[37] Mugambi's understanding of the afterlife is also evident. He criticizes the negative impact of the missionary thought on African culture and he often views aspects of Western theology, particularly the historic creeds, with suspicion.

There is similarity between the views held by the World Council of Churches (WCC) and those held by Mugambi's theological perspective but there is a difference between his view of the eschaton and some theologians in the Concilier Movement. Mugambi argues,

> It has been pointed out that, according to traditional African understanding, the universe is one, and reality consists of two aspects – the visible and the invisible. Duration in this worldview is continuous, with no break in actual events. Logically, this worldview is wholly integrated and consistent. Conceptually, it entertains no possibility of other planets or other worlds. Therefore, God and all other ontological entities exist in this one universe, without end. There may be a change in the mode of existence, but both the visible and the invisible continue to exist in this one universe. In such a view, Christian eschatology is therefore not only meaningless but irrelevant.[38]

Since Mugambi follows this cosmology,[39] his view of the *eschaton* varies from what other Christians accept as a reflection of 2 Peter 3:10 and Revelation 21:1, two of many scriptures which refer to the recreation of this present material world order as a place for God and people to live in together. Before I discuss Mugambi's views on eschatology, I will discuss eschatology in some African contexts.

Eschatology and Africa

African people have a profound understanding of spirit beings which leads to a belief in life after death, future rewards, punishment, and re-incarnation. Turaki comments, "Traditional African concepts of reality and destiny are deeply rooted in the spirit world, for the activities and actions of spirit beings are believed to govern all social and spiritual phenomena."[40] The African concepts of end times are reflected in African people's understanding of human death and rituals about and time of death. Since Africans think that the human soul is immaterial and survives death, it follows that the end time for Africans cannot be conclusive. African eschatology reflects dual submissions; the first is that at the end time, after the death of humans, the creator will require an account of everything done on earth by each. The second is that at death people with good moral deeds will come back to earth from the abode of the ancestors, either as new born babies or as masked visitors at ancestor festivals. This belief is held about the *Egungun* mask in Yoruba society. However, not every person makes it to the abode of the ancestors. The cycle of African belief in end times, therefore, comprises a baby that is born, lives a life, dies and returns to the abode of the ancestors from where the cycle begins again. Mbiti calls this "individual resurrection."[41]

The uppermost incentive for good moral conduct in African societies is tied to benefits accruable at the end of life. Whereas it is true that moral guidelines are instituted to ensure the well-being of members of the society, the idea of recompense at the end of life also calls forth good behavior in people. Similarly, the expectation of reward, promotion, and goodness after death deters individuals from being immoral. Africans avoid sanctions and strive to be good so that nothing hinders their qualifying for the abode of the ancestors after death. African traditional eschatological concepts thus play a major role in sustaining the moral coherence of African societies. Therefore, one may conclude that the African concept of eschatology has acted as a form of checks and balances between members and leaders of the society.

Funerals are important occasions where statements about the social accomplishments of the dead and the status of his or her family are pronounced. Because Africans believe that death is a transition the land of the spirit provision is made for the envisaged needs of the deceased. The belief that life continues after death reflects the people's theology of the end time transmitted through oral history and their contents are also part of the moral norms held by the clan. These oral transmissions are recited and performed in the form of songs, praise names and eulogies at funerals to show that the dead person was a morally upright, lived well, and died a good death. A general practice during burials in African societies is the act of sending messages through the dead to ancestors who had long departed from the society. These messages may ask for help, requests for retribution to be made on evil doers, especially those suspected of having killed the deceased are also made. Burial ceremonies among the Igbo of Nigeria will be explained here to further highlight the link between morality and eschatology in African Traditional Religion. The Igbo people of Nigeria perform two types of burial ceremonies for every dead elder. The first is the burial of the physical body while the second comprises of sacrifice and festivities to enable the deceased to take their rightful place among the ancestors. Festivity marks both ceremonies, various kinds of food items, singing, drinking, and booming of guns. The first ceremony may last for many days after which a cock is killed and buried with the corpse. At a later date chosen by the family, the second ceremony is performed. The Igbo belief is that until this second ceremony is performed the deceased continues to roam about because he is denied admittance into the abode of the ancestors. Roaming about without a rest among one's ancestors is unpleasant for both the dead and the living who may be haunted until the dead settles in the new abode with other ancestors. Heirs of the deceased often perform this second ceremony which is characterized by feasting, singing, drumming, dancing, and eating.

The conclusion drawn from the above is that belief in an afterlife is common in African culture. There is, however, a negative in the equation. Mbiti disagrees with the notion of a future existence being part of African thought: "With the resurrection (immortality and rejuvenation) placed "in front" of it, biblical Eschatology does offer and provide a living hope. This is entirely absent in African religiosity, however rich and strong it might otherwise be."[42] Adamo[43] agrees with Mbiti:

> The central motivation in AIR is the quest for life and its security. This is because life in African indigenous tradition is conceived as a continuum, with a dynamism of rhythm and circles that follow the process of birth, death, and rebirth. What is of paramount interest is that people can still have access to the eschatological realm of existence through rituals by invoking the powers of divinities to renew and revitalize their potentials, to put right any broken relationship during their lifetime. People's hope is to join the rank of the ancestors in the spirit world, with all its rights and benefits and used their enhanced powers for the benefit of their families and clans. . . . Life is also conceived as communion and is not limited only to the relationship with the created order, the

> universe, the spirits, ancestors, one's family and community, but also with the Creator God. However, the most loathsome expectation in the afterlife is to end up as a wandering spirit, vagabond, cut-off from the community and one's family. This means that in AIR, there is an afterlife that has to do with the continuing relationship of the dead with the living, but not as the end of humanity or the world. . . .[44]

Change in African society is, according to Mbiti,[45] a relatively unknown factor. In traditional African life with its mainly two-dimensional concept of the time life is relatively stable and, according to him, almost static. "A rhythm of life is the norm, and any radical change is either unknown, resented, or so slow that it is hardly noticed." However, since the mid-1900s rapid change has taken place in African culture and society. These changes have had a marked effect on the normal rhythm of life and resulted in the invasion of modern technology and modern societal norms. I think that the influence has been mutual, with African Traditional life having to cope with invasive Western capitalist consumerism, but, in a similar way African tradition has impacted Western notions and worldviews that have been subjected to its influence. One instance of such reverse influence is the impact made by the concept of Ubuntu on management styles and decision-making processes on the African continent. I find it significant that in a major publication on eschatology that deals with every religion and culture, there is no mention of African eschatology, thus bearing out Mbiti's conclusion.[46]

When it comes to the kingdom of God Mbiti[47] refers to the harm done by the Christian notion of a linear second coming which he describes as the sudden return of Jesus as portrayed in traditional Christian thinking. I think he has legitimate concerns about escape from the present leading to a focus on the coming of the Lord and not on living the Christian life in the present. In his study of the Akamba Christians who are influenced by the AIM (African Inland Mission), he concludes that such a return does not fit into African belief because "African hereafter is not in the future but the past."[48]

Having laid a foundation regarding African Traditional approaches to cosmology and eschatology; and having glanced at Mugambi's cosmology and view of destiny, I will now approach Mugambi's teachings on eschatology.

Mugambi's eschatology

The use of symbolism in eschatological discourse is widespread, particularly in the apocalyptic literature of the Bible. Mugambi often refers to Ninian Smart who combines two categories which are important to Mugambi, namely myth and symbol.[49] Throughout his writings, Mugambi tries to revitalize African traditional cultural values, norms, myths, and symbols. He endeavors to recast them in an African format that will meet the needs of African Churches and still faithfully convey the biblical message.[50] Contrary to Bultmann's demythologizing, Mugambi calls for remythologizing in which the theologian gauges and develops new symbols and metaphors and represents old myth in such a way as to express the central message of the gospel.[51] In this regard, three scholars, Tillich, Buber, and Jaspers, have influenced Mugambi, particularly in the area of the metaphorical form, new metaphors and a positive appraisal of mythical thinking, and he has carried this appreciation into his reconstruction theology.[52] It is reasonable to suggest that demythologization would be a more effective response when metaphors and idioms become obsolescent, irrelevant or out of context. Theological reconstruction is a project of demythologization, "in which the theologian thus engaged, discerns new symbols and new metaphors in which to recast the central message of the gospel."[53] The different symbols used in eschatology are the traditional (past orientation), the prophetic (present orientation), and the apocalyptic (future orientation). In Mugambi's writings, other symbols predominate such as origins, purpose, destiny, the second coming of Christ, judgment, and the reign of God.

General eschatological influences on Mugambi's thinking

Some influences have informed Mugambi's views. While these views derive mainly from different approaches to eschatology, it should be noted that the field is so broad that it is beyond the scope of this paper to offer an in-depth analysis of these different views. I have simplified the task by dividing the influences on Mugambi's thinking into four basic categories.

These are:

- The influence of Buber, Cone, and Tillich;
- Liberation theologians in Africa and, secondarily, those in South America;
- The development of notions of God in the WCC;
- Currently-popular views on the reign of God.

Mugambi's eschatology is mainly informed by some issues related to African Christian theology. He is negative about what he terms the "neo-Platonic notions encrypted in the Nicene and Chalcedonian formulations of Christian doctrine."[54] In his view, the creeds express a worldview that is not Hebrew. Mugambi also regards the Trinitarian formulae of the early Church as being formed out of Neo-Platonism and not a true reflection of Hebrew notions of God. Oden, however, makes a strong case in the opposite direction when he examines the early Church in Libya.[55] The point Mugambi makes is that there is an almost total absence of neo-Platonic doctrinal formulations in the creeds of African Instituted Churches.

Hebrew ontology resonates with African ontology. Both are neither otherworldly nor futuristic.[56]

African ontology is neither Trinitarian nor Salvationist. It is communally pragmatic and existentialistic.[57]

One may derive certain conclusions from the above statements by Mugambi:

When Mugambi denies the "other-worldliness" of Western eschatology, he refers to the commonly held notion of "heaven" as another place to which people go. He expresses his belief in the single reality of African Traditional culture. This reality is found in both a visible and an invisible entity. Mugambi rejects the three-tier reality expressed in the creeds. Thus, in his eschatology, there is no place for anyone leaving this reality for another separate one (heaven). In denying a futuristic ontology, Mugambi is expressing his view that there is no future existence in "another" place. Everything that takes place and will take place is in this present reality. Others may argue this position leaves no room in his eschatology for the "coming reign of God" different from what exists today. Both Wright and Wittner argue that the redemption of the earth and the resurrection coincide with the new heavens and new earth.[58]

When Mugambi uses the term "communally pragmatic," he refers to the way he understands the make-up of the Church in African Christianity and may imply neither a transcendentalist nor futuristic view of African Christianity.[59] African Christians are excited about "salvation" because they see in Jesus of Nazareth the possibility of overcoming the constraints and limitations imposed by imperial and local politics, economics, ethics, aesthetics, kinship, and religion.[60] Additionally, by referring to the "existentialist" dimension of African Christianity, Mugambi emphasizes the experiential nature of African Christianity against the mainly cerebral Christianity of the West. Mugambi argues that it is easy for African Christians to identify with Jesus the Rabbi of Nazareth because his teachings resonate with their worldviews.

Mugambi's radical stance against anything that resembles Western missionary theology or has vestiges of imperialism contests Western approach to eschatology. I must concede that Mugambi is close to mainstream understanding of a *telos* when he speaks of a perfect earth (utopia) which will only come about with God's intervention. I wonder if this utopia will be a perfected present world or a "resurrected" world described in Revelation 21:1–5. To this extent, I find myself at variance with both Mugambi and most Western "escapist" eschatology. Destiny is not merely an overhauled current cosmos nor is it escape into some cosmic cloud. The Christian hope is that God will finally establish a reign where righteousness prevails, and the evils of this current existence are eradicated, not simply changed.

Julius Gathogo indicates that Mugambi's ATR roots which have influenced his theology can be traced to his grandparents who still practice ATR.[61] Mugambi's Anglican background is rooted in the East African revival when his parents came to faith in the revival. Mugambi's brother and sister are both academics, and his first-born sister is a retired minister in the Anglican Church of Kenya. I find it strange that his Anglican background has not rooted him in traditional Christian orthodoxy as it has done with me. His view of the "other world" of the eschaton is very like the biblical notion of new heavens and a new earth. Strangely, we are promised utopia: a reversion to something far better than the garden of Eden. In saying this, I must concede that my notion of some disembodied existence in a far-off place called "heaven" has had to undergo certain corrections, corrections which bring me closer to Jesse Mugambi than I was before.

Notes

1 J. S. Mbiti, *Introduction to African Religion.* (Nairobi: East African Educational Publishers, 1991), 124.
2 J.N.K. Mugambi, *Christianity and African Culture.* (Nairobi: Acton, 2009), 51.
3 Mbiti, 1991, 35–6.
4 Mugambi, 2009, 51.
5 Y. Turaki, *Foundations of African Traditional Religion and Worldview.* (Nairobi: World Alive, 2006), 32.
6 K. Bediako, *Christianity in Africa: The Renewal of a Non-Western Religion.* (Edinburgh: Edinburgh University Press, Orbis, 1995), 95.
7 Sharing the Burden of Defending the Gospel | World. http://wrfnet.org/resources/2008/01/sharing-burden-defending-gospel (accessed July 26, 2017).
8 J. S. Mbiti, *Concepts of God in Africa.* (Nairobi: Acton, 2012), 35.
9 J. S. Mbiti, *African Religions and Philosophy.* (Oxford: Heinemann, 1969), 21.
10 Mbiti, 2012, 35.
11 See Mugambi, 1989, 137.
12 Turaki, 2006, 32.
13 E. D. Oji, "Ikpu Alu (atonement) in Igbo Traditional Religion." BA Thesis, Jos ECWA Theological Seminary, 1988, 15.
14 Bediako, 1995, 95.
15 John Pobee, African Instituted (Independent) Churches. *Dictionary of the Ecumenical Movement.* (Geneva: WCC and Eerdmans, 2002).
16 P. Makhubu, *Who Are the Independent Churches?* (Johannesburg: Skotaville, 1988), 61–2.
17 I will refer to this again later.
18 Genesis 35:29. Then he (Isaac) breathed his last and died and was gathered to his people, old and full of years.
19 Makhubu, 1988, 61.
20 Pobee, 2002, 2.
21 Moore and Sanders, 2001, 206–25. Select Committee on Social Services 1998.
22 Bediako, 1995.
23 In Patte, *The Modern Theologians*, 2010, 1331.
24 Cf. Romans 8:18–25, 2 Peter 3:10–13.
25 Mugambi, 2002, 50.
26 See Mugambi, 2005, 51–52.
27 Mugambi, 1989, 143.
28 The quote from Moore and Sanders also refers to the census which gives 80 percent of South African as claimed Christians.
29 See Mugambi, 2002, 52.
30 J.N.K. Mugambi, *African Christian Theology: An Introduction.* (Nairobi: Heinemann, 1989), 143.
31 J.N.K. Mugambi and M. R. Guy, *Contextual Theology Across Cultures.* (Nairobi: Acton, 2009), 316.
32 Mugambi sees the god of Africa as the same God who is worshipped by Christians.
33 J. S. Mbiti, *African Religions and Philosophy.* (Oxford: Heinemann, 2006), 16–17. See also Kagame And Mbiti On the Traditional Bantu View Of Time.

www.cavehill.uwi.edu/fhe/histphil/chips/archives/2006/docs/kalumbaii.aspx (accessed July 26, 2017).

34 Mugambi, 1989, 137.

35 Ibid.

36 Mugambi, 2009, 318.

37 Ibid.

38 Mugambi, 1989,143.

39 See J.N.K. Mugambi and M. R. Guy, *Contextual Theology Across Cultures*. (Nairobi: Acton, 2009), 316.

40 Y. Turaki, *Foundations of African Traditional Religion and Worldview*. (Nairobi: World Alive, 2006), 26. See also Africa Traditional Religious System as Basis Of. . ., www.lausanne.org/content/west-african-case-study (accessed July 26, 2017).

41 J. S. Mbiti, *New Testament Eschatology in an African Background: A Study of the Encounter between New Testament Theology and African Traditional Concepts*. (Oxford: Oxford University Press, 1971), 158.

42 J. S. Mbiti, *New Testament Eschatology in an African Background: A Study of the Encounter between New Teastament Theology and African Traditonal Concepts*, (London: Oxford University Press, 1971), 159.

43 D. T. Adamo, *Christianity and African Traditional Religion: The Postcolonial Round of Engagement*. (Pretoria: AOSIS, 2011).

44 Christianity and the African Traditional Religion(s): The http://brewminate.com/christianity-and-the-african-traditional-religions-the-pos. (accessed July 26, 2017).

45 J. S. Mbiti, *African Religions and Philosophy*. (Oxford: Heinemann, 2006), 211.

46 A. Walls, *The Oxford Handbook of Eschatology*. (New York: Oxford University Press, 2008).

47 Mbiti, 1971.

48 Ibid., 64.

49 N. Smart, *Dimensions of the Sacred: An Anatomy of the World's Beliefs*. (Berkeley: University of California Press, 1996), 52.

50 See V. Dedji, *Reconstruction and Renewal in African Christian Theology* (Nairobi: Acton, 2003), 45.

51 H. W. Kinoti and J. M. Waliggo, *The Bible in African Christianity: Essays in Biblical Theology* (Nairobi: Acton, 1997), 73–8.

52 See Kinoti and Waliggo, 1997.

53 Ibid., 75. See, Sharing the Burden of Defending the Gospel World http://wrfnet.org/resources/2008/01/sharing-burden-defending-gospel. (accessed July 26, 2017).

54 I. M. T. Mwase and E. K. Kamaara, *Theologies of Liberation and Reconstruction*. (Nairobi: Acton, 2012), 374.

55 T. C. Oden, *Early Libyan Christianity: Uncovering a North African Tradition*. (Downers Grove: IVP Academic, 2011).

56 Mwase and Kamaara, 2012, 374.

57 Ibid., 375.

58 N.T. Wright, *How God Became King*. (New York: Harper Collins, 2001); M. E. Wittmer, *Heaven Is a Place on Earth*. (Grand Rapids: Zondervan, 2004).

59 Mwase and Kamaara, 2012, 375.

60 Mugambi in Mwase and Kamaara, 2012, 375.

61 Gathogo, *Liberation and Reconstruction in Africa*, 16–68.

Bibliography

Adamo, D. T. *Christianity and African Traditional Religion: The Postcolonial Round of Engagement*. Pretoria. AOSIS, 2011.

Balogun, O. A. The Concepts of Ori and Human Destiny in Traditional Yoruba Thought: A Soft Deterministic Interpretation. *Nordic Journal of African Studies* 16, no. 1 (2007): 116–130.

Bediako, K. *Christianity in Africa: The Renewal of a Non-Western Religion*. Edinburgh: Edinburgh University Press, 1995.

Bujo, B. *African Theology in Its Social Context*. Nairobi: Paulines, 2003.

Bujo, B., and I. M. Juvénal. *African Theology: The Contribution of the Pioneers*. Volume 1. Nairobi: Paulines, 2003.

———. *African Theology: The Contribution of the Pioneers*. Volume 2. Nairobi: Paulines, 2008.

Conradie, E. ed. *African Christian Theologies in Transformation*. Stellenbosch: EFSA, 2004.

Dedji, V. *Reconstruction and Renewal in African Christian Theology*. Nairobi: Acton, 2003.

Engdahl, H. John Mbiti. "Double Consciousness": Notes on Mbiti's Philosophy and Theology. Paper presented at UWC Colloquium, 2016.

Gathogo, J. *Liberation and Reconstruction in Africa: A Critical Analysis of the Works of JNK Mugambi*. Saarbrücken: LAP Lambert Academic Publishing, 2016.

Kato, B. H. *Theological Pitfalls in Africa*. Kisumu: Evangel Publishing House, 1975.

Kinoti, H. W., and J. M. Waliggo. eds. *The Bible in African Christianity: Essays in Biblical Theology*. Nairobi: Acton, 1997.

Makhubu, P. *Who Are the Independent Churches?* Johannesburg: Skotaville, 1988.

Magesa, L. *Anatomy of Inculturation: Transforming the Church in Africa*. Nairobi: Paulines, 2004.

Martey, E. *African Theology: Inculturation and Liberation*. Oregon: Wipf and Stock, 2004.

———. *African Theology Comes of Age*. Nairobi: Paulines, 2009.

Mbiti, J. S. *African Religions and Philosophy*. Oxford: Heinemann, 1969.

———. *Concepts of God in Africa*. Nairobi: Acton, 2012.

———. *New Testament Eschatology in an African Background: A Study of the Encounter Between New Testament Theology and African Traditional Concepts*. Oxford: Oxford University Press, 1071.

———. *Introduction to African Religion*. Nairobi: East African Educational Publishers, 1975.

Mugambi, J. N. K. *African Christian Theology: An Introduction*. Nairobi: Heinemann, 1989.

———. *Christianity and African Culture*. Nairobi: Acton, 1989/2009.

———. *From Liberation to Reconstruction: African Christian Theology After the Cold War*. Nairobi: Acton, 1995.

———. *Christian Theology and Social Reconstruction*. Nairobi: Acton, 2003.

Mugambi, J.N.K., and M. R. Guy. *Contextual Theology Across Cultures*. Nairobi: Acton, 2009.

Mugambi, J.N.K., and L. Magesa, eds. *Jesus in African Christianity: Experimentation and Diversity in African Christology*. Nairobi: Acton, 2003.

Mununguri, M. *The Closeness of the God of Our Ancestors*. Nairobi: Paulines, 1998.

Mwase, I,M.T., and E. K. Kamaara. *Theologies of Liberation and Reconstruction*. Nairobi: Acton, 2012.

O'Donovan, W. *Biblical Christianity in African Perspective*. Sri Lanka: New Life Literature, 1996.

Oden, T. C. *Early Libyan Christianity: Uncovering a North African Tradition*. Downers Grove: IVP Academic, 2011.

Oji, ED. "Ikpu Alu (atonement)." In *Igbo Traditional Religion*. BA Thesis, Jos ECWA Theological Seminary, 1988.
Orobator, A. E. *Theology Brewed in an African Pot*. Nairobi: Paulines, 2008.
Pobee, J. S. "African Instituted (Independent) Churches." In*Dictionary of the Ecumenical Movement*, edited by Losky Nicholas. Grand Rapids, and Eerdmans, 2002.
Ramose, M. B. *African Philosophy Through Ubuntu*. Harare: Mond Books, 2005.
Setiloane, G. M. *African Theology: An Introduction*. Johannesburg: Skotaville, 1996.
Smart, N. *Dimensions of the Sacred: An Anatomy of the World's Beliefs*. Berkeley: University of California Press, 1996.
Stinton, D. B. *Jesus of Africa: Voices of Contemporary African Christology*. Maryknoll: Orbis, 2004.
Taylor, J. V. *Christian Presence Amid African Religion*. Nairobi: Acton, 2001.
Turaki, Y. *Foundations of African Traditional Religion and Worldview*. Nairobi: World Alive, 2006.
Walls, A. *The Oxford Handbook of Eschatology*. New York: Oxford University Press, 2008.
Wittmer, M. E. *Heaven Is a Place on Earth*. Grand Rapids: Zondervan, 2004.
Wright, N. T. *How God Became King*. New York: Harper Collins, 2011.

6 The church of the future

Dialogue on the ecclesiology of Mugambi

Elias Kifon Bongmba

The Kenyan theologian Jesse N.K. Mugambi has contributed thoughtful theological perspectives on ecclesiology in Africa. In this chapter, I discuss Mugambi's perspective on the Church and the prospect of ecumenism. I argue that if the Church is to have a viable future as Mugambi calls for, the African Churches must build intersubjective bonds by recovering the art and practice of listening. Mugambi calls the Church the community that promotes the witness of Christ through its praxis.[1] The Church then must be grounded in African culture and "its whole body-soul, the entire organism called Church must acquire an African character."[2] Its theology should be rooted in the African heritage and provide a broad vision for the community to enable that "the African Church [to] confront face to face the concerns that contradict that rule throughout the continent."[3] Mugambi has called for a new typology of the Church that re-examines the nature of the Church, the role of women, the centrality of the family and youths, its views on human rights, as it adopts the African notion of ancestral life as a model.

The African Church should be renewed through the deployment of an African imagination to address the needs of its people.[4] The East Africa revivals of the 1920s led to the formation of new fellowships within the Christian tradition.[5] The revivalists criticized other Christian denominations for moral and spiritual laxity and promoted a spiritual identity that idealized the Church as a family. In the Catholic Church, Small Christian Communities stressed renewal and the cultivation of a Christian identity in an increasingly secular society.[6]

Mugambi argues that reform movements in Africa have transformed the Church within their different polity but some of the changes were contested. Earlier religious movements were not break away groups but were pushed aside by the criticism from the rest of the Christian communities.[7] Pentecostal Churches have emphasized the presence and control of the Holy Spirit, speaking in tongues, miracles, gifts of healing and prophecy, preaching, and interpretation. Today Christian communities must develop mutual respect for others, work to close the generation gap between the older Christians and the younger Christians, and pay close attention to the message of the gospel and local culture.[8] In addition, the revivalist exercised freedom in different areas of their lives including the freedom to choose their spouses. Revival was and is also supposed to be accompanied by reforms which promote fellowship, justice, tolerance, flexibility on fashions, and promote moral values that would enable faith communities understand their African heritage.

Mugambi has promoted ecumenism nationally, regionally and internationally. While denominationalism has provided diversity, it has also posed some challenges that continue to haunt the Church today. Ecumenism derives from the Greek term, *oikumene*, which refers to the whole inhabited world and Christians today use the term to refer to the Christian tradition and its different faith communities rather than the early Church councils which were called ecumenical councils. The heart of the theological imagination on which the idea of ecumenism is constructed is the prayer of Jesus in the Gospel, according to John 17:6–11, where Jesus prays for his disciples asking that they should be one as Jesus is one with God.[9] Church schism, the reformation, and developments in the modern period, turned the African Church into a recipient of missionaries and reduced African participation in ecumenical initiatives. Vatican II's decree on Ecumenism called for a restoration of unity because Christ founded one Church.[10]

Ecumenism was motivated by missionary concerns that Church cannot preach a Christ and remain so divided. In East Africa, Protestants called for an ecumenical spirit even though mission activity in the post World War I period, strengthened denominational Christianity.[11] The Kikuyu Conference agreed that Churches work together and set the same standards of Church membership, moral conduct, and tried to set similar standards but this was not realized. Later, Bible translation contributed to an ecumenical spirit because those engaged in translation worked together to standardize biblical terms and theological insights. Ecumenical groups, like the Association of Theological Institutions in Eastern Africa (ATIEA), were formed in the East African region. Beginning in 1959 Church leaders started serious dialogue ecumenism. The Lutherans and Catholics agreed in Arusha, Tanzania to create an atmosphere in which members of different religious communities would get to know others. Unfortunately, few Africans were invited to participate in those conversations.

The Vice President of the Evangelical Lutheran Church of Northern Tanganyika invited other Churches to a dialogue on ecumenism and this led to the East African Church Union consultation. The plans were expanded to include Anglicans. Several meetings were held in the early 1960s and produced fruitful results in liturgy and Eucharist, but no agreement was reached on episcopal ministry and ordination. The discussions have not continued even though there is a great need now for such discussions. Ecumenical initiatives failed because of theological disagreements on matters of ministry, a lack of enthusiasm, and lingering fears by Churches that they could lose their own identity in an ecumenical setting.

One enduring legacy of ecumenical dialogue is the All African Conference of Churches (AACC) that was formed in 1963 in Kampala, Uganda.[12] The objectives of the new organization was to end colonialism in Africa and the move towards independence; define the selfhood of the African Church; affirm a Christian perspective and responsibility of economic and social development in Africa; develop a theological perspective to facilitate nation building; and promote Christian perspectives on the family, and Christian communal responsibility.[13] While the AACC has not always achieved all its aims, the organization demonstrates that when ecumenism is given a chance, member Churches experience a new bond and assume a new voice to engage in the reconstruction of society. The AACC is a model of ecumenism in Africa, working on issues that have marginalized millions of Africans. Its leaders have included bold activist theologians like the late Reverend Burgess Carr and Archbishop Desmond Tutu, who placed the well-being of Africa and Africans on the agenda of that ecumenical body. The AACC as an ecumenical institution remains committed to liberation, justice, peace, and security in Africa.

Mugambi on the future of the Church

In his *From liberation to Reconstruction*, Mugambi contended that Africa was portrayed negatively because the its political crisis, which resulted from poor governance even though Africa was experiencing a robust growth in Christianity.[14] Africans face serious health crises with HIV and AIDS, and the Ebola Virus Disease. The scourge of hunger has devastated parts of the Sahel region of West Africa. The debt crisis which decimated African economies in the past has not completely gone away.[15] In religion, African Christianity has experienced exponential growth; driven for the most part by the excitement and enchantment generated by the Pentecostal, charismatic and Neo Pentecostal Churches. African Christianity now thrives in the diaspora and is changing the face, tone, spirit, and nature of the ecclesial community.[16]

While the African Church has asserted its independence it has developed its own version of western cultural wars that has heightened debates on abortion, homosexuality, condoms, etc.[17] On contested issues such as abortion or same sex relations, Africans have grounded their opposition on claims that these practices are antithetical to African culture, the Bible, and the natural order of things. Yet in these debates Western Christians have found in Africa new allies in the long cultural wars that have shaped political and theological culture in the West and this has raised the specters of dependence and tutelage from the west. It would be a folly to claim that on contentious issues like same sex relations that African Christians merely echo western Christian donors because many Church leaders who express extreme homophobic positions speak for themselves. The question for African Churches remain what they think of the love of God since these debates have brought stigmatization, violence, death, and laws proscribing homosexuality; actions supported by the Church.

On a bright note, even in the post moratorium era, African Christianity has enjoyed an excellent relationship with many Faith Based Organizations and Faith Inspired Institutions who have worked, especially in the health care domain where African Christianity had made significant contributions to their localities, by addressing pandemics never seen before in human history and made a difference in the age of HIV and AIDS and the Ebola Virus Disease.[18] Aspects of extraversion in this collaboration cannot be denied, but it is also the case that these global interventions speak to many issues in postcolonial societies where the prophetic voice for justice has declined. There is no doubt that as the African Christians face the future, they would have to fight suffering in a new, critical, and sustainable manner.[19]

We should ask Mugambi's question again: "What kind of religiosity have African Christians embraced? Will it help Africans as individuals, families, nations and as a continent, to cope with the challenges we face as the 20th century comes to an end and the 21st century commences?"[20] Mugambi asserts correctly that the Church can contribute to the solutions of the continent today as it did during colonial resistance. Mugambi argues that hunger is linked to civil strife often "funded and armed by external bodies, which are keen to test new weapons and dump obsolete ones in Africa."[21] Regardless of the influence of outside forces, responsibility for the civil strife lies within the African continent itself. African Churches should continue to address conflicts by supporting and strengthening peace and conflict resolution projects. Mugambi argues that unnecessary competition between the Churches hinders efforts at peace. Where Churches have worked in an ecumenical spirit like Namibia, South Africa, and Mozambique, they have achieved reconciliation.

Mugambi also insists that the Church's essential task is evangelism because "no movement can merit the title 'church' unless it is a missionary community,"[22] Mugambi challenges the Church to explore new frontiers of mission. "The new frontiers are no longer geographical. They are social and conceptual."[23] The new frontier calls for several things. First, it requires an African driven theological approach to faith and order. Second, Churches must bridge the knowledge gap and create useful knowledge for the future. To achieve this, Churches should promote and facilitate dialogue between theologians and scientists to promote development and improve human conditions. Mugambi argues that science and technology should be treated as a new missionary frontier for the Church.[24] Third, the Church should embrace technology but study the ethical implications of technological advancement. Since Mugambi made this claim, the cell phone revolution has taken over Africa, and social media is offering kinds of spiritual resources for Churches in Africa today. The World Wide Web and social media has revolutionized African Christianity and made the Church a very different organization from what it used to be. Fourth, the Church should promote pastoral care at a time when Africans face many challenges. Fifth, Mugambi returned to the theme of ecumenism and argued that the Church in Africa needs ecumenical unity:

> African Christians and churches must come to terms with the theological insight that evangelical unity and ecumenical unity are necessary and complementary aspects of the same challenge of Jesus to his followers. . . . African Christians [should] revive the process of promoting visible expressions of united Christian witness, fellowship, and service-between and amongst Catholics, Protestants, Pentecostals, charismatics, orthodox, and independents.[25]

Sixth, the new frontier of missionary work is healing. This demands an integrative approach that brings together all the stakeholders in health. Seventh, the new frontier also includes appropriate management of all the resources of the Christian community. This is an enormously important observation at the time Mugambi published his proposal for a theology of reconstruction. We know today that some African Churches and leaders are guilty of mismanagement of resources just as the politicians of the continent have done.[26] Mugambi argued then that if the Church was concerned about its future, it ought to change its outward character to maintain the inner character and emphasize love. Mugambi privileged *agape* love, but I would argue that other dimensions of love such as *eros* offer a more broad and engaging perspective to love and interpersonal relations for a broad community.[27] Such a spirit of love should promote liberation, support internally displaced persons, promote reconciliation, promote gender equality, and pay attention to youths of the continent who need critical support, and embrace a full integrated ministry for persons living with disabilities. Mugambi called for the Church to do its own structural adjustment of its programs and finances.

The Church of the future: towards an intersubjective community

Mugambi's concerns and insights for the ecclesial community in Africa invite a reset of social relations in the community. I argue that reconfiguring the social vision of the Church calls for strong intersubjective bonds sustained through critical dialogue in which the Church must practice anew, the art of listening. The growth of the Church in Africa demonstrates its relevance, even if we must also mourn the decline of a critical prophetic voice. Churches have focused on institutions, leadership, programs, major interventions in healthcare, the building of alliances with faith based organizations and non-governmental organizations to cultivate the image of a robust community in the face of mounting crisis. These institutional arrangements have enabled the African Church to engage with society at different levels.

It is time that institutional relations must be strengthened through a primary relationship with each other to build stronger intersubjective bonds.

One fascinating development in African thought in recent decades is the articulation and appropriation of *ubuntu* as a philosophical ideal to describe intersubjective relations. The Collins English Dictionary defines *ubuntu* as humanity or fellow feeling. The Oxford Dictionary describes *ubuntu* as action characterized by sympathy, consideration for others, compassion, or benevolence.[28] The term comes from *ubu*, a state of being, and *ntu*, a person. It has been used in South Africa to refer to interpersonal relations and stress human interconnectedness. The IsiZulu expression, "*Umuntu umuntu ngabantu*," means a person is a person because of another person. The Kikuyu term *umundu* is a variant for *ubuntu*. The Tsonga language term is *vumuntu* and the Killaya language in Tanzania uses to the term *bumunto* and the Kinkongo term is *gimuntu*. The Dean of African theologians, John Mbiti, described African social relations when he stated, "I am because we are, and since we are, therefore I am."[29] According to Archbishop Desmond Tutu, *ubuntu* "speaks of the very essence of being human."[30] It is an ideal that paints a compelling relational praxis. Magobe Ramose is correct that *ubuntu* is an important philosophical concept.[31]

Late in his short ministry on earth, Jesus told the disciples, "A new command I give you: love one another. As I have loved you, so you must love one another. By this everyone will know that you are my disciples if you love one another" (John 13:35–36). This is an interesting periscope with three distinct parts. First, Jesus commanded the disciples to love one another. Second, he described the nature of the love. They were to love one another as he Jesus had loved them. Third, Jesus said that such love would indicate to others that they were his followers. This is a vision of social relations in the Church in Africa especially at a time of such great stress and need.

Listening as a precondition for a new intersubjective community[32]

To build strong intersubjective bonds and serve one another, members of the Church and the Church itself should cultivate the art of listening. Listening is a challenge for some Churches because the previaling model for new Churches is to claim the Holy Spirit hold regular meetings, sing, shout, dance, command demons and satan, and guarantee wealth and wellbeing in the mighty name of Jesus.[33] One cannot question the biblical injunction to sing or make a joyful noise. During the last few decades of neo Pentecostal revolution the joyful noise has become louder and louder, even during prayers. Some believe that the louder one shouts during prayers, the closer he or she is to God's will. If Christians are not making joyful noises of their own, they are listening to loud proclamations of the Word, and testimonies that demonstrate the Satan bursting powers of the new preachers. Testimonies are often punctuated with shouts of praise.

Churches have become such loud places where even leaders who are responsible for the despoilation of Africans also claim the power and anointing of God. I wonder what that means in light of the story Jesus told about two people who went into the temple to pray. The one thanked God that he was not like some who did many wrong things, and went on to boast about the good things he did. However, the other man came in and could barely speak aloud, and in his quiet corner, merely asked that God be merciful to him a sinner. In these days of the misuse of "prophetic" pronouncements, praise and shouts of hallelujah, or tough pronouncements from the pulpit it is difficult to hear the quiet prayer – God be merciful to me a sinner. Church members are victors when they recognize their dependence on God and when they recognize and listen to each other.

Elochukwu E. Uzukwu in *A Listening Church: Autonomy and Communion in African Churches* argued that the historical despoliation of Africa by both colonial and postcolonial practice invites an ethic of reconstruction that is grounded in reconciliation in an interdependent and non-violent world.[34] Africans need democratic principles and respect for human rights to promote reconstruction. The Church is an image of the renewal and must, therefore, respond to the needs through practices rooted in African culture. The Church is a family where members should cultivate and facilitate new relationships in an interdependent world. The Church then ought to cultivate a relational ecclesiology, rethink the notion of the Church from the perspective of small Christian communities, and work against the abuse of ecclesiastical power. This requires a collaborative ministry instead of clericalism.[35]

Uzukwu argued that the Church should listen: "The most arresting imagery of being fully initiated into this ministry or service is the image of the 'large ears.'"[36] For a community that is used to preaching, proclaiming, predicting, prophesying, programming, listening is important "because it implies consultation or deliberation at all levels of community, it becomes an imagery which testifies, according to Cyprian [of North Africa] that the will of God may triumph in the Church-community over human presumption or error."[37] When the Church listens, it also hears God's voice clearer. More importantly for our purpose here, a listening Church also hears the voices of others who live and work together.

Listening is an individual and corporate act. People in the Church ought to listen to each other to hear what keeps them up at night; know their concerns about family, friends, work, farms, illnesses, and politics. We often think we know our neighbors based mostly on our own perceptions. However, when we sit down and to talk with our neighbors, we will realize we do not know our neighbors that well. Our communities are in urgent need of a one-on-one dialogue in which each of us is invited to be the listener. If I cannot listen to someone else, I cannot expect another person to listen to me. The Church as Church, locally or nationally, must listen. Listening includes hearing what members of the community have to say about the Church, its mission, its involvement in the community, and its message for the times. Such an approach will also give members of the Church an opportunity to hear other voices on our common humanity and habitat.

Seth Horowitz has argued, "Listening is a skill that we're in danger of losing in a world of digital distraction and information overload." Listening goes beyond hearing because when you listen, "you actually pay attention to something you're listening to, the signals are conveyed through a dorsal pathway in your cortex, part of the brain that does more computation, which lets you actively focus on what you're hearing."[38] Listeners do not merely hear words and sounds, but pay attention with a desire to understand and comprehend what the other person is communicating. Listeners seek not to note differences and offer counter arguments, but seek understanding in order to appreciate what is at stake, and understood the other person on his or her own terms.

Why should the Church listen?

First, listening establishes a humble beginning for service and praxis. One of the criticisms of missionary Christianity is that western missionaries arrived in Africa and assumed that they knew the needs of Africans. The Church community cannot claim to know everything about the people and the communities they serve. I use humility here deliberately because the Church and its constituents must refrain from claiming and imposing some divine revelation to people, especially facing challenges in life. The social facts, which the Church can gather from talking to people, often do not require divine revelation. The Church can have access to the information about the social conditions of people and their communities if it is willing to listen to the people and the leaders of the community. For some in the Church, refraining from proclaiming a revealed message or prescribing a divine agenda for change or development would be a hard lesson to learn in a context where it is always assumed that certain individuals or communities of discourse have all the answers and ideas about what is needed to make the world a better place.

Second, listening establishes the basis of a dialogue. The distinctions Christians draw between the Church and the world can hinder constructive dialogue between Churches and the communities they serve. The Church cannot have a dialogue with the rest of the world if they come insisting as Hendrik Kramer did that the Church has a specific message for the non-Christian world.[39] The Church is called to be in dialogue with other communities of discourse regardless of their positions on contested issues. Therefore, it is necessary to open doors for a sustained dialogue to find ways in which *diakonen* will not be a competition, but complementary of what others offer for human liberation and reconstruction.

Third, listening is a teachable moment for the Church and its members. Those who listen to people hear other perspectives of the world. They learn about what those people think are the ideals, principles, and actions could help them find meaning in life. They also learn from those they listen to what they can contribute to the ecclesial and community and the things they aspire to do to make the work a better place. When people learn about others, they can gather historical information about individuals and their heritage and find ways of using that heritage to meet their needs and be blessed by them.

To whom should the Church listen?

The Church should listen to members of their faith community as well as others in the local context in which the Church operates. First, the Church should talk to ordinary people. I am using this term to refer to members of the Church whom Gerald West and others have referred to in their studies of reading the Bible in South Africa.[40] Many times this term refers to the non-technical readers of the Bible, or non-academic readers of the Bible. These ordinary readers have ideas, views, and perspectives on the Bible, and one can expect that they also have perspectives on the nature of the Church, its mission, and role in society. These people may include peasants and the dwindling number of people in the African community who have not gone to school. They may be members of the lower class. But what people have in common is that they are human beings who according some religious positions are created by God and for that reason the Church should be open to learn from them as it seeks to serve them better.

Listening is a challenge for the Church today because its leaders and the other members have some big ideas about changing the world. Some believe that witches do not exist, but if they do, they really cannot do any harm. Some Church leaders believe that witches exist and cause harm, but they, as ministers of Jesus, are ordained to drive out these witches in the name of Jesus. Some of the Christian leaders who believe in the power of witches have also been known to torture in order to deliver people from the stronghold of demons. As someone who is familiar with the literature on spirits and spirit possession, my task here is not to disprove such beliefs, but to point out that even when people hold claims that some people consider outlandish, it is still the responsibility of the members of the Church to listen to these people.

Second, the Church ought to listen to women.[41] The Church's practice of listening to women has been hindered by many roadblocks, which include African cultures which have relegated women to the back. The misuse of the bible has created other roadblocks for the Church to listen to women on grounds that in Church women should follow the leadership of men. Ecumenical groups in Africa like All African conference of Churches and the Circle of Concerned Woman theologians (The Circle) have called on the Church to listen to and engage women in the total ministry of the Church. Listening to women would enable its members to understand what disease or poverty means for many women who often go hungry to feed their families.

Listening to women will give the Church insights into the violence against women in the home, at work, and in society at large.

Listening to women would enable the Church which defends African culture to recognize that the African women actually want to protect African culture. This is what the American anthropologist Dorothy Hodgson found out when she studied Christianity among the Maasai women of Tanzania.[42] Listening to women will give insights that will grow and strengthen the Church. This has been the agenda of the Circle from its inception when Mercy Amba Oduyoye invited them to arise and speak for themselves and in speaking; the Circle gave the Church an opportunity to listen and learn from more than half of its members and leaders.[43] During the last 30 years, women have invited the Church in Africa to listen and understand the world from the viewpoint of women who have carried an undue disease burden in the context of HIV/AIDS. Their cries remind the Church that women are people and not vectors of infection. Therefore, listening to women will provide critical perspectives on infectious diseases and strengthen Churches to reject stigma and marginalization of women. In calling on the Church to listen, Circle members have given the Christian tradition lessons about what it means to work for justice.[44] Today Church leaders could learn a lesson from Ali Mazrui who lamented that women still lag behind in positions of power:

> As combatants, African women were part of the crusade for the empowerment of the continent. As diplomats, African women later represented the sovereignty, which they had helped Africa to acquire in world affairs. But as power-brokers, African women seem to have been on the whole part of the periphery rather than at the center of politics.[45]

Garth K. Baker-Fletcher in *Xodus* has argued that an African American male journey ought to include what he calls "love-listening."[46] We have come to think that the voice of the man is more important and that all in the family including the women must listen to male voices. Such an approach to life and especially for service in the Church is no longer sustainable for the simple reason that it is now clear that the men do not know all the answers. In order to succeed either in the Church or at home and wherever we live and work, it is important that we listen to all voices, including the voice of women in our communities. They have something significant to share and we must hear them say it in their own words. The ecclesial community should be a space where members, men and women, "can hear each other's pain, insecurities, sufferings, and longings without reproach, fear, or intimidation."[47]

Third, the Church should listen to all people in and outside the Church. The list of people should include Christians and non-Christians. Among the Christians, this means people from different denominations and for some people it means members of other Churches, which you do not consider Christian enough. The Church needs to listen to those who are not members not because the Church wants to convert them, but because the Church functions better if it understands the diverse views. Interdependency requires that the Church should be aware of the diverse viewpoints in contemporary society. In Nigeria where Boko Haram perpetrates violence, Christians should be willing to sit down and talk, if members of the group are willing to sit down and talk, rather than post messages on the World Wide Web. Some may want to establish preconditions for those talks, but in general, the Church must be in dialogue with all members of the political community and learn from them to model the kind of relations and services that would promote the wellbeing of all in the political community.

Fourth, the Church should listen to members of the Lesbian, Gay, Bisexual, and Transgender and Queer (LGBTQ) community. Many in the Church do not want to listen to them, but insists on talking with them only to tell them that they have departed from biblical teaching and African culture, African values, and biblical norms. Because many people in the Church do not want to listen to members of the LGBTQ community, it is hard for some in the Church to recognize that God loves them and they love God. It is difficult for many in the Church to realize that closing the listening ear precludes dialogue and service. Since many have not taken time to listen, the pronouncements in many contexts have only judged, condemned, and set the stage for some people to promote acts of violence and call for the killing of members of our LGBTQ brothers and sisters.

Finally, the Church in Africa should listen to the children of Africa whose image has been the face of poverty, hunger, HIV/AIDS, neglect; yet their faces have also been an amazing story of resilience, optimism, joy, laughter, smiles, and determination to be what they want to be because they can do anything if given the opportunity. Children are part of families and members of the political community who are guaranteed the same rights to liberty, freedom, justice, and equal protection under the law. To call attention to the plight of children, the African Union adopted the African Charter on the Rights and Welfare of the Child (ACRWC), first adopted by the defunct Organization of African Unity and enforced by the African Union in 1999. The Charter described a child as anybody below the age of 18 years.[48] The first part of the Charter stipulates the rights, freedoms, and responsibilities and duties to which children are entitled, and in the second section, the Charter stipulates the responsibilities of the states to enforce the Charter. The Charter addresses the conditions of children in context of discrimination, practices that not only discriminate against children, but also practices which cause harm such as female genital cutting, conflicts and displacement of children, the rights of children whose mothers have been incarcerated, and poverty and the living conditions of children on the continent. The Church ought to listen to children, many of whom belong to what some consider the lost generation because many do not have access to educational and economic opportunity because of political corruption, neglect, and abuse. If the Church is to develop a theology that speaks to the needs of children and one that is representative of children's voices, their faith, hopes, dreams, and role in the Church and community, it is important that the Church listens to children. The Child Theology Movement has invited the Church around the world to place children at the center of theological reflection and action.[49] In a recent publication, *The Bible and Children in Africa* provides in depth analysis of children in the bible, probing children in the bible, and the metaphoric use of children. The contributors to the volume addressed children in the African context today, examining their status in the family and society, local views of children, their circumstances under poverty, illnesses and pandemic, and violence. The authors have also examined bible influences on the views people have of children, rights of the children, difficult passages for children to read, etc.[50]

Notes

1 Jesse N. K. Mugambi and Laurenti Magesa, eds., *The Church in African Christianity: Innovative Essays in Ecclesiology*. (Nairobi: Initiatives, 1990), 1.
2 Laurenti Magesa and Jesse N. K. Mugambi, "Introduction," 1990, 2.
3 Ibid.
4 See David Barratt, *Schism and Renewal in Africa*. (London: Oxford University Press, 1968).
5 J. E. Church, *Quest for the Highest: An Autobiographical Account of the East African Revival*. (London: Paternoster Press, 1981); J. N. K. Mugambi, ed., *A Church Come of Age: Fifty Years of Revival in the COK Diocese of Embu, 1942–1992* (Nairobi: Acton Press, 1992); Kevin Ward, "Tukutendereza Yesu: The Balokole Revival in Uganda," in Z. Nthamburi, ed. *From Mission to Church: A Handbook of Christianity in East Africa*. (Nairobi: Uzima Press, 1991).
6 Mugambi, *From Liberation to Reconstruction*, 113–15.
7 Ibid., 123.
8 Ibid., 130.
9 Norman Tanner, "The African Church and the First Five Ecumenical Councils," *African Ecclesial Reiview*, 33, no. 4 (August 1991): 201–13.
10 Jesse N. K. Mugambi, "The Ecumenical Movement and the Future of the Church in Africa," in Jesse N. K. Mugambi and Laurenti Magesa, eds. *The Church in African Christianity: Innovative Essays in Ecclesiology*. (Nairobi: Initiatives, 1990), 5–28, 5.
11 Roland Oliver, *The Missionary Factor in East Africa*. (London: Longman, 1962); M. G. Capon, *A History of Christian Co-operation in Kenya*. (Nairobi: Christian Council of Kenya, 1952).
12 Hamilton Mvumelwano Dandala, "The Challenge of Ecumenism in African Christianity Today," in Diane B. Stinton, eds. *African Theology on the Way: Current Conversations*. (London: SPCK Press, 2010), 101–6, 102.
13 Dandala, 2010, 103.
14 Jesse N. K. Mugambi, "The Church of the Future and the Future of the Church," in Jose B. Chipenda, André Karamaga, Jesse N. K. Mugambi and C. K. Omari, eds. *The Church of Africa: Towards a Theology of Reconstruction*. (Nairobi: All African Conference of Churches, 1991), 29.
15 Jesse N. K. Mugambi, 1995, 160–1.
16 Gerrie ter Haar, ed. *Religious Communities in the African Diaspora*. (Nairobi: Acton Publishers, 2001); Hermione Harris, *Yoruba in the Diaspora: An African Church in London*. (New York: Palgrave Macmillan, 2006); Moses O. Biney,

From Africa to America: Religion and Adaptation among Ghanaian Immigrants in New York. (New York: New York University Press, 2011); Afe Adogame, *The African Christian Diaspora: New Currents and Emerging Trends in World Christianity*. (New York: Bloomsbury, 2013).

17 Elias Kifon Bongmba, "Homosexuality, Ubuntu, and Otherness in the African Church," *Journal of Religion and Violence*, 4, no. 1 (2016): 15–37. Kapya Kaoma, *American Culture Warriors in Africa: A Guide to the Exporters of Homophobia and Sexism*. (Sumervile: Political Research Associates, 2014).

18 Elias Kifon Bongmba, "From Medical Missions to Church Health Service," in Elias Kifon Bongmba, ed. *The Routledge Companion to African Christianity*. (New York: Routledge, 2015), 502–23; For more discussion of the collaboration of FBO and FIO, see, James R. Cochrane, Barbara Schmid, Teresa Cutts, eds. *When Religion and Health Align: Mobilising Religious Health Assets for Transformation*. (Pietermaritzburg: Cluster Publications, 2011).

19 Jason A. Carter, *Inside the Whirlwind: The Book of Job Through African Eyes*. (Eugene, Oregon: Pickwick Publications, 2017).

20 Jesse N. K. Mugambi, 1995, 163.

21 Ibid., 164.

22 Ibid., 167.

23 Ibid., 169.

24 Ibid., 171.

25 Ibid., 172.

26 Paul Gifford, 1998.

27 See Elias K. Bongmba, *African Witchcraft, and Otherness: A Philosophical and Theological Critique of Intersubjective Relations*. (Albany: State University of New York Press, 2001).

28 Material in this section comes from Elias Kifon Bongmba, 2016, 15–37.

29 John Mbiti, *African Religions and Philosophy*. (London: Heinemann, 1969), 108–9.

30 Desmond Tutu, 1999, 34–5.

31 Magobe Ramose, 1999, 49.

32 The research for this essay was made possible by a generous support from the Dean of Humanities, Rice University. I thank Dean Shumway for funding my trip to Zambia to deliver this keynote address.

33 Barbara M. Cooper, *Evangelicals in the Muslim Sahel*. (Bloomington: Indiana University Press, 2006).

34 Elochukwu E. Uzukwu, 1996, 33.

35 See also Bénézét Bujo, *African Theology in its Social Context*. (Maryknoll: Orbis Books, 1992).

36 Elochukwu E. Uzukwu, 1996, 137.

37 Ibid., 137.

38 Seth Horowitz, "The Science and Art of Listening," www.nytimes.com/2012/11/11/opinion/sunday/why-listening-is-so-much-more-than-hearing.html?_r=0 (November 9, 2012) (accessed April 21, 2016).

39 Hendrik Kraemer, *The Christian Message in a Non-Christian World*. (London and New York: Harper & Brothers, 1938).

40 Gerald West, "The Inerface between Trained Readers and ordinary Readers in Liberation Hermeneutics: A Case Study: Mark 10:17–22," *Neotestamentica*, 27, no. 1 (1993), 165–80.

41 Elochukwu E. Uzukwu, 1996, 139.

42 Dorothy Hodgson, *The Church of Women: Gendered Encounters between Maasai and Missionaries*. (Bloomington: Indiana University Press, 2005).

43 Marcy Amba Oduyoye and Musimbi R. Kanyoro, eds. *The Will to Arise: Women, Tradition, and the Church in Africa*. (Maryknoll: Orbis Books, 1992).

44 Isabel Apawo Phiri, Beverley Haddad and Madipoane Masenya (ngwana' Mphahlel), eds. *African Women HIV/AIDS and Faith Communities*. (Pietermaritzburg: Cluster Publications, 2003); T. M. Hinga, A. N. Kubai, P. Mwaura and H. Ayanga, eds. *Women, Religion and HIV/AIDS in Africa: Responding to Ethical and Theological Challenges*. (Pietermaritzburg: Cluster Publications, 2008).
45 Ali A. Mazrui, "Introduction," *UNESCO General History of Africa*, 8; Africa Since 1935, A. A. Mazrui and C. Wondji, eds. (Berkeley: University of California Press, 1993), 17. Cited in Uzukwu, 1996, 139.
46 Garth Kasium Baker-Fletcher, *Xodus: An African American Male Journey*. (Minneapolis: Fortress Press, 1996), 35.
47 Garth Kasium Baker-Fletcher, 1996, 40.
48 African Union, African Charter on the Rights and Welfare of the Child, http://au.int/en/treaties/african-charter-rights-and-welfare-child. (accessed March 11, 2016).
49 The Child Theology Movement is registered as a charity in the United Kingdom that has an international Board of Directors that addresses issues that affect children from a theological perspective. See www.childtheology.org/about-ctm/. (accessed April 1, 2016).
50 Lovemore Togarasei and Joachim Kügler, eds. *The Bible and Children in Africa*. (Bamberg: University of Bamberg Press, 2014).

Bibliography

Adogame, Afe. *The African Christian Diaspora: New Currents and Emerging Trends in World Christianity*. New York: Bloomsbury, 2013.

African Union. *African Charter on the Rights and Welfare of the Child*. http://au.int/en/treaties/african-charter-rights-and-welfare-child. Accessed March 11, 2016.

Baker-Fletcher, Kasium. *Xodus: An African American Male Journey*. Minneapolis: Fortress Press, 1996.

Barrett, David. *Schism and Renewal in Africa*. London: Oxford University Press, 1968.

Biney, Moses O. *From Africa to America: Religion and Adaptation among Ghanaian Immigrants in New York*. New York: New York University Press, 2011.

Bongmba, Elias K. *African Witchcraft, and Otherness: A Philosophical and Theological Critique of Intersubjective Relations*. Albany: State University of New York Press, 2001.

———. "From Medical Missions to Church Health Service." In *The Routledge Companion to African Christianity*, edited by Elias Kifon Bongmba, 502–23. New York: Routledge, 2015.

———. "Homosexuality, *Ubuntu*, and Otherness in the African Church." *Journal of Religion and Violence* 4, no. 1 (2016): 15–37.

Bujo, Bénézét. *African Theology in Its Social Context*. Maryknoll: Orbis Books, 1992.

Capon, M. G. *A History of Christian Co-operation in Kenya*. Nairobi: Christian Council of Kenya, 1952.

Carter, Jason. *Inside the Whirlwind: The Book of Job Through African Eyes*. Eugene, Oregon: Pickwick Publications, 2017.

Church, J. E. *Quest for the Highest: An Autobiographical Account of the East African Revival*. London: Paternoster Press, 1981.

Cochrane, James R., Barbara Schmid, and Teresa Cutts, eds. *When Religion and Health Align: Mobilising Religious Health Assets for Transformation*. Pietermaritzburg: Cluster Publications, 2011.

Cooper, Barbara M. *Evangelicals in the Muslim Sahel.* Bloomington: Indiana University Press, 2006.

Dandala, Hamilton Mveumelwana. "The Challenge of Ecumenism in African Christianity Today." In *African Theology on the Way: Current Conversations*, edited by Diane B. Stinton, 101–6, London: SPCK Press, 2010.

Harris, Hermione. *Yoruba in the Diaspora: An African Church in London.* New York: Palgrave Macmillan, 2006.

Hinga, T. M., A. N. Kubai, P. Mwaura, and H. Ayanga, eds. *Women, Religion and HIV/AIDS in Africa: Responding to Ethical and Theological Challenges.* Pietermaritzburg: Cluster Publications, 2008.

Hodgson, Dorothy. *The Church of Women: Gendered Encounters between Maasai and Missionaries.* Bloomington: Indiana University Press, 2005.

Horowitz, Seth. "The Science and Art of Listening." www.nytimes.com/2012/11/11/opinion/sunday/why-listening-is-so-much-more-than-hearing.html?_r=0 (November 9, 2012) Accessed April 21, 2016.

Kaoma, Kapya. *American Culture Warriors in Africa: A Guide to the Exporters of Homophobia and Sexism.* Summerville: Political Research Associates, 2014.

Kraemer, Hendrik. *The Christian Message in a Non-Christian World.* New York: Harper & Brothers, 1938.

Mazrui, Ali A. "Introduction." In *UNESCO General History of Africa, Vol 8: Africa Since 1935*, edited by A. A. Mazrui, and C. Wondji. Berkeley: University of California Press, 1993.

Mbiti, John. *African Religions and Philosophy.* London: Heinemann, 1969.

Mugambi, Jesse N. K., and Laurenti Magesa, eds. *The Church in African Christianity: Innovative Essays in Ecclesiology.* Nairobi: Initiatives, 1990.

———. "The Church of the Future and the Future of the Church." In *The Church of Africa: Towards a Theology of Reconstruction*, edited by Jose B. Chipenda, André Karamaga, J.N.K. Mugambi, and C. K. Omari. Nairobi: All African Conference of Churches, 1991.

———. "The Ecumenical Movement and the Future of the Church in Africa." In *The Church in African Christianity: Innovative Essays in Ecclesiology*, edited by J.N.K. Mugambi, and Laurenti Magesa, 5–28, Nairobi: Initiatives, 1990.

———. *From Liberation to Reconstruction: African Christian Theology After the Cold War.* Nairobi: East African Publishers Ltd, 1995.

———. ed. *A Church Come of Age: Fifty Years of Revival in the COK Diocese of Embu, 1942–1992.* Nairobi: Acton Press, 1992.

Oduyoye, Marcy Amba, and Musimbi R. Kanyoro, eds. *The Will to Arise: Women, Tradition, and the Church in Africa.* Maryknoll: Orbis Books, 1992.

Oliver, Roland. *The Missionary Factor in East Africa.* London: Longman, 1962.

Phiri, Isabel Apawo, Beverley Haddad, and Madipoane Masenya (ngwana' Mphahlel), eds. *African Women HIV/AIDS and Faith Communities.* Pietermaritzburg: Cluster Publications, 2003.

Tanner, Nathan. "The African Church and the First Five Ecumenical Councils." *African Ecclesial Reiview* 33, no. 4 (August 1991): 201–13.

Ter Haar, Gerie, ed. *Religious Communities in the African Diaspora.* Nairobi: Acton Publishers, 2001.

Togarasei, Lovemore, and Joachim Kügler, eds. *The Bible and Children in Africa.* Bamberg: University of Bamberg Press, 2014.

Uzukwu, Elochukwu, E. *A Listening Church: Autonomy and Communion in African Churches*. Eugene: Wipf and Stock Publishers, 1996.

Ward, Kevin. "Tukutendereza Yesu: The Balokole Revival in Uganda." In *From Mission to Church: A Handbook of Christianity in East Africa*, edited by Z. Nthamburi. Nairobi: Uzima press, 1991.

West, Gerald. "The Interface Between Trained Readers and Ordinary Readers in Liberation Hermeneutics: A Case Study: Mark 10:17–22." *Neotestamentica* 27, no. 1 (1993): 165–80.

7 Christian councils in Africa

Whence? whither?: impressions

Harold Miller

Introduction

In mid-year 1965, I accepted the staff position of Secretary for Relief and Service in the Christian Council of Tanzania (CCT), headquartered in the coastal port city of Dar es Salaam. A more idyllic physical locale could hardly be imagined. A statuesque Lutheran "cathedral" graced the picturesque harbor front. Close by, State House, cloaked in coastal colonial architecture, graced the banks of the harbor entrance from the open sea.

Several streets inland from this placid scene, President Julius Kambarage Nyerere was at the height of his powers, proclaiming the virtues of "Ujamaa," popularly referred to as "African socialism" or "familyhood," not to be confused with Marxism or Communism. A prominent building on Lumumba Street served as a favored venue for lectures on topical issues, open to the public virtually every day of the week. Scattered throughout the city were the tiny offices of liberation movements from countries to the south, including Rhodesia (later Zimbabwe), South West Africa (later Namibia), Mozambique, Angola, South Africa, Guinea Bissau, among others. In Dar es Salaam the respective (often rival) would-be representatives from those countries were presenting their credentials to the Liberation Committee of the Organization of African Unity of which President Nyerere was chair and thus seeking recognition as leaders in their hoped-for independent countries. Independence from colonial rule in sub-Saharan Africa had been launched in Ghana in 1957 and was sweeping across the continent. Countries to the south of Tanzania were among the recalcitrant latecomers.

Within the CCT's department of Relief and Service, a pastor to representatives of liberation movements and the related plethora of urban refugees was posted. As it happened, he was extraordinarily knowledgeable about Africa's independence dynamic and with the multiple related movements and personalities. A tri-partite agreement between the United Nations, the Lutheran World Federation and the government of Tanzania had birthed an organization known as the Tanganyika Christian Refugee Service, mandated to administer refugee settlements scattered in western and southern Tanzania. It reported in dotted-line fashion on its activities to the Churches of Tanzania through the "good offices" of the CCT's Relief and Service Department.

In these direct and indirect ways was the CCT serving as mid-wife attendant to the high drama of transition. Liberation was in the air, geo-politically at state level, but also within the ecclesial establishment; everywhere missionaries were being replaced by indigenous African Church leaders.

Following a six-year stint with the CCT, I was seconded to the Sudan Council of Churches (SCC) with its head offices in the capital city of Khartoum. In the wake of an 18-year civil war, the 1972 Addis Ababa Peace Agreement had just been concluded between the "Muslim Arab" government of Sudan and the "African Christian" Any'nya rebel movement of southern Sudan. Both the World Council of Churches (WCC) and the All Africa Conference of Churches (AACC) had been deeply involved as mediators and brokers in the peace process. As follow-up to the peace agreement, a senior staff member of the National Council of Churches in Kenya (NCCK) was seconded to the SCC for purposes of administering its relief and rehabilitation programme in war-ravaged southern Sudan. After nearly two years with the SCC, I was seconded to the NCCK's Rural Development Department for an eight-year stint. And then from 1989 to 1999 I was seconded to the All Africa Conference of Churches (AACC)'s Department of International Affairs.

This exposure to several segments of the African ecumenical community during a time of intense and often conflictual transition offered entry into an alternate world. My own Mennonite faith community was rooted in the "historic peace Churches," marginally conversant on select issues with the ecumenical community within which I now found myself active in several staff positions for a quarter of a century and informally engaged for additional decades. My understandings regarding the African ecumenical dynamic, as well as the global ecumenical story, developed piecemeal, not as the result of focused research, but as an accumulation of select impressions amidst programmed activity. Apart from specific self-identity descriptors of individual national Christian councils, relatively little was written – then and now – in assessment fashion re the character and function of National Council of Churches in Africa. In this regard, the personal impressions comprising this reflection must be considered an exceedingly modest contribution. An exhaustive inquiry into the rich African ecumenical lode must await an exercise much more vigorous than the one on offer here.

Christianity in Africa

Christianity in 21st century Africa cannot be understood without taking account of the modern, largely "western" missionary movement with its beginnings in the middle of the 19th century. Today its tentacles and effects are felt across the whole continent. Nevertheless, it is a mistake to overlook the existence and significance of the ancient Churches of Africa, namely the Coptic (Egyptian) Church and the Ethiopian Tewahedo Orthodox Church, respectively founded in *c.* 62 AD and *c.* 331 AD. Today these Churches are considered integral to the larger "oriental" as opposed to the "eastern" Orthodox Church tradition. Leaders from Africa's ancient Churches such as Origen, Tertullian, and St. Augustine are widely claimed and included within the common Christian heritage. But during the period from 1050 AD to 1948, the ancient or Orthodox Churches were quite separated and "hidden" from their western counterparts. However, since 1948 when Orthodox Churches joined the World Council of Churches, western Protestant and Catholic Churches have become well acquainted with Orthodoxy, thanks to prolific and articulate writings by its theologians. Today both western missionary-founded Churches in Africa and the continent's ancient Churches claim membership in the World Council of Churches and in the All Africa Conference of Churches.

For purposes of this reflection, Africa's Christian Councils are best understood as "western" ecclesial institutions, lodged within the global ecumenical movement which in turn is heir to the global Christian missionary tradition. One of the early reference points for the modern ecumenical movement was the advent of the historically significant Edinburgh Mission Conference, convened in 1910, which led in turn to the formation of the International Missionary Council in 1921, a forerunner institution of the World Council of Churches. Christian Councils were recognized in their institutional form within the context of the establishment of the World Council of Churches in 1948. Thus, is the genealogy of Christian Councils in Africa marked by these several reference points.

While it is beyond the scope of this brief review to comment on the efficacy of the global missionary experience, it is important to cite some of the underlying assumptions generated by it. Already in 1910 and certainly by 1941, there was a strong sense among western Church leaders and missiologists that the "Christian Church" now constituted a global phenomenon. Given the wisdom of the day which called for this newly established global Church to function as a self-supporting, self-administering, and self-propagating entity, the corollary assumption that called for large western missionary establishments to be phased out eventually, is easily understood. It was envisaged by missiologists of the day that the global, western-initiated mission apparatus would be replaced by ecumenical institutional structures and relationships, reflecting a significant degree of parity between the respective Churches scattered around the world.

At the end of the great missionary century, marked by the Edinburgh convocation, there was little sense amongst those gathered, that Africa would someday – even before the close of the century – become one of the centres of world Christianity. Indeed, there was the contrary sense that Islam would probably become the dominant "missionary" religion in Africa and that the continent's strong religio-cultural heritage would not yield readily to Christianity. But it is now widely acknowledged that Africa is home to an unprecedented expansion of the Christian faith, recognized as a significant locus of world Christianity in the 21st century.

African Christian councils

From 1900 to the 1960s, the direct antecedents of Africa's Christian Councils took the form variously of missionary councils or "fellowships" which had been formed as a response to the need for coordinated approaches to Bible translation and its concomitant literature publication and distribution, to medical care and to education, activities deemed integral to evangelization. In select situations, missionaries expressed "political" concerns about the oppressive relationships between the respective colonial governments and their African subjects. At other times missionaries were identified as collaborators with colonial regimes; in popular secular parlance, "the colonialist and the missionary were the same." Beginning in the 1960s and coinciding dramatically with the political shifts of the day, leadership in Churches across the continent was transferred from expatriate missionaries to indigenous African Church leaders, a transition also effected in the leadership of African Christian Councils. This shift took place within the context of far-flung continental African "nationalism," taking the form, eventually, of more than 50 politically independent states; its ecclesial counterparts were taking the form, ideally, of self-governing, self-propagating, and self-supporting Churches, though various dependency and reciprocal ties with erstwhile "mother Churches" in the west persisted.

Development

It will be recalled that the 1960s and 1970s were designated, respectively, by the United Nations as the First and Second Development Decades. This designation can be understood in the context of the post-World War II period characterized by massive American aid (the Marshall Plan) to a devastated Europe and the return to their homelands of African soldiers who had fought against European totalitarianism on behalf of colonial powers! The promise of political independence and the prospects of economic development provided powerful stimuli to the African imagination, not least the imagination of African Church leaders.

The basic assumptions supporting the expectations of the development decades were positive, up-beat; it was assumed that given sufficient support of the right kind, Africa, like the industrialized world, would also develop. These assumptions and expectations took shape against the backdrop of a series of United Nations-sponsored global conferences (a total of 18 between 1972 and 1982) on subjects as diverse as environment, food, water, population, women, and health. Each of these conferences resulted in global surveys and prescribed coordinated global action in efforts to achieve acceptable standards for people living in the so-called "third world." With the coming of independence to peoples of Africa, it was widely assumed that the sky was the limit to possibilities now unfolding; there was the sense that Africans with their strong survival abilities would be released to realize their true potential. This optimism flourished even as the UN's global conferences defined Africa as grossly underdeveloped. At best these contrasting views could be interpreted as complementary; at worst they constituted a shift from initial optimism to protracted remedial initiatives, the fruits of which were mixed, but on-going. In retrospect, it can be queried whether the "global" development standards advocated at the time and the concomitant specter of the West's excessive and wasteful affluence, could be rightly be advocated as a measure of sustainable lifestyles for all peoples on this planet.

Refugees

During this remarkable momentum, the AACC in collaboration with the WCC initiated a massive refugee-cum-development program under the rather complex rubric of an Ecumenical Programme for Emergency Action in Africa (EPEAA). With an initial budget of ten million US dollars, the program addressed the continent's growing refugee population, triggered by the massive transition from colonialism to independence that was underway. For this purpose, the field staff collaborated closely with AACC member Churches, with African Christian Councils and with a range of non-Church, quasi nationalist institutions (e.g., the Dar es Salaam-based Mozambique Institute, the education wing of FRELIMO, struggling at the time for the political independence of Mozambique). Altogether, the program initiative of the EPEAA was an attempt to address the most pressing fallout (refugees) of a rapidly changing continent and to strengthen the leadership and institutional capacity of the Churches in Africa, the former an acknowledgement of Africa's acute problems and the latter an investment in hope for the future. In contrast to significant portions of subsequent ecumenical and partner funding processes, the monies supporting the EPEAA were genuinely ecumenical, solicited from Churches in the west through the good offices of the WCC. Meanwhile western humanitarian agencies, including Church-related service agencies – many of them birthed during or immediately after World War II as relief agencies – metamorphosed into development agencies and thus identified new leases for their institutional lives by shifting programmatic operations to Africa.

For western Church-related humanitarian agencies, Christian Councils in Africa provided precisely the kind of partner linkages required in an emerging but still relatively under-institutionalized African continent. This partnership was supported by ever mushrooming funds, initially from purely ecumenical sources, but later from the coffers of donor governments, funneled through ecumenical institutions. During the 1970s and 1980s, Christian Councils in Africa developed substantial budgets, expanded personnel rosters and launched extensive development programmes. Some Christian Councils became programme implementers in their own right, sometimes in competition, sometimes in collaboration with their own member Churches.

It was, at macro-level, a shift from the generic missionary rubric of "evangelism" to the EPEAA agenda on refugees and thence toward the promotion of "development," including many overlapping continuities and discontinuities, to broad-based education and leadership training, all within the context of Africa's enthusiastic ecclesial and political development.

With the dawn of the 1990s, new relational configurations within the ecumenical community took shape, triggered, among other factors, by the remarkable changes in Eastern Europe. Churches in Africa, like Churches in the west, had been strongly influenced by the post-World War II east-west ideological divide. Some portion of the financial largesse available from North Atlantic ecumenical donors to Christian Councils during the 1970s and 1980s rested on Africa's "pawn value"; western aid to Africa was not without strings attached. When it became apparent that communism in its monolith "soviet" form had "lost the cold war," western aid added conditionalities. Now western aid – meanwhile significantly reduced – became available under the rubric of support for "democratization," an emphasis readily adopted by Christian Councils. Funds for "democratization" activities augmented Christian Council budgets, but for a relatively brief period. Indeed, the democratization venture brought several Christian Councils to the brink of financial collapse, in part because the ready availability of funds had bloated staff and budget figures in ways that could not be sustained.

The achievement of majority rule in South Africa was realized as the culmination of the struggle for continental independence, championed already in the late 1800s/early decades of 1900 by activists among the Afro-Caribbean diaspora. By mid-20th century, the South African Council of Churches (SACC) was championing the anti-apartheid cause with great intensity, fully supported by the global ecumenical community. And rightly so, for South Africa's official apartheid governance policy was recognized by the modern democracies and Churches around the world as a heretical relic from another age, based as it was on highly questionable ideological and theological foundations.

Post-apartheid era – councils in turmoil

With the advent of majority rule in South Africa on April 27, 1994 the SACC virtually collapsed. Approximately half of its staff joined the new majority government (catalyzed by the powerful African National Congress party) while ecumenical funds quickly dried up. Subsequently, the SACC was slowly re-constructed around new realities prevailing in the country and in the region. Additionally, it was adjusting afresh to the changed international donor climate. If the struggle against apartheid toward majority rule had occupied the SACC and the wider ecumenical community with a consuming concern for more than three decades, the agenda of reconstruction and reconciliation soon came into focus.

Apart from the dramatic happenings in South Africa, April 1994 was significant for another reason. It was the month during which a genocide in the tiny central African country of Rwanda took place. Between 500,000 and 800,000 people are said to have perished in "hand-to-hand" combat during that tragic month. In consequence, the whole of the Church structures in Rwanda for all practical purposes collapsed, including the Conseil Protestant du Rwanda (CPR) (Christian Council of Rwanda). Only after protracted effort to reconstitute the ecumenical life of the Church in Rwanda was it possible, finally, in 1996, to re-establish the CPR. In its first General Assembly following the genocide of 1994, the CPR could elect officers and appoint a General Secretary. In one of his first communications to the All Africa Conference of Churches, the new General Secretary requested assistance with the formulation of a proposal that would bring together leaders of the Rwanda Church from both inside and outside the country. The CPR's reconciliation task proved to be herculean; as the most pressing agenda, it engaged all the CPR's creative powers with substantial support from the AACC and Councils in the region.

During the 1980s, in another troubled arena, Sudan featured two Christian Councils, together "giving shape to a single ecumenical reality." In the capital city of Khartoum was located the head office of the Sudan Council of Churches (SCC); on the headquarters compound of the AACC in Nairobi, Kenya were located the offices of the New Sudan Council of Churches (NSCC), registered in Kenya as a non-governmental organization (NGO), serving the needs of the Churches in the war zones of southern Sudan. In collaboration with the WCC, the AACC provided an ecumenical forum within which the SCC and the NSCC could articulate and sustain their common vision for the Church in the Sudan, a country torn by 40 years of civil war, a recent segment of which had extended from 1983 to 2005. From 2005, when a comprehensive peace agreement was signed between the Sudan People's Liberation Movement and the government of Sudan, until 2011 when South Sudan became independent as the youngest country in the world, the fortunes of Sudan's ecumenical institutions were mixed. Today there is a Sudan Council of Churches with headquarters in Khartoum, Sudan and a South Sudan Council of Churches with headquarters in Juba, the capital of independent South Sudan, each actively involved with their respective demanding circumstances.

During the 1997 AACC General Assembly convened in Addis Ababa, Ethiopia, the Desmond Tutu Peace Prize was awarded to two Liberians, one a Muslim and the other a Christian. In the context of initiatives by the Liberian Council of Churches, representatives of the two faith traditions had launched an inter-faith initiative to heal a country torn by civil strife. In an earlier AACC General Assembly, convened in Harare, Zimbabwe, the Desmond Tutu Peace Prize was awarded to two Mozambicans, one a Catholic Bishop from an area dominated by the RENAMO rebel movement and the other an Anglican Bishop acting from a Mozambique Christian Council base, located in an area controlled by the ruling party, FRELIMO. Amidst complex political and ethnic divides, these Church leaders had worked for the peace of the land. Sometime after Nelson Mandela had been installed as President of post-apartheid South Africa, he appointed Bishop Desmond Tutu, former General Secretary of the SACC, as chairman of the government-initiated Truth and Reconciliation Commission. In his book, *No Future without Forgiveness*, Tutu recorded emotive episodes in the quest for national reconciliation. Betwixt and between these and other undertakings by Church leaders in Africa, Christian Councils played significant direct and indirect mid-wifery roles in the quest for a peaceful African continent.

April 1994 stands out as a pivotal turning point for the African ecumenical/conciliar community. With the achievement of majority rule in South Africa, the 1960s liberation agenda was finally "fulfilled." Rwanda and other points of tension across the continent gave expression to an altered agenda for the future. Much was written, subsequently, in an attempt to understand the past, to understand the meaning of April 1994 and its implications for the future. As indicators of the times, Christian Councils engaged with diverse agenda: of war and peace, of forgiveness and reconciliation, of Church-state relational issues, of Muslim-Christian relations, and with traditional religious understanding vs. Christian faith as introduced by missionaries. Conciliar structures and conciliar relationships as they became known and as they functioned in Africa were poised to engage with these and other dynamics. As they embraced fresh emerging mandates, they were working to reconstruct an African world both comfortable with itself and communicating at par with the global ecumenical faith community. In the words of Jesse Mugambi, these initiatives called for an embrace of *reconstruction* in contrast to the Exodus *liberation* metaphor, the latter having for decades inspired ecumenical discourse and action in Africa in its accompaniment of the dramatic shift from colonial and missionary tutelage to political and ecclesial independence.

Meanwhile, African ecumenical institutions have acquired a remarkable profile. Today there are 30 national councils of Churches in Africa, 24 of them claiming associate membership in the AACC. Although initiative for the formation of national councils of Churches emanated primarily from the Protestant Church community, 13 of Africa's councils include Roman Catholic Churches as members. Beyond the respective national councils of Churches, four regional collectivities of national councils have taken shape. These are the: Fellowship of Christian Councils and Churches in Central Africa (FOCCOCA); Fellowship of Christian Councils and Churches in the Great Lakes and the Horn of Africa (FECCLAHA); Fellowship of Christian Councils and Churches in Southern Africa (FOCCISA); and the Fellowship of Christian Councils and Churches in West Africa (FOCCIWA). According to a quick internet survey, issues being addressed by these regional configurations include climate change, agricultural policy, and a broad range of societal issues.

In 1963 the AACC was established several months prior to the establishment of its political counterpart, the Organization of Africa Unity (now the African Union [AU]). Since then the two agencies have initiated and nurtured discourse on a range of issues, commensurate with the general transition dynamics of the African continent. For its part, the AACC has for some years maintained a liaison office with a full-time representative in Addis Ababa, Ethiopia, nurturing relationships with the AU on matters of both common and special interests. In 2014 AU representatives met with African religious (Christian, Muslim, Bahai, Sikh) leaders in meetings convened by the AACC to consider "the Africa we want in 2063," the centenary anniversary year of both organizations. Since then leaders of the AU have approached the AACC to provide guidance with regard to moral and ethical foundations for the future of the African continent. It is a challenge which the leadership of the AACC has accepted and acted upon with alacrity.

Christians in Africa are articulating new understandings of the Christian Gospel, understandings long imbued with western biases. If the ecumenical journey in Africa is to be authentic, it will need to be leavened and enriched with the "corrections" offered by Africa's dynamic engagement with Christianity against the backdrop of its immensely rich religious-cultural heritage, now widely acknowledged as African Religion. Growth points in collective ecumenical understandings will become manifest in a variety of ways, not least by the nature of the engagement through and with Africa's conciliar communities and institutions, such as Christian Councils. Christian Councils are not ends in themselves. They function merely (imperfectly, always) in ecclesial midwifery roles through which and around which common learnings can be shared and to a greater or lesser extent, acted upon within an ever-expanding ecumenical faith community.

Bibliography

All Africa Conference of Churches Team. *African Agenda 2063. Consultation With the African Faith-Based Organisations on African Agenda 2063.* (Organised by the African Union Commission in Partnership with the All Africa Conference of Churches) Nairobi, Kenya, 2014.

Assefa, H. *Mediation of Civil Wars: Approaches and Strategies – The Sudan Conflict.* Boulder: Westview Press, 1987.

Byaruhanga, Christopher. *History and Theology of the Ecumenical Movement in East Africa.* Kampala, Uganda: Fountain Publishers, 2015.

Chepkwony, Agnes. *The Role of Non-Governmental Organizations in Development: A Study of the National Christian Council of Kenya (NCCK) 1963–1978.* Sweden: University of Uppsala, 1987.

McCullum, Hugh. *The Angels Have Left Us: The Rwanda Tragedy and the Churches.* Geneva: World Council of Churches, 2004.

Mugambi, Jesse. *The Church of Africa: Towards a Theology of Reconstruction.* Nairobi, Kenya: All Africa Conference of Churches. P. O. Box 14205, 1991.

National Council of Churches of Kenya. *A Century of Ecumenism and Mission: The Story of National Council of Churches of Kenya 1913–1013*. Nairobi: National Council of Churches of Kenya, 2013.

Okullu, Henry. *Church and Politics in East Africa*. Nairobi, Kenya: Uzima Press Ltd., P. O. Box 48127, 1974.

Tutu, Desmond. *No Future Without Forgiveness*. New York: Image Doubleday Publishers, 1999.

Utuk, Efiong. *Visions of Authenticity: The Assemblies of the All Africa Conference of Churches 1963–1992*. Nairobi, Kenya: The All Africa Conference of Churches, 1997.

Part II

Liberation and reconstruction

8 Postcolonial positions – Jesse N. K. Mugambi and the Christian responsibility in the socio-political sphere

Mika Vähäkangas

The aim of this chapter is to deliberate the social and political responsibility of a Christian academic theologian in a postcolonial situation. I deliberately leave out the question of cultural and religious reconstruction, while by no means thereby assigning it an inferior position about the political sphere.[1] Jesse Mugambi's life and work will be used both as an impetus for this quest but also as the scene in which variations of the theme are played out. I refer to Professor Mugambi's publications but much has also been gleaned from our numerous informal, non-recorded discussions, and I try to use this material carefully in the sense of both retaining confidentiality and acknowledging that my own interpretation strongly shapes memories of those conversations. Likewise, the historical contextualization serving as the backdrop of this discussion is purely mine.

Mugambi's Kenya as the context of Christian life

Jesse N. K. Mugambi was born in 1947 in Kenya where Christianity and Western ways of life were making rapid inroads into the lives of the people; thus his parents were devout Anglican Christians whereas his grandparents were strongly rooted in African traditional religion. The British yoke was growing increasingly heavy on the shoulders of Kenyans, and colonial annexation of the best farmland coupled with population growth was turning native Kenyans into paupers. Meanwhile, the First World War in which Mugambi's grandfather had fought, and subsequently the Second World War, in which Mugambi's father served in the King's African Rifles in the Far East, had proved to the colonized that their colonial masters were also vulnerable.[2]

Yet partly due to the fact that the population of European origin was relatively big and well-connected to ruling circles in London, Kenya, unlike its southern neighbour Tanganyika, did not get the opportunity to move towards independence with relatively little suppression of African patriotism. Furthermore, Kenya was a long-term colony whereas Tanganyika was a League of Nations mandate handed over by the Germans after World War I. World War II had caused an increased demand for agricultural products which prompted the settlers in Kenya to expand, grab lands and force local populations into the service of the commercial farms with the help of the government.[3]

Nonetheless, the freedom movement and the voices raised in support of *Uhuru*, independence, were on the increase. Colonial violence gradually met with independence-minded violence as the Gikuyu gradually began to take up arms in order to fight for their land and freedom. Orchestrated by the white settler community, a colonialist panic about the possibility of increasingly violent future developments led to highly questionable methods of repressing the independence movement dubbed as Mau-Mau. This was coupled with a "Christian and civilized" moral panic about the non- and allegedly anti-Christian nature of the independence movement epitomized by the Mau-Mau oath. The conjuncture led to an escalation of violence.[4]

The British government declared a state of emergency from 1952 until 1962 when the transition towards independence became complete. Mugambi was thus only a small boy when living in a country torn by war, and a teenager when the war was over. He and his family had their share of the sufferings inflicted on the freedom fighters, their families, their supporters, their sympathizers, or anyone suspected of being such. They too were enclosed in a concentration camp designed to cut off support by the local people to the freedom fighters.[5] Simultaneously, the so-called loyalists, Africans serving the colonial power with unwavering allegiance, were showered with booty that included non-loyalists' farmlands.[6]

The human rights abuse record of the British and their cronies makes shocking reading. Numerous interviews with Kenyan concentration camp survivors, whose narratives replicate, and thereby support each other, list routine torture, arbitrary killings, starvation, and denial of medical services, not to mention illegal detention and confiscation of the victims' properties. It is estimated that the Kenyan atrocities carried out by the British colonial government decimated up to 300,000 Kenyans, even if more conservative figures usually remain in the tens of thousands. The craftily spun lies, media blockade, and even destruction of archival evidence both in Kenya and the UK maintained the international public, as well as ordinary Britons, in the naïve belief that what was going on was a struggle between a moral Christian colonial power and the bloodthirsty pagan Mau-Mau. The British hero, Winston Churchill, after liberating the German holocaust survivors, was himself now responsible for similar atrocities under the colonial *Lebensraum im Süden* policy. In 2013, the British foreign minister William Hague finally had to admit that the atrocities had taken place even though he denied the UK government's responsibility, but due to a UK court decision, the government finally had to compensate the few survivors of the concentration camps who had taken the British government to court, although the vast majority of the victims remain empty handed.[7]

Mugambi's formative years, including his primary school education, thus took place in very difficult circumstances under a brutal colonial power that would stop at nothing to crush those Africans who were demanding their rights. Meanwhile, the Churches and missions headed by the whites supported the colonial regime, a state of affairs which led to young Jesse's disillusionment with Western approaches to Christian faith.[8] He entered secondary school at the time of gradual transition from state of emergency to independence of 1964. In the course of this process, the British were able to secure the interests of their past supporters, so the loyalists were largely able to keep their loot and thus benefit from better access to educational facilities, the excuse being that both parties had perpetrated atrocities so it was better to let sleeping dogs sleep. Kenya's new economic and administrative ruling classes mostly comprised people who had been the beneficiaries of colonialism and the state of emergency,[9] meaning that postcolonial, independent Kenya was thus constructed out of colonial lies. Built on the foundation of armed robbery, Kenya became a haven of corruption: merely the means of extortion had changed. Underneath the thin veneer of independence, democracy, and open market economy, colonial structures and injustices survived almost intact, although at least the colour bar largely disappeared. In Jean-Baptiste Alphonse Karr's words, "*plus ça change, plus c'est la même chose*" (January 1849 issue of *Les Guêpes*).

In the following, I outline some different ethical and practical positions Kenyan intelligentsia could take, sketching their contextual theological implications.

Prophetic voice – partisan opposition

There is an old joke from the Cold War era: "If you are not a Communist at the age of twenty, you have no heart and if you still are a Communist at the age of forty, you have no brain." The dilemma of a liberation theologian is similar. The world is full of (colonial) injustices and implementing the natural ethical reaction feels like assaulting windmills – it must be done and yet so little change results. Or so it appears from the responsibility point of view. However, if considering the consequences, the picture becomes more complex.

Kenyan Marxist author Ngũgĩ wa Thiong'o, a sharp prophetic voice on Kenyan society, has a background that also contains the deep shadows of colonial violence and resistance.[10] His vision of an exploiting society built on fraud and corruption is most openly described in his theologically-titled novel, *Devil on the Cross*,[11] a bitter and unforgiving volume that encourages violent overthrow of the oppressive structures. This is hardly a surprise considering that he wrote the work on toilet paper after having been jailed for his political views. This voice in the wilderness later had to emigrate from his motherland.

Taking up one's cross and playing the role of prophetic voice in society involves considerable risks. Cameroonian Jesuit, Engelbert Mveng, for example, was assassinated in 1995 – presumably because of his liberation theological message – and the case remains, unsurprisingly, unsolved today;[12] Mveng's colleague Jean-Marc Éla had to flee the country to save his own life.[13] These heroic voices are needed but the more they are needed, that is, the more oppressive the regime, the more briefly these voices can be heard on the spot.

Theologically this kind of approach can be built on an understanding of discontinuity between creation and redemption whereby the present world is seen as a thoroughly corrupt place of sin: this may lead either to radical activism which draws its inspiration from the Gospel values while admitting that a perfect society is not attainable, thereby advocating constant opposition; or, alternatively, to spiritualizing political passivism. On the other hand, for those who subscribe to a level of continuity between creation and redemption, there is a subsequent responsibility to present a better alternative society. In the World Council of Churches this latter approach has been dubbed "eschatological realism," that is, that the realization of a better society will take place in the *eschaton*.[14] This position need not presuppose a discontinuity between the present and the future – this will depend on whether one is post- or premillennialist. Jesse's theology does not seem to fit into any of these categories, however. His theology of reconstruction is oriented to the present situation, and he is far from spiritualizing Evangelical approaches.[15]

A distant analyst – the intelligentsia emigré

As seen above, prophetic voices may, of necessity, become emigrants, a state which inevitably distances people from everyday life back home. In the case of forced emigration, as in the case of expelled prophetic voices, the alienation is painfully deepened by the impossibility of even visiting the land of one's ancestors. This position runs the risk of giving rise to a romantic vision banking on past glories and transforming African traditions into an almost faultless Eldorado of wisdom, harmony, and communality. A telling example is an interchange on the position of women in African traditions between John S. Mbiti and Mercy Amba Oduyoye. In his "Flowers in the Garden," for example, Mbiti presents a rather idealized picture of the role of women, whereas Oduyoye challenges his views pointing to several oppressive structures in African traditions.[16] Naturally, much of the difference between their positions also stems from the fact that they represent different genders.

In some diaspora African (and resident African) theology, there is the temptation to compare African real or imagined values with Western realities. This is very much akin to the early Christian missionary approach to African cultures. David Livingstone's journals, for example, reveal an emphatic observer of African ways of life who, however, was convinced of the superiority of Western values. He did not spare his words in condemning the slave trade or colonial exploitation. Benevolent colonialism was rather his goal: colonialism that would be true to the European values. It was hardly surprising that African realities (as observed by a European) did not reach the heights of European ideals.[17] When comparing reality and values, values will usually triumph regarding the ideal.

In his theology, Jesse has not been alienated from the harsh realities of life; rather, his theologizing has been concerned with where the rubber hits the road. I remember how, during a WCC environmental theological consultation, we visited villages in the Kenyan countryside to observe several successful sand-dam communal projects that had turned semi-arid areas into lush gardens. In the last village, we got the chance of getting our hands dirty carrying stones and participating in the communal labour. That is called embodiment![18] In spite of the fact that Jesse tends to be at times very concrete and realistic, he still exhibits a strong dimension of idealism in the sense of a man truly striving to fulfill his ideals, and his enthusiasm spreads easily to the people around him. It also seems that he has programmatically resisted the urge to emigrate, thereby claiming the role of a son of the soil rather than that of emigrant observer.

Liberation theology in the service of the powers that be

There is also that kind of liberation theology that does not build on the discontinuity about the present state of affairs but rather sees current socio-political developments as steps towards liberation. This is a natural move when an oppressive situation, like colonialism, has been dismantled, and power has been shifted into the hands of representatives of the people. However, there is also the danger of theology becoming a source of legitimation for the powers that be. Tanzanian Ujamaa theology, for example, produced impressive theological ideas about the ideological foundation of that form of African socialism. On the level of theory, Ujamaa and liberation theology merged beautifully together, resulting in a harmonious political-theological balance in which, for instance, Ujamaa principles of communal life could be seen as a reflection of the holy Trinity.[19] The ideological proximity to the state ideology on the part of some of the theologians of the two biggest Churches in Tanzania – the Roman Catholic and Lutheran – may also have contributed to their paralyzing silence with regards state excesses and mismanagement. The Ujamaa villagization program of the 1970s, for example, involved the army forcibly removing citizens from their homes to places where the government wanted them to settle, sometimes with no services at all. One may wonder what forms of responsibilities a theologian deserving the name of liberation theologian should have in such a situation.[20] In Jesse's analysis, the roots of the tendency of Churches to attempt to locate themselves close to the powers that be lie deep in colonial Africa where Christianity was connected to the ruling elite; he thereby distances himself from this kind of position.[21]

Critical solidarity

Having outlined a couple of postcolonial theological perspectives that cannot be used to describe Jesse's stance, I move on to discuss that which probably most closely approaches it: namely, critical solidarity, the position claimed by several theologians of reconstruction. Jesse is the leading representative of the theology of reconstruction in East Africa, while it also has a strong foothold in South Africa.[22] The point made by critical solidarity is that while the changes propagated by liberation theologians have been carried out, like ousting the Apartheid regime in South Africa or introducing multi-party democracy in Kenya, theologians are supposed to support the reconstruction of their countries.[23] At the same time, however, they need to safeguard their independence from the state machinery. For example, in Kenya, the Churches played a central role in civil society challenges to the one party system. After that, the Churches had a choice between becoming apolitical, supporting the powers that be or remaining critical but constructive players in the society.[24]

Critical solidarity is a realistic position in the sense that it takes human fallenness seriously. It does not imagine that a perfect society will be reached in the here and now, while acknowledging, simultaneously, both the good that a working political system can generate for the people, as well as the constant possibility of its failing expectations.[25] Thus, it is a stance that is only possible when rulers and theologians are in basic agreement about what constitutes good life: a Black theologian could never have been in critical solidarity with the Apartheid regime despite, perhaps, appreciate that the currency rate of Rand was stable at a certain point. The fact that the political system was flawed would have made solidarity impossible. However, when the basic values of the government are more or less acceptable from a theological and ethical perspective, solidarity is possible. The critical aspect is then directed towards the implementation of the political ideals or some less than constitutive ideological dimensions. This is where I would place Jesse, as a supporter of a democratic, fair, and open Kenya.

On one of the University of Nairobi campuses there was, and probably still is, a "Hidden Agenda Café," the name probably referring to the idea that the hidden agenda in politics is often the real agenda. What if the political elite pays lip service to sound and wholly acceptable principles, but the hidden agenda is the "politics of the belly"[26]? Is there any point, in that case, to have solidarity with the principles that are not followed and only criticism for all that is done? How long can such solidarity survive? What is to be done when the South African police force shoots down striking miners in Marakana? Should there be any solidarity left towards a state machinery that has abandoned its basic principles to act like the oppressor of old? Is reconstruction possible when the destruction continues? Do many African political realities leave us space for much other than a theology of deconstruction?[27]

We live in an imperfect world where faith, hope, and love are under constant threat. While whether and when one should shift from critical solidarity mode to liberation theology may sound like an academic question, that is not the case. My interpretation is that Professor Mugambi has long pondered this question, and it is still very much in his mind, as is indicated by the changes in his position during the years of his career.[28] For me, as it probably is also for him, the question of which theological paradigm to espouse – liberation or reconstruction – is, ultimately, an ethical issue, with the choice depending heavily on the prevailing situation and the analysis one makes of it. Any theology is contextual,[29] and therefore no theology can claim universal applicability. The choice between theological paradigms becomes thus not an ontological question of truth but an ethical question of being true to the Gospel values. Whether one opposes an oppressive or kleptocratic government or is in critical solidarity with it makes a great difference: critical solidarity is possible when only minor repair is needed but not when a complete overhaul is essential.

In a mode of conclusion

Jesse once told me that his children were wondering at the time why he was still rooted in his post- or anticolonial approach; they were born well after *Uhuru*. However, I have tried to argue above that postcolonialism does not mean the end of colonialism but, rather, a new stage in colonial domination in which no party remains uncontaminated and unchanged: colonialism constantly produces peculiar hybridities. The Kenyan economic and political situation is a case of yet another round of variations on the theme.

Furthermore, in Cheikh Anta Diop's words: "*ceux qui sont morts ne sont jamais partis*."[30] The victims and the perpetrators of Kenyan colonial atrocities are not resting in peace. These ancestors of contemporary Kenya are restless in the societal structures, historical consciousness, political li(v)es and souls of the daughters and sons of the soil. The blood of Abel is crying out from the ground. Having myself grown up in a community haunted by the memories of a highly brutal civil war, I can only exhort the younger Mugambi (and Kenyan) generation to listen to the stories of the past to put matters finally to rest. The ancestors are not sleeping dogs; they are the moral guardians, and, where the immoralities of the past are institutionalized in the economic and political structures of the present, they cannot rest in peace but will continue to haunt the nation, just like prophetic voices in the wilderness. True reconstruction of Kenya involves a radical rearranging of the societal power structures to provide for proper justice and reconciliation. It is never too late because the ancestors are with us; the memories are alive.

Notes

1 For Mugambi, the cultural and religious foundation is absolutely central, a position which I share. No political or economic renewal is sustainable unless it has a stable cultural and ethical grounding. See J. Mugambi, *From Liberation to Reconstruction: African Christian Theology after the Cold War*. (Nairobi: East African Educational Publishers, 1995), xiv.

2 For Mugambi's background see Julius M. Gathogo, "Post-Liberation Theology: A Critical Appreciation," In Isaac M. T. Mwase and Eunice K. Kamaara, eds.

Theologies of Liberation and Reconstruction. (Nairobi: Acton, 2012), 59–74. Many of the details have also been confirmed in private discussions between me and Mugambi.

3 For Mau Mau social and economic background, see e.g. Caroline Elkins, *Britain's Gulag: The Brutal End of the Empire in Kenya*. (London: Pimlico, 2005), 1–30.

4 Elkins, *Britain's Gulag*, 31–61. Brendon Nicholls and Ngũgĩ wa Thiong'o, *Gender, and the Ethics of Postcolonial Reading*. (Farnham, Surrey: Ashgate, 2010), 61–8.

5 Gathogo, "Post-Liberation Theology," 68.

6 See Elkins, *Britain's Gulag*.

7 See Elkins, *Britain's Gulag*. On the compensations and the court case: "UK to compensate Kenya's Mau Mau torture victims" in *The Guardian* June 6, 2013, www.theguardian.com/world/2013/jun/06/uk-compensate-kenya-mau-mau-torture. (accessed October 7, 2014).

8 See J. Mugambi, *From Liberation to Reconstruction*, 229. See also J. Mugambi, *Critiques of Christianity in African Literature*. (Nairobi: East African Educational Publishers, 1992), 100; J. Mugambi, *Christian Theology and Social Reconstruction*. (Nairobi: Acton, 2003), 84–9.

9 Elkins, *Britain's Gulag*, 354–5, 359–63.

10 Nicholls and Ngũgĩ wa Thiong'o, 89.

11 Ngũgĩ wa Thiong'o, *Devil on the Cross*. (London: Heinemann, 1982).

12 Meinrad P. Hegba, "Engelbert Mveng: A Pioneer of African Theology," in Bénézet Bujo and Juvénal Ilunga Muya, eds. *African Theology: The Contribution of the Pioneers* vol 1. (Nairobi: Paulines Publications Africa, 2003), 40.

13 Bujo, Bénézet. "Jean-Marc Ela: Champion of a Theology under the Trees," in Bénézet Bujo and Juvénal Ilunga Muya, eds. *African Theology: The Contribution of the Pioneers* vol 2. (Nairobi: Paulines Publications Africa, 2006), 184.

14 Michael Kinnamon. "Theology of Prophetic Witness," in Peter Holtzel, ed. *Chalice Introduction to Disciples Theology*. (Atlanta: Chalice Press, 2008), 253.

15 See J.N.K. Mugambi, "Evangelistic and Charismatic Initiatives in Post-Colonial Africa," in Mika Vähäkangas and Andrew A. Kyomo, eds. *Charismatic Renewal in Africa: A Challenge for African Christianity*. (Nairobi: Acton, 2003), 114–16.

16 John S. Mbiti, "Flowers in the Garden: The Role of Women in African Traditional Religion," in Jacob Olupona, ed. *African Traditional Religions in Contemporary Society*. (St. Paul: Paragon House, 1991), 59–72 and Mercy Amba Oduyoye, "A Critique of Mbiti's View on Love and Marriage in Africa," in Jacob Olupona and Sulayman S. Nyanga, eds. *Religious Plurality in Africa*. (New York: Mouton de Gruyter, 1993), 341–65.

17 See, David Livingstone, *African Journal* 2 vols. (London: Chatto & Windus, 1963).

18 For the sand dam projects, see Joshua S. Mukusya, "Responding to Global Warming: A Community Based Approach," in J.N.K. Mugambi and Mika Vähäkangas, eds. *Christian Theology and Environmental Responsibility*. (Nairobi: Acton, 2001), 131–7.

19 Peter Kijanga, *Ujamaa and the Role of the Church in Tanzania*. (Arusha: The Evangelical Lutheran Church in Tanzania, 1978); Christopher Mwoleka, "Trinity and Community," in Gerald Anderson and Thomas F. Stransky, eds. *Mission Trends no. 3: Third World Theologies*. (New York: Paulist Press, 1978), 151–5.

20 For further analysis and critique, see Mika Vähäkangas, "Ukristo, uzima na ujamaa: The Theology of the Evangelical Lutheran Church in Tanzania in Relation to Tanzanian Socialism." Unpublished MTh thesis. University of Helsinki, 1992. For more acerbic critique, see Gwamaka Mwankenja, "Church and State Amid Political Changes in Tanzania: A Case Study of the Evangelical Lutheran Church in Tanzania." Unpublished MTh thesis, Makumira University College, Tanzania, 1999.

21 Mugambi, *From Liberation to Reconstruction*, 44.
22 For South Africa, see e.g. John W. De Gruchy, "Midwives of Democracy," *Journal of Theology for Southern Africa*, 86, no. 1, 14–25.
23 See, for example, J. Mugambi, "Theology of Reconstruction," in M. T. Mwase and Eunice K. Kamaara, eds. *Theologies of Liberation and Reconstruction.* (Nairobi: Acton, 2012), 24–8.
24 For criticism of Kenyan Churches being too lenient towards the corrupt government, see Paul Gifford, *Christianity, Politics and Public Life in Kenya.* (London: Hurst & Company, 2009).
25 See my discussion of Mugambi's theology of reconstruction as a complement to Luther's teaching of God's twofold rule over the world, thereby resulting in a politically relevant though not dependent theology Mika Vähäkangas. "Church-State Relations in Theology of Reconstruction," in M. T. Mwase and Eunice K. Kamaara, eds. *Theologies of Liberation and Reconstruction.* (Nairobi: Acton, 2012), 245–60.
26 Jean-François Bayart, *L'état en Afrique: La politique du ventre.* (Paris: Fayard, 1989).
27 For critiques of critical solidarity see e.g. Vuyani S. Vellem, "Ecumenicity and a Black Theology of Liberation," in Ernst M. Conradie, ed. *South African Perspectives on Notions and Forms of Ecumenicity.* (Stellenbosch: Sun Press, 2013), 177–8.
28 Compare, e.g. J. Mugambi, *African Christian Theology: An Introduction.* (Nairobi: Heinemann Kenya, 1989), 51–60 and J. Mugambi, *From Liberation to Reconstruction.*
29 Jesse Mugambi, "Theology of Reconstruction," 22–3.
30 Birago Diop, poète et écrivain du Sénégal: "Souffles" (Leurres et Lueurs); *Editions Présence Africaine*, Paris 1977; Cited in *Doumbi-Fakoly: Cheikh Anta Diop expliqué aux adolescents.* (Paris: Editions Menaibuc, 2006), 67.

Bibliography

Bayart, Jean-François. *L'état en Afrique: La politique du ventre*. Paris: Fayard, 1989.

Birago Diop, poète et écrivain du Sénégal: "Souffles" (Leurres et Lueurs); Editions Présence Africaine, Paris, 1977.

Bujo, Bénézet. "Jean-Marc Ela: Champion of a Theology under the Trees." In *African Theology: The Contribution of the Pioneers vol 2.*, edited by Bénézet Bujo, and Juvénal Ilunga Muya. Nairobi: Paulines Publications Africa, 2006.

De Gruchy, John W. "Midwives of Democracy." *Journal of Theology for Southern Africa* 86, no. 1 (March 1, 1994): 14–25.

Elkins, Caroline. *Britain's Gulag: The Brutal End of the Empire in Kenya.* London: Pimlico 2005.

Fakoly, Doumbi. *Cheikh Anta Diop expliqué aux adolescents.* Paris: Editions Menaibuc, 2006.

Gathogo, Julius M. "Post-Liberation Theology: A Critical Appreciation." In *Theologies of Liberation and Reconstruction*, edited by Isaac M. T. Mwase, and Eunice K. Kamaara, 59–74. Nairobi: Acton, 2012.

Gifford, Paul. *Christianity, Politics and Public Life in Kenya.* London: Hurst & Company, 2009.

Kijanga, Peter. *Ujamaa and the Role of the Church in Tanzania.* Arusha: The Evangelical Lutheran Church in Tanzania, 1978; Mwoleka, Christopher. "Trinity and

Community." In *Mission Trends no. 3: Third World Theologies*, edited by Gerald Anderson, and Thomas F. Stransky, 151–5. New York: Paulist Press, 1978.

Kinnamon, Michael. "Theology of Prophetic Witness." In *Chalice Introduction to Disciples Theology*, edited by Peter Holtzel. Atlanta: Chalice Press, 2008.

Livingstone, David. *African Journal 2 vols*. London: Chatto & Windus, 1963.

Mbiti, John S. "Flowers in the Garden: The Role of Women in African Traditional Religion." In *African Traditional Religions in Contemporary Society*, edited by Jacob Olupona, 59–72. St. Paul MN: Paragon House, 1991.

Meinrad, Hegba, P. "Engelbert Mveng: A Pioneer of African Theology." In *African Theology: The Contribution of the Pioneers vol 1.*, edited by Bénézet Bujo, and Juvénal Ilunga Muya. Nairobi: Paulines Publications Africa, 2003.

Mugambi, Jesse N. K. *African Christian Theology: An Introduction*. Nairobi: Heinemann Kenya 1989.

———. *Critiques of Christianity in African Literature*, 100. Nairobi: East African Educational Publishers, 1992.

———. *From Liberation to Reconstruction: African Christian Theology after the Cold War*, xiv. Nairobi: East African Educational Publishers, 1995.

———. *Christian Theology and Social Reconstruction*. Nairobi: Acton, 2003.

———. "Evangelistic and Charismatic Initiatives in post-Colonial Africa." In *Charismatic Renewal in Africa: A Challenge for African Christianity*, edited by Mika Vähäkangas, and Andrew A. Kyomo, 114–6. Nairobi: Acton, 2003.

———. "Theology of Reconstruction." In *Theologies of Liberation and Reconstruction*, edited by M. T. Mwase, and Eunice K. Kamaara, 24–8. Nairobi: Acton, 2012.

Mukusya, Joshua S. "Responding to Global Warming: A Community Based Approach." In *Christian Theology and Environmental Responsibility*, edited by J.N.K. Mugambi, and Mika Vähäkangas, 131–7. Nairobi: Acton, 2001.

Mwankenja, Gwamaka. "Church and State amid Political Changes in Tanzania: A Case Study of the Evangelical Lutheran Church in Tanzania." Unpublished MTh thesis, Makumira University College, Tanzania, 1999.

Ngũgĩ wa Thiong'o. *Devil on the Cross*. London: Heinemann, 1982.

Nicholls, Brendon. *Ngũgĩ wa Thiong'o, Gender, and the Ethics of Postcolonial Reading*. Farnham, Surrey: Ashgate, 2010.

Odouyoye, Mercy Amba. "A Critique of Mbiti's View on Love and Marriage in Africa." In *Religious Plurality in Africa*, edited by Jacob Olupona, and Sulayman S. Nyanga, 341–65. New York: Mouton de Gruyter, 1993.

The Guardian. "UK to compensate Kenya's Mau Mau Torture Victims." In *The Guardian*, June 6, 2013, www.theguardian.com/world/2013/jun/06/uk-compensate-kenya-mau-mau-torture Accessed October 7, 2014.

Vähäkangas, Mika. "Church-State Relations in Theology of Reconstruction." In *Theologies of Liberation and Reconstruction*, edited by M. T. Mwase, and Eunice K. Kamaara, 245–60. Nairobi: Acton, 2012.

Vähäkangas, Mika. "Ukristo, uzima na ujamaa: The Theology of the Evangelical Lutheran Church in Tanzania in Relation to Tanzanian Socialism." Unpublished MTh thesis. University of Helsinki, 1992.

Vellem, Vuyani S. "Ecumenicity and a Black Theology of Liberation." In *South African Perspectives on Notions and Forms of Ecumenicity*, edited by Ernst M. Conradie, 177–8. Stellenbosch: Sun Press, 2013.

9 Relating peace in African religion to theologies of liberation and reconstruction[1]

John S. Mbiti

Introduction

The crusade of the Liberation Theologies expanded from Latin America to become the global fashion in the last three decades of the 20th century. They addressed aspects of economic, educational, ethnic (racial), political, social, and sexual structures of exploitation, injustice, and oppression. Collectively, Liberation Theologies highlighted these (then) alarming structures and practices of oppression and subjugation, in their different global settings and forms. They spoke loudly, clearly, and ecumenically, with particular references to local, regional, and national situations. They generated strong, subjugated, or whispered echoes in every compass direction of the earth, and provoked a rainbow of responses.

After the liberation yearning and attainment, Professor Jesse Mugambi, with deep insight, anticipated a possible or indeed necessary theological paradigm. Consequently, in the last decade of the 20th century, he initiated, promoted, published,[2] and argued for a Theology of Reconstruction. He depicted this after the Biblical task of Nehemiah. He said, "If Moses is the epitome of a liberator, then Nehemiah serves as a model of social reconstruction." The name means: *comforted by Jehovah*. This is Nehemiah who, while in the Babylonian Captivity (Exile), learned of the pathetic state of Jerusalem, the land of Judah and the remnant of the people. He wept, fasted, prayed, and with permission and support of the King of Babylon he returned and rallied the subdued people to "let us rise, and rebuild" (2:17 f.). Moreover, there was plenty to be built and rebuilt, reconstructed: physical items like buildings, city wall, and gates of Jerusalem, the Temple; as well as social, religious, and economic institutions.

Nehemiah was a trusted cupbearer to the Persian king Artaxerxes, the most powerful ruler in the world at that time. He left his post to rebuild the land of Judah and Jerusalem its great city. He was made governor of Judea, and he rallied the people to "rise and rebuild." They rebuilt Jerusalem, the community became vibrant, the country prospered, and the religious life revived. Eventually, they could build the Second Temple 353 BCE–349 BCE. In the account of this rebuilding spearheaded by Nehemiah and Ezra, to "rise and rebuild," there is no mention of bribery, corruption, political fights, or stealing of public resources. Moreover, that was some 2400 years ago. It is reported that it took 52 days to finish restoring the walls of Jerusalem. Other restoration work continued. The fascinating biblical accounts of Ezra, Nehemiah, and Esther deal with Israel's restoration (reconstruction) at that time.

Nehemiah knew that rebuilding was not going to run smoothly. The enemies would fight to prevent the work from proceeding. So, he set half of his workers and equipped them to keep watch and ensure peace. Without peace, his rallying "let us rise, and rebuild" would be only hypothetical. Without peace, "let us rise, and rebuild" would become a laughing stock. Without peace, "let us rise, and rebuild" would be an illusion worse than the captivity in Babylon.

The Theology of Reconstruction after the Theology of Liberation requires and anticipates peace as well. From early times, through a colonial phase, and after colonialism, somewhere there have been fights, conflicts, and wars, on local, regional, national levels. As a whole, the vast continent of Africa and its islands has hardly experienced continuous, let alone universal peace. However, it knows peace, has constantly sought peace, and in places, it has experienced peace. In particular, the struggle for independence from colonial occupation was not a peaceful phase of our history: it was barbaric, bloody, brutal, deadly, fierce, and fiery. Immediately after formal independence from colonial rule, some different countries waged (especially) internal wars, often fostered by financial (economic), ideological, political, and ex-colonial motives behind the facade. This fracture of African life stretched everywhere: economic, ethical, internal structures; international relations; political, religious, social, and spiritual realms. Moreover, it has not ceased,[3] and it erupts during and after national elections, or through political rivalry and the manipulation of some leaders and their parties to hold onto power beyond constitutional limits.

Following the decades of Liberation Theology and witnessing some concrete attainments of political liberation, Mugambi with profound insight, took up the rallying call of Nehemiah to "rise, and rebuild," as being also suitable for our time. So, through publications, teaching, and lectures, Mugambi pioneered his "Theology of Reconstruction." It is a valid, appropriate, and urgent call, like Nehemiah's rally, to rise "from liberation to reconstruction." Like in Jerusalem and Judah at Nehemiah's time, much had fallen to ruins in African life, during the colonial period, during the struggle for independence, and even in independent countries. Everywhere African life has needed to heed the Nehemian call to "rise, and rebuild."

The ruined and injured vast areas of African life have been in want of liberation and reconstruction, reaffirming, renovation, creative renewal, and forging new goals. There are two outstanding and important features in the rebuilding work of Nehemiah. It may be possible from them to draw parallels and inspiration, for the African work of reconstruction.

One: Nehemiah and his workers could use the stones of the ruined wall of Jerusalem and keep its city gates, and (eventually) the erection of the Second Temple. In African life, there are injured and ruined traditional walls and temples, concepts and practices that could inspire, invigorate, and stabilize the reconstruction of African life after political and theological Liberation.

Two: Nehemiah realized that peace was indispensable for the realization of the collective call to "rise, and rebuild." He armed half of his workers and set them to watch and keep guard, to maintain peace while the rebuilding went on and after that. Two thousand and five hundred years later, peace is also and still indispensable for the theology of reconstruction in Africa. The Babylonian Exile ended in 538 BCE when the Persian King Cyrus conquered Babylon and set free the Jews. They could return and build, eventually including the Second Temple.

Mugambi has made a challenging call for the Theology of Reconstruction. Several other theologians have followed and taken up further discussion of this theological stream. In this chapter, I discuss traditional African concepts of Peace. From ruined traditional bricks of peace, maybe our time can rescue some and reuse them, in the contemporary discussion of peace. Africa needs peace today, as ever, and our traditional concepts could shed some light on understanding and implementing peace in our time. I feel that Reconstruction and Peace have much to do with each other, the latter undergirding the former and the former consuming the fruits of the latter. Mugambi is very much aware of the place and necessity of peace in our times. He has also addressed the issue of peace in connection with reconstruction.[4]

The distorted shaping of Africa and occupation by the colonial powers of Europe in the 19th and 20th centuries did not happen peacefully. In the 60-year period between 1950 and 2010, all African countries gained back their political independence and (part of) their cultural dignity. Colonial powers did not hand over independence as a present, wrapped up in beautiful gift paper. It was the result of painful struggles, with words and weapons, which I experienced as a young man. Following that phase, many of the independent countries have gone through rough tumults. These included major political changes, internal struggles for power, military rule, civil wars, and the flight of millions of people as refugees within their countries or mostly to other countries in Africa and beyond. Even the current affirmation of or search for political stability is not always taking place peacefully.

Africa is severely wounded by the "roughness" of ugly struggles and conflicts in political, social, economic, and religious spheres. These have inflicted deep wounds from ruthless blows on the body, the mind, and the soul, which affect the whole of society. This is an alarming face of African history, from ancient to contemporary conflicts. Africa has been wailing and weeping for peace here, and everywhere, now and then. Therefore, the significance of peace is not a foreign notion, and its intensity has accelerated, whether we look at it from secular or religious considerations.

This paper gives a brief outline of concepts and practices on that theme, from the perspectives of African Religion. That is the indigenous religion of every African people, which evolved from ancient times, without individual founders. We find it in creedal formulations, the oral culture of proverbs, ritual formulas, prayers, and symbols. Its beliefs are centered on the monotheistic acknowledgment of God as the invisible Creator of all things, to whom people pray, give praise names, and attribute many concepts. In every African language, there is a word for God and many attributes about God.[5]

Its ethics and morality regulate the social interrelationships among both the living and in relation with the departed. While each people have particular ways of expressing its religious life, there are many similar features that make it meaningful to speak collectively of African Religion in the singular, albeit without uniformity or centralized institutions. It is deeply integrated into the total life and worldview of the people, without delineating life into religious and secular components.

Religion is part and parcel of traditional life. While both Christianity and Islam also impact upon the religious landscape of Africa today, and both are the visible statistical giants of religious affiliations, African Religion is still very present. It is mainly in the background of these other religions, generating an on-going (sometimes silent) dialogue with them. When followers of African Religion convert to Christianity or Islam, they neither dispense with their traditional religiosity nor do they embrace their new faith with empty hands. In a fairly similar process, (Western and Eastern) secularism is not (yet?) squeezing out African religiosity from the people. Perhaps, instead, it is provoking them to affirm their religiosity versus the apparent challenge of secularism. So, religion is very much involved in the political, religious, economic, educational, historical, and communication transformation of Africa, and this has accelerated since the second half of the 20th century.

Religion plays a very dominant role in matters of peace and reconciliation. There is no space to consider the other religions of Africa in this connection, but we will focus on the perspectives of African Religion only.

Prayers for peace and reconciliation

Peace has always been a major need in society, on personal, family, communal, national, and international levels. Through various means, African Religion has addressed this need, one way of which is through making prayers. We take some examples of such prayers.

The Wapokomo people of Kenya make the following invocations for peace, rain, and health:

> O God, give us peace, give us tranquillity, and let good fortune come to us. . . .
>
> O God, give us rain; we are in misery, and we suffer from our sons and daughters. Send us the clouds that bring the rain.

We pray Thee, O Lord our Father, to send us the rain.
Let her who is sick, O God; receive from thee health and peace, and her village and her children and her husband.
Let her get up and go to work, let her work in the kitchen, let her find peace again.[6]
Several concepts about peace emerge in this prayer.

First, God is the Author and the Giver of peace. This means that peace is God's gift to the world, to human beings in particular and nature at large. Peace is an expression of divine will towards all creation, humans, and nature.

Second, one expression of peace from God is the supply of rain. Rain is water and water is life. God gives peace to sustain and propagate the life of all living creatures. God wills that there be peace, abounding like water in the world. Life is a unity, and human life depends on other life as well as non-living objects and laws of existence. Water is the most explicit symbol of life. Life and peace go hand in hand. Where there is peace, there is an abundance of life. The absence of peace is a threat to life, a reduction of life, a destruction of life; it is the suffering of life, leading to annihilation. Peace and water go hand in hand to sustain life.

Third, peace means tranquillity, good fortune, good health, with the freedom to live and to work. "*Let her get up and go to work!*" is one of the petitions in this prayer. Where there is no peace, there is no fortune, no joy, no freedom, no happiness, no strength or incentive to work, and no motivation to live. The absence of peace means suffering, for people and nature.

Fourth, the presence of peace has both communal and personal dimensions. This one is a communal prayer; hence, the use of the pronouns *we, us, our*, petitioning God for rain. Rain is never a gift to an individual. Rain is for the whole community, nation, and nature; and only within that framework can the individual "benefit" from it, by using its water and being sustained by that water. Likewise, peace comes upon the community of human beings and nature first and foremost. At the same time, there is a personal aspect to peace, the appropriation, and experience of peace. The last stanza is devoted to this personal dimension. It petitions the restoration of health for a sick woman, her village, her children, and her husband. This petition can be applied to anyone, in a personal way. Peace penetrates into the heart of the individual and does not vanish into thin air. Where there is no peace, there is suffering for the individual and the wider community: clan, children, family, husband, neighbors, wife, village, society, and the environment (nature), even extending to the peoples of the world.

Fifth, peace is grounded in a spiritual dimension. People raise their spiritual eyes towards God and petition God for peace. Alone, humans cannot generate lasting peace. Therefore, they do not seek peace merely from fellow humans, but first and foremost from God, after which humans become instruments of God's peace within their souls, within their community, and within creation at large.

We take another prayer, from the Gikuyu people, also of Kenya. It is a traditional litany recited while people are moving back to their villages after attending a sacrifice or other ceremony at the sacred tree (*mogumo*). It is addressed to God, even if the word God does not appear. The ritual leader (elder) recites one part, while the people respond to the other:

Leader:	*Other people:*
Say peace!	O peace!
Peace to children!	O peace to children!
Peace to the country!	O peace to the country!
Peace to the gardens!	O peace to the gardens![7]

The following are short comments about this prayer.

First, the word peace dominates the whole prayer. People are saturated with this one thought: peace. Leaders and laity are concerned with the one item: peace. It is as if everything else depends on peace and peace alone. When there is peace, there is plenty of what is necessary for life.

Second, peace is not just for grown ups only. It is also necessary for children and young people. If they learn early the ways of peace, this is a sound foundation for the rest of their lives. Peace must begin at the cradle. Only when there is peace can the children grow up well, be integrated, and be able to use their abilities to the full.

Third, peace is needed for the country, for human relations, for the carrying out of national activities: cultural, economic, social, political, and religious activities. Peace must have ramifications for the whole country. It is not a private commodity to be acquired and monopolized by an exclusive elite. Peace knows no discrimination and no favoritism, based on creed, gender, health, race, or wealth.

Fourth, as in the previous prayer, peace is necessary also for nature – human "gardens." Without peace in nature, there is no peace for human life and vice versa. If there were peace among people, there would be peace in nature (gardens). Gardens symbolize the supply of food – aesthetic, cultural, physical, social, and spiritual. They also symbolize where life is propagated, nourished, affirmed, sustained, safeguarded, and interrelated in its manifold forms on earth.

Fifth, as in the previous prayer, peace is grounded in a spiritual dimension.

A third example of prayer for peace comes from the Ewe peoples of Ghana and Togo. It is a prayer for universal peace:

May peace reign over the earth,
May the gourd cup agree with the vessel.
May their heads agree

Moreover, every ill word be driven out
Into the wilderness, into the virgin forest.[8]

Again I offer only a few comments to this prayer.

First, as it is addressed to God even without mentioning that word, it assumes that God is the author of peace.

Second, it sees peace in universal dimensions. The whole earth needs peace, not just one country or one part of it. People are interdependent, and real peace must be comprehensive enough to cover the peoples of the entire earth.

Third, this prayer seems to petition peace and reconciliation, for leaders of the world: "*May their heads agree!*" It implies that where there is agreement, there is peace. We know all too well that when "leaders" disagree, peace evaporates and conflicts or wars may break out, devastating people, property, and environment, often while such leaders remain safe and secure. An African proverb describes this well: "*When elephants fight, it is the grass that suffers most.*" It is the "ill word" which destroys peace, in the family, in the community, in the nation, in the world. Therefore, this prayer appropriately pleads that "*every ill word be driven out into the wilderness, into the virgin forest.*" That means the words that bring about disagreement, dispute, division, quarrels, and fights should be sent far away, to places where there are no people, and should be abandoned completely.

Fourth, this prayer petitions that: "*May their heads agree!*" When reconciliation is worked out, peace ensues where otherwise conflict has torn people apart. The agreement is a great step towards peace. The process can also work in the opposite direction: when peace is restored, reconciliation follows.

The next and final prayer illustrates that in African Religion, peace functions not only on a human level but also in the dimension of spiritual realities. African Religion has a deep awareness of spiritual realities. It portrays existence regarding visible and invisible realities, human and spiritual dimensions. These are normally the spirits of family members who are still remembered by name and whom we call the living-dead. There are, however, other spirits of the unknown dead, as well as nature spirits, which are associated with or are personifications of natural phenomena and objects, such as thunder, earthquakes, big rocks, lakes, and epidemics.

The relation between the living and the departed is very important, and where it is disturbed, there is a feeling of "no peace." Therefore, the living endeavor to "please" the living-dead, through proper funeral rites. When necessary, they also do so through offerings and sacrifices, or the fulfilling of requests from the other world, which may come through divination, dreams, or visions. The following prayer comes from the Banyoro of Uganda:

My father built,
Moreover, his father built,
Moreover, I have built.

Leave me to live here in success,
Let me sleep in comfort,
Moreover, have children.
There is food for you.[9]

In this prayer, there is, *first*, clear communication between the world of the living and the world of the living-dead, the physical and the spiritual. The petitioner asks that the spirits of his or her father and grandfather would "*Leave me to live here in success.*" That means he or she wants to live with the spirit world in peace. Only when there is such peace can he or she prosper, have success, and lead a meaningful life. The spiritual world is not indifferent to the physical world; the departed are not indifferent to the living. Comprehensive peace means harmony between the spiritual and the physical worlds, between those who are alive now and those who have gone on into the next world. African Religion affirms and acknowledges the continuation of life beyond death. Human life is affected by the invisible world. Peace with the invisible world is necessary for peace on the visible level.

Second, to bear children is a great privilege and responsibility. This should be done ideally in a setting and an environment of peace – in the family, in the community, in the nation, in the world. Children are the enhancement and beautification of life. For that reason, the petitioner asks to "*Sleep in comfort, And have children.*" The word "comfort" here is meant to signify peace. Ideally, the most desirable thing in life is to propagate life in peace, to bear children in peace, to raise them up in peace, and for them in their time to 'build' a home and raise a family in peace, as the petitioner has done. The prayer implicitly asks eventually for one to die in peace and have the soul rest in eternal peace. Peace has dimensions that stretch into the visible and the invisible worlds. We have already seen that peace is ultimately a gift of God.

Measures that enact peace and reconciliation

In African Religion, there is more action on peace and less speculation about it. This functions all the time at many levels of life. These include peace and reconciliation in person-to-person relations, in the family, in the neighborhood, in the community, and among peoples (tribes) that may have disputes or fights with one another. Peace is not taken for granted; the fact that people quarrel, have disputes and serious differences, fight, and even injure or kill one another is a tragic reality of life. Though not necessarily with success, religion provides ways of bringing about reconciliation and peace where and when such fights ensue.

Take for example measures that have profound religious significance for putting peace and reconciliation into action. Here is one out of thousands that take place daily all over Africa. This ritual example is observed among the Luo and Maasai peoples in Kenya when disputes or fights have arisen. According to this traditional method:

The elders arranged for peace parleys, and after both sides had agreed on the need and satisfactory terms for peace, a great inter-societal rally was convened on the border where the battles had been fought. Men, women, youth, and children convened along the border on the covenant day. They chopped down trees whose white sap is used as a poison for arrow tips. These poison trees were formed into a fence along the common border, with the antagonists facing one another across the newly formed poison-tree fence. The weapons of warfare were placed along the fence: spears, bows and arrows, swords and shields. This fence of poisonwood and weapons was a symbol of the war that had divided the two communities.

Then they took a black dog and laid it across the fence. The dog was cut into two and blood was allowed to flow through the fence and onto the ground, on both sides of the fence. Then the mothers with suckling babies exchanged their young back and forth across the fence, so that Maasai mothers could suckle Luo babies and Luo mothers suckle Maasai babies. Prayers followed this, in which the respective elders beseeched God to bless the covenant of peace. The participants pronounced anathemas on any one who ever crossed that fence to do evil.

The covenant had united the two sides in a bond of peace. The evil (*enmity*) of the societies, as it were, had been vicariously cleansed through the sacrificial death of the dog. The blood had transformed the war barrier into a sign of peace. The warring parties had become brothers (*and sisters*) by suckling one another's babies.[10]

This is a beautiful example of deeply religious measures that are carried out daily among African societies. We see some important points in it, which are also in other measures that try to restore peace and reconciliation. *First*, both parties show a willingness and readiness to work out peace. They face each other. *Second*, there are witnesses from both sides to these acts of reconciliation and peace. In this case, they include men, women, youth and children, babies, and above all God. These strengthen the bonds, which the rite and ceremony cement between both parties.

Third, there is a willingness to lay down "the weapons of warfare"; these are material weapons, weapons of words, and weapons that may linger in the mind or community, such as bitterness, grudges, hatreds, mutual fears, and suspicions. This makes the people free and open for peace and reconciliation. Each side gives up something for the sake of peace and reconciliation: it gives up that which otherwise could injure, damage, or destroy the other.

Fourth, the blood of an innocent animal is shed to serve as the blood of reconciliation and peace. Instead of human beings shedding one another's blood, they use an innocent and neutral animal. The blood of the animal saves, replaces, and stops further shedding of human blood. This is a profoundly meaningful act: one life dies so that many lives may be saved. Peace and reconciliation can be extremely expensive if paid for by the innocent blood of fellow humans. Of course, not every case of disputes and quarrels at personal, family, and communal levels result in blood being shed or included in measures of bringing peace. But where and when blood is shed, it is a very serious affair. Life is in the blood, and blood can save a life.

Fifth, there is "common" sharing of food. In this case, mothers from both parties suckle the babies from the opponent party. Again, this is also deeply symbolic: babies are for all practical purposes innocent, the living symbols of peace and joy. They have no open enmity between them. They have no weapons of warfare. Here they symbolize peaceful communal eating and drinking; they join both sides through drinking from mothers of both parties, "enemy mothers," as it were. Babies are the hope of society; they point to peaceful coexistence across barriers. They build bridges across chasms of enmity and pave two-way roads of communication. Through them, the warring parties become "brothers" and "sisters," even if brothers and sisters also fight! In the sense that, they are potentially one: human beings who should live in peace and harmony with one another and nature around.

Sixth, the offering of prayers to God recognizes the spiritual dimension of peace and reconciliation. This is a recognition that peace is a gift from God, where and when people genuinely want it. Furthermore, offering prayers is recognition that God's will for society and nature is peace. God will and does bless human measures for peace and reconciliation. We have already seen the role of prayers for peace.

The seventh point is that, pronouncing formal curses (*anathemas*) upon those who break the peace accord and arrangements, strengthens the spiritual dimension. African societies take formal curses very seriously. Because peace is such an important state, it is protected not by human police or watch persons but by the powers of the curse upon those who break it. Ultimately it is God who sees to it that the consequences of the curse take effect. God is the just Judge of the world. Again, we point out that not every act of peace making is necessarily concluded with either prayers or the pronouncing of curses upon those who break it.

The role of women in peace making and reconciliation in African society is tremendous, and all due tribute should be paid to them. Let me quote an illustration that speaks for itself. It comes from the Zande people of Southern Sudan, about which it is reported:

> If war broke out among the Zande, the oldest women of the clan would go to meet that opposing clan and interpose themselves between the fighters to make them see reason. When words proved fruitless, the women would threaten to expose their nakedness or to go down on their knees. In either case, the gesture signified a curse for those who bore the responsibility for such grave acts. Because of the respect that the enemy soldiers had for the women, they would usually put down their weapons before the fateful acts were accomplished.

Continuing, the same report suggests that, if there were no laying down of arms, the old women, naked and on their knees, would crawl towards the foolhardy combatants and say to them:

> We are your mothers,
> We do not want war,
> We do not want bloodshed.
> Do not fight with your brothers.
> They have sent us to sue for peace.

"[Moreover], if the assailants still refused to see reason and marched on the village, they would suffer the ultimate punishment for having disobeyed and obliged their 'grandmothers' to expose their nakedness."[11]

Covenants of peace

In all African societies, there are covenants that people draw up to cement a wide range of relations, such as marriages, agreements, settling of disputes, adoption of children or other people, admission into "societies," employment arrangements, borrowing of property, and various promises. Some of these are drawn more formally than others. We take one example from Nigeria to illustrate the importance and seriousness of covenants.

The late Professor E. Bolaji Idowu (1913–1993) writes,

> In the ethical system of the Yoruba, covenant plays an important role. In fact, the whole of person-to-person, and divinity-to-person, relations have their basis largely in covenants. The covenant between person and person is usually a parity covenant in that it is 'reciprocal – that is, both parties bind themselves to each other by bilateral obligations.' It appears that, originally, the Yoruba made this kind of covenant before the tutelary divinity of the Earth, and hence the generic name for covenants is *Imulè*, which means literally, 'Drinking the Earth together' or 'Drinking together from the Earth.'

The ritual, in general, is as follows: A shallow hole is dug in the ground; water is poured into it, and a kola nut is split and cast into the water. Two people who are entering the covenant kneel face to face with the hole in between them. Then one says, "O Earth . . . come and preside as we make this covenant: if I should break the covenant, may the Earth carry me away (may I disappear from the face of the earth)." Then he stoops down and sips some water from the hole, at the same time picking up and eating a piece of the kola nut. The second person does the same, and the covenant is thus concluded.

But although the generic name for the covenant is thus suggestive of a particular ritual, covenant-making actually takes various forms. It may be done before any of the divinities, but especially before Ogun. Besides these ritualistic forms of covenant-making, it is believed that to be trusted by a friend, to be bosom friends, to eat together, or to be received hospitably as a guest, is to enter into a covenant which involves moral obligations. "A covenant between two parties means, negatively, that they must think or do no evil against each other's body or estate, and positively, that they must cooperate in active good deeds towards each other in every way."[12] [10]

Covenants serve as preventive measures against the potential threat to peace and tranquillity. They cement the parties involved into a mystical relationship. They carry obligations of giving and receiving. Their intention is to cultivate peace, good relations, ties, mutuality, friendship, respect, and love between people, between people and nature, and between people and spiritual realities (God, divinities and spirits, as the case may be). In many African societies there are "blood brotherhoods and sisterhoods," drawn at such a deep level of relationship that those who enter into them become literally brothers and sisters to each other. Part of the covenant rituals leading to this is the exchanging of personal blood with one another.

The summary that David Shenk makes at the end of his survey of different covenants in African life is very appropriate here. He writes,

> First, covenants establish relationships, which are different from kinship ties. Second, a covenant is a very serious and profound matter. . . . It affects the entire community and is witnessed and endorsed by the community, the living-dead, and often by God as well. The covenant is everlasting. To break a covenant is to invite a curse. Third, the covenant attempts to affirm and recreate the person's original ontological unity with God and humanity. It is a quest for and a sign of the primal harmony of life and community. . . . Fourth, the covenant can be established only when there is openness and transparency. . . . Fifth, covenants which are sought because of a breakdown in relationships often require restitution before the covenant can be established.
>
> Sixth, covenants require sacrifice. . . . [They] are for the preservation of life through the solidifying of the community. . . . Seventh, the covenant is celebrated by feasting together. . . . The eating is a communion, a celebration of life in a community. Finally, the covenant is affirmed by the community, by the elders, by the living-dead, and often also by God.[13]

Proverbs about peace and reconciliation

Traditional African culture is a primarily oral culture. What people communicate and transmit orally in proverbs, among other ways, is of great value in society. I give here the example of a few proverbs that address the issue of peace and reconciliation in society. Every African people has its wealth of proverbs, wise sayings, riddles, songs, and symbols. As proverbs are public property, it should not be necessary to cite in details the sources from which I draw this list. A comprehensive bibliography on collections of proverbs would contain more than 2,000 items. An estimated ten million proverbs circulate orally, of which a small portion is available in written form.[14] The Internet has several websites with African proverbs.

A short list of African proverbs speaking and teaching about peace and reconciliation[15]

A loose tooth will not rest until it is pulled out. (Ethiopia)
A quiver placed upside down will drop arrows. (Kenya)
A shepherd does not strike his or her sheep. (Nigeria)
Abstaining from fighting is not timidity. (Malawi)
After an injury to the heart, an animal is killed and shared to make peace. (Ethiopia)
Hate has no medicine. (Africa)
He who sows peace reaps peace. (Kenya)
I have never heard someone say, "Let's go to visit a person wounded in a fight!" (Kenya)
If a person loves peace, it does not make him/her a coward. (Nigeria)
If we do not forget yesterday's quarrels, we will not have somebody to play with tomorrow. (Nigeria)
If you get peace, you get a life. (Somalia)
If you trample on another person's property in looking for your own, you will never find your own. (Ghana)
It is better to be a victim of injustice than to be unjust yourself. (Cameroon)
It is peace, and not food provisions that you always carry with you. (Somalia)
Let us eat out of the same spoon and drink from the same cup. (Sudan)
No matter how hot the water is, it can never set fire to a house. (Kenya)
One does not like heat, and the other does not like cold; make it tepid and still remain friends. (Madagascar)
The house of a person who negotiates survives. (Lesotho)
The one who does not fight is an ass; the one who fought and would not reconcile is a devilish person. (Ethiopia)
The teeth and tongue quarrel together, but they eat together. (Africa)
The toad likes water, but not when it is boiling. (Guinea)
There is no loser if all can listen to each other. (Kenya)
Those who refuse to forgive, break a bridge on which they must pass. (Cameroon)
When two people fight, the third one is the peacemaker. (Ghana)

Conclusion

Africa is a deeply religious continent, blessed with three major religions (African Religion, Christianity, and Islam), and many small ones, regarding adherents. At the same time it is groaning under the ravages of conflict, wars, violence, and injustices, to say nothing of natural calamities such as drought, famine, and disease. This human agony is a challenge to the religious heritage. Each of these many religions can contribute something towards peace and reconciliation, to ameliorate the suffering and foster prosperity (security, health, justice, and quality of life). We have seen that potentially African Religion is committed to peace, and in various ways, it undertakes ways that teach, encourage, and promote it. It has many channels of communicating this message: through traditional values and worldviews, rituals, social relations, and the increasing use of modern communication.

People want peace in our time, peace tomorrow, and peace in this new millennium. We want religion to be an asset for peace and not a liability, and African Religion is potentially one such strong asset. It does not preach, foster, or justify war between communities or nations. That makes it a challenge to the institutions of the other religions, to engrave the message of peace at all levels of life, in both internal and international relations.

Adherents of neither African Religion nor Christianity nor Islam are innocent of engaging, aggravating, or promoting conflicts and wars. However, their teachings can challenge people to make and practice peace at all levels: peace among people, peace between people and nature, and peace between people and God. As long as there are religious insights, they should continue to inspire and challenge society to move in the direction of peace. This is not to overlook the many forces that cause conflicts and make it so difficult to put peace into practice in the family, at work, in the community, in the nation, in the world, and with nature at large.

Nehemiah's call to "rise, and build" after the ruins in Jerusalem and the Babylonian captivity, and Jesse Mugambi promotion of the Theology of Reconstruction after the Theology of Liberation, presume that there be peace in the land (locally, regionally, and internationally) where the necessary building and reconstruction may be implemented. Only "the God of peace" (Romans 15:33; Hebrew 13:20) can help us to deepen our practice and experience of peace every day, individually, collectively, and universally. May God please help our world, which is thirsty for peace and reconciliation that we can rise, to build and reconstruct all areas of human existence and Nature at large.

Notes

1 The bulk of this essay is a reprint of material published in *Dialogue & Alliance*, Spring / Summer 1993, Vol. 7 No. 1, pages 17–32: "Peace and Reconciliation in African Religion and Christianity." The author has written a foreword and revised the essay for this chapter.

2 Professor Jesse Mugambi has published enormously on the Theology of Reconstruction. Among others are books and essays / articles including:

Christian Mission and Social Transformation, ed. 1989; God, Humanity and Nature in Relation to Justice and Peace, WCC/Church and Society Documents, No. 2, Geneva 1989; From Liberation to Reconstruction: African Christian Theology After the Cold war, Nairobi, EAEP 1995; Religion and Social Construction of Reality 1996; Churches and the Reconstruction of Society in Democracy, 1996; African Churches in Social Transformation, 1996; The Church and Reconstruction of Africa: Theological Considerations, editor 1997; African Theologians and the Reconstruction of Africa's Social Consciousness, 2001; Christian Theology and Social Reconstruction, Acton, Nairobi 2003; "Theologies of Reconstruction," in Diane B. Stinton, ed., African Theology on the Way, London SPCK 2010; "Justice, Participation and Sustainability as Prerequisite for Peaceful Coexistence," in: Applied Ethics in Religion and Culture: Contextual and Global Challenges, Acton Nairobi, 2012; Isaac M.T. Mwase and Eunice K. Kamaara, eds., Theologies of Liberation and Reconstruction: Essays in Honour of Professor Jesse N.K. Mugambi, Acton Nairobi 2012.

3 "It encompasses colonial wars, wars of independence, secessionist and separatist conflicts, major episodes of national violence (riots, massacres, etc.), and global conflicts in which Africa was a theatre of war," https://en.wikipedia.org/wiki/List_of_conflicts_in_Africa.

4 See, inter alia: J.N.K. Mugambi, 1989; "African Church Leadership: Between Christ, Cultures and Conflicts," in Responsible Leadership: Global and Contextual Ethical Perspectives," (Geneva, Nairobi: Globethhics.net/Acton, 2008); J. N. Kanyua Mugambi and David W. Lutz, eds. *Applied Ethics in Religion and Culture: Contextual and Global Challenges*. (Nairobi: Action Publishers, 2012); J.N.K. Mugambi, 2012.

5 Cf. John S. Mbiti, *Concepts of God in Africa*. Second Edition. (Nairobi: Acton Publishers, 2012). The book contains 1,600 African words and attributes about God, from some 550 peoples and languages.

6 John S. Mbiti, *The Prayers of African Religion*. (London and New York: SPCK, Orbis Books, 1975), 162.

7 Ibid.

8 Mbiti, op. cit., 163.

9 Aylward Shorter, *Prayer in the Religious Traditions of Africa*. (New York and Nairobi: Oxford University Press, 1975), 71.

10 David W. Shenk, *Peace and Reconciliation in Africa*. (Nairobi: Uzima Press, 1983), 68 f. (Italics mine).

11 Miriam Agatha Chinwe Nwoye, "Role of Women in Peace Building and Conflicts in African Traditional Societies: A Selective Review," Article in the Internet: www.afrikaworld.net/afrel/chinwenwoye.htm. (Accessed September 27, 2017).

12 See, for example, Stan Nussbaum, ed. *The African Proverbs: Collections, Studies, Bibliographies, CD-ROM*. (Colorado Springs: Global Mapping International, 1996). This CD-ROM contains nearly 30,000 proverbs and 1,000 bibliographical entries to date (1996).

13 Sources: Annetta Miller, compiler. *African Wisdom on War and Peace*. (Africa and Nairobi: Pauline Publications, 2004); J. Obi Oguejiofor, "Resources for Peace in African Proverbs and Myths," Article on the Internet Website: www.afrikaworld.net/afrel/obioguejiofor.htm; Kofi Asare Opoku, lecture: "African Perspectives on Peace," at Claremont Colleges, Claremont, US on April 14, 2008, in a personal communication (April 2010).

14 See, for example, Nussbaum, ed. *The African Proverbs*, 1996. This CD-ROM contains nearly 30,000 proverbs and 1,000 bibliographical entries to date (1996).

15 Sources: Annetta Miller, 2004; J. Obi Oguejiofor, "Resources for Peace in African Proverbs and Myths," Article on the Internet Website: www.afrikaworld.net/afrel/obioguejiofor.htm; Kofi Asare Opoku, April 2010. For current initiatives on peace, see: Grace Maina and Erik Melander, eds., Peace Agreements and Durable Peace in Africa, University of Kwazulu, Scottsville, South Africa 2016. See the very comprehensive list of conflicts, uprisings, wars, civil wars, internal wars, wars between African countries or nations, https://en.wikipedia.org/wiki/List_of_conflicts_in_Africa.

Bibliography

Barrett, David, et al., eds. *World Christian Encyclopaedia*. Oxford, 2001.

Maina, Grace, and Erik Melander, eds. *Peace Agreements and Durable Peace in Africa*. Scottsville: University of Kwazulu Press, 2016.

Mbiti, John S. *Concepts of God in Africa*, Second Edition. Nairobi: Acton Publishers, 2012.

———. "Peace and Reconciliation in African Religion and Christianity." *Dialogue & Alliance* 7, no. 1 (Spring/Summer 1993): 17–32.

———. *The Prayers of African Religion*. London: SPCK, 1975.

Miller, Annetta, compiler. *African Wisdom on War and Peace*. Nairobi: Paulines Publications Africa, 2004.

Mugambi, J.N.K. *God, Humanity and Nature in Relation to Justice and Peace*. Geneva: WCC, 1987.

———. "Justice, Participation and Sustainability as Prerequisites for Peaceful Coexistence." In *Applied Ethics in Religion and Culture: Contextual and Global Challenges*. Nairobi: Acton, 2012.

Mugambi, J.N.K., N. Kanyua, and David W. Lutz, "African Church Leadership: Between Christ, Cultures and Conflicts." In *Responsible Leadership: Global and Contextual Ethical Perspectives*. Geneva, Nairobi: Globethhics.net, Acton, 2008.

———. eds. *Applied Ethics in Religion and Culture: Contextual and Global Challenges*. Nairobi: Action Publishers, 2012.

Nussbaum, Stan, ed. *The African Proverbs: Collections, Studies, Bibliographies*, CD-ROM. Colorado Springs: Global Mapping International, 1996.

Nwonye, Miriam Agatha Chinwe. "The Role of Women in Peace Building and Conflicts in African Traditional Societies: A Selective Review." Article in the Internet: www.afrikaworld.net/afrel/chinwenwoye.htm.

Oguejiofor, J. J. Obi "Resources for Peace in African Proverbs and Myths." Article on the Internet Website: www.afrikaworld.net/afrel/obioguejiofor.htm.

Opuko, Kofi Asare. "African Perspectives on Peace." Lecture presented at Claremont Colleges, Claremont, US on April 14, 2008, in a personal communication (April 2010).

Shenk, David W. *Peace and Reconciliation in Africa*. Nairobi: Uzima Press, 1983.

Shorter, Aylward. *Prayer in the Religious Traditions of Africa*. New York: Oxford University Press, 1975.

10 Re-orientation

Theology of reconstruction and intercultural theology

Franz Gmainer-Pranzl

The African *theology of reconstruction* has much to do with "re-orientation," as Jesse Mugambi makes clear in his book, *Christian Theology, and Social Reconstruction*.[1] People who have experienced oppression and dependence, who have lost their self-confidence and courage, need to find themselves again and to *reconstruct* their families and societies, communities, and Churches – the entire African continent, in fact. This reconstruction has a very real effect on the infrastructure of a country, its economy, and politics, but also on its consciousness, creativity and intellectuality, its hope and confidence. If therefore a *theology of reconstruction* strengthens people's self-awareness, fosters a capacity for critical discernment,[2] and provides the impetus for the reconstruction of social life, it functions as a socially oriented discourse, as a form of theology which is constantly relating to actual developments in society. Mugambi himself repeatedly emphasizes this inner connection between Christian proclamation, faith reflection, and social reconstruction: "If evangelization in Africa does not help Africans in the social reconstruction of their environment, such an enterprise is like salt that has lost its taste" (Matt. 5: 13–16).[3]

This social and political aspect of the theology of reconstruction is comparable with the social debate conducted by intercultural theology. Intercultural theology also explores the interaction between Christian faith and diverse societal contexts, and analyzes the corroborative and critical power of the Christian message that motivates people to engage with political issues. Hence a comparison of these two approaches to "political theology," examining the relationship between the theology of reconstruction and intercultural theology and considering ways in which the theology of reconstruction can offer impetus to intercultural theology. With this in mind, I wish in this reflection to (1) introduce the field of work and research entitled, *intercultural theology*, (2) define the social relevance of the *theology of reconstruction*, and (3) highlight possible ways in which the theology of reconstruction can provide stimuli to intercultural theology.

The intercultural theology research project

Since the 1990s the subject of *intercultural theology* has been taught at some universities in the German-speaking world. Whereas Protestant theology in Germany has established several professorships, institutions, and departments of intercultural theology, in Austria, for example, there is only one professor of intercultural theology at the Catholic faculty of theology (at the University of Salzburg). However, that does not mean that the concerns of intercultural theology are being overlooked; at many institutions and all theological faculties intercultural theology is represented in research and teaching programs, even though there is no actual Chair of Intercultural Theology.

The foundation for the subject of intercultural theology is to be found in the criticism of the hitherto Eurocentrism of theology. Early in the 20th century, missiologists had already established that non-Christian religions showed tremendous potential for ethics and spirituality; systematic and practical theologians drew attention to the effects of colonialism and demanded the formation of an indigenous Church and theology. Also, concepts that had previously been taken for granted were questioned and a critical analysis of terms such as "mission," "culture," "context," "religion," was undertaken. Moreover, Christian Churches and their theologies were confronted with new developments to which they were now compelled to find answers: the increasing pluralization of society; the altered role of religion in public life; cultural upheavals which had an impact on religious practice such as migration, religious traditionalism, extremism; and fundamentalism. Intercultural theology examines these issues. It has to be said that it does not consider itself a school of thought as such, but rather a network of disciplines engaging primarily with intercultural and interfaith challenges encountered by the Christian faith.

The large, sometimes unwieldy, research field of intercultural theology can be disaggregated into four major work areas.

- To the extent that the complex subject matter of intercultural theology is viewed from the perspective of culture, and indeed at the level of actual communication, it is concerned with (a) *Contextual Theologies*. These examine the degree to which the encounter between the Christian faith and new cultural contexts has led to distinctive forms of theology, how different contextual theologies can be compared and what correlations exist between societal contexts and Christian theologies. For example, it examines theologies in China, Latin America, South Africa, or central Europe. However, it considers geographical regions and the cultural traditions associated with them, together with specific contexts of experience and their influence on the development of theology, such as the gender perspective (feminist theology) or the experience of social exclusion (Dalit theology).
- When the cultural dimension of intercultural theology is viewed, not at the level of the history of the actual encounter but the level

of epistemological preconditions, it is concerned with (b) *Intercultural Theological Epistemology*. Here concepts such as "context," "culture," and "interculturality" are given critical consideration; in other words, it investigates the operating system of intercultural theology. Which understanding of "culture" is taken as a premise? Which approach does a specific argumentation take to intercultural hermeneutics? Which models of theological contextualization can be distinguished? Moreover, when there is a reference to a correlation between faith and society, how are "faith," "society," and "politics" to be understood? Moreover, finally: which theological logic is being applied here?

- The third and fourth working fields of intercultural theology stem from the perspective of religion. Different religious traditions and elements of various religions are compared with each other at the level of actual communication and encounter. This is the approach taken by (c) *Comparative Theology*, which is interested in particular motifs that find expression in different religious traditions, in symbols, in rituals and religious practices such as prayer, fasting, and social involvement. This type of comparison requires a distinctive criteriology of interreligious comparison which does not simply cross-reference superficial similarities but compares elements of different religions by their theological meaning. Comparative theology also reflects on the different observational, analytical, and discourse methods used in the interreligious comparison, scrutinizing the approaches adopted by interreligious dialogue and making a critical examination of specific religious models.
- When the implications of the religious plurality are examined regarding their theological epistemology, the (d) *Theology of Religions* comes into play. Here we are dealing with comparisons and methodological reflection and with the question of what the claim to "salvation" and "truth" made by Religion A means for Religions B and C. The explosive nature of this question only becomes clear if we take seriously the fact that religions constitute different pathways to salvation which cannot be traced back to a common unity. A theology of religions is not a comparison from a religious studies perspective, which simply presents different religions; rather, it is the pressing question as to the significance of another religion for one's faith conviction. What does it mean for a Buddhist to see liberation from the cycle of suffering as *the* path to salvation, for a Muslim to see salvation in the revelation of the Koran? What does it mean for a Jew, when Christians describe the Jewish Bible as the "Old Testament," and how do Christians cope with the fact that the Jews do not recognize Jesus as the "Son of God?" The theology of religions has developed particular models for addressing these challenging questions and engages in a critical discussion of concepts such as revelation, the claim to exclusivity and salvation. The exclusivist/inclusivist/pluralist model accepted since the 1980s[4] has become problematic in recent years

since it is too strongly oriented towards the cognitive dimension of religion and pays too little attention to the societal conditions of religious "truth."

These four working fields (contextual theologies, intercultural theological epistemology, comparative theology and theology of religions) cannot be strictly demarcated; to engage with specific challenges, intercultural theology must think contextually and connect different research topics. Some of the challenges include, as mentioned above, the correlation between migration experience and religiosity, the complex interaction between religion and society, the question of the (intrinsic) religious potential for violence and its relationship with fundamentalism and extremism, religious criticism and atheist currents in different societies, new religious movements (for example Pentecostalism, esotericism, and Islamic groups), "spirituality" (as an umbrella term for a broad interest in non-institutional religion), new forms of Christianity in the urban centres of the global south, and religious or anti-religiously encoded racism and xenophobia. Here intercultural theology is required to reflect on the complex correlation between religion/Christianity and society in different contexts and to couple its specific theological competence (intellectual reflection on the hope of faith) with interdisciplinary expertise. Intercultural theology applies the convictions of the Christian faith to the problem areas of society and engages in theological reflection in collaboration with other disciplines, including empirical religious studies, particularly sociology of religion, psychology of religion, ethnology of religion, and economics of religion, with philosophical expertise (in particular philosophy of religion and intercultural philosophy), with the cultural, political, and social sciences, together with those sciences that examine societal contexts from particular problem perspectives (gender studies, migration studies, postcolonial studies, global studies, and development studies).

Intercultural theology's academic self-understanding has been particularly influenced by the *Cultural Turn*; the recognition that "culture" is not merely a topic, but the medium of intercultural theological reflection and has had a decisive influence on its work. An important premise of cultural science is that religion is not merely a subject area to be handled historically and systematically, but it has to do with "meanings." Rituals and symbols represent a specific worldview and ethic. They are interrelated with the social "web of significance" (Clifford Geertz) or are in tension with it: they "mean" something for people. Such a cultural science approach has, with good reason, criticized positivist conceptions of religion and had taken the interpenetration of culture and religion into account. At the same time, intercultural theology's strong cultural science emphasis has somewhat disregarded the social, political and economic dimensions of religion and society. As important as it is to interpret religious traditions in light of dimensions of cultural meaning, it is also vital not to forget the hard facts regarding globalization, economics, social living conditions, and political conditions. Political scientists rightly criticize a naturalization of social issues, which, for example, presents the subject of the Islamic head-covering as the central issue of migration/integration without even mentioning the problems of poverty, unemployment, social exclusion, and racism. While it is true that intercultural theology operates with an appreciation of cultural science issues, for this very reason it must not fall prey to a naturalization of social issues; it must combine cultural scientific and socio-scientific methods and adopt an interdisciplinary approach to theological analysis, always keeping in mind current social questions.

This is precisely where the theology of reconstruction takes its place within the working field of intercultural theology. "Social Reconstruction is a process in which all sectors of the population are invited to participate in the inauguration of a new social order,"[5] stresses Jesse Mugambi, emphasizing the broad social aspect of the theology of reconstruction. This new approach to theological thinking aims to introduce the ethical and social resources of the Christian faith into the social debate, thereby contributing to a reconstruction at various levels of life.[6] So what is the specific social relevance of the theology of reconstruction?

The theology of reconstruction as social and socio-critical discourse

While not claiming to offer a comprehensive survey of the theology of reconstruction, what follows will highlight five aspects of the social relevance of this theological approach.

The *Kairos* starting point: Mugambi sees the *theology of reconstruction* as having its origin in a specific event, a decisive point in time. This *kairos* consists in a profound upheaval which took place at the beginning of the 1990s, at the end of the Cold War (following the demise of the Soviet Union), at the time of Nelson Mandela's release from prison (1992). Mandela's election as president of the post-apartheid South Africa signaled a new era calling for a new paradigm of theology: a theology of reconstruction in place of a theology of liberation. Mugambi sees this upheaval as a *kairos*, to which theology must respond. It was impossible for Christian Churches to remain unaffected by what was happening, both socially and politically. In contrast to a "purely spiritual" theology, preoccupied with questions of faith within the Church, the theology of reconstruction manifests great social sensitivity; social and political changes have an impact on theological discourse as well – and what is more, the *kairos* of the end of the cold war gave a once and once-only inspiration to theology. The opportunity of such a *kairos* could be used or wasted, as is illustrated by many examples from recent history.[7]

While it is true that the theology of reconstruction is not a socio-political strategy, but a form of academic debate, it nonetheless reflects in a special way on the potential of the Christian faith to encourage and empower people, to take them seriously as subjects of political action and to enable them to resolve crises and problems. The biblical figure of Nehemiah symbolizes this *empowerment* when he persuades the people of his time (the middle of the 5th century before Christ) to reconstruct the temple in Jerusalem:

> You see the trouble we are in, how Jerusalem lies in ruins with its gates burned. Come, let us build the wall of Jerusalem, that we may no longer suffer disgrace. . . . Moreover, they said: Let us rise and build.
>
> (Nehemiah 2:17–18)[8]

Mugambi portrays Nehemiah as an example of a charismatic leader who wins people over for the reconstruction project. "It seems that at this time in history, the figure of Nehemiah is the most encouraging and most inspiring for Africa today,"[9] writes Mugambi. His reconstruction theology approach has as its objective the empowerment of the excluded, the hopeless and the disappointed, to enable them to be independent participants in the process of social renewal.

The inspiration of the Christian, which Mugambi wants to introduce into the social debate, has, on the one hand, a personal dimension, because it seeks to empower real people, but also a social dimension, consisting in the strengthening of social cohesion. There are some points worth noting here. First, it is primarily the reconstruction of society, not of the Church, which is at stake. Second, social competence becomes the credibility criterion of Christian Churches. Alternatively, to put it another way: Christians are recognized by their constructive, cooperative, and communicative participation in the social debate. Moreover, third, it is not a question of promoting the theological contribution to become part of the political decision-making process; the theology of reconstruction seeks to take its place alongside other disciplines and initiatives in supporting the reconstruction of Africa.[10] This sends a clear religiopolitical signal: Christianity does not intend to enter a "competition between religions," but to be effective as a socially constructive force for peace.

However, the ability to cooperate, solidarity, and social competence does not mean simply adapting to societal norms. On the contrary, the theology of reconstruction raises objections if human dignity, social justice or political freedom are at stake. In this context, Mugambi always refers to the text of Romans 12:2–4: "Do not be conformed to this world, but be transformed by the renewing of your minds, so that you may discern what is the will of God – what is good and acceptable and perfect." It is precisely by means of the critical distance it maintains from mainstream thinking, politics and cultural practices that the theology of reconstruction does society a special service; it does not seek to rescue "values" or "traditions," but to be the critical thorn of Christian hope in the side of a society which may already have resigned itself to "reality." Authoritarian politics, corruption, discrimination against the rights of women, and the disadvantaged of minorities are not simply accepted as unalterable facts but are addressed as problems to be remedied. The medium employed by the theology of reconstruction, however, is not a political struggle,[11] but consciousness-raising. "Not to be conformed to this world" means preserving an *attitude of critical discernment* – even towards one's preferences and (theological) opinions. It is ultimately not the rubber-stampers and conformists but the critical thinkers who make the best contribution to the democratic development of society.

A fifth mark of the theology of reconstruction, one specific to African societies, describes the role played by religions. "Religion, as one of the pillars of culture, is at the core of people's identity,"[12] stresses Mugambi. The contribution made by the Christian Churches to the social reconstruction of African societies consists neither in the repression of other religions (to establish itself more firmly) nor in adopting the western concept of secularization.[13] Rather, Christianity cooperates with the representatives of other religions in the social reconstruction of social and political life; an exclusion and repression of religions would remove the forces which have characterized and structured public life in Africa for millennia. This fifth aspect reflects a clear contrast to European conceptions of religion and society. Whereas Mugambi holds religion to be essential to Africa and believes that its social development is resistant to secularization, in Europe concepts of a "post-secular society" (Jürgen Habermas) have evolved, which assume that religious and secular citizens can learn from each other. Religions possess resources which can be important and helpful for society, although they are not "essential" in the way Mugambi's theology of reconstruction presents them.

These five aspects set out the social relevance of the theology of reconstruction together with the inner correlation between the intercultural theology research program and the specific concerns of the theology of reconstruction. Its inception at a specific *kairos*, which has become a theological "sign of the times," represents the counter-programme to a traditionalism which always views the decisive truths (of theology) as being in the past. The empowerment and encouragement it has given to the citizens of society stand in direct contrast to right-wing populist movements, which are primarily concerned with inciting fear and maintaining the idea that citizens are in any case mere victims, helplessly at the mercy of political developments and authorities. The societal and socio-political perspective, as it is developed by the theology of reconstruction, constitutes an alternative to those forms of a "theology of prosperity" which see a sign of God's blessing in the happiness and prosperity of the individual, but not in social justice. The gift of critical discernment which Mugambi demands by Romans 12:2–4 represents a clear contrast to an established Church which has long since lost its intellectual and political mobility. Moreover, Mugambi's emphasis on the role of religions stands in direct contradiction to a secularist attitude which does not merely argue for freedom of religion (as taken for granted in a secular society) but wants a categorical exclusion of religion from public debate.

To what extent can these aspects of the (East African) theology of reconstruction now be seen as forming part of an intercultural theology which is concerned with the relationship between religion/Christianity and society from the standpoint of various issues and perspectives?

Various ways in which intercultural theology can be given impetus by the theology of reconstruction

So far our reflections have shown that neither intercultural theology nor the theology of reconstruction can be viewed as clearly delimited work areas or disciplines. It is not that there is a competition between the two or some attempt at a total integration of the theology of reconstruction into intercultural theology. Rather, we should be asking what someone working in the field of intercultural theology can learn from the theology of reconstruction. It seems that there are three things to be learned.

- Intercultural theology must become more *interdisciplinary*. Even though intercultural theology already represents a significant step forward from the integralism of earlier periods (i.e., the attempt to explain all social and scientific issues from a purely theological point of view), it should be engaging still more intensively with those disciplines which analyze social and global developments. Very few of the methods and insights of the social sciences, global studies, and development studies have been adopted up to now – and the theology of reconstruction also has some catching up to do in this area. However, if the Christian message is to contribute anything to the reconstruction of society, and if this contribution is also to be considered from a theological point of view, it is vital that there be an intensification of interdisciplinary collaboration. Likewise, intercultural and interfaith dialogue must be viewed more in the light of social and economic conditions, so that theology does not fall victim to essentialist or culturalist explanations.
- Intercultural theology must become more *political* – not by having a direct influence on the realm of politics, but by becoming conscious that its academic work needs to be connected with societal challenges. Subjects such as interfaith dialogue, mission, or the Church in the global south must be connected with issues such as migration, discrimination against women, or political extremism, meaning that its theological expertise must be coupled with socio-political sensitivity. Unlike fundamentalist concepts of theocratic dominance or purely individualized and spiritualized concepts of religion, intercultural theology considers that the task of Christian proclamation is to contribute to social progress. Intercultural theology's methods must also reflect this political orientation.

- Intercultural theology must become more *ethical*. Here too, it is not a strategy for the direct application of ethical concepts that is intended, but a closer consideration of the way in which religion acts and is oriented. It is precisely in the context of difficult or conflict-ridden social relationships that there is a greater need for ethics. Intercultural theology can learn from the theology of reconstruction in its handling of questions of culture, religion and academic scholarship under the influence of social re-orientation. This does not mean that scientific findings are replaced by ethical rules, but that the question of the future orientation and self-understanding of a society is recognized as the prerequisite for scientific research. Intercultural theology does not work on the neutral ground, but in a political context shaped by questions of people's meaning and future. In a nutshell: the theology of reconstruction provides intercultural theology with a form of re-orientation that is of crucial significance for the further development of this discipline.

Whether it is concerned with issues such as democracy, social inclusion, the handling of refugees, or social justice as a whole, intercultural theology can learn much from the theology of reconstruction – as a current and creative form of contextual theology – and can thus improve its own methodology, leading to a more discriminating understanding of the relationships between cultural traditions, religious convictions, societal challenges, and global dynamics.

Notes

1 Cf. J.N.K. Mugambi, *Christian Theology and Social Reconstruction.* (Nairobi: Acton, 2003), 59f.
2 Jesse Mugambi emphasises, on the basis of Romans 12:2–4: "Please do not be conformed to the norms of this world. Rather, through the renewal of your minds, transform the world" (Ibid., v).
3 J. N. K. Mugambi, *From Liberation to Reconstruction. African Christian Theology After the Cold War.* (Nairobi: East African Educational Publishers Ltd, 1995), 151.
4 The models can be described as follows: Only one religion is a valid pathway to salvation (exclusivism); in principle one religion is a valid pathway to salvation, although incipient traces of salvation and truth are found in other religions (inclusivism); more than one religion is a valid pathway to salvation, and one and the same truth lies behind different religions (pluralism).
5 Mugambi, *Christian Theology and Social Reconstruction*, 166.
6 Cf. Mugambi, *From Liberation to Reconstruction*, 15–17.
7 Jesse Mugambi recognized and appreciated the kairos offered by the upheaval associated with the year 1989, but he also criticized the erroneous conclusions drawn – for example the demand made by the western world that Africa must democratize itself: "It is an ironical twist of history that Euro-American interests in the 'democratization' of Africa accelerated after the collapse of the Soviet Union in 1990, rather than at the establishment of African republics following decolonization in the 1960s. African struggles for national independence

in the 1940s and 1950s did not get much support, moral or otherwise, from Western Europe and North America, even though in the North Atlantic nations freedom was cherished as one of the basic 'human rights' and 'democracy' was championed as the ideal form of government. The rich nations now interested in 'democratization' of Africa did not consider 'democracy' a priority for the continent in the 1960s, 1970s and 1980s – ideological considerations took precedence over Africa's 'democratization'" (Mugambi, *Christian Theology and Social Reconstruction*, 78f.).

8 Quoted from: Ibid., 172.

9 Ibid., 173.

10 This is emphasized by Mugambi in the introduction to his book From Liberation to Reconstruction: "This theology should be reconstructive rather than destructive; inclusive rather than exclusive; proactive rather than reactive; complementary rather than competitive; integrative rather than disintegrative; programme-driven rather than project-driven; people-centred rather than institution-centred; deed-oriented rather than word-oriented; participatory rather than autocratic; regenerative rather than degenerative; future-sensitive rather than past-sensitive; co-operative rather than confrontational; consultative rather than impositional" (Mugambi, *From Liberation to Reconstruction*, xv).

11 This is the basis of Mugambi's criticism of traditional liberation theology; cf. Mugambi, *Christian Theology and Social Reconstruction*, 74.

12 Ibid., 119.

13 Mugambi strongly criticizes this model: "In contemporary Africa, religion is so influential that social consciousness cannot be re-shaped without the participation of religious institutions – especially Christianity, Islam and Traditional African Religion. Unfortunately, a secularist model of 'modernization' was adopted and promoted in the progress of decolonization. This secularist model erroneously presupposed that religion was a hindrance to progress, and sought to build 'welfare states' in tropical Africa. The consequence has been total disaster in state formation. . . . " (Ibid., 126).

Bibliography

———. *Christian Theology and Social Reconstruction*. Nairobi: Acton, 2003.

Mugambi, Jesse N. K. *From Liberation to Reconstruction. African Christian Theology After the Cold War*. Nairobi: East African Educational Publishers Ltd, 1995.

11 Reconstruction theology in action

Exploring the significance of Jesse N. K. Mugambi's theological contribution through a case study of Nairobi Chapel/Mavuno church in Nairobi, Kenya

Diane Stinton

"Letter to my Child"
Africa, my only child, my only home,
You are a child no more.
Cry aloud no more like a suckling baby,
Do not fail to blow the golden fire before it dies,
To kindle the golden flame that has always blown
At the Central Heart of your African brain. . . .
Africa, you are now a man of age,
For you have borne your initiation rites
Like a hero sanely bred from your mother's breast; . . .
Yes, Africa,
You are my only child, my only home,
And this is why I will neither rest nor sleep
Until your sinews are fully grown.
Now that you have come of age
In adolescent eruptions of hope and power,
Shun all your boastfulness, but bear with pride
Your early pains of second-birth and circumcision.
There is a lengthy winding stair
That you must spiral through, my child,
A bumpy stair that you must climb with total care,
Before I contently sign and spit blessings
Upon this bony frame that weathers day by day,
To see you crowned in world esteem
Upon the Tower of Liberty.[1]

Jesse N. K. Mugambi is distinguished as an African theologian of international repute. He is less well known as a poet, yet the poem cited above, published over 40 years ago, artistically renders the heart of his theological project since then: to "kindle the golden flame that has always blown" within Africans, so that they arise in self-dignity, freedom, and confidence to take their rightful place within the global Kingdom of God.

Born in Embu District, Kenya, to first-generation Anglican parents, Mugambi grew up in the 1950s during Kenya's war of independence from British rule.[2] This childhood experience marked him for life, particularly his encounters with missionaries in this setting. On the one hand, his early friendships with missionary children from Australia and Britain "helped me to appreciate the unity of the human race, and the stupidity of racial bigotry."[3] On the other hand, he found the conduct of some missionaries during the war to be inconsistent with the gospel. He explains,

> The Gospel proclaims liberty to the captives, but we were taught to acquiesce in our oppression and aspire only for "freedom in Christ." This was hypocritical, because they were free, and we were captive. They seemed not to mind about the loss of African lives, including devout Christians, during that war. There was a great deal of emphasis on "new life in Jesus Christ." However, there was hardly any willingness to talk publicly about the necessity to end colonial rule. In their public profile, they portrayed hardly any difference between themselves and the colonial oppressors. This conduct had a lasting impact on me, and helped me to distinguish between the Gospel and missionary appropriations (or misappropriations) of it.[4]

Accordingly, the desire to see the gospel accurately understood and authentically rooted in Africa has been a major driving force within Mugambi's life and leadership within the academy, the Church, and society.[5] Over the past few decades, his name has become closely associated with Reconstruction Theology, a new paradigm Mugambi proposed which forms a leading contribution to the development of African theology.[6] The purpose of this paper is to examine the contribution of Jesse N. K. Mugambi's Reconstruction Theology through twofold means: first, to revisit his proposal for Reconstruction Theology, particularly his prophetic call to the Church for Social Reconstruction, and second, to explore indications of this theological reconstruction in action through a brief consideration of the Nairobi Chapel/Mavuno Church story. Critical analysis will then focus on aspects of the significance of Mugambi's Reconstruction Theology that are reflected in the contextual data from these two organically related Churches, and about ongoing developments in African theology. Concluding reflections then highlight the significance of Reconstruction Theology to African and world Christianity.

The methodological approach for this paper integrates textual analysis with qualitative field research undertaken among Kenyan Christians more broadly, and within Nairobi Chapel more specifically.[7] My methodological stance is that of an insider-outsider: as an active member of Nairobi Chapel, I write from first-hand observation and experience of this Church over the past 25 years. As a scholar committed to ongoing learning in the field of world Christian, I seek to engage both sympathetically and critically with current developments in African Christianity, including those expressions arising from the Nairobi Chapel/Mavuno story.

A call for social reconstruction

A closer look at Mugambi's call for Social Reconstruction must be set within the wider scope of his Reconstruction Theology, including the context, rationale, and main proposals for his theological project.[8] In brief, Mugambi explains that the theme of reconstruction was motivated partly by the dramatic changes throughout Africa in the 1960s, 1970s, and 1980s, with rapid decolonization followed by widespread disillusionment with independence, and partly by the "New World Order" of the 1990s with the end of the Cold War and the colonial era, including apartheid.[9]

The problem, as Mugambi saw it, was that "Christian theology in Africa, particularly during the 1960s and 1970s, emphasized very much the theme of liberation as Exodus from colonial bondage, without highlighting the transformative and reconstructive dimensions."[10] While liberation had become "a dominant paradigm on the continent," as well as in Latin American, African American, and other global theologies, Mugambi queried, "If most of Africa had been 'liberated' in the 1950s and 1960s, what happened to that 'liberation'?"[11] He therefore called for theological reflection to move beyond the paradigm of liberation, with its frequent reference to the Exodus and Luke 4:16–22, and to discern other biblical imagery currently relevant to African experience such as the Exilic motif (Jeremiah), the Deuteronomic motif (Josiah), the Restorative motif (Is. 61:4), or the Reconstruction motif (Haggai and Nehemiah).[12]

Mugambi first voiced his preference to the All Africa Conference of Churches Executive Committee in 1990: "We need to shift paradigms from the Post-Exodus to Post-Exile imagery, with *reconstruction* as the resultant theological axiom."[13] The call was timely since the 1990s were viewed as a decade of reconstruction in various areas such as constitutional reform and economic revitalization. He identified the terms "construction" and "reconstruction" as deriving from engineering, and the notion of "social reconstruction" as deriving from the social sciences. Given the gravity and complexity of the social reconstruction required across Africa in the 1990s, Mugambi advocated Reconstruction as a "necessarily multi-disciplinary, ecumenical and inclusive" paradigm requiring theologians to work with other specialists to incorporate the social and the natural sciences, as well as the humanities and the creative arts.[14] In sum, he asserts,

> African Christian theology in the twenty-first century will be characterized by these themes of social transformation and reconstruction. The shift from liberation to social transformation and reconstruction begins

> in the 1990s. This shift involves discerning alternative social structures, symbols, rituals, myths and interpretations of Africa's social reality by Africans themselves, irrespective of what others have to say about the continent and its peoples. The resources for this re-interpretation are multi-disciplinary analyses involving social scientists, philosophers, creative writers and artists, biological and physical scientists. Theology, as the systematic articulation of human response to revelation in particular situations and contexts, will be most effective in the Africa of the twenty-first century if, and only if, the social and physical reality of the continent and its peoples is accurately and comprehensively understood and re-interpreted.[15]

To tackle this comprehensive project, Mugambi recommends three levels of reconstruction: first, personal reconstruction, on the stated grounds that productive change must begin with the character and motives of the individual. Pointing out New Testament examples of Jesus' encounters with different persons, and citing revivalist hymn writers who echo this theme, Mugambi concludes, "The key to social transformation is appropriate disposition of the individual members of the community concerned, especially its leaders."[16] Second, he calls for cultural reconstruction along the lines of each foundational component of culture: politics, economics, ethics, aesthetics and religion.[17] Notably, in relation to the present paper, he states, "Reconstruction of religion is perhaps the most vital project amongst a people undergoing rapid social change."[18]

The third level of reconstruction Mugambi delineates is that which pertains most significantly to the present research: ecclesial reconstruction. Three inter-related observations warrant attention. First, Mugambi points to the Church as "the organizational framework within which a people's world-view is portrayed and celebrated," with dimensions including "mythological reformulation, doctrinal teaching, social rehabilitation, ethical direction, ritual celebration, and experiential (personal) response."[19] He then calls for ecclesial reconstruction in broad areas such as management structures and financial policies, research and human resources development, education, pastoral care, service, and witness. Elsewhere he questions how the Church can manifest its witness to new life in Christ, and concludes with both the importance of preaching and the need to live out the witness in deeds more than words.[20]

The second observation is related to the point above but is worth highlighting separately: namely, evangelization as the essential task of the Church. Mugambi underlines, "The Christian faith demands of all its adherents, as individuals, communities and organisations, continuous involvement in missionary work; the work of evangelisation. No movement can merit the title 'Church' unless it is a missionary community."[21] He describes evangelization as a cyclic process analogous to a farmer undergoing three stages of (1) planting seeds, (2) the seeds germinating and growing, and (3) the plant flowering and reproducing. He also refers to Meryll C. Tenny's analogy of the Christian missionary process consisting of three cyclic phases: inception, expansion, and consolidation. According to this model, Mugambi states that the Church in Kenya is entering the third phase of consolidation, which "will require new methods, strategies, and skills for the new age."[22] In sum, he asserts,

> The consolidation of Christianity in Africa will require a contextualization of both the Church and its doctrines, so that African Christians can articulate their commitment in their own language, idiom and symbolism. This project of contextualization leads to new frontiers of mission.[23]

The third inter-related observation concerns the role of the theologian in ecclesial reconstruction, which Mugambi explains as follows: "The theologian, at best, should be a catalyst – a facilitator – who makes it possible for the Church to adjust itself to the new social demands of the society to which its members belong."[24] He further notes that within this role,

> [t]he theologian is assumed to be a responsible leader of opinion in the community of faith for whom his or her theology is articulated. The responsibility extends beyond description, analysis and synthesis to reconstructive action, participating together with other members of the community to bring about the change implied in the four levels outlined above.[25]

Finally, Mugambi emphasizes that the theologian's primary audience must therefore be his or her own community of faith, and that the theological quest must respond to their joys, sorrows, hopes, and fears.[26] He also notes the considerable amount of theological literature which young African theologians produced in the 1990s for an African readership. However, some of this literature has reached Europe and North America, stimulating responses that have in turn reached Africa. He underlines that this global exchange is vital for the development of Christian theology at the universal level.

In conclusion, Mugambi's reconstruction theology sounds a clarion call for "a new understanding of the *Church* and a new corresponding *theology*,"[27] as well as new challenges for *theologians* as catalysts of social reconstruction. Perhaps the boldest expression of his theological paradigm is as follows:

In Africa, Christianity has been used for too long to destroy the cultural and religious foundations of African peoples. In the 1990s and beyond, African Christian theology (including Catholic, ecumenical and evangelical strands) should have a reconstructive function, comparable to the role of Protestant theology during the European Reformation and Renaissance;

Africa deserves to celebrate its Reformation and its own Renaissance. The Churches should be the catalysts of this process, as they were in Europe at the end of the medieval period.[28]

Given this very bold claim, what indications, if any, can be found in the local context of Kenya to exemplify Mugambi's Reconstructive Theology in action? In other words, what is the significance of his Reconstruction Theology to the life and witness of the Church in Africa today? To explore these questions, the next section explores contextual data from two organically related Churches in Kenya: Nairobi Chapel and Mavuno Church.

A case of social reconstruction in action

This section considers the significance of two concurrent developments: J.N.K.'s articulation of reconstruction theology and the emergence of the Nairobi Chapel/Mavuno Church story. No claim is made for any direct causal relationship between the two, yet it is worth considering any connections, whether explicit or implicit, for two reasons. First, the timing: it is striking to note that the same year in which Mugambi publicly articulated his proposal for Reconstruction Theology, 1990, is the year of Nairobi Chapel's birth, or rebirth, to be explained further below. Second, the organic relationships involved are crucial. These hinge primarily on Mugambi's first-born son, Kyama Mugambi, who has been a key leader in Nairobi Chapel since 1992 and a pastor in the Church(es) since 1999. Having naturally imbibed his father's theological perspectives while growing up in the 1980s and 1990s, Kyama Mugambi comments, "My father is a prophet! What he called for in the 1990s is currently being played out in the Nairobi Chapel/Mavuno movement."[29] Moreover, while Jesse N. K. Mugambi is a member of the Anglican Church of Kenya, he regularly attends Mavuno Church, where Pastor Kyama serves, and so he has witnessed first-hand the growth of these Churches. A brief synopsis of these developments within Nairobi Chapel and Mavuno Church, focusing on their strategies for social transformation, provides contextual data for critical engagement with Jesse N. K. Mugambi's Reconstruction Theology.

Nairobi Chapel was originally birthed as a non-denominational fellowship in 1952 when Kenya was a British colony. The congregation was primarily composed of British expatriates, many of whom returned to Britain following Kenya's Independence in 1963. Attendance at Nairobi Chapel continued to decline dramatically during the 1970s and 1980s, reaching approximately 20 people by 1989. The Chapel then sought assistance from Nairobi Baptist Church, and together they invited Oscar Muriu and his wife Beatrice to serve as the first African pastor at Nairobi Chapel. Under Muriu's leadership since 1990, the Chapel has experienced dramatic growth with new initiatives in African leadership, specifically in cultivating a large pastoral team of men and women as well as dozens of other ministry leaders and an internship program that attracts participants from around the world.

Further innovations included worship styles with greater appeal for Africans, creative outreach to the neighboring University of Nairobi students, and pastoral care for young families.[30]

The heartbeat of Church life occurs in small cells or "E-groups" (formerly "Ekklesia") which meet weekly for worship, Bible study, prayer, pastoral care, plus evangelism and social transformation ministries. Nairobi Chapel's outreach reflects two central foci: first, a deep commitment to Church-planting locally (for example, in several informal settlements within Nairobi), nationally, and internationally. The Chapel has planted well over 100 Churches to date, including over 60 daughter Churches, over 20 Churches in partnership with other Churches and ministries, and over 20 grand-daughter Churches. [31] The second focus is a strong commitment to social transformation ministries, such as Christian education, medical clinics in slums, justice ministries, and other specialized ministries in response to poverty, sexual exploitation, HIV and AIDS, prisoners, disadvantaged teenage girls, and street children.[32]

In August 2005, Nairobi Chapel subdivided into five distinct congregations spread out across the city to engage more of the members in ministry and to enhance its transformative impact on the city, the nation, and beyond.[33] One of these five congregations was Mavuno Church, which began with a staff of five members under the leadership of Pastor Muriithi Wanjau and approximately 400 adults and children.[34] Since then, Mavuno has planted eight additional Churches: one in downtown Nairobi (2006), Eastlands, Nairobi (2010), Kampala, Uganda (2010), Dar es Salaam (2010), Berlin, Germany (2011), Lusaka, Zambia (2013), Kigali, Rwanda (2013), Blantyre, Malawi (2013), and Johannesburg, South Africa (2014).[35]

Aside from dramatic growth, the two organically related Churches continue to share much in common regarding mission, teaching, and strategies about social transformation. Nairobi Chapel's mission statement is "Growing D.E.E.P. to reach W.I.D.E.," with the "I" in the acronym representing a crucial component of its vision: Impact. This is delineated as "social impact that will change the lives of our people significantly, especially by the poor and needy around us," through ministries of poverty alleviation and social justice.[36] The gospel is regularly proclaimed in both its vertical dimension, in loving God, and its horizontal dimension in loving neighbor. For example, Pastor Nick Korir delivered a six-week sermon series in October/November 2014 entitled, "Beyond Sunday: Transforming All Sectors of Society." The website introduction to the series states,

> '[B]eyond Sunday' is a shift of focus away from Sunday and a journey of discovery of God's Purposes for us from Monday to Saturday in our respective sectors of society: be it [1] Media, Arts & Entertainment; [2] Science, Technology & Medicine, Health; [3] Business & Commerce, Economy, Agriculture; [4] Education and Family, Community; [5] Politics & Governance; [and 6] Church & Religion.[37]

Likewise, the mission statement of Mavuno Church is even bolder in expression than that of Nairobi Chapel: "Turning Ordinary People into Fearless Influencers of Society." Concerning the same six sectors of society adopted from Nairobi Chapel, the mission is elaborated as follows:

We exist to see real people with real issues, coming to Jesus, having their lives transformed, and becoming change agents to transform society. Our focus is to enable every member of Mavuno to become a fearless influencer in one of the sectors of society. As a result, our city, nation, and continent will be transformed positively.[38]

The overall strategy to fulfill this mutual mission is outlined in the strategic system of Church ministry known as "The Transformation Track (T-Track)" in Nairobi Chapel (Figure 11.1). The first part of the T-Track focuses on reaching out to invite newcomers to Church, either through extending personal invitations to those within one's social networks or through mission events. The next part seeks to connect visitors with the Church community, particularly through one major strategy called the "Plug-in" program. This is an intensive small-group experience of Bible study, prayer, spiritual disciples, outreach in evangelism and social justice ministries, and a final weekend retreat of further instruction. Following this in-depth training, the Plug-in groups become full-fledged "E-groups," the ongoing small groups organized that focus geographically on spiritual growth, pastoral care, and outreach to the community. The third section of the T-Track also seeks to

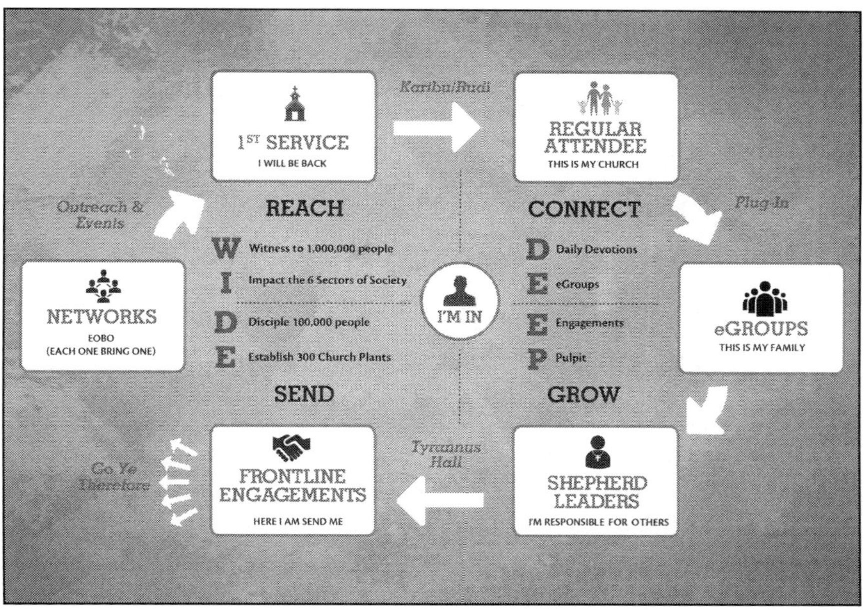

Figure 11.1 The Transformation Track (T-Track)[39]

raise up lay leaders to exercise pastoral oversight and to participate in the Chapel's key leadership decisions.

The final part of the T-Track then focuses on further leadership training of pastors, Church planters, and social justice leaders, particularly through Nairobi Chapel's in-house school of leadership development called "Tyrannus Hall." The vision is to further equip those who will engage in "Frontline Ministries" of direct involvement in society, based on the Apostle Paul's discipleship approach in Ephesus (Acts 19:9–10). Key types of "front liners" are distinguished as follows: (1) Frontline Warriors, who initiate ministries to care for the poor and underprivileged; (2) Frontline Partners, who support the frontline warriors in various ways such as serving on their ministry boards, guiding, networking, and mobilizing resources; (3) Frontline Professionals, who use their profession as an avenue to impact their own sphere within the six sectors of society; and (4) Frontline Missionaries, who engage in evangelism, discipleship and Church-planting, both locally and internationally.[40] Examples of Frontline Ministries in Nairobi Chapel include Tumaini Clinics, providing medical care in Korogocho and Kibera informal settlements; One Lamb, working with communities against the prostitution of children; and Safe Families, extending compassion, hospitality, and support to vulnerable families in crisis.[41]

The T-Track at Nairobi Chapel has been adapted to the "Mavuno Marathon" in Mavuno Church. The equivalent process is simplified and set forth in four phases: "1. From Complacent to Consumer; 2. From Consumer to Connected; 3. From Connected to Committed; and 4. From Committed to Compelled."[42] Frontline Ministries in Mavuno are promoted in each of the six sectors of impact: first, Church and Mission includes, for example, Africa Aflame, doing outreach among unreached communities of coastal Kenya, and I stopped, seeking to assist recovery among pornography and sex addicts.[43] Second, Family and Education Frontline initiatives include, for example, the Lulu and Kwetu Trusts, fostering education and empowerment for underprivileged girls and communities, and Back to Beginning, assisting recovery and offering mentoring for abused teenaged girls.[44] Third, Politics and Governance prompts a key Frontline Ministry, Transform Kenya, which seeks to equip leaders to spearhead societal change in family, politics, and governance.[45] Fourth, Media and the Arts call forth several frontline initiatives such as Filamujuani, which teaches youth in informal settlements the skills to earn income and tell their stories through video, and other ministries among writers, editors, journalists, and entertainers who seek to promote uplifting content in the media.[46] Fifth, Business and Economics includes various initiatives like microfinance programs among the poor, assisting marginalized handcraft producers to connect with global markets, and organizing business breakfasts for encouragement and networking among entrepreneurs.[47] Finally, Health and Environment forms the sixth sector of societal impact in Mavuno's vision. While no distinct Frontline Ministry has yet emerged in this sector, Mavuno has shared in Nairobi Chapel's longstanding involvement in the Tumaini Clinics and in occasional congregational clean-up events held in various informal settlements.

One last, significant observation regarding these Churches' strategies for social transformation is their integral relationship with Church-planting. The priority of Church-planting is pursued not only in response to the biblical mandate for evangelism and discipleship but also as an intentional strategy for sustainable community engagement. Muriu explains, "As part of our committed value regarding Church-planting, we always try and engage the community around us, and try and allow the community to define how we should be engaged."[48] In a context where Church ministries are often under-resourced, the policy of Nairobi Chapel is to require that any new frontline initiative must become self-sufficient and self-sustaining within a set period before the Church discontinues its financial support. Sustainability applies equally to the Church at large, as Muriu explains further:

> As a Church, our community engagement also needs to be sustainable. Moreover, the only model we have that we feel is sustainable – our communities understand it, they embrace it, they are willing to finance it – is a Church. So if we want to go into a community to engage with them socially and bring about change, we will plant a Church there, because the community will own the Church, the community will pay towards the Church. The Church can then turn those sorts of finances and tithes back into the community, to develop leadership, etc. So we use Church-planting as a strategy to community engagement, because it is a sustainable model.[49]

A full-blown analysis of the Church's social engagement lies beyond the scope of the present paper. However, it is noteworthy that the Chapel is involved in each type of service outlined in Donald Miller and Tetsunao Yamamori's typology, set forth and explained as follows:

1 Mercy ministries (providing food, clothing, shelter)
2 Emergency services (responding to floods, famine, earthquakes)
3 Education (providing day care, schools, tuition assistance)
4 Counseling services (helping with addiction, divorce, depression)
5 Medical assistance (establishing health clinics, dental clinics, psychological services)
6 Economic development (providing microenterprise loans, job training, affordable housing)
7 The arts (training in music, dance, drama)
8 Policy change (opposing corruption, monitoring elections, advocating a living wage)

At one end of the spectrum are programs that focus on relief, while at the other end are programs intended to effect systemic change. Crossing this spectrum is another polarity – namely, programs that minister primarily to individuals versus those that seek to change the conditions of an entire population of people with shared characteristics.[50]

A consideration of reconstruction theology

Like sunlight refracted through a prism, what distinctive aspects of Reconstruction Theology come to light in living color through a consideration of the Nairobi Chapel/Mavuno Church story? Moreover, what do these developments signify, regarding Reconstruction Theology's contributions to the ongoing development of African theology? To begin with, most fundamentally, the driving force of Mugambi's theological project, for the gospel to be accurately understood and authentically rooted in Africa, is certainly attested in the life and ministry of these two Churches. The wellspring of this shared vision is African agency, empowered by the Holy Spirit to live out the gospel of Jesus Christ within the contexts of Africa. Just as Africans – Church founders, preachers, teachers, catechists, and other laypeople – have been the primary agents in the historical expansion of Christianity in Africa, particularly in its phenomenal growth throughout the 20th century, so in the 21st century, African Christians are the primary agents in the continued expansion of the Church in Africa. This is certainly attested in the case of Nairobi Chapel/Mavuno Church, where Oscar Muriu played a pivotal role in the revitalization of this Church, through his leadership and through mobilizing and mentoring hundreds of young pastors, lay leaders, and Church planters who have fuelled the movement's expansion. Indeed, Pastor Kyama Mugambi identifies Mavuno Church as an African Initiated Church, despite its progenitor in the British missionary fellowship established in the 1950s. Here, then, is a classic case of renewal or rebirth, which Mugambi calls for in his Reconstruction Theology.

This reawakening of Nairobi Chapel and its daughter Churches also affirms the three levels of reconstruction Mugambi advocates: first, personal reconstruction as the foundation for social reconstruction. For example, a Nairobi Chapel pastor reiterates that "when you see the transformation happen to an individual, it almost always translates to transformation in the community," citing examples from the Church's ministries among marginalized peoples. Moreover, just as Mugambi underlines the crucial role of leaders as key to social transformation, so Nairobi Chapel and Mavuno Church prioritize leadership training within the life and witness of the Church. Indeed, their Kinara leadership training program draws interns from around the world, just as the discipleship materials the leaders publish are being accessed by Churches around the world.[51]

Second, the cultural reconstruction that Mugambi calls for in the realms of politics, economics, ethics, aesthetics, and religion are also reflected in Nairobi Chapel and Mavuno Church's holistic ministries within the six sectors of society. As indicated above, this comprehensive approach to gospel transformation is intentionally set forth and lived out through the "Transformation Track" or the "Mavuno Marathon." This ministry paradigm illustrates the outworking of one of Mugambi's core convictions within his project of reconstruction theology: the need to overcome any false divide between "salvation," understood primarily as spiritual conversion, and "liberation," often interpreted regarding the "social gospel." Mugambi concludes,

> The polarization indicated above presupposes that liberation and salvation are mutually exclusive, or mutually incompatible. However, it is quite clear that Jesus, in His public ministry, was actively and simultaneously involved in both personal and social reconstruction. He mobilized his followers to become involved in social change, having convinced them of the necessity and urgency to change their attitudes towards themselves and the world. The logical implication of this integral approach to evangelism is that liberation and salvation are theologically complementary.[52]

In Mugambi's view, and in this Church movement, social transformation entails an integral approach to the gospel, so that spiritual conversion cannot be separated from an actual witness in society. Moreover, while fostering engagement in all dimensions of society, Nairobi Chapel, and Mavuno Church insist upon the Church being the primary agent of social transformation, attesting to Mugambi's observation that the reconstruction of religion is the most vital project for people undergoing rapid social change.

Finally, the ecclesial reconstruction that Mugambi calls for is certainly attested in the Nairobi Chapel/Mavuno Church story. Even a brief consideration of these Churches provides evidence of developments in certain directions that Mugambi urged, such as refashioning and celebrating people's worldviews as African Christians through various dimensions like "mythological reformulation, doctrinal teaching, social rehabilitation, ethical direction, ritual celebration, and experiential (personal) response." Participant observation in the worship, preaching, fellowship, and outreach of these Churches leaves little doubt that believers are taught and nurtured in the universal Christian faith while approaching life and ministry from local African perspectives. As a result, their initiatives in evangelism and mission – the essential task of the Church, as Mugambi points out – have contributed to the phenomenal growth experienced in 25 years, from an original congregation of 20 to approximately 15,000 people in over 100 Church plants throughout Kenya, Africa and beyond. While undoubtedly contributing to the consolidation of Christianity in Africa, these Churches also demonstrate Christian Mission as a holistic living out of the gospel in every dimension of life and every sphere of society. Lastly, Mugambi's appeal for theologians to serve as catalysts or facilitators, enabling the Church to participate together with the other members in reconstructive action, also comes to light through the witness of Nairobi Chapel and Mavuno Church. While Mugambi rightfully acknowledges the presence and role of lay theologians within African Christianity, he also advocates for specialized theologians trained at advanced levels and in multi-disciplinary fields to guide the Church in its contribution to social reconstruction. While Nairobi Chapel and Mavuno Church benefit from pastors and other Church leaders trained in the natural and human sciences, these Churches also invest in the specialized training of theologians like Kyama Mugambi and Maggie Gitau, both of whom completed their Ph.D. research on Mavuno Church as a renewal movement within contemporary African Christianity.[53]

Overall, then, Reconstruction Theology calls for "a new understanding of the Church and a new corresponding theology," as well as new challenges for theologians as catalysts of social reconstruction. Since the Kingdom of God is its subject, the theological project is already and not yet fulfilled. Likewise, the growth of African Christianity, like that of the apostolic Church, is neither linear nor tidy. Within the ongoing expansion of the Church in Africa and beyond, Nairobi Chapel and Mavuno Church provide glimpses, or mere snapshots, of Reconstruction Theology in action.

Naturally, Mugambi's interlocutors have voiced critiques of reconstruction theology that serve constructively to extend the conversation in the continued development of African theology. For example, Julius Gathogo argues that the new metaphor of reconstruction tends to overemphasize "social reconstruction" at the expense of "individual" reconstruction; hence he underlines the need for personal responsibility and radical change on the part of individual Christians.[54] He and others, including Elelwani Farisani and Musa Dube, question the adequacy of Mugambi's critical engagement with Nehemiah's reconstruction project, for example, in not addressing its alleged ideological underpinnings in politics, patriarchism, and classism.[55] Ernst Conradie makes the accurate observation that the strength of the reconstruction paradigm is also potentially its main weakness: while the metaphor allows "for a multi-disciplinary approach of social engineering in which the role of the social sciences is pivotal . . . its theological content may easily become rather shallow."[56] He cautions against the tendency to reduce reconstruction to human initiative and responsibility, without adequately acknowledging the soteriological import of God's grace and human gratitude.

More substantial are the critiques of Tinyiko Maluleke and Valentin Dedji, that Mugambi's reconstruction paradigm does not do justice to the prior developments in 20th-century African theology. Maluleke, perhaps the most outspoken critic of reconstruction theology, sums up, "I have also been critical of the fact that both Mugambi and Villa-Vicencio appear to minimize the value of previous African theologies of inculturation and liberation."[57] Moreover, Maluleke asserts,

> The proposal for some theology of reconstruction is not new in the Third World. Most Third World theologies, insofar as they have been local initiatives aimed at local renewal, have been kinds of theologies of reconstruction. Africans and churches north of the Limpopo have for a long time been engaged in theologies of reconstruction of one sort or another.[58]

He concludes, "From a black and African perspective, therefore, the proposal for a theology of reconstruction, *instead of*, and even alongside black and African theologies of liberation, is misplaced and unacceptable."[59] Thus a major line of critique is that Reconstruction Theology is not as new or as original as it claims since the growth of the Church in African and elsewhere has always been characterized by Spirit-prompted, locally initiated renewal movements. Therefore Mugambi's critics concur with Isaac Mwase, that "Mugambi's focus on the paradigm shift from Liberation to Reconstruction should be appreciated as a continuation, rather than as a break from the past."[60]

Perhaps the most incisive assessment, however, comes from Laurenti Magesa. Pointing out that every metaphor within theological discourse is necessarily limited, Magesa concludes that Mugambi's main contribution lies in the new horizons that this reconstruction metaphor opens in shaping the future of African theology in all its dimensions.[61] He also notes personally and poignantly the remarkable significance of this paradigm within Mugambi's theological project, and concomitantly, within the wider context of African theology. Magesa admits his deep sense of shock in discovering, after almost 30 years of close collaboration with Mugambi, that Mugambi spent ten years of his childhood in a British concentration camp during the Mau Mau Emergency from 1952 and 1962. Magesa interprets Mugambi's silence about this obviously painful experience as cardinal to the very essence of his entire theological journey. Magesa comments, penetratingly,

> It seems to me that he has chosen to '*reconstruct*' this profound personal experience he underwent as a young man in line with the theological project he proposes. For him, the way of reconstruction constitutes the wisdom of Jesus, the wisdom . . . not of bitterness at injuries suffered, but of 'befriending and winning over' the oppressor, or, in other words, 'reconstruct[ing] . . . relationships.'[62]

As opposed to the more adversarial approaches of liberation theology, Magesa continues, Mugambi unequivocally advocates the approach of reciprocity in which all parties, oppressors and oppressed, are called "to participate in the inauguration of a new social order" – hence reconstruction. From this perspective, reconstruction as restored relationships, Mugambi's theological paradigm, carries profound significance in conveying the gospel anew in its entire cosmic scope of God reconciling all of humanity and creation to himself. Hearing the good news of the Kingdom of God afresh in this way, who among us, whether theologian, Church leader, or layperson, would not heed the resounding call of Nehemiah's cry also resonating across Africa and beyond today: "Let's rebuild!"

Conclusion

While the scholarly assessment of Reconstruction theology continues, Maluleke makes an astute observation. He notes that Reconstruction theology is a kind of blueprint or program of action for the Church, and hence it is "a missionary theology – a kind of 'program of Christian witness.' It is not just another academic theology, but a constructive theological engagement in all the public issues of a democratic theology."[63] From this perspective, the consideration of Nairobi Chapel/Mavuno Church as an example of reconstructive theology in action takes on heightened significance. Whatever the status of its development within African theology, Mugambi's prophetic call for personal, social, and ecclesial reconstruction within Africa is indeed being lived out through this Church movement. Like the parables of the Kingdom of God – a mustard seed that, despite its small size, grows into the greatest shrub so that birds can rest in its branches (Mk. 4:30–32 and parallels), or a little yeast that penetrates the flour until it is all leavened (Mt. 13:33 and parallel) – so this single congregation of approximately 20 believers has now grown into a movement integrating spiritual conversion and social transformation in over 100 congregations across Kenya, Africa, and beyond. If this be but one case of reconstructive theology in action, then Mugambi's early poetic cry and his later theological contribution coalesce, to "kindle the golden flame that has always blown" within Africans, with deep significance for the local and global Church.

Notes

1 J.N.K. Mugambi, *Carry It Home*. (Nairobi: East African Literature Bureau, 1974), 85–7. Used with permission of the Kenya Literature Bureau.
2 For a recent historical examination of this war, see David Anderson, *Histories of the Hanged: Britain's Dirty War in Kenya and the End of Empire*. (London: Weidenfeld & Nicolson, 2005).
3 Personal interview with J. N. K. Mugambi, Nairobi, Kenya, June 8, 1998.
4 Ibid.; cited in Diane B. Stinton, *Faces of Africa: Voices of Contemporary African Christology*. (Maryknoll: Orbis Books, 2005), 26–7.
5 Mugambi earned his Ph.D. from the University of Nairobi and has taught in the Department of Philosophy and Religious Studies since the late 1970s and as a Full Professor since 1993. Mugambi is a member of the Kenya National Academy of Sciences and received the Presidential honour of the Elder of the Order of Burning Spear in 2010, in recognition of his distinguished service to the nation.
6 Mugambi's proposal came closely together with that of Charles Villa-Vicencio, *A Theology of Reconstruction: Nation-Building and Human Rights*. (Cambridge: Cambridge University Press, 1992).
7 See Stinton, Faces of Africa, and " 'This Kairos of Our Time': African Christian Spirituality in Relation to Social Transformation in Kenya Today," in G. M. Bediako, B. Y. Quarshie, and J. K. Asamoah-Gyadu, eds. *Seeing New Facets of the Diamond: Christianity as a Universal Faith – Essays in Honour of Kwame Bediako*. (Akropong-Akuapem, Ghana: Regnum Africa, and Oxford: Regnum Books, 2014), 336–58.
8 For further discussion of Mugambi's *Reconstruction Theology*, see Stinton, *Faces of Africa*, 222–6.
9 J.N.K. Mugambi, *From Liberation to Reconstruction: African Christian Theology After the Cold War*. (Nairobi: East African Educational Publishers, 1995), x.
10 Ibid., 39.
11 Ibid., 5.
12 Ibid., 39.

13 Ibid., 5.
14 J.N.K. Mugambi, "Theological Method in African Christianity," in Mary N. Getui, ed. *Theological Method and Aspects of Worship in African Christianity*. (Nairobi: Acton Publishers, 1998), 5–40, 34.
15 Mugambi, *From Liberation to Reconstruction*, 40.
16 Ibid., 16.
17 For further discussion of these cultural components, see J.N.K. Mugambi, *The African Heritage and Contemporary Christianity*. (Nairobi: Longman Kenya Ltd., 1989). In relation to reconstruction theology, see also J.N.K. Mugambi, "Social Reconstruction of Africa: The Role of Churches," in J.N.K. Mugambi, ed. *The Church and Reconstruction of Africa: Theological Considerations*. (Nairobi: All Africa Conference of Churches, 1997), 1–25.
18 Mugambi, *From Liberation to Reconstruction*, 40.
19 Ibid., 17.
20 J.N.K. Mugambi, "The Future of the Church and the Church of the Future in Africa," in *The Church of Africa: Towards a Theology of Reconstruction*, African Challenge Book Series No. 2 (Nairobi: All Africa Conference of Churches, 1991), 44.
21 Ibid., 36.
22 Ibid., 38.
23 Ibid.
24 Mugambi, *From Liberation to Reconstruction*, 17.
25 Mugambi, "The Future of the Church and the Church of the Future," 31. To clarify his last statement concerning "four levels outlined above": in this case, he is not referring to the levels of reconstruction. Rather, in discussing the inductive method for theology he draws upon Bernard Lonigan's notion of human intentionality which operates at four levels of consciousness: 1) the empirical level of sense perception and feeling; 2) the intellectual level of understanding and expressing what is understood, with awareness of presuppositions and implications; 3) the rational level of reflecting and passing judgment on what is thought; and 4) the responsible level which concerns the self, with the goals established and the evaluation and implementation of courses of action.
26 Mugambi, *From Liberation to Reconstruction*, 11.
27 Ibid., xv.
28 Ibid., xiv. See also Malegapuru William Makgoba, *African Renaissance: The New Struggle*. (Cape Town: Mafube Publishing (Proprietary) and Tafelberg Publishers, 1999).
29 Paraphrased from personal conversation with Kyama Mugambi, Karen, Nairobi: June 22, 2014. I am indebted to Kyama for his collaboration in this research. Since he has completed PhD research based on Mavuno Church, his perspective on this dual Church movement warrants close consideration. See Kyama Mugambi, "Leadership Development in Progressive Pentecostal Churches: Three Case Studies from Nairobi, Kenya." PhD dissertation, Africa International University, Nairobi, 2017.
30 For further details of Nairobi Chapel's origins and early history, see http://nairobichapel.net/about-us/beginnings/. (accessed October 28, 2016).
31 For a list of the daughter, partner-assisted, and grand-daughter Churches, see http://nairobichapel.net/church-directory/. (accessed October 28, 2016).
32 For an overview of these ministries, see http://nairobichapel.net/. (accessed October 28, 2016).
33 These five Churches took on new names, aside from the original name being retained by the mother congregation led by Pastor Oscar Muriu. The others include Mamlaka Hill Chapel on the original property, Mavuno Chapel on Mombasa Road, Mashariki Chapel on Jogoo Road, and Covenant Community

Chapel in Westlands, which has recently merged with another Church to form Kileleshwa Covenant Community Church. Nairobi Chapel also re-teamed up with two of its earlier Church plants, Lifespring Chapel and Karura Community Church, so that the seven congregations work closely together in pursuing their joint vision. While these other congregations feature occasionally in the data, the preliminary findings presented here derive almost entirely from the mother congregation, Nairobi Chapel, located off Ngong Road, Nairobi.

34 "Mavuno" means "harvest" in Kiswahili. For further details of Mavuno Church's origins and early growth, see www.mavunochurch.org/content.php?id=51. (accessed October 29, 2016).

35 See "Locations" at www.mavunochurch.org/index.php and the 5 year strategic plan under way at www.mavunochurch.org/content.php?id=242. (accessed October 29, 2016).

36 http://nairobichapel.net/about-us/our-mission/. (accessed October 28, 2016).

37 www.nairobichapel.org/NC/beyond-sunday-october.php. (accessed October 28, 2016).

38 www.mavunochurch.org/content.php?id=50. (accessed October 29, 2016).

39 http://nairobichapel.net/adult-church/t-track/. (accessed October 28, 2016).

40 Oscar Muriu, Sermon Manuscript, "I Love this Place: Frontliners – Making a Difference," June 7, 2010. Sermon manuscript made available by Muriu. See the further specification of these frontline leaders as "Frontline Initiators, Frontline Supporters, Frontline Professionals, Frontline Disciplers, Frontline Missionaries, Frontline Partners, and Frontline Evangelists," at http://nairobichapel.net/adult-church/t-track/. (accessed October 28, 2016).

41 See "Social Justice" at http://nairobichapel.net/. (accessed October 28, 2016).

42 www.mavunochurch.org/content.php?id=52. (accessed October 29, 2016).

43 www.mavunochurch.org/content.php?id=252. (accessed October 29, 2016).

44 www.mavunochurch.org/content.php?id=253. (accessed October 29, 2016).

45 www.mavunochurch.org/content.php?id=254. (accessed October 29, 2016).

46 www.mavunochurch.org/content.php?id=255. (accessed October 29, 2016).

47 www.mavunochurch.org/content.php?id=256. (accessed October 29, 2016).

48 Interview with Pastor Oscar Muriu, May 19, 2010. See also his sermon series, "Walking with the Poor: Helping without Hurting," starting Sept. 6, 2009, most of which are available online at http://nairobichapel.net/sermon-archives/. Sermon manuscripts made available by Muriu.

49 Interview with Pastor Oscar Muriu, May 19, 2010.

50 Donald E. Miller and Tetsunao Yamamori, *Global Pentecostalism: The New Face of Christian Social Engagement*. (Berkely: University of California Press, 2007), 28. The authors formed this typology on the basis of their research over four years on Pentecostalism and social engagement in 20 countries in Asia, Africa, Latin America and eastern Europe.

51 See http://nairobichapel.net/leadership-development/ and www.mavunochurch.org/content.php?id=320. (accessed October 29, 2016).

52 Mugambi, *From Liberation to Reconstruction*, 6.

53 Margaret Wanjiru W. Gitau, "Focusing Scholarly Discourse on African Megachurches: The Evangelical Revitalizations Movements' Theory in a Case Study of Mavuno Church, Nairobi, Kenya." PhD dissertation, Africa International University, Nairobi, 2015; Kyama Mugambi, "Leadership Development in Progressive Pentecostal Churches: Three Case Studies from Nairobi, Kenya."

54 Gathogo, "Post-Liberation Theology: A Critical Appreciation," 84; "Genesis, Methodologies, and Concerns of African Theology of Reconstruction," *Theologia Viatorum: Journal of Religion and Theology in Africa, South Africa*, 32, no. 1 (2008): 23–62.

55 Gathogo, "Post-Liberation Theology," 84; Elelwani B. Farisani, "The Post-Exile Motif in Mugambi's Theology of Reconstruction," *Theologies of Liberation and Reconstruction*, 210–12 edited by Mwase, Isaac T, Kamara, Eunice, (Nairobi: Acton Publishers, 2012).
56 Ernst Conradie, "African Perspectives on the 'Whole Household of God' (Oikos)," *Theologies of Liberation and Reconstruction*, (unpublished; cited in John Hugo Fischer, "The Relationahisp beteen the Church and the Reign of God in the Reconstruction Theology of JNK Mugambi: A Critical Analysis," PhD. Dissertation, The University of the Western Cape, 2013, 310.
57 Tinyiko Sam Maluleke, "Half a Century of African Christian Theologies: Elements of the Emerging Agenda for the Twenty-first Century," *Journal of Theology for Southern Africa* 99 (November 1997): 23; Valentin Dedji, *Reconstruction and Renewal in African Christian Theology*. (Nairobi: Acton Publishers, 2003), 75; "The Reconstruction Paradigm in Mugambi's Theology," in *Theologies of Liberation and Reconstruction*, 128. See also Tinyiko Sam Maluleke, "Recent Developments in the Christian Theologies of Africa: Towards the Twenty-First Century," *Journal of Constructive Theology*, 2, no. 2 (December 1996): 33–60.
58 Tinyiko Sam Maluleke, "The Proposal for a Theology of Reconstruction: A Critical Appraisal," *Missionalia* 22, no. 3 (1994): 255–6.
59 Ibid., 256.
60 Isaac M. T. Mwase, "African Religious Scholarship as the Context of Mugambi's Works," *Theologies of Liberation and Reconstruction*, 184.
61 Ibid., 196.
62 Laurenti Magesa, "A Portrait of J.N.K. Mugambi's Theological Project of Reconstruction: A Review Article of Theologies of Liberation and Reconstruction: Essays in Honour of Professor J.N.K. Mugambi, Ph.D., edited by Isaac M. T. Mwase and Eunice K. Kamaara," *Studies in World Christianity* 19, no. 2 (2013): 189.
63 Maluleke, "The Proposal for a Theology of Reconstruction," 251.

Bibliography

Anderson, David. *Histories of the Hanged: Britain's Dirty War in Kenya and the End of Empire*. London: Weidenfeld & Nicolson, 2005.

Dedji, Valentin. *Reconstruction and Renewal in African Christian Theology*. Theology of Reconstruction Series. Nairobi: Acton Publishers, 2003.

Gathogo, Julius M. "Genesis, Methodologies, and Concerns of African Theology of Reconstruction." *Theologia Viatorum: Journal of Religion and Theology in Africa, South Africa* 32, no. 1 (2008): 23–62.

Gitau, Margaret Wanjiru W. "Focusing Scholarly Discourse on African Megachurches: The Evangelical Revitalizations Movements' Theory in a Case Study of Mavuno Church, Nairobi, Kenya." Ph.D. dissertation, Africa International University, Nairobi, 2015.

Magesa, Laurenti. "A Portrait of J. N. K. Mugambi's Theological Project of Reconstruction: A Review Article of *Theologies of Liberation and Reconstruction: Essays in Honour of Professor J. N. K. Mugambi, Ph.D.*, edited by Isaac M. T. Mwase and Eunice K. Kamaara." *Studies in World Christianity* 19, no. 2 (2013): 187–97.

Makgoba, Malegapuru William. *African Renaissance: The New Struggle*. Cape Town: Mafube Publishing (Proprietary) and Tafelberg Publishers, 1999.

Miller, Donald E., and Tetsunao Yamamori. *Global Pentecostalism: The New Face of Christian Social Engagement*. Berkely: University of California Press, 2007.
Mugambi, J.N.K. *Carry It Home*. Nairobi: East African Literature Bureau, 1974.
———. *The African Heritage and Contemporary Christianity*. Nairobi: Longman Kenya Ltd., 1989.
———. "The Future of the Church and the Church of the Future in Africa." In *The Church of Africa: Towards a Theology of Reconstruction*, African Challenge Book Series No. 2, 29–50. Nairobi: All Africa Conference of Churches, 1991.
———. *From Liberation to Reconstruction: African Christian Theology After the Cold War*. Nairobi: East African Educational Publishers, 1995.
———. "Social Reconstruction of Africa: The Role of Churches." In *The Church and Reconstruction of Africa: Theological Considerations*, edited by J. N. K. Mugambi, 1–25. Nairobi: All Africa Conference of Churches, 1997.
———. "Theological Method in African Christianity." In *Theological Method and Aspects of Worship in African Christianity*, edited by Mary N. Getui, 5–40. Nairobi: Acton Publishers, 1998.
———. *Christian Theology & Social Reconstruction*. Theology of Reconstruction Series. Nairobi: Acton Publishers, 2003.
Mwase, Isaac M. T., and Eunice K. Kamaara, eds. *Theologies of Liberation and Reconstruction*. Nairobi: Acton Publishers, 2012.
Maluleke, Tinyiko Sam. "The Proposal for a Theology of Reconstruction: A Critical Appraisal." *Missionalia* 22, no. 2 (August 1994): 245–58.
———. "Recent Developments in the Christian Theologies of Africa: Towards the Twenty-First Century." *Journal of Constructive Theology* 2, no. 2 (December 1996): 33–60.
———. "Half a Century of African Christian Theologies: Elements of the Emerging Agenda for the Twenty-First Century." *Journal of Theology for Southern Africa* 99 (November 1997): 4–23.
Stinton, Diane B. *Faces of Africa: Voices of Contemporary African Christology*. Maryknoll: Orbis Books, 2005.
———. "'This *Kairos* of Our Time': African Christian Spirituality in Relation to Social Transformation in Kenya Today." In *Seeing New Facets of the Diamond: Christianity as a Universal Faith – Essays in Honour of Kwame Bediako*, edited by G. M. Bediako, B. Y. Quarshie, and J. K. Asamoah-Gyadu, 336–58. Akropong-Akuapem, Ghana: Regnum Africa, and Oxford: Regnum Books, 2014.
Villa-Vicencio, Charles. *A Theology of Reconstruction: Nation-Building and Human Rights*. Cambridge: Cambridge University Press, 1992.

12 Theology of reconstruction

A paradigm for reflection on revitalization in African Christianity

Kyama Mugambi

Jesse N.K. Mugambi defined the *theology of reconstruction* as that theology which "provides conceptual tools in anticipation of the new society that results from successful struggles for liberation. Since the struggle for liberation is a process, it necessarily overlaps with social construction."[1] He argued that theology will, in the future of Africa, provide for and act as a catalyst to the future African "renaissance and reformation."[2] In this way Mugambi is suggesting that the theology of reconstruction is both practical and conceptual. It will be argued here that the theology of reconstruction, as laid out by Mugambi in the 1990s, provides tools for the evaluation of new "post-liberation" Church expressions. Such a theology is also helping to clarify the relationship between gospel and culture, particularly in the African context.[3]

Themes in the theology of reconstruction

We now turn to important themes in Mugambi's *theology of reconstruction*. The first theme is the ontology of African Christianity. Mugambi stressed the importance of what he described as relationships of being in his discussion of method in Christian theology. He proposed an "introspective method in theology" that would have "great creative potential in the future of African Christianity."[4] He recommended intentionality at four complementary levels. The first level is where Africans learn to *experience* "their own experiencing." They are to understand, judge, and decide for themselves as they process their realities, ontologically. The next level involves *understanding* the unity and the relationships between what they experience, understand, judge, and decide. The third level builds on the second, namely, the *affirmation* of the reality of what Africans experience, understand, judge, and decide. At the fourth level, not only do Africans experience, understand, and affirm their collective experiences, Africans *decide to operate* in accordance with the norms imminent in the spontaneous relatedness of their experience.[5] Through this ontological discussion, Mugambi suggests that when Africans have engaged and implemented these levels of consciousness they grow in self-confidence and commitment to their own future. These levels of engagement involve the respective sectors of social construction.

Reconstruction theologians, according to Mugambi, practice theological introspection through self-criticism and self-reflection. He argues that Good News, that is the Gospel, will only be valid to the extent that it helps Africans to relate with their context. Good News addresses what dehumanises them while opening possibilities for total liberation. Through this kind of reflection, the Christian missionary enterprise in the future will not be dwelling on the failures of the past, rather it will move beyond them toward liberation. Self-criticism is therefore important for the future success of Christianity in Africa. Mugambi argued that this is an important task of reconstruction.[6] "The challenge posed by the theme of reconstruction is that progressive activism need not always entail apportioning blame to others; it should, as a priority, focus on self-criticism, self-evaluation and re-dedication," he said.[7]

Another theme of Mugambi's theology of reconstruction is the holistic, integrative approach to theology. Mugambi's understanding of the theology of reconstruction is that it is multi-disciplinary, multi-sectoral, and cross-cultural in its approach. The theology of reconstruction takes its cue from the African worldview, theology, and ontology. It is holistic just as the African worldview is holistic, and the way African theology ought to be. The theology of reconstruction is not only multi-disciplinary, but also integrative. It moves away from the dialectical thought and moves into reciprocity.[8] Two texts worth quoting extensively here illustrate these insights.

Mugambi quoted Archbishop John Habgood:

> "No matter how much Christians may stress the objective, historical aspects of their faith, and claim that theirs is the faith of an historical community, there remains a large personal element in it. To know God is not to add an extra card labelled 'God' to our mental card index; it is to become a changed person. To a lesser degree, to lean on science is to become a changed person also. But whereas in science the process of change is largely unconscious and often unrecognised, in religion it is paramount."[9]

Mugambi interacts with these thoughts in the following way:

> These remarks lead us to conclude that the various disciplines through which we endeavour to comprehend ourselves and the reality around us, will serve us best if we appreciate them as complementary parts of a very complex jigsaw puzzle, of which we ourselves are an integral part. Theology cannot dispense with the empirical sciences without impairing its objectives. Nor can science and technology dispense with theological insights without losing direction. Unfortunately, they seem to have already lost their bearings, and they may have to count on theological

insights for a new orientation. This re-orientation will need the contribution of those cultural and religious traditions which have so far been considered marginal, despite their being deeply human.[10]

Ecumenism is a central theme in Mugambi's theology of reconstruction. He proposes that an ecumenical approach is important for the growth and development of the theology of reconstruction. He is aware of the challenge of approaches to ecumenical questions. For example, he cites the challenge of dialogue in ecumenical contexts where such denominationally diverse activities as the Eucharist are carried out.[11] In such instances there arise challenges of meaning which are likely to affect mutual sharing. That said, Mugambi recognizes that the future of the African Church lies not in its divisions, but in its unity. "The Church of the future, the Body of Christ, the Community of Believers, those who gather together, in all their various expressions, to break bread, should be coming together to ensure our survival," he said.[12] Ecumenical and cross denominational conversations, in his view, would bring about the necessary unity of understanding that is required for the social and theological reconstruction of Africa. From what can be seen among revitalization movements on the continent today, these movements are not alien. Scholars have described that emerging Christianity as post-denominational and one in which traditional boundaries are broken in order to advance the gospel.[13]

Revitalization and reconstruction

Reconstruction provides useful tools toward an understanding of revitalization movements in Africa. Mugambi suggests that the need in Africa is for a religious commitment that leads to social reconstruction, moving beyond passive piety.[14] This resonates with recent reflections on revitalization by Asamoah-Gyadu who points out that revitalization is important in producing communities that exhibit health and wholeness.[15] Healing in this context includes those elements that comprise the fullness of life that God makes available in Jesus Christ.[16]

Revitalization in Africa is a part of the ongoing global renewal of Christianity. Ireland correctly observes that the revitalization that we see in one place, in a particular era, is linked to the continual revitalization and renewal of the Church throughout history.[17] In addition to this, Karkkainen wrote that revitalization must be seen in the context of the understanding of a triune God, acting in historical, cultural, social, and spiritual contexts so that the community can experience enlivening and reawakening.[18] Mwaura's perspective sheds light on this from an African Christian scholar's perspective: revitalization is about "creating a community of hope; it gives life to the Church and energises it. It is evidence of God moving into history. Revitalization may occur where there is spiritual lethargy and the Church is compromised by worldliness."[19]

Mark Shaw suggests that global revitalization movements have an impact in the world as they mediate the transfer of power through the translation of Christian truth into the local context.[20] Spiritual dynamics of this revitalization provide the individual with a sense of liberation and a move towards a radical hope. Cultural dynamics of revitalization include indigenization, inculturation, and contextualization. Indigenization, he argues, is the transfer of power into the hands of local people. Inculturation is when the gospel is spoken and received into the deep worldview of the hearer. Contextualization is when revitalization begins to tangibly affect the world. It is the historical dynamic of revitalization where Shaw, making reference to Anthony Wallace, summarizes revitalization into three stages: the problem stage, the paradigm change, and the power stage.[21]

Mugambi's theology of reconstruction could be framed within this understanding. The problem stage, according to Shaw, is when the old way of doing things interrupts and hinders the normal way of life. Mugambi articulated the fall of the Iron Curtain between the former Soviet Union and western countries and the subsequent emergence of a new world order as a problem that required theological attention. It served as an historical marker of a new set of problems that emerged facing the African continent at the end of the 20th century.

This problem stage, according to Shaw, is countered by a new paradigm stage. Here new leaders emerge introducing new ways of doing things. This is what Shaw calls the new light.[22] In Mugambi's theology of reconstruction, the need for rebuilding in these different social sectors points to a new paradigm. Here Mugambi suggests that a new way of thinking and a new way of evaluating the society must be developed, including the move away from an old paradigm of liberation to the new paradigm of rebuilding.

Finally there is the power stage. Here, according to Shaw, there is a transfer of power from the old light into the new light. New leaders emerge and develop new ways of processing their realities.[23] It is here that Mugambi's theology of reconstruction provides insight into emerging revitalization movements. Revitalization movements emerging and growing after the crises of the 1990s seem to be addressing these new problems. In other words, Mugambi and his theology of reconstruction provide insights regarding the conditions for the emergence of revitalization movements and their key concerns in the African context.

We now examine the revitalization movement history in East Africa. Mwaura outlined four stages of the renewal movement history.[24] Revitalization began with the Roho movement. This took the form of the classic African Indigenous Churches (AICs) founded at the beginning of 20th century. They were characterised by charismatic, often eccentric individuals who led a community with an acute sensitivity to and an appreciation for pneumatological resources. After these came the nationalist movements. These are also called Ethiopian movements. They were a religious as well as a political response by Africans to "missionary paternalism and tensions created by colonialism and its attendant oppressive policies and practices." Founded in the 1920s–30s, these were followed by renewal movements within mainline Churches. The classic example of this was the East African Revival which had its beginnings in the 1930s and extended into the 1950s. Its effects were still being felt in the latter part of the 20th century. The 1960s saw the emergence of neo-Pentecostal or charismatic movements.[25]

Karanja places revitalization in Kenya within the context of the history of the world Christian missionary enterprise.[26] This period began in earnest in the years between 1844 and 1862. The Church Missionary Society began its work in 1844. The Methodist Missionary Society began in 1862. Much of the missionary work at the time was focussed on the coastal region of Kenya. The next major wave of missionary activity took place in the years between 1895 and 1914. This was characterized by a rapid expansion into the interior and an increase in Protestant missions. Key mission initiatives included the Africa Inland Mission in 1895, the Church of Scotland Mission in 1898, the Friends African Industrial Mission in 1902, and the Seventh Day Adventists in 1906. These missions spread from the Kenyan coast into central and western Kenya.[27]

In the years between 1919 and 1963 there was an unprecedented increase in the number of African Christians. This came with the indigenization of leadership within traditional western mission-founded Churches as well as the rise and growth of African Instituted Churches (AICs). Between 1963 and 1985 Church leadership became almost fully indigenized. African Christians had developed fairly good relations with leaders of the new state. Later on new faith missions, mostly from the United States arrived, emphasizing healing, speaking in tongues, prophecy, and prosperity through giving. These new missions attracted many young people from mainstream Churches. From 1985 to 2008 new evangelical "ministries" emerged as part of the ongoing revitalization. At the same time, Karanja observes, there was a polarization of Christians with regard to the question of political participation.[28]

Reconstruction and revitalization in perspective: reflections involving New Pentecostal and Charismatic Churches (NPCCs) from Kenya

As noted above, reconstruction and revitalization are related. Reconstruction is a rebuilding of the society, while revitalization movements in Christian history are an attempt by Churches to rebuild Christianity and to address the issues of their respective contexts, at a particular time. The operative questions are these: How can we evaluate, reflect, and critique revitalization movements in Africa today? Do we have frameworks that can be used to reflect on the nature, scope, and the effectiveness of revitalization movements in Africa? I argue here that the theology of reconstruction provides useful tools to engage in reflection.

We can deploy salient aspects of the theology of reconstruction as a beginning point for reflection on revitalization today. Here NPCCs in Nairobi serve as case studies. First we address the question of self-awareness and then identify introspective theology. After this we examine the holistic approach to theology, and finally, the concept of constructive ecumenism.

Self-awareness, identity, and the NPCCs

The theology of reconstruction invokes questions of self-awareness and identity. These are ontological questions that must be addressed as the African Church seeks selfhood. In our reflection it must therefore be asked: If the ontological question of self-awareness and identity is important for theology in Africa, to what extent is it reflected in the life of the African Church?

Gifford thinks that the sense of African identity in the NPCCs has been negatively affected by pervasive American influences.[29] On the surface, Gifford's observations seem to be accurate. The language, dress, and technology in these Churches may not immediately strike the observer as African. Many Churches, both charismatic and Pentecostal, use English as the main language of communication.[30] The dress code among members of the congregation, and the leaders alike, in many of the Churches in Nairobi cannot be said to be traditional African. The architecture of many Churches is not particularly African in design. And certainly, the technology that is used in many of these Churches is sourced from and commonly found in Churches from the west. However, Gifford misses the point ontologically in his assessment of the contemporary Pentecostal charismatic Churches in Africa.

Beginning with language, many of the leaders and congregation members speak English as a second or third language. Therefore, the command and use of the language will have been influenced by the culture of the land and will not be used exactly as it is in the west. More specifically, the grammar, intonation, and the syntax in the use of the western languages in the services is distinctly African. In Nairobi, Churches such as the Nairobi Chapel, Mavuno Church and Deliverance Church use a rich spontaneous mix of languages in which English is the main language interspersed with phrases from other languages including Swahili.[31] Music is sung in two or more languages in nearly all Pentecostal and charismatic Churches in Nairobi. Frequently one finds that 50 percent or more of the total singing time is in Swahili or other African languages.[32]

Some Churches designate special dress for ministry teams involved in the worship services. In others such as the Nairobi Chapel, there will special dress for the ushers, the choir, and sometimes the preacher reflecting contemporary African design. Some Churches such as the Nairobi Chapel and Mavuno Church will use special dress patterned on contemporary African designs to be used during Church celebrations and for weddings.[33]

There is a strong sense of identity and belonging in what appears to be a foreign expression of the faith. The ontological question of self-awareness penetrates beyond what on the surface seems western or American. The content of the sermons and discipleship materials and conference themes reveal a deep sense of self-awareness in the African Church.[34]

Are newer Churches self-aware and are they confident of their identity as Africans, as Christians? The answer is, yes. Churches that originally emerged out of western denominational missionary initiatives now see themselves as distinctly African and Christian. Churches such as the International Christian Centre (ICC) that developed from the American Assemblies of God, CITAM that emerged from the Canadian Assemblies of God; these see themselves as fully African in their identity in the same way that locally-initiated NPCCs such as the Deliverance Church and the Redeemed Gospel Churches of Kenya do.[35] As such there is no identity confusion as Gifford seems to suggest.

Introspective theology in NPCCs

Gatu's reflection in the early 1970s on the state of the Church in Africa led to a call for a moratorium on missionaries for at least five years.[36] Though this debate faded in the 1980s, there has been continued reflection on the role of the Church in Africa with respect to global missions.[37] The question arises: What is the role of the African Church in global missions? The other related question that could be raised is: What does the Church need to do differently in its engagement within its context here in Africa, and, more specifically here in Kenya?

The example of the Church and its engagement in politics and governance here in Kenya in the period beginning in the year 2000, is instructive. In the referendum that followed the quest for a new constitution, ethnic division in 2005 emerged as a key issue both within and outside the Church. At the time, the Church in Kenya was said to have assumed ethnic positions on the issue.[38] In the year 2010 a second referendum finally enacted a new constitution. This time the Church adopted a more issues-oriented posture and assumed a more self-critical perspective. The Church in Kenya as represented by ecumenical associations, reflected on its role in the first referendum and adjusted its approach in the second. This same attitude of self-reflection could be discerned after the general election of 2007 which resulted in violence, followed by the next election in 2012.[39] During the latter election the Church was more deliberate in presenting a united front against ethnic positions, and in its advocacy for better high-quality leadership in governance. The Church was also more deliberate in terms of its quest for peace in the country.[40]

There is a need for the continual development of a practical theology and ecclesiology that promotes self-criticism and self-reflection within the local Church and the Church in general. Some of this is taking place at the local Church level where the development of materials that address marriage as a Christian rite of passage in the African context. This can be seen in Churches such as the Nairobi Chapel, CITAM, and ICC.[41] There has also been the development of Christian materials and scholarship on the topic of leadership, which the Church has actively confronted in the past 20 years of Kenya's political history. Church leaders such as Oscar Amisi, Gibson Anduvate, and Tim Kiruhi have reflected on leadership in the country from a Christian perspective.[42]

Hence the question: Are revitalization movements in Nairobi engaged in introspective theology? There is evidence of self-criticism and reflection on matters of national importance. And there is evidence of self-criticism with regard to the Church's engagement politically, socially, and culturally in order to bring about change in society. More needs to be done on the question of self-criticism and debate on the issues of identity, praxis, economics, and aesthetics. There needs to be more locally developed theological response to questions touching on global economic, political, moral, and cultural issues.

NPCCs and the holistic approach to theology

The Church in Africa has been characterized as being an inch deep and a mile wide.[43] It is widely reported that Christian values have failed to permeate African society. It is possible that inadequate discipleship may be responsible for this state of affairs. The Church seems unable to produce Christians who exercise their faith in the marketplace. This may well be the result of a largely western, missionary catechism which assumed a Cartesian worldview that linked knowledge with identity or belief.

Discipleship is a broad term describing the process of instruction in which Christians grow in their understanding of the practice of their faith. Catechism comprises instruction on the principles of Christianity primarily through the dialectical approach of question and answer. Discipleship was accomplished through catechism in the traditional Church denominations prior to the missionary era. Such catechism developed in Europe, with roots in Hellenistic epistemology, built upon Greco-Roman foundations and revised in post-Reformation Europe within the context of a dialectic, rational approach to knowledge and belief.

Africa with its holistic worldview requires a different approach to discipleship, specifically to the catechism. It requires a holistic catechism encompassing all aspects of the believer's life. The theology of reconstruction proposes a holistic theology that encompasses all aspects and sectors of public and private life. A catechism birthed out of this theology must therefore be holistic in nature. Recently there has been development of a discipleship catechism within the revitalization movements such as ICC, Mavuno, CITAM, and Nairobi Chapel.[44] This catechism takes the form of discipleship materials that address the issues of the day from a contextual standpoint.[45]

In the case of Mavuno, the discipleship process is depicted as a cycle, beginning when an individual is drawn from society, enters into the community which is the gathered Church, engages with a micro community, and is then sent back into society where the person is intended to have an impact. Such impact unfolds in concentric levels of influence from the individual, to family, to workplace and into society at large.[46]

Mavuno's discipleship programme takes the individual through biblical principles, developing a theology of personal victory over sin, an understanding of community and its role in one's personal life, an understanding of God, and a commitment to impact the world through God's leading. The discipleship journey takes the participant through Simama, a discipleship experience with a specific emphasis on one's life, with special focus on the family.[47] It takes the participants through Ombi, which is a practical theology of prayer by the believer and its impact on the work front.[48] It also takes the participant through Hatua, an understanding of the Old Testament, drawing on the principles for social justice and societal impact.[49] Practical initiatives have emerged from Hatua in which participants have engaged with policy issues such as the sensitization of rural communities with regard to land policy.[50] A unique feature of the type of discipleship offered by Mavuno and other Churches is the emphasis on a holistic, community based approach.[51] This is one example of revitalization being sustained through discipleship as described by William J. Abraham.[52]

The theology of reconstruction extends beyond theologians into society. This is the kind of engagement seen in discipleship in some of the revitalization movements as described above. Mugambi says, "It will be necessary for African biblical scholars to work closely with African professionals in other disciplines to avoid a situation in which theologians operate in isolation."[53] He goes on to say,

> This multi-disciplinary cross-reference will help African theologians move from their academic isolation to the general pool of African expertise. Thus the theology of reconstruction implies a re-definition and re-assessment of the task of African theologians as members of the elite in Africa and in the world.[54]

Mavuno and other NPCCs actively engage in this holistic practice of theologization in their approach to ministry.

Other examples of this holistic approach to theology are seen in initiatives such as the engagement of CITAM in politics, leadership, and governance issues through their Bishop.[55] Scholars such as Timothy Kiruhi and Jonathan Maritim have researched leadership behaviour in the Kenyan marketplace from a Christian perspective.[56] The Mavuno Church has launched initiatives such as "spread the love" and the Fearless Summit Conference to challenge participants in their engagement with society.[57] ICC has developed discipleship material for marriages. Philip Kitoto, the

ICC Bishop, is a regular contributor in the secular print media on marriage and relationships.[58] CITAM have acquired a radio and television media house that, in addition to evangelism, addresses personal, professional, and national issues.[59] Reconstruction theology presents a holistic and an all-encompassing paradigm that erases the lines of division between the public and the personal, the secular and the sacred. In reflecting on revitalization movements in Nairobi, a practical approach to theology in the life of Church can be seen as evidence of the holistic paradigm that reconstruction theology proposes.

Post-denominationalism in NPCCs

In his reflections on the effectiveness of the Church, Karanja has suggested that ethnic allegiances rendered the Church somewhat ineffective in the democratic process in the 1990s because of ethnically based denominational divisions.[60] Karanja's assessment of these ethnically aligned denominational divisions was reflected in the period just prior to the 2007 general elections in Kenya. Ethnicity is one factor that complicates interdenominational unity and hinders ecumenism in Kenya.

Urban centres account for a large proportion of the Kenyan population which is ethnically diverse within high density population areas.[61] This introduces ethnic complexities that have missiological implications.[62] It is worth noting here that ethnic divisions along denominational lines have their historical origins in the apportioning of the country to different Christian missions in the early 20th century. These divisions were followed by intense rivalry among the missionaries which found its way into the Churches.[63] It did not help that the colonial governments were well served with the divide and rule principle, a philosophy that enhanced ethnic divisions. In this way ethnic animosity could be seen in governance structures, and was present in Christian denominations. One early and very notable exception, though, was manifested in the East African Revival Movement in which ethnic and national identities were obliterated in a singular expression of Christian solidarity.[64]

Recently more constructive ecumenism in the nation has begun to take shape. This is indicative of a shift into new paradigms of Christian mission that have for various reasons been "de-territorialized and re-territorialized."[65] When Kenyan Churches united for peace and an appreciation of ethnic diversity after the deadly post-election clashes in Kenya in 2008, this shift was in evidence. Coming together across denominations they preached peace and brought about reconciliation under the Msafara initiative in 2008.[66] This initiative continued in various parts of the country just prior to the 2012 elections with the Peace Caravan, a follow-up initiative to Msafara. We have also seen unity on issues of security in this country in the last three years. The National Council of Churches in Kenya (NCCK) and other ecumenical institutions have stood shoulder-to-shoulder to condemn insecurity, and to provide solutions for the ongoing security crisis in Kenya.

We also see unity among Church leaders with regard to select social and political agenda that are driven by western governments and Churches.[67]

At the local Church level, it is common to find members of the traditional Churches attending charismatic Pentecostal prayer gatherings. Gatherings of this nature may be hosted by a denomination, but they attract people from other denominations. This is true of revival conferences and women's gatherings.[68] This also includes leadership development conferences such as Viral, Veritas and the Fearless Summit.[69] The Viral Conference is attended by leaders from different Churches and denominations locally and around the world.[70] CITAM is one of several Churches that has hosted an annual conference providing a Christian response to the plight of Africa. The Springboard conference has been hosted in Nairobi, drawing audiences from different denominations locally and from across the continent.[71]

Can we see ecumenism in revitalization movements in Kenya today? The answer is, yes. The purpose of the Church today, through its theology and praxis, is to enhance the quality of life as promised in scripture. To this end Mugambi states, "Enhancement of quality of life should be the priority of all evangelization, bearing in mind that such enhancement is measurable in quantitative terms such as adequate food, adequate shelter, and satisfactory health."[72] The theology of reconstruction pointed to the coming of what Donald Miller and Tetsunao Yamamori refer to as a socially conscious post-denominational Christianity.[73] The intention of the efforts in these revitalization movements is to present the gospel in relevant ways through constructive collaboration beyond traditional denominational boundaries.

Looking ahead: prospects for the theology of reconstruction

The theology of reconstruction provides a grid with which to reflect on the growth of revitalization in Africa. I have argued in this paper that the theology of reconstruction through its salient themes provides useful tools for the reflection of the theology and praxis of the Church in Africa. In the foreseeable future, this theology will continue to open dialogue in the various facets of social reconstruction on the continent. Mugambi is confident that such reflection will provide hope for the continent of Africa in future. He says, "I am convinced that the 21st century will be the century of Africa, depending on how her thinkers participate in the shaping of the continent's social consciousness."[74]

The theology of reconstruction is not only cognitive or reflective, but also participatory. It engages the Church, its leaders, and the congregation, demanding from them a response to their world. This theology is forward-looking, pro-active, and optimistic providing hope for the Church and the future of the continent. Mugambi says,

> Each of us is challenged to add his or her brick towards rebuilding the wall of Africa, then towards the rebuilding of our societies now in ruins. This is not the time to apportion blame. It is the time to build.

> Are you and I a part of the solution or part of the problem? Are you and I a builder, or a destroyer? Are you a producer or a consumer of theology? This is your challenge and mine, in the theology of reconstruction. There is no time for academic rhetoric. There is time only for re-constructive reflection and action.[75]

The theology of reconstruction also provides a glimpse into the future by challenging the Church to consider new frontiers in mission. Previously, the Church engaged in mission from an evangelistic point of view. The theology of reconstruction proposes that the future of the Church is bound up in a quest for an evangelization the result of which would be a total liberation of the individual and society. For this reason the new mission frontiers are no longer geographical, but sociological, ecological, and cultural.[76] It is to these areas that the theology of reconstruction directs the Church community through its congregations, leaders, and theologians.[77]

Notes

1 J.N.K. Mugambi, "African Theologies of Reconstruction," in Daniel Patte, ed. *The Cambridge Dictionary of Christianity*, First Edition. (Cambridge, New York: Cambridge University Press, 2010).
2 J.N.K. Mugambi, *Christian Theology and Social Reconstruction*. (Nairobi: Acton Publishers, 2003), 106.
3 Mugambi, "African Theologies of Reconstruction."
4 Mugambi, *Christian Theology and Social Reconstruction*, 27.
5 Ibid.
6 J.N.K. Mugambi, *From Liberation to Reconstruction: African Christian Theology After the Cold War*. (Nairobi: East African Educational Publishers, 1995), 72.
7 J. N. K. Mugambi, "The Social Reconstruction of Africa: The Role of Churches," in *The Church and Reconstruction of Africa: Theological Considerations*. (Nairobi: All Africa Conference of Churches, 1997), 14.
8 Mugambi, *Christian Theology and Social Reconstruction*, 166.
9 J. Habgood, *Religion and Science*, 132; Mugambi, *God, Humanity and Nature in Relation to Justice and Peace*, Church and Society Documents. (Nairobi: World Council of Churches, 1987), ii.
10 Mugambi, *God, Humanity and Nature in Relation to Justice and Peace*, 69.
11 J.N.K. Mugambi, *Christian Mission and Social Transformation: A Kenyan Perspective*. (Nairobi: National Council of Churches of Kenya, 1989), 115.
12 J.N.K. Mugambi, "The Social Reconstruction of Africa: The Role of Churches," 234.
13 Donald E. Miller, and Tetsunao Yamamori. *Global Pentecostalism: The New Face of Christian Social Engagement*. First Edition, Includes DVD Edition. (Berkeley: University of California Press, 2007); Dale T. Irvin "The Church, the Urban, and the Global: Mission in an Age of Global Cities," *International Bulletin of Missionary Research*, 33, no. 4 (October 2009). Dale Irvin observes that "Spatial configurations of the personal body, the congregation, the denomination, the city, the culture, and the nation are all being increasingly deterritorialized and reterritorialized, resulting in new spatiotemporal configurations and combinations."
14 Mugambi, *From Liberation to Reconstruction. African Christian Theology After the Cold War*, 150.

15 J. K. Asamoah-Gyadu, "We Are Here to Heal: Revitalisation Movements as Charismatic Communities in Africa," in J. Steven O'Malley, ed. *Interpretive Trends in Christian Revitalization for the Early Twenty First Century*. (Lexington: Emeth Press, 2011), 272.
16 Ibid.
17 Ireland, "The Church Alive: Beyond the Commonalities and Anomalies of Revitalisation Models."
18 Karkkainen, "Lessons for Revitalisation from the Broader, Missional Phenomenology of the Holy Spirit as Found in the Data," 102.
19 Mwaura, "Practices for Sustaining Revitalization in Local Communities: Perspectives from Africa."
20 Shaw, *Global Awakening*, 17.
21 Ibid.; Wallace, "Revitalization Movements."
22 Shaw, *Global Awakening*, 17.
23 Ibid.
24 Mwaura, "Practices for Sustaining Revitalization in Local Communities: Perspectives from Africa."
25 Ibid.
26 Karanja, "Evangelical Attitudes toward Democracy in Kenya."
27 Ibid.
28 Ibid.
29 Gifford, *Ghana's New Christianity*, New Edition, 198–9; Gifford, "A View of Ghana's New Christianity."
30 "Mavuno Sermons I Blog.Mavuno."; Jessica Warren, *Worship at Nairobi Chapel*; "Hope FM – Citam."
31 "Mavuno Sermons I Blog.Mavuno."
32 Ibid.; "Mavuno Worship Project"; Richard Njau, 10. Ombi – The Mavuno Worship Project. (www.google.com/+CTA101); Richard Njau, 2. Leo – The Mavuno Worship Project (MWP) (www.google.com/+CTA101).
33 "African Wear Nairobi Chapel."; "African Wear Mavuno Church."; "African Wear Mavuno Church."
34 Wanjau, Mizizi; Ochola-Adolwa, Hatua; Mbevi, Ombi: Making Prayer an Adventure; Fearless Summit 2015: Position Yourself.
35 International Christian Center, "About Us I I.C.C Church"; CITAM, "Citam History and Background."
36 Gatu, *Joyfully Christian. Truly African*, 163–76.
37 Muriu, *Urbana Missions Conference 2006: Interdependence Model of Missions*, 4:51.
38 Owiso, "Post-Election Violence Even Divided Priests and Churches."; "Kenya's Churches Stand Accused Too."
39 "Q&A"; Branch, "Kenya's Referendum 'in the Name of God, No!' "; Mutua and Kemei, "Referendum Date Set as Church Insists 'No.' "
40 Mue, "Regaining Our Saltiness."
41 Wanjau and Wanjau, *Ndoa: Investing in the Marriage of Your Dreams*; Kitoto and Kitoto, *The Other Side of Bliss*.
42 Amisi, *Generation Y: Engaging and Impacting This Generation*; Anduvate, *Leading Young*; Kiruhi, "Navigating Uncertain Times: Perspectives of African Leaders on Key Global Change Drivers over the Next Ten Years."
43 Muriu, *Urbana Missions Conference 2006: Interdependence Model of Missions*, 9:08.
44 "Nairobi Chapel DNA."; "Mavuno Church – Discipleship – Marathon."; "Nairobi Chapel Plug-In."; "Christ Is the Answer Ministries – The Safari."
45 "Mavuno Church – Discipleship – Marathon."; "Nairobi Chapel DNA."

46 "Mavuno Church – Discipleship – Marathon."
47 Wanjau, Simama.
48 Mbevi, *Ombi: Making Prayer an Adventure.*
49 Ochola-Adolwa, *Hatua.*
50 "Mavuno Church – Discipleship – Marathon."
51 "Christ Is the Answer Ministries – The Safari"; "Mavuno Church – Discipleship – Marathon."
52 Abraham, "Catechesis and Revitalisation."
53 Mugambi, *Christian Theology and Social Reconstruction*, 152.
54 Ibid.
55 Oginde, "We Must Confront the Question of Religion in the War on Terror."
56 Kiruhi, "Navigating Uncertain Times: Perspectives of African Leaders on Key Global Change Drivers over the Next Ten Years."; Maritim, "Perceptions of Appropriate Leader Behavior."
57 *Fearless Summit 2015: Position Yourself*; "Mavuno Spread The Love – September 2010."; "Mavuno 'SPREAD THE LOVE FESTIVAL' Presents Kirk Franklin."
58 Kitoto, "My Husband Is a Serial Cheater and My in-Laws Want Me to Raise."; Kitoto, "KITOTO."
59 "Hope FM | Listen and Live."
60 Karanja, "Evangelical Attitudes toward Democracy in Kenya."
61 "Kenya Population Census 1999: Analytical Report on Migration and Urbanisation. Volume VI."; "Kenya Population Census 1989: Analytical Report Volume VI. Migration and Urbanisation."
62 Mutua, "Complexity of Migrant African Urbanites and Its Missiological Implications for the Church."
63 Barrett, *Schism and Renewal in Africa: An Analysis of Six Thousand Contemporary Religious Movements*, 264–78. In his extensive analysis of African renewal movements, Barrett attributed mission agency rivalry and competition to the failure of Christian love.
64 Gatu, *Joyfully Christian. Truly African*, 17; Dancun and Kalu, "Bazukufu: Revival Movements and Indigenous Appropriation in African Christianity," 246.
65 Irvin, "The Church, the Urban, and the Global."
66 "Msafara Wheels of Hope | Rescue Kenya."; "Msafara Muriithi Wanjau."
67 Muriu, *Urbana Missions Conference 2006: Interdependence Model of Missions*, 4:58.
68 "Daughters of Zion."; "Queen Esthers Generation."
69 Nairobi Chapel, *The 2015 Viral Conference*; "Veritas Bible Exposition Conference"; Fearless Summit 2015: Position Yourself.
70 Nairobi Chapel, *Viral Conference 2015 – Pst Oscar Muriu – Plenary Session One.*
71 "Springboard Convention."
72 Mugambi, *From Liberation to Reconstruction. African Christian Theology After the Cold War*, 151.
73 Miller and Yamamori, *Global Pentecostalism*, 39.
74 Mugambi, *Christian Theology and Social Reconstruction*, 130.
75 Ibid., 176.
76 Mugambi, *African Christian Theology: An Introduction*, 130.
77 Mugambi, *From Liberation to Reconstruction. African Christian Theology After the Cold War*, 170–3.

Bibliography

Abraham, William J. "Catechesis and Revitalisation." In *Interpretive Trends in Christian Revitalization for the Early Twenty First Century*, edited by J. Steven O'Malley, 245–52. Lexington: Emeth Press, 2011.

"African Wear Image Nairobi Chapel." Accessed September 1, 2015. www.google.com/imgres?imgurl=http://d.christiantoday.com/en/full/5734/oscar-muriu-senior-pastor-of-nairobi-chapel-in-kenya-tells-more.jpg&imgrefurl=www.christiantoday.com/article/global.shift.in.christianity.requires.new.paradigm.missionaries/8900.htm&h=525&w=350&tbnid=R3b_be4kU0cEeM:&docid=VvI9uFceZtFbhM&ei=HqHlVYXXMoX0-QGzg4voAw&tbm=isch&ved=0CEAQMygZMBlqFQoTCIXegu7x1ccCFQV6Pgods8ECPQ.

"African Wear Mavuno Church Image1." Accessed September 1, 2015. https://fbcdn-sphotos-f-a.akamaihd.net/hphotos-ak-xpf1/t31.0-8/p480x480/11875018_1046744838677534_7856591550360684425_o.jpg.

"African Wear Mavuno Church Image2." Accessed September 1, 2015. https://fbcdn-photos-d-a.akamaihd.net/hphotos-ak-xpa1/t31.0-0/p480x480/10484519_1046745138677504_7550845224467321256_o.jpg.

Amisi, Oscar. *Generation Y: Engaging and Impacting This Generation*. Nairobi: Oscar Amisi Publishers, 2015.

Anduvate, Gibson. *Leading Young*. Nairobi: Berean Communications, 2013.

Asamoah-Gyadu, J. Kwabena. "We Are Here to Heal: Revitalisation Movements as Charismatic Communities in Africa." In *Interpretive Trends in Christian Revitalization for the Early Twenty First Century*, edited by J. Steven O'Malley, 263–74. Lexington: Emeth Press, 2011.

Barrett, David B. *Schism and Renewal in Africa: An Analysis of Six Thousand Contemporary Religious Movements*. Oxford University Press, 1968.

Branch, Daniel. "Kenya's Referendum 'in the Name of God, No!'." *The African Executive*, August 2010. www.opendemocracy.net/daniel-branch/kenya%E2%80%99s-referendum-%E2%80%9Cin-name-of-god-no%E2%80%9D.

"Christ Is the Answer Ministries – The Safari." n.d. www.citam.org/index.php/component/content/article?id=209.

CITAM. "Citam History and Background." n.d. http://citam.org/index.php/about-us/history-and-background.

Dancun, Graham, and Ogbu Kalu. "Bazukufu: Revival Movements and Indigenous Appropriation in African Christianity." In *African Christianity: An African Story*, edited by Ogbu Kalu. Pretoria: University of Pretoria, 2005.

"Daughters of Zion." n.d. www.doz.co.ke/vision.htm.

Fearless Summit 2015: Position Yourself. Mavuno Church, 2015.

Gatu, John G. *Joyfully Christian: Truly African*. Nairobi: Acton Publishers, 2006.

Gifford, Paul. "A View of Ghana's New Christianity." In *The Changing Face of Christianity Africa, the West, and the World*, edited by Lamin O. Sanneh and Joel A. Carpenter, 81–96. New York: Oxford University Press, 2005. http://site.ebrary.com/id/10103687.

———. *Ghana's New Christianity, New Edition: Pentecostalism in a Globalising African Economy*. New Edition. Bloomington: Indiana University Press, 2004.

Habgood, John. *Religion and Science*. London: Hodder & Stoughton, 1971.

"Hope FM | Listen and Live." Accessed September 1, 2015. www.hopefm.org/.

"Hope FM – Citam." *Hope FM*. Accessed September 1, 2015. http://citam.org/index.php/units/hope-fm.

International Christian Center. "About Us | I.C.C Church." Accessed April 23, 2015. http://icc-kenya.org/about-us/.

Ireland, Daryl. "The Church Alive: Beyond the Commonalities and Anomalies of Revitalisation Models." In *Interpretive Trends in Christian Revitalization for the Early Twenty First Century*, edited by J. Steven O'Malley, 57–66. Lexington: Emeth Press, 2011.

Irvin, Dale T. "The Church, the Urban, and the Global: Mission in an Age of Global Cities." *International Bulletin of Missionary Research* 33, no. 4 (October 2009): 177–82.

Jessica Warren. *Worship at Nairobi Chapel*. Accessed September 1, 2015. www.youtube.com/watch?v=TPv9rSpSOqE.

Karanja, John. "Evangelical Attitudes toward Democracy in Kenya." In *Evangelical Christianity and Democracy in Africa*, edited by Terence O. Ranger, 67–94. New York: Oxford University Press, 2008.

Karkkainen, Veli-Matti. *Kenya Population Census 1989: Analytical Report Volume VI. Migration and Urbanisation*. Nairobi, Kenya: Central Bureau of Statistics, April 1996.

———. *Kenya Population Census 1999: Analytical Report on Migration and Urbanisation*. Volume VI. Nairobi, Kenya: Central Bureau of Statistics, November 2004.

———. "Lessons for Revitalisation from the Broader, Missional Phenomenology of the Holy Spirit as Found in the Data." In *Interpretive Trends in Christian Revitalization for the Early Twenty First Century*, edited by J. Steven O'Malley, 101–7. Lexington: Emeth Press, 2011.

"Kenya's Churches Stand Accused Too." Text. *The Hague Trials Kenya*, May 1, 2014. https://thehaguetrials.co.ke/article/kenyas-churches-stand-accused-too.

Kiruhi, Timothy Mwangi. "Navigating Uncertain Times: Perspectives of African Leaders on Key Global Change Drivers over the Next Ten Years." *Leadership Advance Online* no. XVII (Summer 2009).

Kitoto, Dinah, and Philip Kitoto. *The Other Side of Bliss*. Nairobi, Kenya: Ascent, 2010.

Kitoto, Philip. "KITOTO: Trying for a Baby Is Ruining Our Relationship." Accessed September 1, 2015. www.nation.co.ke/lifestyle/DN2/KITOTO-Trying-for-a-baby-is-robbing-us-joy/-/957860/2853092/-/cqbg0nz/-/index.html.

———. "My Husband Is a Serial Cheater and My in-Laws Want Me to Raise." *Daily Nation DN2*. Accessed September 1, 2015. www.nation.co.ke/lifestyle/DN2/KITOTO-HELP – My-husband-is-a-serial-cheater/-/957860/2853090/-/tmwmis/-/index.html.

Maritim, Jonathan Cheruiyot. "Perceptions of Appropriate Leader Behavior: A Comparative Study of the Kalenjin, the Kikuyu, and the Luo." D.Miss., Fuller Theological Seminary, School of World Mission, 2002. http://search.proquest.com/docview/276150729/abstract/F0A6C475E32549E3PQ/2?accountid=8380.

"Mavuno Church – Discipleship – Marathon." *Mavuno Church*, April 22, 2014. www.mavunochurch.org/new/content.php?id=52.

"Mavuno Sermons | Blog.Mavuno." Accessed May 8, 2015. https://mavuno.wordpress.com/category/mavuno-sermons/page/28/.

"Mavuno 'SPREAD THE LOVE FESTIVAL' Presents Kirk Franklin." *Capital Lifestyle*. Accessed September 1, 2015. www.capitalfm.co.ke/lifestyle/2009/09/14/mavuno-spread-the-love-festival-presents-kirk-franklin/.

"Mavuno Spread The Love – September 2010," n.d. https://mavuno.wordpress.com/2010/09/04/spread-the-love/.

"Mavuno Worship Project." *Blog.Mavuno*. Accessed September 1, 2015. https://mavuno.wordpress.com/mavuno-worship-project/.

Mbevi, Simon. *Ombi: Making Prayer an Adventure*. Nairobi: Fearless Publications, 2007.

Miller, Donald E., and Tetsunao Yamamori. *Global Pentecostalism: The New Face of Christian Social Engagement*. First Edition, Includes DVD Edition. Berkeley: University of California Press, 2007.

"Msafara Wheels of Hope | Rescue Kenya." *Msafara*. Accessed September 1, 2015. https://rescuekenya.wordpress.com/category/msafara-wheels-of-hope/.

Mue, Njonjo. "Regaining Our Saltiness: The Role of the Church in Post Election Kenya." *Kenyan Analyst*, May 10, 2008. https://kenyananalyst.wordpress.com/2008/06/05/regaining-our-saltiness-the-role-of-the-church-in-post-election-kenya/.

Mugambi, J.N.K. *God, Humanity and Nature in Relation to Justice and Peace*. Church and Society Documents. Nairobi: World Council of Churches, 1987.

———. *African Christian Theology: An Introduction*. Nairobi: East African Educational Publishers, 1989.

———, ed. *Christian Mission and Social Transformation: A Kenyan Perspective*. Nairobi: National Council of Churches of Kenya, 1989.

———. *From Liberation to Reconstruction: African Christian Theology After the Cold War*. Nairobi: East African Educational Publishers, 1995.

———. *Christian Theology and Social Reconstruction*. Nairobi: Acton Publishers, 2003.

———. "The Social Reconstruction of Africa: The Role of Churches." In *The Church and Reconstruction of Africa: Theological Considerations*, 1–24. Nairobi: All Africa Conference of Churches, 1997.

———. "African Theologies of Reconstruction." In *The Cambridge Dictionary of Christianity*, edited by Daniel Patte, First Edition, 940–1. Cambridge, New York: Cambridge University Press, 2010.

Muriu, Oscar. *Urbana Missions Conference 2006: Interdependence Model of Missions*, 2006. https://vimeo.com/69504380.

Mutua, Henry. "Complexity of Migrant African Urbanites and Its Missiological Implications for the Church." In *African Missiology*, edited by Steven Rasmussen, Henry Mutua, Alemayehu Mekonnen, Josephine Mutuku Sesi, Stephen Mutuku Sesi, and Caleb Chul-Soo Kim, 40–54. Nairobi, Kenya: Uzima Publishing House, 2009.

Mutua, Martin, and Kipchumba Kemei. "Referendum Date Set as Church Insists 'No'." *Standard Digital News*. Accessed September 1, 2015. www.standardmedia.co.ke/article/2000007637/referendum-date-set-as-church-insists-no.

Mwaura, Philomena Njeri. "Practices for Sustaining Revitalization in Local Communities: Perspectives from Africa." In *Interpretive Trends in Christian Revitalization for the Early Twenty First Century*, edited by J. Steven O'Malley, 177–84. Lexington: Emeth Press, 2011.

Nairobi Chapel. *The 2015 Viral Conference*. Accessed October 15, 2015. www.youtube.com/watch?v=O4QZA7NO78A.

———. *Viral Conference 2015 – Pst Oscar Muriu – Plenary Session One*. Accessed October 15, 2015. www.youtube.com/watch?v=wOQl84454ZM.

"Nairobi Chapel DNA." n.d. www.nairobichapel.org/NC/our-DNA.php.

"Nairobi Chapel Plug-In." n.d. http://nairobichapel.org/NC/plugin.php.

Ochola-Adolwa, Linda. *Hatua*. Nairobi: Fearless Publications, 2009.

Oginde, David A. "We Must Confront the Question of Religion in the War on Terror." *Standard Media*, n.d. http://standardmedia.co.ke/article/2000157285/we-must-confront-the-religion-question-in-war-on-terror?articleID=2000157285&story_title=we-must-confront-the-religion-question-in-war-on-terror&pageNo=2.

Owiso, Jackie. "Post-Election Violence Even Divided Priests and Churches." Text. *The Hague Trials Kenya*, December 8, 2013. https://thehaguetrials.co.ke/article/post-election-violence-even-divided-priests-and-churches.

"Pastor M's Blog: Msafara Website." Accessed September 1, 2015. http://greatness-now.blogspot.co.ke/2008/02/msafara-website.html.

"Q&A: Kenya's Constitution Referendum." *BBC News*. Accessed September 1, 2015. www.bbc.com/news/world-africa-10729860.

"Queen Esthers Generation." n.d. http://queenesthersgeneration.com/qeg-mandate/.

Richard Njau. *2. Leo – The Mavuno Worship Project (MWP)* (www.google.com/+CTA101). Accessed September 1, 2015. www.youtube.com/watch?v=DqoqLWERqpQ.

———. *10. Ombi – The Mavuno Worship Project* (www.google.com/+CTA101). Accessed September 1, 2015. www.youtube.com/watch?v=_SJPE426XIk.

Shaw, Mark. *Global Awakening: How 20th-Century Revivals Triggered a Christian Revolution*. Downers Grove: IVP Academic, 2010.

"Springboard Convention." n.d. https://citamblog.wordpress.com/2014/09/05/the-springboard-convention-2014/.

"Veritas Bible Exposition Conference." n.d. http://nairobichapel.net/veritas-conference/.

Wallace, Anthony F. C. "Revitalization Movements." *American Anthropologist* 58, no. 2 (April 1956): 264–81.

Wanjau, Carol. *Simama*. Nairobi: Fearless Publications, 2012.

Wanjau, Muriithi. *Mizizi*. Nairobi: Fearless Publications, 2007.

Wanjau, Muriithi, and Carol Wanjau. *Ndoa: Investing in the Marriage of Your Dreams*. Nairobi: Fearless Publications, 2010.

13 ". . . Then towards the rebuilding of our societies now in Ruins"

Ntozakhe Simon Cezula

Introduction

In this chapter, I discuss aspects of Mugambi's proposal for a theology of reconstruction beginning with an analysis of the changes in the political landscape which called for such a theological reflection. It is important to note that while Villa-Vicencio's book, A *Theology of Reconstruction*, was published in 1992,[1] three years before Mugambi's *From Liberation to Reconstruction*[2] which was published in 1995, Mugambi first articulated the idea before Villa-Vicencio published his book.[3] John Samuel Mbiti remarked that one of the areas in which Mugambi has pioneered theological discussion is in the paradigm shift from the theology of liberation to the theology of reconstruction, but pointed out that the theology of reconstruction had not generated the kind of excitement and heat that liberation theology did in its heyday. This chapter discusses Mugambi's important contribution to theology in Africa by discussing the political landscape that warranted the call for reconstruction and examines the notion of reciprocity of reconstruction theology. It contributes to the discussion by arguing that the Ezra Nehemiah paradigm of reconstruction was problematic. To expand the insights of reconstruction in African societies today, I will draw from the Chronicler to argue that one of the key messages of the Chronicler was that Israel, described as a people of God, ought to change their habits and turn to God for God to heal the land. The broad landscape of this chapter is Africa, and the thought patterns of this chapter are informed by the South African context.

Change in political landscape

Mugambi introduced his theology of reconstruction in the context of a new world order. He argued at the time, "The world in general, and Africa, in particular, has undergone profound political change since 1990."[4] Designating this changed context "the New World Order," he argued that it demanded a new paradigm for African Christian theological reflection which he calls *reconstruction*.[5] I share that broad vision, but question Mugambi's view that liberation as a framework for theological theory and practice (paradigm) in the 21st century has been exhausted because I think that liberation as a paradigm still has a key role to play. The difference between Mugambi and my approach lies in the way we perceive the postures of these paradigms on the historical time line. For him the two are consecutive; liberation first and reconstruction follows.[6] I think liberation and reconstruction processes are not solid but fluid, and liberation remains important if the lives of people have not chanted in a democratically elected government.

The release of Mandela on February 2, 1990 and the first democratic elections on April 27, 1994 in South Africa are significant events that will be remembered in the history of the country. Most people in South Africa, 23 years down the line, have not yet experienced socio-economic freedom. Following those political developments, government structures, the Constitution, state institutions, commissions, and other related structures were established to facilitate processes of reconciliation, reform, and reconstruction and to facilitate a transformation that would also undo the harms that oppression, racism, conflict, and instability did in South Africa. For that reason, reconstruction as a paradigm for doing theology is necessary but liberation and reconstruction must complement each other in South Africa. Justin S. Ukpong argues that situational hermeneutics suggests that should the people's circumstances change, liberation and Black theology would lose its appeal, but that is not the case in South Africa today.[7]

Therefore, an inverse relationship between the intensity of liberation theology and the pace of the liberation process is necessary. The more liberated the nation becomes, the less intense liberation theology should become. This phenomenon does not affect the necessity of reconstruction theology since structures to facilitate the process of reconstruction may already be established in the liberation process, and for that reason, the two paradigms do not negate each other. If the liberation paradigm is still viable in the 21st century in (South) Africa, why another paradigm. Rothney S. Tshaka and Karabo M. Makofane in response to a reconstruction paradigm of theology in (South) Africa argue,

> While scholars such as Mugambi in his famous book (From liberation to Reconstruction: African Christian Theology after the Cold War, 1995) suggest a move from 'liberative metaphor' to a new paradigm of 'theology of reconstruction' we are still operating with the liberation paradigm but seeking to expand its scope. The demise of apartheid requires for the liberation dimension of South African Black Theology to broaden its scope (in the sense of being engaged in the struggle for liberation from the contemporary causes of human suffering such as oppression of women, corruption by government officials, class issues, HIV/Aids, poverty, Xenophobia, Third World debt etc.).[8]

The reference to broadening the scope of the liberation dimension of South African Black Theology acknowledges that pre-1994 theological strategies to fight against injustice do need some adjustments. The question remains:

If an adjustment can take place within the parameters of liberation, why reconstruction? The plight of the poor, for example, in some quarters has degenerated so that poverty means hunger because many people have no food to sustain themselves and their families. This calls for an urgent poverty relief program, and it is in such a context that reconstruction theology is a viable additional strategy to motivate people to fight against injustice in society.

Reciprocity of liberation and reconstruction theology

Mugambi argues that a theology of reconstruction in Africa presupposes a process which is not adversarial but reciprocal. He further argues that liberation is a process in which the oppressed direct their actions against oppressors who often resist. In contrast, social reconstruction is a process in which all sectors of the population are invited to participate in the inauguration of a new social order.[9] The strategy of a theology of reconstruction in Africa should be to bring the previously antagonistic stakeholders in each political community together. Because of its significance, a plurality of approaches could play a significant role in the process of reconstruction where political, social, and economic power should be deployed in the joint project of liberation and reconstruction.

A theology of reconstruction in Africa must focus on identity formation processes unfolding in the "New World Order." Shuch a theology should recognize and affirm the identities of members of the community to facilitate reconstruction. Therefore, reconstruction should begin by defending social identity groups that are unjustly treated. It should reject injustice against the poor, victims of xenophobia, victims of homophobia, victims of racial prejudice, and people who are physically challenged. This calls for theological convictions that will facilitate *unity*, *cooperation*, and *contention*. The focus on social identity formation processes should be anchored in the principle of community solidarity to enable members of the community to address social conflict and facilitate reconstruction which is often retarded by social conflicts. Theological thought should make unity, cooperation, and contention key words of liberation and reconstruction.

To make sense of identity formation, it is important to consider the social psychological insights from the Social Identity Approach (SIA) of Henry Tajfel and the Social Covariation Theory (SCT) of Jean-Claude Deschamps.[10] Tajfel's SIA is a theory that focuses on differences and ignores commonalities. It leads to the simple categorization of "we" and "them." It explains identities that need discrimination to flourish. Deschamps' SCT, on the other hand, focuses on commonalities and emphasizes them more than differences. It leads to cross categorization which emphasizes commonalities among different identity groups and thus common interests. Simple categorization aggravates social conflict. Cross categorization on the other hand, by its diminishing effect on differentiation, decelerates social conflict.

Because social conflict is not in the interest of reconstruction, simple categorization needs to be avoided and cross categorization emphasized. This discussion gives a picture of how reconstruction theology should look like or what it should entail. To do that, I will address the issue of a biblical paradigm for a theology of reconstruction in Africa.

Biblical paradigm for reconstruction

Mugambi used a biblical paradigm. Mugambi argued that this theology, like liberation theology which had Moses and Exodus as a biblical paradigm, has Nehemiah as a biblical paradigm because he recognized the need to rebuild Jerusalem and took action to carry out the massive reconstruction project. He argues that Africa in the 21st century is in a very analogous situation as Judah in the days of Nehemiah, and the figure of Nehemiah should be the most encouraging and most inspiring for Africa today. However, he declared that Nehemiah was not perfect, just as there is nobody who is perfect. Nevertheless, contemporary Africa can learn more from Nehemiah about the demands and challenges of leadership than from Moses, he continues.[11]

Farisani argued that in his proposal for a theology of reconstruction, Mugambi offered an uncritical reading of the Ezra-Nehemiah paradigm.[12] Farisani decried the discriminatory tendencies in the Book of Ezra-Nehemiah. He argued that such a reading of Nehemiah may be counter-productive because instead of supporting and advancing the cause of the poor, it may further marginalize and enslave the poor with the "revealed word of God."[13] The sentiment expressed by Farisani here is echoed in a statement made by Gerrie Snyman about the Ezra-Nehemiah narrative when he says, "After apartheid, I am left with some serious questions about the story's moral vision, even when God is drawn into the argument."[14] Farisani calls for the de-ideologization of the Ezra-Nehemiah text by identifying the role of the dominant group.[15]

In a direct critique of reconstruction, Tinyiko S Maluleke argued, "From a black and African perspective, therefore, the proposal for a theology of reconstruction, *instead* of, and even alongside black and African theologies of liberation, is misplaced and unacceptable."[16] Maluleke decried replacing the inculturation-liberation paradigm without engaging it but warmly recommends Mugambi's *From Liberation to Reconstruction* as a book "projecting the genuine concerns of a passionate and committed African churchman, theologian and continental patriot of our times."[17] Mugambi also seems to have taken note of the remark for his tone somewhat softened later, acknowledging the role of liberation theology.[18]

Despite these criticisms, one should be aware that Mugambi makes an important point by suggesting that Nehemiah saw a need and came up with a project to meet that need. As Sara Japhet indicated more than two decades ago, "The Book of Ezra-Nehemiah is the principle (*sic*) source for our knowledge of the Restoration period."[19] Nevertheless, it is still the case that the figure of Nehemiah might not have been a proper paradigm for a theology of reconstruction in Africa. While I sympathize with the position taken by Farisani, I recognize its limitations because he does not propose a biblical paradigm. Mugambi specifically identified the post-exilic period in the Old Testament as a resource for reconstruction. I agree, but think that the Book of Chronicles or the Chronicler, is a better example.

Scholars of the Hebrew Bible and Second Temple studies refer to Chronicles when Ezra-Nehemiah is discussed and to Ezra-Nehemiah when Chronicles is discussed. The theologies grounded on the Chronicles have not been extensively explored about Africa. Illuminating this point, Steven L. McKenzie says,

> Williamson focused on the 'all Israel' motif in Chronicles, contending that its interest in including the northern tribes among the chosen people of Israel contrasted with the narrowness of Ezra-Nehemiah, which regarded true Israel as exclusively the returnees of Judah and Benjamin.[20]

The Chronicler probably wrote after Ezra-Nehemiah and perhaps even in response to it.[21] I also maintain that the Chronicler was responding to Ezra-Nehemiah. A brief background can place the books into perspective. Both books originated from the post-exilic period. Although they were freed from exile, Judah was no more an independent kingdom but a province of Persia. This implied co-existing with foreigners. The exiles were returning to their fellow Judeans who did not go to exile. Daniel Smith-Christopher observes, "The separation of the community in 597–586 began to create long-standing divisions that persisted after groups of diaspora Jews returned to Palestine under Persian patronage."[22] This also had implications for their exiles/non-exiles relations. Additionally, Hugh Williamson asserts,

> It is clear beyond a shadow of a doubt that throughout the Persian period there continued to be fundamental differences of opinion in Judah concerning the attitude which should be adopted towards the descendants of the former northern kingdom of Israel.[23]

Williamson here refers to the ten tribes that broke away from Judah and Benjamin during the time of Rehoboam. Generally, according to Williamson and John A Thompson, there is evidence of considerable disagreement at the time of Chronicles concerning how "open" or "exclusive" a stance should be taken to those outside the confines of the group centered in Jerusalem."[24] Against this background, Ezra-Nehemiah employed an exclusive ethnic theology and Chronicles employed an inclusive ethnic theology.[25]

It is interesting to note that both Ezra-Nehemiah and the Chronicler appealed to history writing to advocate their theological views. Ezra-Nehemiah wrote the history of the return of exiles and the Chronicler rewrote the history of Israel in 1 Samuel-2 Kings. Both Ezra-Nehemiah and the Chronicler used the Priestly and Deuteronomistic documents, among others, as sources. However, they presented different theological points of view. The inclusive theology of the Chronicler is also perceptible in books like Ruth, Jonah, and Trito-Isaiah. Concurring this observation, McKenzie remarks on the Book of Jonah as follows:

> Some late linguistic features in the book indicate a date in the postexilic period (around 400 BCE). This date fits well with the themes of Yahweh's universal dominion and concern for all people, which surface in Jonah and which became especially pointed issues of debate in the postexilic period. These matters loom large in other biblical books from this period, such as Chronicles and Ezra-Nehemiah. Jonah was likely written to contribute to this theological debate.[26]

To me, the Ezra-Nehemiah view was not popular even in its own time among the Judeans. This is also demonstrated by the fact that the followers of Ezra and Nehemiah kept on deviating from their teachings.[27]

Lastly, one of the methods these authors used to justify their points of view is genealogies. I argue that genealogies can also be devices to project ideological viewpoints. An interesting observation about the genealogies in Chronicles and Ezra-Nehemiah is by James T. Sparks. The parallel of 1 Chronicles 9 is Nehemiah 11. According to Sparks, "Both profess to be lists of Jerusalem dwellers in the postexilic province of Yehud (1 Chr. 9:3; Neh. 11:3)."[28] In Chronicles, Ephraim and Manasseh are included while in Nehemiah they are excluded. Referring to these two texts (1 Chr. 9 and Neh. 11), Knoppers observes, "The differences between the catalogues enables one to see how the editors of each work have each gone their way with earlier material. Each has contextualized, edited, and supplemented the catalogue according to his interests."[29] Ezra-Nehemiah's interest was to exclude some, and the Chronicler's interest was to include all. The Chronicler held firmly to the conviction of *unity*, *cooperation*, and *contestation*.

By starting his historical retelling with Adam, the Chronicler pinpointed common origin for all humanity and thus a commonality within diverse ethnic groups. Commentating on this literary strategy, Jonker asserts, "Unlike the Deuteronomistic version, [the Chronicler][30] situates the history of God's people within the history of humankind." The Chronicler indicated his universalist or inclusivist approach while presenting the Pentateuch as a point of entry for his reconstruction of the history of Israel. This universalist or inclusivist approach "is also echoed in the closing of the book in 2 Chron. 36:22–23, where Cyrus, the Persian Emperor, is described as the great liberator of God's people."[31] Here, the Chronicler was fostering *unity* in diversity.[32] Also, the collaboration with King Hiram to build the temple in 2 Chronicles 2:11–16 indicates the importance of *cooperation*. This cooperation had been indicated earlier in the preparation of the building of the temple in 1 Chronicles 22:2–4 during the last days of King David as follows:

> [2]And David commanded to assemble the resident aliens who were in the land of Israel and appointed stone craftsmen to cut dressed stones to build the house of God.[3] And David provided much iron for nails for the doors of the gates and the seams, and abundant copper that could not be weighed,[4] and cedar timbers without number, for the Sidonians and Tyrians brought abundant cedars to David.

These verses do have parallels in Ezra 3:7; however, the foreigners are not mentioned, and the interaction with the Sidonians and Tyrians was "according to the authorization over them of Cyrus king of Persia," clearly distancing the exiles from interacting with foreigners. Lack of cooperation with King Neco of Egypt in the case of King Josiah led to a disaster. Lastly, the Chronicler also maintained *contestation* where he disagrees so as not to compromise his faith. Despite fostering unity with foreigners and encouraging cooperation with them, he maintained that there was one God; YHWH. He puts in the mouths of foreign kings praises of YHWH although they had their deities and the Chronicler praises none of those deities. He upheld unity, cooperation, and contestation. The arguments forwarded above should suffice to demonstrate why the Chronicler is a more appropriate candidate for a biblical theology in Africa.

To conclude this section, despite having argued for the Chronicler as a proper biblical paradigm, I do not claim that he is perfect. The Exodus paradigm was not perfect either but played the role of biblical paradigm for liberation theology successfully in Latin America and Africa. Eleazar S. Fernandez demonstrates this sentiment clearly when he says:

> Palestinians, as pointed out by Naim Ateek and Mitri Raheb, find the Exodus narrative extremely disturbing. When they read it, they do not identify with the conquering Israelites but with the resident Canaanites. Exodus, for them, becomes a mirror of their oppression as well as of God's identification with the oppressors. For the Palestinians, exodus signifies conquest, not liberation. As such, the exodus narrative becomes a narrative of terror. In resonance with the Palestinians, Robert Allen Warrior argues that American Indians identify with the Canaanites on the land, not with the conquering Israelites, in the exodus narrative. Like the biblical Canaanites, American Indians have also suffered conquest and genocide at the hands of those who escaped from the 'Old World' and laid claim to the promised land of the 'New World.' For American Indians, therefore, the exodus narrative proves a narrative of terror as well, an exodus-conquest narrative.[33]

A follow-up question would be if that is the case, why should Mugambi's Nehemiah not be a biblical paradigm for a theology of liberation in Africa? The answer is two-fold. First, Nehemiah stands for an adversarial theology, against a reciprocal theology. This contradicts what Mugambi himself is calling for. Joseph Blenkinsopp says,

> Nehemiah is presented not only as a member of the upper-class *golah* segment of the population but also as an exponent of the rigorist legalism which characterized Ezra and his associates. This quasi-sectarian orientation, with its roots in the eastern diaspora and its orientation heavily dependent on Deuteronomistic theology and the teaching of Ezekiel and his school, was a significant factor in Nehemiah's conflictual relations with the lay and especially the priestly aristocracy in the province. His ejection of Tobiah from the temple precincts and ritual purification of the space he had occupied (13:4–9) is one pointer in this direction.[34]

The point Blenkinsopp makes is that Nehemiah should not be understood separately from the ideology for which he staunchly stood. For example, in South Africa, it is difficult for non-white populations to make a model of a leader who entrenched Apartheid just because he had good economic policies for the minority white population. Second, Nehemiah has already been used before by the Apartheid, and Nazi ideologues[35] and the consequences were terrible. Such ideologues may re-emerge in the future and reconstruction theology should not make the soil fertile for them. As Farisani suggests, for Nehemiah to be meaningful for reconstruction, the text needs to be de-ideologized. At a time when sporadic xenophobic attacks have been experienced in South Africa and some parts of Africa, the xenophobic attitude in Ezra-Nehemiah should be discouraged. Also, given that ethnicity is a force to be reckoned with in Africa, Nehemiah should help us to be warned against exclusive ethnicity.

Reconstruction today

If the Ezra-Nehemiah model is problematic, reconstruction in Africa today needs to be a reciprocal project that engages all in the political community. Exiles and those who have stayed under political dictatorships have things they can and should contribute. In the current configurations in African countries, it need not be those who have gone into exile, but those members of the political community who have been side-lined for a long time – those men and women, boys and girls, who have been left in the political wilderness in Africa. Such an approach would embrace a theology which Mugambi suggests should be reciprocal and not adversarial. By reciprocal is meant that it must promote a spirit of partnership among different stakeholders instead of opposition. It should strive for community solidarity vis-à-vis social conflict. If one takes a perspective from social psychology, particularly those of Henri Tajfel and Jean-Claude Deschamps, one would argue that reconstruction should draw inspiration from covariation social categorization instead of simple social categorization. Such an approach is necessary because community solidarity facilitates reconstruction and social conflict retards it. In its endeavors to promote partnerships, it must uphold the principles of unity, cooperation, and contention. All this should be pursued to protect disadvantaged identity groups and recognize that traditional social categorizations have been challenged by the change in the social identity landscape.

Therefore, it is important for this forward-looking agenda to consider as a biblical paradigm for a theology of reconstruction in Africa the approach of the Chronicler. Like us today, the two books responded to their circumstances in the face of a changed political landscape. Ezra-Nehemiah did this by writing history after the exile to influence Second Temple thought patterns. For the same reason, the Chronicler re-wrote history before the exile. In McKenzie's words, "In the Bible . . . [h]istory was written for an ideological purpose. History writing was theology."[36] Ezra-Nehemiah embraced an exclusive ethnic theology while Chronicles embraced an inclusive one. Ezra-Nehemiah discriminated against non-exiled Judeans, the ten northern tribes of Israel, and non-Israelite ethnic groups. Chronicles, on the other hand, was impartial towards these groups. Ezra-Nehemiah's discriminatory tendencies led to a social conflict that stalled the reconstruction of the temple for no less than 20 years. Solomon's temple, which was bigger and more splendid, was built in seven years. Moreover, Ezra-Nehemiah was used by Apartheid and Nazi ideologues to perpetrate human rights violations against sections of their respective populations. These ideologues can be revived in the future and reconstruction theology should not help them. Third, the Chronicler displayed a unity-cooperation-contestation attitude that can be helpful for reconstruction. For the above reasons, I propose the Chronicler. I hope that this contribution is an additional "brick towards the rebuilding of the wall of Africa, then towards the rebuilding of our societies now in ruins."

Finally, the Chronicler calls the nation to a life of repentance and a return to God.[37] The Chronicler gives an insight into the spiritual conditions necessary for reconstruction. Although the text states that after Solomon dedicated the temple, God appeared to him and told Solomon that he would withhold blessings from the people if they sinned, what is significant then is the promise: "If my people who are called by my name, will humble themselves and pray and seek my face and turn from their wicked ways, then I will hear from heaven and I will forgive their sin and will heal their land." It is clear that the Chronicler highlights a text that is associated with Solomon's Temple. The text offers Africans today a model that calls for the examination of the life history of its nations – one that encourages taking a broad look in the search for appropriate paradigms of reconstruction. In this particular text, the message calls for a spiritual disposition that looks to

God for renewal. It is a return to God that is intentional, one that involves turning away from evil (unethical) practices to prepare for a season of blessing that will usher in reconstruction. The contrition necessary for reconstruction cannot be limited to what we see in Pentecostal spirituality today.[38] While Ezra and Nehemiah are strong leaders and exemplars of a focused vision, a spiritual disposition that embraces virtues of humility, especially by the political class, would go a long way in the reconstruction of Africa.

Notes

1 Villa-Vicencio Charles, *A Theology of Reconstruction*. (Cape Town: David Phillip, 1992).
2 J.N.K. Mugambi, *From Liberation to Reconstruction: African Christian Theology after the Cold War*. (Nairobi: East Africa Educational Publishers, 1995).
3 Elelwani B. Farisani, "The Use of Ezra-Nehemiah in a Quest for a Theology of Renewal, Transformation and Reconstruction in the (South) African Context." PhD dissertation, University of KwaZulu-Natal, 2002, 63.
4 J.N.K. Mugambi, "Theology of Reconstruction," in Isaac M. T. Mwase and Eunice K. Kamaara, eds. *Theologies of Liberation and Reconstruction*. (Nairobi: Acton, 2012), 18.
5 Mugambi, 1995, 2.
6 Mugambi, "Text and Context," 61; Ntozakhe Simon Cezula, "Identity Formation and Community Solidarity: Second Temple Historiographies in Discourse with (South) African Theologies of Reconstruction." PhD dissertation, Stellenbosch University, 2013, 33.
7 J. S. Ukpong, *The Emergence of African Theologies in Theological Studies* 45 (1984): 525.
8 Rothney Tshaka and Karabo Makofane, *The Continued Relevance of Black Liberation Theology for Democratic South Africa Today in Scriptura* 105 (2010): 543.
9 J.N.K. Mugambi, "Text and Context in Applied Christian Theology," in *Christian Theology and Social Reconstruction*. (Nairobi: Acton Publishers, 2003), 166.
10 Cf. Cezula, "Identity Formation," 41–9.
11 Mugambi, "Text and Context," 173.
12 Farisani, "The Use of Ezra-Nehemiah," 2002. See also Elelwani B. Farisani, "The Post-Exile Motif in Mugambi's Theology of Reconstruction," in I. M. T. Mwase and E. K. Kamaara, eds. *Theologies of Liberation and Reconstruction*. (Nairobi, Kenya: Acton Press, 2012), 219.
13 Farisani, "The Use of Ezra-Nehemiah," 86–7.
14 Ibid., 79.
15 Ibid., 86–7.
16 Tinyiko Maluleke, "The Proposal for a Theology of Reconstruction: A Critical Appraisal," *Missionalia*, 22, no. 2 (1994): 252–6.
17 Tinyiko Maluleke, "Mugambi, J.N.K. From Liberation to Reconstruction. African Christian Theology after the Cold War," *Missionalia*, 24, no. 1 (1996): 473.
18 Mugambi, "Theology of Reconstruction," 25.
19 Sara Japhet, Sheshbazzar and Zerubbabel, "Against the Background of the Historical and Religious Tendencies of Ezra-Nehemiah," *ZAW*, 94, no. 1 (1982): 67.
20 Steven L. McKenzie, *Introduction to the Historical Books: Strategies for Reading*. (Grand Rapids: Eisenbrauns, 2010), 21.
21 Ibid., 113.

22 Daniel L. Smith-Christopher, "Exile," in D. N. Freedman, ed. *Eerdmans Dictionary of the Bible.* (Grand Rapids: Eerdmans, 2000), 440. See also Waiting for the Lord: The Fulfilment of the Promise of . . ., http://scriptura.journals.ac.za/pub/article/download/1304/1227 (accessed September 6, 2017).
23 Hugh G. M. Williamson, *Studies in Persian Period History and Historiography.* (Tübingen: Mohr Siebeck, 2004), 23.
24 Williamson, "Studies in Persian Period," 24; J. A. Thompson, *1 & 2 Chronicles, New American Commentary*, v. 9 (Nashville: Broadman & Holman, 1994), 33.
25 Cezula, "Identity Formation," 118–93.
26 Steven L. McKenzie, *How to Read the Bible.* (Oxford: Oxford University Press, 2005), 19.
27 Ezra 9, Nehemiah, 9 and 13.
28 Thomas J. Sparks, *The Chronicler's Genealogies: Towards an Understanding of 1 Chronicles 1–9* (Atlanta: Society of Biblical Literature, 2008), 334.
29 Gary N. Knoppers, *1 Chronicles 1–9: A New Translation with Introduction and Commentary.* (New York: Doubleday, 2004), 80.
30 The insertion is the author's.
31 Louis C. Jonker, *1 and 2 Chronicles.* (Grand Rapids: Baker Academic Press, 2013).
32 Also 2 Chronicles 30 and 2 Chronicles 35 concerning unity with the northern tribes.
33 Eleazar S. Fernandez, *Exodus-toward-Egypt: Filipino-Americans' Struggle to Realize the Promised Land in America in The Postcolonial Biblical Reader*, R. S. Sugirtharajah, ed. (Oxford: Blackwell Publishing, 2006), 291.
34 Joseph Blenkinsopp, *Judaism, The First Phase: The Place of Ezra and Nehemiah in the Origins of Judaism.* (Grand Rapids: Eerdmans, 2009), 115.
35 Cezula, "De-Ideologizing Ezra-Nehemiah," 150–3.
36 McKenzie, "Introduction," 12.
37 I am indebted to Matthias Henze and Elias Kifon Bongmba for insights on this section of this chapter.
38 See Naomi Haynes, "Zambia Shall be Saved!': Prosperity Gospel Politics in a Self-Proclaimed Christian Nation," *Nova Religion, Journal of alternative and Emergent Religions*, 19, no. 1 (2015): 5–24.

Bibliography

Blenkinsop, Joseph. *Judaism, The First Phase: The Place of Ezra and Nehemiah in the Origins of Judaism.* Grand Rapids: Eerdmans, 2009.

Cezula, Ntozakhe S. "Identity Formation and Community Solidarity: Second Temple Historiographies in Discourse with (South) African Theologies of Reconstruction." Ph.D. dissertation, Stellenbosch University, 2013.

———. "De-Ideologizing Ezra-Nehemiah: Challenging Discriminatory Ideologies." In *Restorative Readings: The Old Testament, Ethics, and Human Dignity*, edited by L. Juliana Claassens, and Bruce Birch, 117–38. Eugen: Wipf & Stock, 2015.

———. "The Chronicler as a Biblical Paradigm for a Theology of Reconstruction in Africa: An Exploration of 2 Chronicles 6:32." *OTE* 29, no. 2 (2016): 277–96.

Farisani, Elelwani B. "The Use of Ezra-Nehemiah in a Quest for a Theology of Renewal, Transformation, and Reconstruction in the (South) African Context." Ph.D. dissertation, University of KwaZulu-Natal, 2002.

———. "The Post-Exile Motif in Mugambi's Theology of Reconstruction." In *Theologies of Liberation and Reconstruction*, edited by Isaac M. T. Mwase, and Eunice K. Kamaara, 198–223. Nairobi: Acton Publishers, 2012.

Fernandez, Eleazar S. “Exodus-toward-Egypt: Filipino-Americans’ Struggle to Realize the Promised Land.” In *America in The Postcolonial Biblical Reader*, edited by R. S. Sugirtharajah, 291–394. Oxford: Blackwell Publishing, 2006.

Gathogo, Julius. “Jesse Mugambi’s Pedigree: Formative Factors.” *Studia Historiae Ecclesiasticae* 32, no. 2 (2006): 173–205. http://hdl.handle.net/10500/4407. Accessed on 20/08/2016.

Japhet, Sara. Sheshbazzar and Zerubbabel. “Against the Background of the Historical and Religious Tendencies of Ezra-Nehemiah.” *ZAW* 94, no. 1 (1982): 66–98.

Jonker, Louis C. *1 and 2 Chronicles*. Grand Rapids: Baker Academic Press, 2013.

Knoppers, Gary N. *1 Chronicles 1–9: A New Translation with Introduction and Commentary*. New York: Doubleday, 2004.

Loba-Mkole, Jen-Claude. “Bible Translation and Reconstruction Hermeneutics” in *Theologies of Liberation and Reconstruction*, eds. I. M. T. Mwase and Eunice K. Kamaara, Nairobi: Acton Publishers, 2012, 146–170.

Mbiti, John S. Preface to *Theologies of Liberation and Reconstruction*, eds. I. M. T. Mwase and Eunice K. Kamaara, Nairobi: Acton Publishers, 2012, 1–4.

Maluleke, Tinyiko S. “The Proposal for a Theology of Reconstruction: A Critical Appraisal.” *Missionalia* 22, no. 2 (1994): 248.

———. “Mugambi, J.N.K. From Liberation to Reconstruction. African Christian Theology after the Cold War.” *Missionalia* 24, no. 1 (1996): 473.

McKenzie, Steven L. *How to Read the Bible*, Oxford: Oxford University Press, 2005.

———. *Introduction to the Historical Books: Strategies for Reading*, Grand Rapids: Eisenbrauns, 2010.

Mugambi, J.N.K. *From Liberation to Reconstruction: African Christian Theology after the Cold War*. Nairobi: East Africa Educational Publishers, 1995.

———. “Social Reconstruction in Africa: The Role of Churches.” In *The Church and Reconstruction of Africa: Theological Considerations*, edited by J. N. K. Mugambi, 1–25. Nairobi: All Africa Conference of Churches, 1997.

———. “Text and Context in Applied Christian Theology.” In *Christian Theology and Social Reconstruction*. Nairobi: Acton Publishers, 2003.

Smith-Christopher, Daniel L. “Exile.” *Eerdmans Dictionary of the Bible*, edited by D. N. Freedman, 439–40. Grand Rapids: Eerdmans, 2000.

Sparks, Thomas J. *The Chronicler’s Genealogies: Towards an Understanding of 1 Chronicles 1–9*. Atlanta: Society of Biblical Literature, 2008.

Thompson, J. A. *1 & 2 Chronicles*, New American Commentary, v. 9. Nashville: Broadman & Holman, 1994.

Tshaka, Rothney S. and M. Karabo Makofane. “The Continued Relevance of Black Liberation Theology for Democratic South Africa Today.” *Scriptura* 105 (2010): 532–46.

Villa-Vicencio, Charles. *A Theology of Reconstruction*. Cape Town: David Phillip, 1992.

Warrior, R. “A Native American Perspective: Canaanites, Cowboys, and Indians.” In *Voices from the Margin: Interpreting the Bible in the Third World*, edited by R. S. Sugirtharajah, 287–295. Maryknoll: Orbis Books, 1991.

Williamson, Hugh G. M. *1 and 2 Chronicles. New Century Bible Commentary*. London: Marshall Morgan & Scott, 1982.

———. *Studies in Persian Period History and Historiography*. Tübingen: Mohr Siebeck, 2004.

14 Reconstructing mission

The church in Africa in the service of justice, peace, and reconciliation

Philomena Njeri Mwaura

Introduction

This chapter addresses the following questions: What is mission today? What is the context of mission in Africa and what are its challenges? What does reconstructing mission mean and is there a need for it? Which are the markers of a mission theology of reconstruction? How can the Church in Africa be better equipped to carry out its missionary mandate?

These questions will be addressed in the light of Jesse N. K. Mugambi's view of the *theology of reconstruction* and the quest of the Church in Africa for justice, peace, and reconciliation in the midst of conflicts, poor leadership, and poor governance of the state. From the outset, mission implies the calling of the Church at every level to participate in the mission of the

> Triune God who created the world as an expression of love, power and creativity; who sustains and rules the universe, and who sent Jesus Christ into the world in the power of the Holy Spirit as a healing, liberating savior, who will bring about final reconciliation and restoration.[1]

This reflection will also consider the theme of the Second Catholic African Bishops Synod that was held in Rome in October 2009, namely, "The Church in Africa in Service to Reconciliation, Justice, and Peace." The subtitle of the theme was: "You are the salt of the earth. . . . You are the light of the world." Other questions to ponder related to the theme are: What does it mean to be the salt of the earth today in a world full of wealth and potential, but a world held captive by poverty, misfortune, disease, and wars? What does it mean to be the light of the world in a continent with a mature Christian faith, but laced with ethnic animosity, superficial faith, and divisions? Which missiological issues and options in this scenario are to be engaged?

Perceptions of mission

The meaning, context, dimensions, and perceptions of mission have changed and become multi-faceted, but Jesus' imperative to make disciples of all nations has not. Mission is not only the Church's activity in another context; rather, it is the frontier of belief, conviction, and commitment. The Catholic Church's understanding of mission is well articulated in the Vatican II document, Ad *Gentes* (Decree on the Church's Missionary Activity),[2] Pope Paul VI's Apostolic Exhortation *on Evangelization of Peoples (Evangelii Nuntiandi [1975])*,[3] and John Paul II's encyclical, *Redemptoris Missio*, among other Catholic social teachings. These documents describe mission as "proclaiming Christ and his Gospel, building the local Church and promoting the values of the Kingdom."[4]

The teachings remind the Church that mission is a divine madate that evangelizes as the Church encounters people with the good news of God's love proclaimed by Jesus Christ (Matt. 22:34–40; Jn. 3:16–17; 15:9–17). Evangelization invites people to accept the good news. It entails converting, heralding, or worshipping and an involvement in the world. The context of evangelization requires a proper understanding of the notion of salvation which implies liberation from all that oppresses and dehumanizes people, whether social, cultural, economic, political, spiritual, or personal. Mission in this understanding means regeneration of people in fundamental ways through the power of the gospel. Evangelization should bring about inner transformation in people, thus rendering them new creatures who witness God's transforming presence and activity in society. John Pobee perceives mission in an African context as enabling people to do the will of God, working for a community of communities, bringing wholeness and healing.[5]

By its very nature, the "Church exists by mission as fire exists by burning."[6] Mission creates the Church and bridges the gap between the Church and the Kingdom of God. The Church is called into being by the Father "who so loved the world that he gave his only Son that whoever believes in Him shall not perish but have eternal life" (John 3:16) and who sent the Holy Spirit to lead believers into truth.[7] The Church is a communion of those who have embraced the word of God and stand in a living relationship with God. The Church participates in the life of the Triune God, the source and focus of all communion. It is both a divine and a human institution. Its members are part of the body of Christ and open to the free activity of the Holy Spirit.

The Church in the world is still subject to the dynamics of the world. According to the World Council of Churches, the Church is open to both positive and negative developments; it is open to decline and distortion; it is open to the individual, to the cultural and historical power of sin, sometimes relativizing, sometimes absolutizing insights and expressions of faith.[8] It is therefore crucial that the Church be attuned to the signs of the times in order to respond creatively to changed and changing situations with new understandings and attitudes regarding its mission mandate.

Defining reconstruction

The term *reconstruction* gained prominence in theological discourse in Africa in the early 1990s in the context of theological consultations convened by the All Africa Conference of Churches. It was a notion inspired by the Russian word, *perestroika* (reconstruction), which inadvertently led to the demise of the Soviet Union and the *cold war* in 1989. Jesse Mugambi, a Kenyan theologian, Charles Villa-Vicencio of South Africa, Andre Karamaga of Rwanda, and Ka Mana of the Democratic Republic of Congo were among the foremost proponents of this theology. Their operating premise was that Christian theology is crucial to the social reconstruction of Africa. Mugambi perceived the emergence of the so-called New World Order as an important historical moment that presented opportunities and challenges for a new theological vision and strategy for action that would deal effectively with colonial and postcolonial legacies in Africa. He challenged African theologians to critically inquire into how Christianity can help Africans in the postcolony escape the vicious cycle of crises. What could the Churches do to promote conditions conducive to national and social harmony? Are Christians and related organizations in the respective countries and regions, agents of reconciliation and promoters of social change?

Mugambi has taken issue with the liberation and inculturation paradigms in theology insisting that those paradigms were no longer adequate as frameworks for African Theology. Both paradigms responded to the ecclesiastical and colonial bondage which no longer obtains and hence have been ineffective in responding to the multi-faceted challenges posed by the postcolonial context. The liberation-inculturation paradigm which was mainly "reactive," ought to be abandoned for a "proactive" *theology of reconstruction.*[9] Instead of "calling for the ascendancy of liberation over inculturation or vice-versa," Mugambi called for an innovative transcendence of both.[10] He proposed the post exilic motif exemplified in the Ezra-Nehemiah model as the embodiment of the new theological challenge, replacing the exodus motif which inspired liberation. Mugambi was convinced that a fresh reading of the Bible by Africans would reveal multiple illustrations of personal renewal and social reconstruction. Such a fresh reading is also derived from Isaiah 65:17–25. This text reflects the post-exilic period of the Jewish pilgrimage with reconstruction – restoration was very slow and difficult; the poor were being exploited. The prophet attempted to restore hope, to renew pure faith within the religious community. The text also envisages the reconstruction of a "new heaven" and a "new earth," a motif for imagining an alternative world, invoked by the World Forum for Theology and Liberation, the theological wing of the World Social Forum.

The notion of reconstruction, Mugambi admits, is borrowed from the disciplines of engineering and social sciences; it implies remodeling, redesigning, and the re-organizing of certain aspects of society to render it more responsive. Reconstruction implies change at the levels of the individual, society, Church, and nation. Reconstruction as a theological paradigm also finds its justification in the life and ministry of Jesus. The Sermon on the Mount (Matt. 5–7) is regarded as the most basic reconstructive theological text in the ministry of Jesus. The theme of reconstruction highlights a new inclusive society transcending barriers of geography, culture, historical moments, gender, age, class ethnicity, and race.

Villa-Vicencio appeals for a post-cold war theology for Africa to engage in serious dialogue with democracy, human rights, legislation, nation building, and economics to improve the quality of human life.[11] A theology of reconstruction as defined by Ka Mana seeks an alternative pattern of human destiny outside the determinism of crisis. He calls for a halt to the all-pervasive crises and for the reconstruction of African societies on a new basis. The task of the theology of reconstruction consists in re-adapting the ethical posture offered by the Christian faith to mobilize afresh creativity, energy, and dynamism with regard to the problems of African societies.[12]

In such a context, the mission of the Church consists in reconstruction through a triple strategy, namely: bringing awareness to Christian communities of the urgent need for self-empowerment vis-à-vis dehumanizing forces in every situation; bringing awareness among Christian communities with regard to the negatives of tribal or ethnic hegemony; and teaching Christian communities ways of living a genuine faith in Christ engaged in public affairs and avoiding a religiosity that is enchanted by the invisible.[13] Ka Mana's vision of mission for the Church in Africa today calls for "the re-evangelization of African societies in order to promote *anti-pharaoh* and *anti-baa* values, to grow seeds of life for the reconstruction of a human sphere in which Christians perform their duties as generators of active and creative hope."[14]

The theological vision articulated by these theologians is crucial to our understanding of the reconstruction mission. It promotes alternative biblical metaphors, symbols, and narratives together with an alternate hermeneutical understanding of African realities for purposes of creating new patterns of social transformation and community in Africa. How does the reconstruction paradigm inform mission theology?

Is there a need to reconstruct mission and to what purpose? Churches and mission scholars have criticized dominant mission paradigms, calling instead for "rethinking mission," "transforming mission," "transfiguring mission," and "new evangelization." Wilbert Shenk contends that mission is always susceptible to distortion or misdirection. Whenever the Church allows herself to be controlled by culture, she loses her sense of being in the stream of God's mission. Such accommodation indicates that a worldview such as modernity rather than the Gospel has become dominant for the Church in its mission.[15]

Some missiologists who have been uncomfortable with the interpretation and implementation of concepts of mission point out that some of the ideas and attitudes conveyed in mission thought and practice are not in accord with the project of Jesus Christ whose fundamental goal was "life in its fullness" for all humanity. The concept of "mission to the nations," dominant since the 15th century, was influenced by the ideology of Christendom but also implied a cultural triumphalism. Churches and missionary movement in the 20th century were plagued by reductionisms that limited the scope of the Gospel as Christians reacted to the challenges of modernism and fundamentalism.[16]

Magesa argues that rather than speaking of "mission to the nations" (*missio ad gentes*), we should speak of mission as "God's activity among the nations" (*missio intre gentes*). The "nations" to which God's mission (*mission Dei*) is targeted in this new understanding are not only peoples of "underdeveloped" or "undeveloped" nations in Africa, Asia, Latin America, and Oceania, but encompasses all people of all races of the world including "us," whoever and wherever "we," the evangelizers, may be.

The consequences of this understanding of mission and missionary activity are enormous and far reaching. First, it renders redundant previous dualistic notions of the missionary mandate which sent missionaries only to certain territories. Theologically, all nations are considered mission lands as far as the work of God is concerned. All human beings, all societies are receivers and potential givers of God's grace. All peoples need to be "discipled" in the way of Christ regardless of when or how long they have been exposed to the faith. Second, this understanding also informs the methods of mission. If every person, nation, or culture is in need of being evangelized, then evangelization cannot be carried out in a uniform manner. It means that considerations of culture, group identity, human dignity, and respect for religious pluralism become imperative. Dialogue is therefore a crucial component of mission. At this point let us briefly consider the African context in which mission is taking place in the 21st century.

The necessity of mission for Africa

Africa is a context that bespeaks two diametrically opposed stories. One is a story of frustration and the cries of children; women and men who are tired of unending debt; poverty; unlimited exploitation of their natural and human resources and who desperately seek to end the misery caused by civil wars; ethnic conflicts; inept and unaccountable leadership; debilitating diseases including Ebola, HIV/AIDS; and the mismanagement of national affairs and resources. The other story is one of a vibrant Christianity, a rich spirituality that engenders hope amid this apparent chaos. There is joy in community life, in the African values of solidarity, mutual caring, reverence for God; a dynamic engagement with spiritual forces is experienced and shared. Nevertheless, the Church is fragmented, seemingly unable to collaborate ecumenically. Night and day exist side by side in modern Africa.

It is a fact that Christianity is growing exponentially in Africa. According to select statistical indicators, in the 20th century, the proportion of Africans who are Christians rose from nine percent of the whole to almost half. According to the *World Christian Encyclopedia*, "African Christians have mushroomed from 9.9 million (0.6 percent) of the world's population to 300 million in 2000 AD (89 percent). The present net increase on the continent is 8.4 million Christians a year (23,000 a day) of which 1.5 million are new converts."[17] As in the rest of the two-thirds world, what is drawing Africans to Christianity is the power of the Gospel to change the individual and the individual's personal circumstances, and it is the key to social transformation of the modern world. The Gospel message of the love of God resonates with those who struggle for survival, for justice, and for peace.

There is tremendous revival in the Church as is evidenced by the multiplication of new Pentecostal Christian groups and charismatic renewal within Protestant and Catholic faith communities. These are reminiscent of the pietistic-Wesleyan movements in the 17th and 18th centuries. Methodism fostered a new religious climate in England, making people more aware of their fellow citizens and more responsive to their needs. It infused a new philanthropic impulse into English society that stimulated humanitarian concern resulting in societal action, a unifying value for the whole nation. Unfortunately for Africa, numerical growth has not resulted in a transformational spirituality that fosters Christian and national identity. Ethnicity is a demon threatening to tear apart both the nation state and the Church.

The *Lineamenta* (the promotion of the Kingdom of God, which is reconciliation, justice, and peace), a preparatory document for the Second Special Assembly for Africa, is regarded as crucial to the identity and relevance of the Church in Africa, hence the choice of these issues in the theme of the 2009 Assembly. The document identified socio-economic, cultural, socio-political, ecumenical, minority, migration, inter-religious dialogue, violence, gender injustice, and environmental concerns, among others, all to be included in the Church's fruitful missionary engagement. The first African Synod held in 1994 under the general theme of "Evangelization" explored topics of inculturation, dialogue, justice, peace, and communication. Its theological vision was captured with the descriptive phrase, "The Family of God," referring to the Church in Africa. Much theological reflection on the theme has been generated; but the Church is far from fully realizing the implied goals.

The disputed 2007/2008 presidential election crisis in Kenya bespoke a deep ethnic hatred, unaddressed historical injustices from the colonial period, social exclusion especially of the youth, unemployment, economic injustice, poverty, and competing political interests; the episode tested the nature and integrity of the Church in Kenya. Her participation in God's mission was questioned, calling for an evaluation and reconstruction of her mission theology.

The Church's initiative in welfare provision, emergency relief, pastoral care, and general presence among the dispossessed is commendable. However, Christians expected more bold and prophetic leadership, demonstrating that the Church is really the *conscience of the nation*, reflecting a preferential option for the poor. Amid political interests, distortion of history, hate and ethnic propaganda proclaimed by competing political parties, generally polarized along ethnic lines, Kenya's Christian population sought guidance from their political and religious leaders. The Muslims took a stand, but most of the Church leaders, whether evangelical, Catholic, Pentecostal, Protestant, or Independent, told their adherents to abide by their respective consciences. This was bewildering advice, given that people in Kenya generally trust and depend on the guidance of their religious leaders. Many Christians are illiterate or semi-literate without the capacity to make informed choices and decisions; their consciences are not well formed, they still rely on the authority of their leaders.

As a consequence there was unprecedented ethnic violence in Kenya, reminiscent of Rwanda's experience of 1994 in which "born again" Christians hacked neighbors to death, maimed others for life, destroyed property and livelihoods, raped women and girls, and displaced over 350,000 people, some of whom are still living in designated camps. In Kenya, the death toll exceeded 1300. The Church responded to the humanitarian crises wonderfully, but what people really wanted to hear was a message of hope, reconciliation, justice, and a creative political intervention in the crisis. The tragedy of December 2007–February 2008 in Kenya shook the Christian Church to its foundations. Christians and clergy were victims of the violence at the hands of fellow Christians. Hallowed Church buildings where people sought refuge were burned to the ground; in one incident 35 people inside a burning Church died. Until now, justice for the victims and reconciliation of the nation has not taken place.

The crisis divided the Church and in some cases led to a splintering of congregations. By its silence, the Church was accused of complicity, abetting the evil. On February 15, 2008, the National Council of Churches of Kenya apologized to Kenyans for its failure to provide moral leadership, while other Churches including the Catholic Church preferred to apportion blame to individuals rather than to Church leadership. In this regard, a priest in one mainline Church later remarked, "Religious leaders persist in keeping a safe distance from the critical effort of reconstruction, choosing instead to criticize politicians as they fumble in their attempts to rebuild our society's relationships."[18]

The Church in Africa has failed in some respects to promote an authentic Christian identity in the form of communities that transcend barriers of ethnicity. At the time, a Catholic priest attributed the failure of Christians to live up to their calling and gospel values in the 2007/2008 political crisis in Kenya to the absence of quality formation. He said there is need for a deep-rooted evangelization in which African values of life such as mutual responsibility, reciprocity, and respect for relationships with people and with the earth, align with Christian values. He also said that there is need for prophetic, spiritual and sincere leadership for the Church in Kenya to regain its moral authority. The Church's ecclesiology and mission needs thorough evaluation; there is need for Christians to understand themselves and their roles in the world following model leaders of the Church. Numerical growth of the African Church must be matched by deep catechesis if it is to escape the fate of the ancient North African Church which expanded numerically, but because of its shallowness could not withstand the encounter with Islam in the 7th century.

Other challenges face the Church in Africa. Today, 19 of the 54 African nations are experiencing conflicts and wars. While we thank God that the Church is growing numerically and that vocations to the priesthood and religious life are increasing, the depth of faithful commitment must be given diligent attention. The task of reconciliation, justice, and peace is of utmost concern and priority.[19] People expect the Church to take leadership. According to Buri,

> Politicians are working hard to connect with the people. But regrettably, religious institutions, which already performed poorly in guiding the country during and after the December 2007 elections are not arising to the occasion. Their presence is hardly felt, and their participation ranks well below that of secular charitable organizations.[20]

There must be a focus on ways to promote genuine peace, premised on justice and development. The Churches' involvement in peace building, conflict resolution, civic education, anti-gun campaigns, and advocacy for human rights and economic justice is remarkable. However more spirited efforts are required, based on Gospel, not on secular approaches.

Another issue related to the promotion of human dignity is that of the HIV/AIDS pandemic and related gender injustice. The HIV/AIDS pandemic requires a holistic approach; it is more than merely a medical or moral issue; it is a matter of social justice aggravated by poverty which is a result of bad governance. The stigma associated with HIV/AIDS prevents "victims" from enjoying life to the full. The Church has not addressed gender issues which include the ordination of women, amongst much else. Women must be involved in decision making at all levels, promoting the rights of the girl and boy child. Gender-based violence must be addressed as a moral, theological, and social issue, buttressed by sermons, catechetical training, and focused discussions conducted by small Christian communities. If the Church is to be relevant, it needs to advocate for social justice, for the equitable distribution of resources and for the dignity of people. Economic growth during the last ten years in countries like Kenya, Malawi, Zambia, South Africa, Tanzania, and Uganda has not translated into marked improvement in the livelihoods of people. The gap between the rich and poor classes has widened; people have expressed their frustration through ethnic and xenophobic violence as witnessed in Kenya and South Africa, especially in 2008.

The Church must create a balance between providing service, proclaiming the Gospel, and exercising the prophetic role, otherwise there will be no difference between it and secular non-governmental organizations. Her commitment to issues of justice, peace, and reconciliation should go beyond pastoral letters that denounce conflicts, corruption, and foreign debt. There must be deep pastoral involvement that fosters faith, promotes the catechesis of children and adults, enhances prayerful liturgies, and inspires the spiritual depth of families toward a genuinely authentic African Church. The Church, especially former mission Churches, must become more self-reliant in terms of its theology and mission, based on a creative and dynamic accountability in all Church affairs. Peter Henriot, in writing about the Catholic Church in Zambia, observed, "We still have a long way to go before we can say that mechanisms of participation, guarantees of human rights and openness of decision making are fully adopted in the Church."[21] What does reconstructing mission mean in the African context? What is the future of mission in Africa? To these issues the discussion now turns.

Towards a holistic mission

Although the future of mission is ultimately in God's hands, it is the privilege of human beings to shape it based on understandings from the past and present. The Church comprises the whole people of God including individuals and groups responding to the law of Christ whose eternal admonition is to express love to others. The Church must continue to renew itself and its mission. For any individual or group to live fully, mistakes of the past must be corrected and a better vision for the future must be charted. Christians live in the spirit of repentance or *metanoia*. What does this mean in practical terms? In the face of seemingly hopeless and precarious situations, the Church must live and exercise its mission in such a manner as to be a sign and an instrument of change and hope that is rooted in the Paschal mystery.

Promoting peace-building, justice, and reconciliation

The deep hurts and pains that the African continent has experienced invite the Church to promote peace, reconciliation, and healing. It calls for an ecumenical mission and vision that accompanies people who are suffering from HIV/AIDS, ethnic conflicts, gender violence, child abuse, and other forms of distress. As people of God it is our moral duty to stand up for justice and to speak out when ethical norms are violated. Ethnic hatred and xenophobia challenge the African Church to live the life and love of Christ. "Othering" regards those unlike "us" as less human or unworthy and turns on differences such as gender, class, race, disability, and even religion/faith. Difference should be celebrated rather than serve as a source of division. The Church must reject the malady of "otherness" and foster what Miroslav Volf calls a "theology of embrace." He observes, "The future of the whole world depends on how we deal with ethnic, religious and gender otherness."[22] Volf considers that the inability to relate to each other touches on the core theological beliefs with regard to reconciliation and the Church's social responsibility.

Furthermore, an individuated pietistic and evangelical Christianity (prevalent in Europe and America) has placed little focus on social reconciliation.

Faith is a matter of the soul's relationship with God; an exclusive emphasis on private morality based on an individual's relationship with God leads to an aversion towards the world and the other. Could this be the problem at the root of ethnic animosity among Christians? The social dimension of reconciliation was central to human and communal relationships in traditional Africa. This is a resource the Church can tap into as it develops new dynamic ways of being Church and as it addresses the injustice of social and political strife.

The Church in Africa should see her mission as bringing wholeness to people as Jesus did. Jesus' ministry was grounded in *Shalom*, an Old Testament concept of peace connoting harmony and wellbeing. Shalom bespeaks justice, healed relations between individuals in society, between God and humanity and between humanity and the rest of creation. One of the greatest challenges for the Church is reconstruction in a post war context. This is where confession, forgiveness, reconciliation, and healing are necessary. Reconciliation should not be a hasty process; it should respect and restore human dignity. It should be seen as a process that leads victims to discover the mercy of God welling up their lives. It is discovering God's reconciliation through Christ. It is allowing the Holy Spirit to bring forgiveness and reconciliation among both victims and perpetrators who were hurting. As Esther Mombo asserts, "For reconciliation to be there, the victim must forgive, the perpetrators cannot forgive themselves. That forgiveness must carry something of the unboundedness of grace that God gives. We must not count trespasses more than God does."[23]

Discipling the nations

Commenting on the apparent superficiality and nominal nature of African Christianity, Madu notes that as long as Africa's cherished ideals and values are not fulfilled by the Gospel, its cogency for the African must be questioned: "Is this the Christ or shall we look for another?"[24] This is a challenge to an uninculturated evangelization. The future of mission and the Church in Africa depends on sound, committed, and honest theological reflection and not merely on numerical strength. There is need for continuous comprehensive, integrated, and systematic formation of the catechesis. The emphasis in the catechesis should be on learning and living the faith, a catechesis that facilitates a living, personal, and communal encounter with the risen Lord. This will promote moral behavior, mutual concern, and responsibility.

The Good News is about transforming cultures. When people have the Good News and turn to God in Jesus Christ, they respond in new ways to community structures, rituals and celebrations, reflection, and spirituality. Doing mission in a holistic and transformational manner implies a surrender of ourselves to Christ to be purified, sanctified, and renewed. It calls for confronting and transforming our lives and institutions to be like him. Until the Gospel effects this transformation by being inculturated in the

African context, we shall continue to lament an "uncompleted mission," a "superficial Gospel" and a "schizophrenic Christianity." Sustained theological engagement and formation constitutes a major challenge to Christian mission in Africa.

Prophetic leadership

For effective mission, there is need for a courageous, empowered, and committed leadership. Our Church leaders must have pastoral integrity. A leader must be dependable, must uphold justice, and must possess convictions and courage. Church leaders must embody integrity, dignity, and humility as modelled by Jesus. The Kenyan Church failed to provide moral leadership by taking sides in the political crises that engulfed the nation in the post-election period of 2008. They failed to serve as the conscience of the nation. Theological education/formation is crucial to developing this type of leadership. A visionary leadership must engage in a dynamic and informed way with the myriad issues confronting the African continent.

Dialogue as a way of mission

Africa is a continent of diverse nations, cultures, and religions. Expressing integrity in mission calls for an awareness of this pluralist context, recognizing that Christians can only fulfill their mission mandate in collaboration. Dialogue has not been a common practice in the Church due to fundamentalist currents, and due to the misuse of the power of religion by economic and political vested interests. We need to listen to one another in order to effectively proclaim the Good News. In the process of mutual listening, there is mutual learning and our common experience of God is deepened, facilitating common living in dignity with others.

Witness to the marginalized

For the Church's mission in Africa to be relevant, it must be inclusive and bring Shalom to the marginalized. To be Church in Africa is to offer "good news" for humanity, for the poor, and for the deprived who seek fullness of life. These are the women, men, and children, victims of economic and political injustices. Women and the girl child are especially oppressed by patriarchy, both in Church and in society. The reconstruction of mission calls for dismantling patriarchal praxis and power structures that prevent people from experiencing the liberating power of God. In an insightful article on the Church and HIV/AIDS, Orobator observes, "In the context of HIV/AIDS, the face of the Church as a multi-sectoral, ministering and healing community has a distinctively feminine profile. This profile or face embodies an important aspect of identity and mission, namely Church as mother."[25]

This dimension is visible in the many ways that women provide care to the infected and affected. The spiritual and social accompaniment, compassion, and commitment provided by women responding to HIV/AIDS are integral to the identity and mission of the Church. The same can be said of women as healers and peacemakers in conflict situations. A renewed or reconstructed mission should value the contribution of women in all situations and accord them greater freedom in representing the profound reality of Church as mother to the rest of society. A renewed Church must deconstruct the structures of gender-based discrimination in Church and society. The image of the Church as a caring community is tarnished by its knowing or inadvertent oppression and discrimination of women.

The youth is another category forgotten by the Church and society. They are acclaimed as leaders of tomorrow, but they wait forever to take the mantle from their elders. They are a resource that the Church is not adequately utilizing. The modern missionary movement owes its success to the committed and untiring efforts of youth worldwide through organizations such the Young Men Christian Association, the Young Women Christian Association, the World Student Christian Federation, and the Student Christian Movement. Youth departments are typically the most underfunded and undervalued sub-sectors in many Churches. This needs to change. It is not surprising that young people are moving to charismatic Churches that feature relatively young membership and provide more fulfilling opportunities for participation and leadership. Unfortunately, some young people drop out of the Church entirely and do not join another one. Some have never been evangelized. These become fodder for politicians in both urban and rural areas. This situation needs serious attention, especially in urban slums. It has been observed that many mainline Churches are reluctant to engage in "slum ministry"; and indeed the Church in the slums does not perceive itself as part of the larger Church. Most of the clergy serving in urban slums are foreign missionaries. The local Church is therefore challenged to be engaged.

Conclusion

The Church in Africa is growing as evidenced by the number on Christians in the continent; by the increase in vocations; by the increasing number of local clergy; by the educational, health, and pastoral institutions; and by the development of projects and programmes aimed at uplifting the lives of people. Mission in terms of proclamation and witness has succeeded. However, this numerical growth is not matched by the moral transformation of people, a malady that is visible in the frequent and persistent ethnic conflicts, corruption, impunity, and disregard for healthy relationships among fellow human beings. Mission is not an event or a condition; it is a process and an ongoing task. We Christians are continually becoming Christians. Therefore discipling is an ongoing task if Christians are to love and live the life to which Christ calls us. With regard to the question: "Africa, where are you going?," I agree with the Lineamenta and Mugambi: there is need for a renewed vision for mission in Africa and for the pursuit of a theology of reconstruction. It must change Africa's destiny so that reconciliation will replace hatred and divisions, and peace and justice will prevail. It is a vision that calls for imagining another world, centered on Christ who is the fullness of life, our Reconciler, our Peace, our Justice, and our Hope.

Notes

1 www.fmc-canada.org/global/resources/theology _mission 2006 pdf. A Theology of Mission for Free Methodist World Mission: 4 Downloaded May 26, 2008.
2 Walter M. Abbot, ed. *Documents of Vatican II.* (London: Geoffrey Chapman, 1967), 580–630.
3 Paul VI, Evangelii Nuntiandi, Austine Flannery, ed. *Vatican Council II, More Conciliar Documents.* (Leominister Herefords: Fowler Wright Books, 1982), 711–61.
4 John Paul II, *Redemptoris Missio.* (Nairobi: Pauline's Publications, 1980), 33.
5 John S. Pobee, "Lord, Creator-Spirit, Renew and Sustain the Whole Creation," *International Review of Mission* 29 (April 1990): 55.
6 Emil Brunner, *The Word and the World.* (London: Student Christian Movement Press, 1931), 108.
7 WCC, *The Nature and Mission of the Church: A Stage in the Way to a Common Statement.* (Geneva: WCC, 2005), 11.
8 Ibid., 30.
9 Mugambi, *From Liberation to Reconstruction*, 11–13.
10 Tinyiko Sam Maluleke, "African Theology," in David F. Ford and Rachel Muers, eds. *The Modern Theologies: An Introduction to Christian Theologies since 1918* (Oxford: Blackwell, 2005), 496.
11 Charles Villa-Vicencio, *A Theology of Reconstruction: Nation-building and Human Rights.* (Cape Town: David Phillip Publishers, 1992).
12 Ka Mana cited in Valentin Deji, *Reconstruction and Renewal in Africa in Christian Theology.* (Nairobi: Acton Publishers, 2003), 120–1.
13 Ibid., 122.
14 Ibid.
15 Wilbert Shenk, ed. *The Transfiguration of Mission: Biblical Theological and Historical Foundations.* (Scottdale: Herald Press, 1993), 11.
16 Shenk, *The Transfiguration of Mission*, 11.
17 David B. Barrett, et al. *World Christian Encyclopedia: Comparative Survey of Churches and Religions in the Modern World. Vol. 1.* Second Edition. (New York: Oxford University Press, 2001), 5.
18 Buri Edward, "The Displaced Are a Test of Our Freedom," *Sunday Nation*, 27th April 2008, 24.
19 For the urgent need to promote justice, peace and reconciliation All Africa Conference of Churches, 10th General Assembly and Golden Jubilee Celebrations Report. (Nairobi: AACC, 2014).
20 Ibid.
21 Peter Henriot, "AMECEA and the Second African Synod," *New People*, no. 114 (May–June 2008), 20.
22 Miroslav Volf cited in Anne-Marie Kool, "The Church in Hungary, Central and Eastern 'Trends and Challenges'," *The Princeton Seminary Bulletin*, XXVIII, no. 2 (2007), 149.
23 Esthe Mombo, "Building a Culture of Peace Through Reconciliation from a Christian Religious Perspective," in Mary N. Getui and W. Musyoni, eds., *Overcoming Violence: A Faith Based Response.* (Nairobi: NCCK, 2004), 144.

24 Madu Emeka, "The Place of African Culture on Christian Practice: Food for Thought for Nigeria's Major Seminaries," *African Christian Studies*, 19, no. 3 (2003), 34.
25 A. E. Orobator, "When AIDS Comes to the Church," in Benezet Buju and M. Czerny, eds. *AIDS in Africa: Theological Reflections*. (Nairobi: Paulines, 2007), 124.

Bibliography

Abbot, Walter M., ed. *Documents of Vatican II*. London: Geoffrey Chapman, 1967.

All Africa Conference of Churches. *10th General Assembly and Golden Jubilee Celebrations Report*. Nairobi: All Africa Conference of Churches, 2014.

Barrett, David B. et al. *World Christian Encyclopedia: Comparative Survey of Churches and Religions in the Modern World. Vol. 1*, Second Edition. New York: Oxford University Press, 2001.

Deji, Valentin. *Reconstruction and Renewal in Africa in Christian Theology*. Nairobi: Acton Publishers, 2003.

Edward, Buri. "The Displaced Are a Test of Our Freedom." *Sunday Nation*, April 27, 2008, 24.

Emeka, Madu. "The Place of African Culture on Christian Practice: Food for Thought for Nigeria's Major Seminaries." *African Christian Studies* 19, no. 3 (2003): 34.

Henriot, Peter. "AMECEA and the Second African Synod." *New People* no. 114 (May–June 2008): 20.

John, Paul II. *Redemptoris Missio*. Nairobi: Pauline's Publications, 1980.

Kool, Anne-Marie. "The Church in Hungary, Central and Eastern 'Trends and Challenges.' *The Princeton Seminary Bulletin* XXVIII, no. 2 (2007).

Maluleke, Tinyiko Sam. "African Theology." In *The Modern Theologies: An Introduction to Christian Theologies since 1918*, edited by David F. Ford, and Rachel Muers. Oxford: Blackwell, 2005.

Mombo, Esther. "Building a Culture of Peace Through Reconciliation from a Christian Religious Perspective." In *Overcoming Violence: A Faith Based Response*, edited by Mary N. Getui, and W. Musyoni, 144. Nairobi: NCCK, 2004.

Mugambi, J.N.K. *From Liberation to Reconstruction: African Christian Theology After the Cold War*. Nairobi: EAPH, 1995.

Orobator, A. E. "When AIDS Comes to the Church." In *AIDS in Africa: Theological Reflections*, edited by Benezet Buju, and M. Czerny, 124. Nairobi: Paulines, 2007.

Paul, Pope VI. "Evangelii Nuntiandi." In *Vatican Council II, More Conciliar Documents*, edited by Austine Flannery. Leominister Herefords: Fowler Wright Books, 1982.

Pobee, John S. "Lord, Creator-Spirit, Renew and Sustain the Whole Creation." *International Review of Mission* 79 (April 1990): 55.

Shenk, Wilbert, ed. *The Transfiguration of Mission: Biblical Theological and Historical Foundations*. Scottdale: Herald Press, 1993.

Villa-Vicencio, Charles. *A Theology of Reconstruction: Nation-building and Human Rights*. Cape Town: David Phillip Publishers, 1992.

World Council of Churches. *The Nature and Mission of the Church: A Stage in the Way to a Common Statement*. Geneva: WCC, 2005.

Part III

Future trajectories on religion and theology in a global context

15 The reality of African religio-cultural identity in the context of globalization

Peter Mutuku Mumo

Introduction

One of the central themes of Professor Mugambi's work has been the cultural and religious identity of the African people. In this chapter, I discuss the reality of African cultural identity in the context of globalization. I use African religio-cultural identity instead of African religious identity because African religious experience is incorporated in all aspects of life. I argue that the African scholars should reclaim the continent's religio-cultural identity especially in the wake of globalization in order to reform and restore their societies.

The centrality of religion in the African culture

Religion plays a key role in giving Africans their identity. Culture and religion are interwoven in Africa and shape identity. John Mbiti has argued, "Africans are notoriously religious and each people have its religious system with a set of beliefs and practices. Religion permeates into all the departments of life so full that it is not easy or possible always to isolate it."[1] Mbiti has called for critical study of the religious system of Africa because it is an important way of understanding the spiritual resources Africans deploy as they wrestle with the complexity of their lives in a modern context.[2]

New religions and modernizing institutions that were introduced in Africa extended the diversity of religions and practices that enhanced a sense of self, identity, and community. The new religions and institutions were intended to transform Africans and develop a new identity based on the values of the new religions and modernity, but the religious traditions have survived and thrived. For example, Islam has been in Eastern African since the 7th century, and Christianity has been in the region longer. Both religions have introduced new cultural forms. The introduction of Islam in the region also introduced Arabization. The interaction between Arabs and Africans led to the development of Swahili culture which enabled African Muslims to retain their African identity. Despite the vigorous missionary enterprises, colonization, modernization, secularization, and globalization,

African religio-cultural identity is still viable. Aspects of African religio-cultural identity have been carried into the African diaspora and today are manifested in the daily lives of Africans in the diaspora and demonstrate that any group of people will only advance when they come to terms with their identity.

Mugambi has championed the protection of African cultural values from his student days at the University in Kenya. In a departmental meeting in honour of one of the founding members of the department Prof. Joseph Nyasani, Mugambi told members how as a first-year student, a lecturer drew the religious geographical map of the world without including African Religion as part of it. This was a class on Comparative Religion, and because the lecturer was absent the head of the department Dr. Stephen Neil stepped in, and it was Dr. Neil who drew a map of the geographical distribution of religions of the world and left out African Religion. The shocked students asked why African Religion was omitted, and Dr. Neil responded that African Religion is not one of the religions of the world. One student in the class responded by saying that J. S. Mbiti had written and shown African Religion as the dominant religion in Africa. Dr. S. Neil laughed and said J.S. Mbiti was neither a scholar nor authority in religion. This encounter moved Mugambi to pursue further studies in religious studies and prove to the world that African Religion is a religion just like the other religions of the world. Mugambi has succeeded enormously because he and many other African scholars have demonstrated convincingly that African Religion is a religion like others and that in the globalized world it has its rightful place.

The significance of African religio-cultural identity

Mugambi argues that no society has ever advanced without first rediscovering its origins and asserting its identity.[3] Citing European countries, he argues that it was after they asserted their identities that they made advancements in all the pillars of their cultures.[4] After colonialism and missionary evangelization of African societies, a dilemma was created on African religio-cultural identity. The beneficiaries of colonialism and evangelization were divided on whether to embrace the new identity introduced by the missionaries and western culture or to go back to their African identity. Africa has gone through drastic changes in the last 100 years. The implementers of the changes were very systematic with already determined outcomes. Due to the socialization in Euro-American cultures, some Africans are attracted by aspects of western culture such as dressing, food, a mass media culture, art, design, and architecture.

The result today is what N.W. Ndung'u describes as the two perspectives with which Africans live: their Christian worldview and African culture and worldview. When people face a crisis, they turn to cultural beliefs and ways of solving those problems and do not see that as a contradiction.[5] Despite prejudices and modern attractions to the western lifestyles that have beset African identity, Africans have not abandoned their cultures. Ndung'u asserts correctly that when Africans are confronted with survival needs, they turn to their heritage. African identity is specifically acquired during transitional rites such as birth, initiation, marriage, and death.[6] This may explain why circumcision rites have persisted among some African communities.

The debate around this cultural practice demonstrates that not everything that was done in the past is accepted by everybody today. In Kenya, for example, the constitution of 2010 prohibits female circumcision, but some communities continue to circumcise girls. In Ngugi Wa Thiongo's classic novel in 1965, *The River Between*, the character of Muthoni insisted that she wated to be circumcised so that she becomes a woman.[7] Muthoni said, "Look, please, I want to be a woman. I want to be a real girl, a real woman knowing all the ways of the hills and ridges."[8] Muthoni wanted to do this and still be a Christian because she did not see any contradiction in being a Christian and living according to the culture of her people. The character of Muthoni represents African desire to live like Christians and celebrate their cultural identity. Muthoni stated,

> I too have embraced the white man's faith. However, I know it is beautiful to be initiated into womanhood. You learn the ways of the tribe. Yes, the white man's God does not quite satisfy. I want, I need something more.[9]

When Muthoni was eventually circumcised, she said, "I am a woman now." However, unfortunately she died. This continues to happen in contemporary Africa. Therefore, my reference to this account does not condone questions raised about the safety or propriety of female genital cutting. I refer to it to demonstrate that Africans have argued that one can balance religion and culture. However, the death of Muthoni in the novel should give readers something to reflect on the propriety of certain practices.

Another area where cultural claims have been contested is in marriage life. Mugambi narrates the court proceedings on the S.M Otieno case in Kenya to show the identity crises Kenyans face in contemporary society. He writes, "It turned out that Kenyans are interested in finding out whether African cultural and religious heritage could serve as the basis for resolving the crisis of identity in a nation undergoing rapid social transition."[10] The Courts ruled in favour of African traditions, and S.M Otieno was buried in Siaya in Kenya.

In recent times, in Africa and especially Kenya has been faced with social problems such as greed, corruption, individualism, selfishness, divorce, promiscuity, drug abuse, and political instability. It is quite evident that foreign ideologies and moral codes have not solved the basic problems African societies are facing in the contemporary society. It goes without saying that Africans would continue to benefit from outside innovations as it often happened when two cultures meet. Certain innovations are not culture bound as they can be applied across cultures. Yet it is the case that other cultures cannot be allowed to dominate and work for the extinction of other cultures. Writing on globalization, Lata Dani says that what the world needs today is unity, harmony and not uniformity of cultures.[11] N.W. Ndung'u writes, "The persistence of African cultural practices which were condemned a century ago by western Christian missionaries is a proof of the importance attached to them by the communities in which they are practiced."[12]

Colonialism, missions, modernity, and globalization on Africa religio-cultural identity

Modernization was introduced in Africa by both the colonialists and western missionaries. Modernization refers to both intellectual and technological advances that have had an impact on the development and the use of technology, introduced different economic theories and practices to promote economic and social development, political ideologies, and different modes of political participation and protest where necessary.[13] Religious missionaries introduced modern practices in Africa. In many places modernization was tantamount to westernization and the transformation of African societies. For example, missionaries demanded that Africans drop their traditional structures and ways of thinking. Conversion for some Africans entailed burning cultural artifacts which missionaries erroneously described as idols and belonged to the devil. In most cases, the items of devil included African aesthetics such as beads, necklaces, and other artistic works.[14] Therefore the version of modernization that denigrated cultural practices eroded African religio-cultural identity. One way this practice was glaring was that on becoming Christians, Africans were required to accept western names. N.W. Ndungu writes,

> To the missionaries, Africans had to be transformed through the gospel for them to acquire a new identity befitting a civilized people. To achieve this goal, traditional cultural beliefs and practices had to be destroyed in order to have a tabula rasa on which the superior European culture and gospel were to be inscribed.[15]

After the Berlin conference of 1884–1885 African countries were shared by the major European countries. Missionaries went along the new political demarcations and together with colonials they introduced changes through schools, health services, new agricultural methods, modern hygienic methods, among others. These developments transformed social and economic moods of production in a colonial context that benefited the colonial powers. From the middle of the 20th century, African countries started attaining their political independence.

Africa in a global era

After the end of colonialism and collapse of communism in Eastern Europe, the dominant economies of the world embarked on globalizing the world. Mugambi defines globalization as

> the hegemony established . . . Monopolar situation. In the name of globalization, goods and services have been dumped from affluent countries which form the Organization for Economic Cooperation and Development (OECD) to the destitute countries especially those in Africa. The latter group of countries has neither the power nor the means to resist this dumping.[16]

While one could debate if globalization was a scheme developed by the powerful economic states, there is no doubt that some argue that the powerful nations have used it to dominate the world culturally and economically. Globalization is an effort to synchronize the world culturally. Mugambi summarizes the intentions of globalization as an attempt to synchronize the whole world with norms and expectations of the reigning ideology of global capitalism.[17] To effect globalization, information technology has been enhanced. Mugambi writes,

> "A new imperial culture characterized by technological advancement in communication, radio, television, and internet as the vehicle for the promotion of a Euro-American way of life."[18]

The promoters of globalization are out to silence all other cultural voices. This is the dilemma of the 21st century. On the impact of globalization, M. Gecaga writes, "It is clear that economic globalization has produced injustices, inequality, and poverty." Globalization targets all aspects of culture. The advertisements in the mass media promote a way of life that denigrates African culture and promotes Anglo-Saxon aesthetics, tastes, and values.[19] On the link between globalization and modern evangelization, Mugambi writes, "The modern missionary enterprise is inseparable from globalization. Religion and cultures from Europe and Asia have become an integral part of religious and cultural diversities especially in the cities and town of tropical Africa."[20] Therefore, globalization has become in some ways a reality that Africans must take seriously. However, such a reckoning must be done in a critical dialogue that recognizes the cultural identity and religions of Africa as African scholars have argued in the past, a subject I turn to in the next section.

African scholars on Africa religio-cultural identity in the wake of global changes

Despite numerous prejudices that have attempted to negate African religio-cultural identity on its worthiness, African scholars have researched and written to assert the significance of African religio-cultural identity. Beginning with *African Religions and philosophy* and other subsequent publications, Mbiti has documented on African religio-cultural identity in all its facets. He argues that the African world view is still intact because "the changes are generally on the surface; affecting the material side of the life . . . traditional concepts still form the essential background of many African peoples."[21] Africnas have retained their elaborate world view which has shaped the African religio-cultural identity. According to Mbiti, "To ignore these traditional beliefs, attitudes and practices can only lead to a lack of understanding African behavior and problems."[22]

In his book *African traditional Religion A definition*, E. B. Idowu has refuted the prejudices and misunderstanding African identity and also argued that African scholars recognize and want to claim their God given heritage and values.[23] Idowu wrote when the African religion cultural identity was under attack, especially by colonial and missionizing agents who questioned not only the viability of African religions but wanted to impose Christian theological categories. Idowu pointed out that African religious heritage remained a significant factor in the development and articulation of Christian theology in Africa. He anticipated the dawning of a new day for African theology when Africans and other faithful people would recognize that "prefabricated" theology that was imported into Africa would no longer serve the academic and spiritual need of the African Church.[24]

In the same reconstructive mode in theology, L. Magesa, a leading African theologian, has addressed African identity and argues that despite the many changes that have occurred in Africa, it is still relevant. Africans have not lost their consciousness as a people.[25] They have benefitted from innovations from the western world and elsewhere, but their worldview and value systems are still operational.[26] Magesa uses the moral traditions of African Religion and through them illustrates the significance of African religion in the contemporary society. He writes, "Africans have been influenced by Islam and Christianity but their inner motivation for religiosity is African religion."[27] As Magesa correctly argues, African religion remains the force behind African religiosity and identity, and even in the contemporary society, it is still the basis of religious meaning.

Magesa has argued that African Religion has persisted in Africa up to the present as a testimony to its influencing power on black Africans.[28] He further argues that African religion must be counted as among the great world religions because it directs lives of millions of people in Africa and diaspora.[29] He concludes by restating the preciousness of African religious heritage and emphasizes that that heritage should not be taken lightly. Rather, Africans should work to rescue its religious heritage from the ridicule it has received from outsiders who did not show appreciation in those religious traditions or understood its practices.[30]

N.W. Ndung'u, a leading researcher on African instituted Churches argues that the interaction between Europeans and Africans has been characterized by violence, exploitation, and oppression.[31] He argues that although western missionaries have attempted to transform Africans into black Europeans, African religio-cultural identity is continued in African instituted Churches. Kikuyu resistance to the demands of western Christian missionaries was an attempt to assert themselves as a community against the domineering external forces which were wrecking their traditional social structures.[32] The Kikuyu wanted to remain with their identity and at the same time remain Christians. He writes, "They were not opposed to the word of God as contained in the Bible but were against the new laws that the missionaries were inventing to undermine the traditional customs, the very basis of their identity."[33] Due to the need to protect their identity, the Kikuyu started an independent Church called Independent Pentecostal Church of Africa (AIPCA). Ndung'u asserts, "One can argue that these churches have at least managed to uphold the African identity by creating a church in which members are true Africans and true Christians at the same time."[34]

Lessons for African religio-cultural identity from India

India just like many African countries was colonized and culturally dominated by Western Europe. Unlike many African countries, India emerged out of colonization, westernization, and secularization with her identity intact. What factors in Indian society, insulated her from being wooed and conquered by western lifestyles? Some scholars have shown that Hindu culture is the oldest and most persistent of the world cultures.[35] In discussing the resilience of Hindu culture Kala Acharya writes, "Those cultures which are based on values and philosophy last long. India has cherished non-injury, non-theft, celibacy and non-accumulation of wealth. The purity of thought, speech and deed and harmony in these three makes a person integrated."[36] The history of India is dominated by a variety of ideas and thoughts. These to a large extent have given the Indian society an edge in the face of competing influences from outside India. The Indian thought has gone through re-interpretations over the years. Indians have been able to compare new lines of thought from other cultures and evaluate them by change or maintenance of the status quo. Hindu reformers have been instrumental in giving Hindu culture a new lease of life. Movements such as Arya Samaj founded by Swami Dayananda, neo-Hinduism founded by Swami Vivekananda, Brahmo Samaj by Ram Mohan Roy, and International society for Krishna consciousness have ensured that Hindu culture remains relevant despite the rapid changes which have rocked the Indian society.

Hinduism to the Indians is a way of life. Raymond Hammer argues, "Whenever Indians have gone, they have taken with them their culture and religious ideas and practices."[37] In recent times some Hindu practices such as yoga, ahimsa (non-violence), the simplicity of life, meditation, vegetarianism, self-denial, charity, among others have acquired universal appeal across many cultures of the world. This has gone a long way in promoting Hindu culture and enhancing its visibility.

Hindu culture has been promoted by both theologians and statesmen. Some Indian political parties are associated with Hindu culture. Through political patronage, Hinduism has been preserved as one of the most significant belief systems of the world. Mahatma Gandhi has played a leading role in making Hinduism respected. He was educated in the western world, and despite its attractions, he remained a Hindu. Although he championed cultural and religious diversity, he affirmed his identity as Hindu through his writings and way of life. He acted as a role model to other Indians on the necessity of religious co-existence, especially between western Christianity and Hinduism, Gandhi wrote as follows:

> Then there is the question of the whole Hindu culture I see, even at the present moment a conflict going on between Hindu culture and Christianity of Indians, the latter is being torn between two almost opposite attractions. Somehow or other, Christianity has become synonymous with western culture. Perhaps rightly so, for, the religion of western people is predominantly Christianity and therefore Hindu culture would certainly be described as Hindu culture.[38]

Mahatma Gandhi confessed that whenever he was in a dilemma, he consulted Hindu scriptures: "I must confess when doubts haunt me when disappointments stare me in the face and when I see no ray of light on the horizon I turn to Bhagavad-Gita."[39] He gave Indians a new spirit, a sense of self-respect and a feeling of pride in their civilization. Unlike what happened to many African countries after independence, Mahatma Gandhi identified himself with Hindu identity. In Kenya, as in other African countries, the elite have been at the forefront of promoting western lifestyles. Even within the mainline Churches and Pentecostal Churches, the elite are still greatly attached to a western identity.

Resurgence of African religio-cultural identity as a counter to globalization

Much awareness on the reality of African religio-cultural identity has been created at all levels in African societies. In the scholarly level, Mugambi has played a key role in sensitizing Kenyans and Africans, in general, to appreciate their identity and utilize it to understand other world identities. He was first trained as a primary school teacher, which accorded him with an opportunity to influence many children.[40] Mugambi was advantaged to interact with policy makers in the area of the teaching of Christian Religious Education (CRE). Together with Protestants and catholic representatives they were given the opportunity of developing the curriculum for the teaching of CRE. During the missionary period, African religious heritage was presented as an inferior heritage which was supposedly fulfilled by the coming of Christianity.

In 1976, together with Nicodemus Kirima, Mugambi prepared materials for the teaching of syllabus 228 of the Kenya certificate of education.[41] This was historical because for the very first time in Kenya, African religious heritage was offered in a course unit of its own and taught for its sake. Young minds were being shaped by African ideas. At the university level, especially in the early years of the development of university education, the University of Nairobi offered African Religion as an equal of other religious traditions of the world. In the M.A Programme of the University of Nairobi, African Religion is given equal status with other world religions. For instance, a student taking Master of Arts in Religious Studies is given an opportunity to specialize on the following options: Christianity, Islam, African Religion, Judaism, and oriental Religions. [42] Mugambi's argument has been that African theologians should focus on what aspects of new cultures to adopt but not on what aspects of African culture to discard. He writes,

> The focus ought to be on the new foreign cultures. What aspects of these cultures should Africa people accept for blending with their heritage? The resilient values of culture will always prevail in varying degrees depending on internal conflicts and external pressures.[43]

The resurgence of Africa religio-cultural heritage was ignited after the Second World War. African soldiers, who fought outside Africa, discovered that Africans and their institutions were the same as those of other countries outside Africa; they experienced a multiplicity of cultures whereas the missionaries and colonialists were fighting African cultures and elevating western culture, in places such as India, Burma, Singapore, each society was proud of its culture. When the soldiers came back home, the struggle for independence commenced. The Mau Mau rebellion in Kenya was fought using African and Christian symbols. After the end of the colonial rule, many African societies started self-discovery of their identities. For example, African instituted Churches became very active. Most of these Churches borrowed heavily from African religio-cultural heritage and became carriers of African identity. The momentum of the rise and spread of these Churches continues to the present. Mugambi writes, "As the twentieth century draws to a close and twenty – first-century sets in, Africa renaissance enters the scene of world history."[44]

In recent years, there is a resurgence of suppressed key elements of African religio-cultural heritage which encourage rites of passage, worship practices, blessing ceremonies, herbal medicine, and use of mystical powers in all aspects of Africans way of life. Due to the emergence of new lifestyles diseases such diabetes and hypertension, Africans are beginning to eat traditional African dishes. In the area of art, design, and architecture African are rediscovering the significance of African aesthetics. Churches and homes are being constructed using African architectural features and decorated with African art. In literature, oral traditions are being used to promote African understanding and interpretation of current realities. Many writers are beginning to use African language in their writings. FM and TV stations have been opened which only transmit in African languages.

In the area of ethics and morality, Africans are beginning to use African proverbs and wise saying. Several books have documented such proverbs. Examples of such books include the Holy book of Neter, the wisdom, and philosophy of the Gikuyu proverbs, the Kihooto worldview, and Kamba Riddles and proverbs. The African communal aspect is slowly gaining currency. In the Roman Catholic Church, this aspect is being promoted through small Christian communities. Africans in urban centers are coming together to form social associations aimed at helping each other during times of need. In the area of conservation of the environment, African indigenous knowledge of preserving the environment is being used. In politics, the idea of consensus building which was significant in the traditional society is becoming common. Political parties are increasingly being used to unite several ethnic groups to compete for power. The role of councils of elders has become common in many African communities.

Reconstruction theology and African religio-cultural identity

Mugambi called for a theology of reconstruction for the 21st century.[45] Global movements which ended colonialism also facilitated the emergence of the new global regime of the capitalist market economy.[46] Despite the attainment of independence and the successful liberation of South Africa in 1994 and the changes which occurred, Africa was still dominated by western and other global forces keen on preserving their economic and strategic interests in Africa. Mugambi contends that a theology of reconstruction differs from liberation theology because liberation is a process in which the oppressed direct their actions against resisting oppressors while the theology of reconstruction is not adversarial but reciprocal.[47] Mugambi argues that the reconstruction could establish a new social order.[48] He roots the theology in the Bible by using Nehemiah as a model leader for social reconstruction. Mugambi writes,

One of the challenges of doing a theology of reconstruction in Africa is the existence of the missionary legacy which has been very critical of African religio-cultural identity. Kibicho observes that when Christianity arrived in Africa, it had adopted a Greco-Roman metaphysic with its exclusive, dualistic understanding of truth.[49]

He notes as follows: "It became a western religion and shared the characteristics of European culture, which considered itself to be both universal and normative."[50] While writing an appreciation of S. K. Kibicho's work Frans Wijsen writes as follows: "Anyone living outside this culture was considered a barbarian who had to be brought into the day light of western culture and religion."[51] Today, a theology of reconstruction must embrace the African religious. Some evangelical theologians in Africa argue that any theology done in African should be done within the biblical/evangelical perspective[52] even though such theologies have been very oppressive of African religio-cultural identity. Mugambi argues that there should be unrestricted movement between the text and context because it is important always to remember that context is the space for operation and serves as a theological platform for critical analysis.[53] A critical dialogue between the text and the new cultural context is required to do reconstruction theology. Africans must overcome the divisive mode of Christianity introduced to different cultues. Catholics have emphasized inculturation theology from the time the Second Vatican Council of 1962–1965 and embraced aspects of African culture which are favorable to the perpetuation of a universal Church. Mugambi argues that Roman Catholics have enriched their practices on African thought to perpetuate their universal appeal. They have not emerged as genuine African Churches but as part the greater Roman Catholic Church.

Kibicho argues that the European Church wants to have its cake and eat it too because whe is concerned with perfect universality but cannot say as Paul said there is neither Jew nor Greek, neither rich nor poor, neither free nor slave, neither male or female, neither young or old, neither white nor black.[54] Reconstruction theology will only begin to bear fruits when the oppressive cultural barriers in the Church are broken. A new world order will emerge as it happened in the early Church where there was an honest attempt to create a society where the gospel story impacts equally on all societies.

Conclusion

The chapter has demonstrated that African religio-cultural identity has always been real to the Africans. Before the coming of new religions in Africa, namely Islam and Christianity, Africans were proud of their unique identity. When modernization came to Africa accompanied by colonialists and missionaries, the once united African identity was divided into several sections depending on the missionaries who evangelized in particular regions. There was concerted effort both from the colonialists and missionaries to discredit African identity.

After African countries were freed from colonial domination, African scholars led by Mugambi have called for a paradigm shift and embraced the theology of reconstruction. This is intended to rebuild African societies by using African religio-cultural identity. The recent resurgence of interest in African identity in all the pillars of African culture holds promise for the theology of reconstruction which could contribute to the emergence of a genuine African identity.

Notes

1 J. S. Mbiti, *African Religions and Philosophy*. (Nairobi: Heinemann, 1969), 1.
2 Ibid., 1.
3 J.N.K. Mugambi, *Christianity and African Culture*. (Nairobi: Acton Publishers, 2002), 111.
4 Ibid., 111.

5 N. W. Ndungu, "Cultural Challenges and the Church in Africa," *African Ecclesial Review*, 50, nos 1 & 2 (2008), 72.
6 Ibid., 84.
7 Ngugi Wa Thiongo, *The River Between*. (Nairobi: Heinemann, 1965), 26.
8 Ibid., 26.
9 Ibid., 26.
10 J.N.K. Mugambi, op.cit., 111.
11 Lata Dani, "Conference Report," *Journal of International Centre for Cultural Studies*, 1 (1997), 2.
12 N. W. Ndungu, Op.cit., 85.
13 S. E. Eisenstadt, ed. *Patterns of Modernity*. (New York: New York University Press), 2.
14 N. W. Ndungu, "Religion and Cultural Identity: The Case of the African Instituted Churches," in J. Bahemuka and J. L. Brockingston, eds. *East Africa in Transition Images: Institutions and Identities*. (Nairobi: University of Nairobi Press, 2004), 237.
15 Ibid., 237.
16 J.N.K. Mugambi, "Religions in East Africa in the context of Globalization," in J.N.K. Mugambi and M. N. Getuni, eds. *Religions in Eastern Africa under Globalization*. (Nairobi: Acton Publishers, 2004), 5.
17 M. M. Gecaga, "Globalization and Churches," in I. Mwase and E. Kamaara, eds. *Theologies of Liberation and Reconstruction*. (Nairobi: Acton Publishers, 2012), 328.
18 M. M. Gecaga, 2012, 329.
19 Ibid., 330.
20 Ibid., 330.
21 J. S. Mbiti, Op. Cit., xi.
22 Ibid., 1.
23 E. B. Idowu, *African Traditional Religion a Definition*. (London: SCM Press Ltd, 1973), x.
24 Ibid., xi.
25 L. Magesa, *African Religion the Moral Traditions of Abundant Life*. (New York: Orbis Books, 1997), xiiii.
26 Ibid., 329.
27 Ibid., xiii.
28 Ibid., xiv.
29 Ibid., 287.
30 Ibid., 287.
31 N. W. Ndungu, J. M. Bahemuka and J. L. Brockington, eds. *East Africa in Transition Images Institutions and Identities*. (Nairobi: University of Nairobi Press, 2004), 240.
32 Ibid., 239.
33 Ibid., 239.
34 Ibid., 239.
35 K. M. Sen, *The World's Oldest Faith*. (London: Penguin Books Ltd., 1963), 5.
36 Kala Acharya, "Whether Global Culture Is Viable?" *Journal of International Centre for Cultural Studies*, 1 (1997), 28.
37 Hammer Raymond, "The Eternal Teaching Hinduism," in R. P. Beaver, et al., eds. *A Lion Handbook the World's Religions*. (Tring, Herts: Lion Publishing, 1984), 171–2.
38 Yogendra Yadav, "Cultural Diversity, Its Development and Mahatma Gandhi." www.internationalpeaceandconflict/org/profiles/blogs/culture. (accessed May 23, 2017).
39 www.mkgandhi.org/religionmk.htm. (accessed May 23, 2017).

40 Julius M. Gathogo, Op.cit., 64.
41 J. Mugambi and N. Kirima, *African Religious Heritage*. A textbook based on syllabus 228 of the Kenya certificate of Education. (Nairobi: Oxford University Press, 1982).
42 University of Nairobi Academic Calendar July 2009/June 2010, 592.
43 J.N.K. Mugambi, *Christianity and Culture*. (Nairobi: Acton publishers, 2002), 114.
44 Ibid., 116.
45 J.N.K. Mugambi, "Theology of Reconstruction," in I. T. Mwase and E. Kamaara, eds. *Theologies of Liberation and Reconstruction*. (Nairobi: Acton Publishers, 2012), 17.
46 Ibid., 17.
47 Ibid., 22.
48 Ibid., 26.
49 Frans Wijsen, "An Appreciation of Kibicho's Work," in S. G. Kibicho, ed. *God and Revelation in African Context*. (Nairobi: Acton Publishers, 2006), 12.
50 Ibid., 12.
51 Ibid., 12.
52 R. J. Gehman, *Doing African Christian Theology: An Evangelical Perspective*. (Nairobi: Evangel Press, 1987).
53 J.N.K. Mugambi, "Theology of Reconstruction," in I. Mwase and E. Kamaara, eds. *Theologies of Liberation and Reconstruction*. (Nairobi: Acton Publishers, 2012), 23.
54 S. G. Kibicho, *God and Revelation in African Context*. (Nairobi: Acton Publishers, 2006), 189.

Bibliography

Acharya, Kala. "Whether Global Culture Is Viable?" *Journal of International Centre for Cultural Studies* 1 (1997).

Dani, Lata. "Conference Report in Journal of International Centre for Cultural Studies." 1 (1997).

Farisani, E. B. "The Post-exile motif in Mugambi's Theology of Reconstruction." In *Theologies of Liberation and Reconstruction*, edited by I. Mwase Kamaara. Nairobi: Acton Publishers, 2012.

Eisenstaedt, S. E., ed. *Patterns of Modernity*. New York: New York University Press, 1991.

Essien-Udom, E. U. *Black Nationalism A search for an Identity in America*. Chicago: University of Chicago Press, 1971.

Gathogo, Julius M. "Post-liberation Theology: A Critical Appreciation." In *Theologies of Liberation and Reconstruction*, edited by I. M. Mwase, and E. K. Kamaara. Nairobi: Action publishers, 2012.

Gecaga, M. M. "Globalization and Churches." In *Theologies of Liberation and Reconstruction*, edited by I. Mwase, and E. Kamaara. Nairobi: Acton Publishers, 2012.

Gehman, R. J. *Doing African Christian Theology: An Evangelical Perspective*. Nairobi: Evangel Press, 1987.

Hammer, Raymond. "The Eternal Teaching of Hinduism." In *A Lion Handbook the World's Religions*, edited by R. P. Beaver et al. Tring, Herts: Lion Publishing, 1984.

Idowu, E. B. *African Traditional Religion a Definition*. London: SCM Press Ltd, 1973.
Kibicho, S. G. *God, and Revelation in the African Context*. Nairobi: Acton Publishers, 2006.
Magesa, L. *African Religion the Moral Traditions of Abundant Life*. New York: Orbis Books, 1997.
Mbiti, J. S. *African Religions, and Philosophy*. Nairobi: Heinemann, 1969.
Mugambi, J.N.K. *Christianity, and African Culture*. Nairobi: Acton Publishers, 2002.
———. "Religions in East Africa in the Context of Globalization." In *Religions in Eastern Africa under Globalization*, edited by J. N. K. Mugambi, and M. N. Getui. Nairobi: Acton Publishers, 2004.
———. "Theology of Reconstruction." In *Theologies of Liberation and Reconstruction*, edited by I. M. T. Mwase, and E. Kamaara. Nairobi: Acton Publishers, 2012.
Mugambi, J. N. K., and N. Kirima. *Religious Heritage a Textbook based on Syllabus 228 of the Kenya Certificate of Education*. Nairobi: Oxford University Press, 1982.
Ndung'u, N. W. "Religion and Cultural Identity: The Case of the African Instituted Churches." In *East Africa in Transition Images: Institutions and Identities*, edited by J. Bahemuka, and J. L. Brockingston. Nairobi: University of Nairobi Press, 2004.
———. "Cultural Challenges and the Church in Africa." *African Ecclesial Review* 50, no. 162 (2008).
Sen, K. M. *The World's Oldest Faith*. London: Penguin Books Ltd., 1963.
Wa Thiongo, Ngugi. *The River Between*. Nairobi: Heinemann, 1965.
Wijsen, Frans. "An Appreciation of Kibicho's Work." In *God and Revelation in African Context*, edited by S. G. Kibicho. Nairobi: Acton Publishers, 2006.

16 Integrity of mission in light of the gospel in Africa

A perspective from an African in diaspora

Tite Tiénou[1]

Introduction

I encountered Professor Mugambi in his scholarship before meeting the man. In the early 1990s, during one of my travels to Nairobi, I purchased his 1989 book *The Biblical Basis of Evangelization*. As I read it, I recognized a convergence of concerns and interests. Over the years, acquiring and reading more books, edited by him and/or with chapters he contributed, has only increased my appreciation for his scholarship. We would not meet face to face until this century in the context of work related to a two-year research project entitled "Christianity and Social Change in Contemporary Africa," funded by the John Templeton Foundation and administered by the Nagel Institute of Calvin College, Grand Rapids, Michigan (US). I serve as the director of one of the initiatives of this research: "Christian Theology: African Realities and African Hope." Mugambi serves as one of the mentors of grant recipients doing research in theology. In our work together, his dedication to careful work in scholarship, his genuine care for the researchers and his commitment to a different view of Africa and Africans have added great value to the research. It has been a great joy to work with Mugambi.

The present reflections on integrity of Christian mission in Africa come from an African in diaspora, an *émigré* presently living in the United States. From this particular viewpoint, three "realities" seem especially relevant and important for framing my ideas. First, the integrity of mission is rooted in the nature of the Gospel and the nature of the Church: the Gospel is for everyone (Romans 1:16) and, in the oft quoted words of Emil Brunner, "The Church exists by mission, just as fire exists by burning."[2] Second, the Church is now solidly rooted in Africa. Third, on the continent the word *mission* is problematic as it is often ambiguous and misunderstood. In light of the foregoing, I have decided to examine the integrity of mission in light of the Gospel by exploring the following issues: the Church as African and its implication for mission; the meaning of mission in Africa; the place of Africa in the world; the opportunities for the integrity of mission in Africa; and the requirement of integrity for the agents of mission.[3]

The Church as African: implications for mission

Today the presence of the Church in Africa should be an important aspect of any discussion of Christian mission to or from the continent. Given the abundant literature documenting the presence of Christianity in Africa, its growth and its impact, it would seem unnecessary to call attention, once again, to the fact that Christianity is alive and well in Africa and bears an African imprint. There are, however, reasons for a reminder that, in Africa, the Church is indeed African and has been so for a very long time. According to Andrew F. Walls,

Christianity is indigenous to Africa, [and] it antedates the oldest African Islam. . . . [M]odern African Christianity is not only the result of movements among Africans, but has been principally sustained by Africans, and is to a surprising extent the result of African initiatives.[4]

In spite of the above, some people either express scepticism about African Christianity or seem surprised to learn that the "continent [is now] a major base of the Christian faith."[5] One even finds statements that give the impression that Christian presence in Africa is a paradox. So, for example, a 1996 publication on mission introduces its survey of Africa with these words:

> In Africa, optimists quickly become realists. Realists become pessimists. And pessimists become cynics. . . . An abysmal education system, along with many other sad measures of economic and social illness. Yet Christians live there. They are sharing Africa's pain and pointing her to a future beyond the worst hurts this world can offer.[6]

Should we really be puzzled to find Christians in places where "sad measures of economic and social illness" prevail? Should we not just acknowledge the fact that "Africa has become, or is becoming, a Christian continent in cultural as well as numerical terms?"[7] For reasons that cannot be fully understood, the human problems of the continent do not seem to have adversely affected the growth of the Church in Africa. One thing is certain: "During the past thirty years, the economy of Africa has deteriorated at the same inverse proportion as Church membership has grown. The more Christian the continent becomes, the more *pauperized* it is increasingly becoming."[8]

It is an undeniable fact that in Africa Christian vitality exists in a context of poverty. What lessons can be learned? This is neither the occasion nor the place for an investigation of lessons to be learned from Christianity in Africa. Rather, I will point out a major mission implication of the present situation; Christian mission in contemporary Africa must address multiple complex issues at once. In this continent doing mission with integrity and with the whole Gospel in mind requires that one accepts the fact that

> with the 1990's a new period of African Church History has begun: *A Church Challenged by a Continent in Crisis*. . . . In this situation the Church has to live up to the challenge and find answers to the cries of

> the time, to the fears and anguish which plague the minds of so many Africans today.[9]

In order for the Church to "live up to the challenge" she must make teaching and training a key aspect of mission. In my experience "mission to and in Africa" often means evangelization and making converts. This conception of mission seldom includes the necessary aspects of pastoral care and the deepening of the faith of those who identify themselves as Christians. Christian mission is not just about gaining converts; it is also about making sure that the converts become mature disciples and servants of Christ. That is why, in the words of Arthur Glasser, "the Christian movement must focus on consolidation while reaching out in expansion."[10] Consequently, one of the greatest missiological challenges of the Christian movement in Africa is the ability to continue the practice of mission as evangelism (meaning the focus on increasing the number of converts) without neglecting the requirement of devoting enough energy and resources to the need "to cope with the elementary issue of absorbing new members, let alone with the deeper issues of formation and training."[11]

While evangelism is still needed in Africa in spite of the exponential progression of Christianity,[12] for the foreseeable future "formation and training" will be significant frontiers of mission because of what Isaac Zokoué calls "the crisis of maturity in Africa."[13] Why is it, then, that evangelism is still considered the primary focus of mission in Africa? I do not presume to know all the answers to this very important question. I think that the lack of a clear ecclesiology may provide a clue. In many cases mission agencies produced what may be called "junior" Churches in Africa, described by Sidbe Sempore as "'missionary' Churches hurriedly built for Africans and without Africans."[14] It is not surprising that these "hurriedly built" Churches have not paid sufficient attention to significant aspects of Church life. Moreover Klaus Fiedler contends,

> When faith missions started their work in Africa, they did not think much in terms of ecclesiology for their converts, because they simply did not expect the developments that took place. . . . This poses for faith missions the challenge to take conscious ecclesiology seriously. . . . The priority of the faith missions was always evangelism.[15]

I do not believe that "faith missions" are alone in giving priority to evangelism. Be that as it may, the question is: What can we expect from "junior" Churches? What does "participation in mission" mean for them?

Mission by Africans?

In 1989 Mugambi made this observation: "Up to the present, there is virtually nothing published by African theologians on the mission of the Church in Africa."[16] Only people unfamiliar with the ambiguities surrounding the word "mission" in Africa can be surprised by that observation. After all, "the missions introduced a clear dichotomy: mission is the foreigners' affair; the Church is for the 'natives.'"[17] It is for this reason that

> We in Africa have misunderstood our call to mission. The word mission itself raises certain ambiguities in our understanding. Mention mission and missionaries and you think of all the foreign brothers and sisters who live in our villages working in hospitals, translating our Bibles and teaching women hygiene and sewing. . . . Thus mission among ourselves and for ourselves is not an issue that keeps up awake with concern.[18]

As long as such misunderstanding persists, there will be no significant qualitative participation of Africans in mission. Africans will continue to position themselves as recipients of mission thereby delaying the requirement to "rethink our mission task as Africans in Africa"[19] and beyond. For me this requirement is essential for the integrity of mission in the continent because "no movement can merit the title 'Church' unless it is a missionary community."[20] However, the Church in Africa will not take her rightful place in mission unless she deals adequately with the numerous issues related to the place of Africa in the world.

Africa in the world

In Europe and in the United States one faces "the constant portrayal of Africa as a place beset by famine, drought, and civil war, or as an open-air ethnographic museum for the West."[21] This portrayal of Africa reinforces the continent's "otherness." The perception of Africa as distant and other may be the result of the particular relationship between Africa and Europe. As Chinua Achebe writes,

> It is a great irony of history and geography that Africa, whose land mass is closer than any other to the mainland of Europe, should come to occupy in European psychological disposition the farthest point of otherness, should indeed become Europe's very antithesis.[22]

In today's world Africa has easily become the "very antithesis" of all continents. One can make the case that this image of Africa describes the continent's place in the world. Africa's "otherness" exposes the continent to all sorts of experiments by and from the outside and pushes Africans to the margins of humanity.[23] No wonder there is so much pessimism about Africa in the world. It would appear that at no time in recent memory has there been as much pessimism concerning the present and the future of the African continent and its nation-states as now. The pessimism is often due to the dire economic conditions of the continent. So, for example, a 2002 publication of the Organization for Economic Cooperation and Development states, "Africa's participation in the world economy has declined alarmingly over the past 50 years in terms of GDP, exports, and foreign investment. Only the continent's share of global population grew as its birth rate accelerated during the 20th century."[24]

For African *émigrés* living in the United States, like myself, the weight of pessimistic news about Africa is sometimes unbearable. In January 2000 in a series of articles the *Chicago Tribune* devoted to Africa someone commented, "No wonder everybody is going *out of Africa*!" Then, in June, Steve Chapman (a journalist of the *Chicago Tribune*) put it succinctly with this title in the Commentary section: "Africa's sad present and its very grim future":

> The opening of the 21st century is a time of optimism about the future of humanity. Until you consider Africa.
>
> For years, the continent has been a bleak landscape of chaos, bloodshed, failure and stagnation. Unhappy as the colonial era was for Africans living under foreign rule, the post-colonial era has been far worse.[25]

Chapman is only one of the more recent Afro-pessimists.[26] Afro-pessimism should, therefore, be the broader context for any reflection on the African continent these days. Even if Afro-pessimism is the background against which one must examine the challenges and opportunities facing Africa, I do not wish to engage in refuting or examining it in detail. Rather against this background I want to consider four major challenges and three great opportunities for Africa and Africans.

Challenges facing Africa and Africans

As Africa enters the 21st century her children face the following four major challenges: they must deal with the lingering effects of Afro-pessimism; they must come to terms with the marginalization of Africa in the present world order; they must refuse solutions to Africa's problems based on ignorance; and they must find room for God and morality in nation building. Afro-pessimism will, for the foreseeable future, represent an important lens through which many people see Africa and react to Africans. Afro-pessimism reinforces the negative image of Africa and Africans. The negative image and the undeniable fact that Africa "trail[s] the rest of the world in practically every area of human endeavour"[27] means that "Africa stands naked before the rest of the world."[28] Since Afro-pessimism contributes significantly to the "nakedness of Africa," Africans need to devise ways of coping with its lingering effects. But how? Should Africans engage in major media campaigns promoting a positive image of the continent? Should they focus on the analysis of the causes for the continent's present predicament with the hope that better understanding will promote a more balanced assessment of

Africa and Africans? Is it more prudent to rally Africans around "a bright vision for Africa" with concepts like "African Renaissance"? Is it not best to ignore Afro-pessimism altogether?

I do not believe that we need to invest time and energy in attempts to mount a rebuttal to Afro-pessimism. Such attempts at rebuttal may concede too much to Afro-pessimism and may at the same time, be overly optimistic. Take the concept of African Renaissance for example. Its proponents use it to point to positive indicators in the continent. These indicators signal re-birth. The very notion of re-birth implies that there is death or general breakdown. But Africa has not died; she has not experienced a general breakdown. She certainly has had, and she continues to have, many problems caused by her sons and daughters as well as by outsiders. Can we seriously equate these problems with death or general failure? Moreover, how sure are we that we are now living at a time of re-birth for Africa? Has Africa not seen other periods of "Renaissance"? What have we learned from them? I recall a history professor from my high school days in Burkina Faso who in 1967 spent much time on the idea that the 19th century was a time of African Renaissance! I have often asked myself, "What is the legacy of this 19th century Renaissance?"

Die-hard Afro-pessimists cannot be silenced with indications of an African Renaissance. Given the complexity of the continent and the multiple challenges it faces, one can always find enough bad news to illustrate "Africa's" sad plight! Afro-pessimism is not, however, just about reporting bad news on Africa. Ultimately Afro-pessimism can cripple the self-confidence of Africans because, as Siradiou Diallo points out, the scorn it generates towards Africa and Africans erodes the dignity of Africans.[29] In light of this, I think that the protection of the dignity of Africans is one of the best ways of dealing with the lingering effects of Afro-pessimism. Africans may sometimes have to appeal to God directly, through prayer, as I did in 1990, and implore God to restore their self-confidence and human dignity.[30] Christians can have a significant role in the restoration of the human dignity of Africans if their theology and practice of mission are solidly based on what the Bible teaches regarding human nature.

The marginalization of Africa in the present world order, which is the second challenge Africans face, is linked to Afro-pessimism. Since it is often taken for granted that Africa is marginal in the world, especially in economics and politics, I will not provide much description here. Africa's marginalization takes many forms. At times she is ignored altogether even by people and nations claimed to be her partners in development. At other times silence and indifference are replaced with comments such as "Africa, the bottomless pit of need"; "On Africa, No Attractive Options for the World" (*Herald Tribune*, November 23–24, 1996, p. 8); "Some Places Globalization Forgot: Africa and Mexico" (*Herald Tribune*, January 2, 1997, p. 2).

The marginalization of Africa also affects events in the continent. It seems to be related to present uncertainties. These uncertainties have implications for nation-building, social stability as well as Christian mission. So, on the one hand, we are witnessing the destruction of many African nation-states by implosion or by the revival of ethnic or micro-nationalism as in other countries in the world. On the other hand, fewer Africans seem to trust in the value of nation building as they point out the failures, the mistakes, the greed, and the impasse to which the past 50 years (or more) of independence have led us. Indeed it appears that we live at a time when Africa is once again ruled by chaos. In such a situation, how does one address the topic of nation building?

I do not believe that Africa's problems – whatever they are – can be solved by outsiders. This means that, in a sense, Africa's marginalization by the outside world (whether such is a possibility, a reality, or fiction) does not have an immediate impact on nation-building. Nevertheless, taken together with the implosion of many African nation-states and many misgivings that Africans have about the worth of nation building at the present time, Africa's marginalization must be taken seriously.

The third challenge Africans face is the need to refuse solutions to Africa's problems that are based on ignorance. The marginalization of Africa, the dysfunctional nature of many of her nation-states and the many doubts that Africans have about the merits of nation-building may promote the idea of looking to outside sources for help and solutions. Indeed, non-Africans sometimes reinforce the idea that positive changes in the continent come from the outside. Consider, for example, what Jacques Godefrain, then France's Minister of Cooperation, declared in 1995: "Fifty years ago we told Africans to become nations and they became nations. Ten years ago we told them to become democrats and they became democrats."[31] No surprise, therefore, that some have wondered if Africa does not need to be re-colonized! Yet, many solutions to Africa's problems may be based on selfishness, even on the part of foreign states or they may be the application of policies formulated out of ignorance. As far as selfishness or self-interest is concerned, we must never forget this sobering statement attributed to Charles de Gaulle: "A state does not have friends, it has interests" (*Un état n'a pas d'amis, il a des intérêts*).

Matters are further complicated by the widespread ignorance regarding African realities. Let me illustrate. *The New York Times* is recognized as a reputable daily newspaper in the United States. One can assume that it can inform its readers accurately. Yet, over the course of 40 years (1955 to 1995), *The New York Times* has consistently portrayed Africa negatively.[32] I note, in fairness to *The New York Times*, that in 2004 Howard C. French, its Africa correspondent, published *A Continent for the Taking: The Tragedy and Hope of Africa* (New York: Knopf), a rather balanced treatment of the continent.

It is, frankly, a pity that so many of us look to the outside for solutions to Africa's problems. What kind of solutions can one expect from states that are bent on protecting their own interests and whose "African" policies are often rooted in negative images of Africa? Elochukwu E. Uzukwu is right: "The solution to Africa's problems is through mobilizing and ably harnessing its internal resources instead of depending on external aid."[33] Let us always remember that nation-building and development cannot be the results of philanthropy.

The fourth challenge – that of finding room for God and morality in nation-building – is especially important for us Christians. Here I only present why and how this is a challenge. I will indicate below how Christians can respond to this challenge positively. The challenge is brought into focus by the following paradox. On the one hand, religious people (Christians in particular) stress the positive role of religion in nation-building. On the other hand, some writers seem to have a particular problem with religion when it comes to nation-building: for them religion represents a negative element in the nation-building and development process. Edem Kodjo's *et demain l'Afrique* (Paris: Editions Stock, 1985) provides an illustration of this attitude. Although the book is an analysis of the African condition and a proposal of hope for the future of the continent, it contains no substantial treatment of the role religion or Christianity can play in what he calls the path to salvation (*la voie du salut*, Chapter 13) for Africa.

There are only oblique and negative references to religion such as "the future of the continent is neither in autarchy (isolationism) nor a new millenarianism" (p. 289: *L'avenir du continent africain ne se trouve ni dans l'autarcie ni dans un nouveau millénarisme*). Edem Kodjo is not alone in viewing religion negatively in matters pertaining to nation building and development. Consider, for example, Daniel Etounga-Manguelle's opinion in "Does Africa Need a Cultural Adjustment Program."[34] He seems to attribute Africa's backwardness and stagnation to the power religion has over Africans. For him Africa will progress only if she is liberated from religion and invisible powers. I find this negative view of religion on the part of an African academic, a serious intellectual bias. Likewise, the dismissal of religion by an African politician of the status of Edem Kodjo represents a fundamental misunderstanding of the continent by a person who is charged with the responsibility of enabling citizens to be about nation-building. No person with religious convictions should allow this bias and this misunderstanding to remain unchallenged!

Opportunities for the integrity of mission in Africa

The present challenges facing Africa may provide us (Africans and non-Africans alike) with the greatest opportunity for a fresh and creative examination of issues related to the integrity of mission in the continent. I see three areas of opportunity for Africa and Africans: Africans can turn marginalization into a resolve to find intra-African solutions to African problems; Africans may be able to think realistically about nation-building and development; Churches in Africa have a window for being hope-generating

Churches. These areas of opportunity are, in my mind, the positive side of the challenges Africa faces at this time.

I have already tipped my hand, as it were, when I presented the third challenge. We can turn our present marginalization in the world order into a resolve to find intra-African solutions to African problems. This collaboration in nation-building is crucial at this time when Africa seems to be facing its greatest challenges since its partition during the age of imperialism. The current situation of the continent also provides the opportunity to think realistically about all aspects of life in Africa: nation-building, development, social harmony, and religion. For me, whatever else nation-building is and means, it is about providing citizens with the conditions to contribute peacefully to the common good of society and nation of which they are members. Given this, freedom and justice are two of the foundational pillars of nation-building. When the state provides these two ingredients or strives to do so, citizens can carry on the task of nation-building. It is in this connection that I think the following words of scripture are particularly meaningful: "Righteousness and justice are the foundations of [God's] throne" (Psalm 89:14) and "Righteousness exalts a nation, but sin is a disgrace to any people" (Proverbs 14:34).

For us to think realistically about nation-building and development, we must ask if the state in its present form in Africa provides its citizens with the necessary conditions for participating in nation-building. In the following analysis of the nation-state I am indebted to Jean-François Bayart's, *L'état en Afrique: la politique du ventre* (Paris: Fayard, 1989); "Les églises chrétiennes et la politique du ventre" in *Politique Africaine*, 35 (Octobre 1989): 3–26; and to Achille Mbembe's, *Afrique indociles* (Paris: Karthala, 1988). According to Mbembe the authoritarian principle best describes how the state functions in post-colonial Africa. This authoritarian principle has led the state into becoming what he calls the theologian-state (l'Etat-théologien), that is, the state claims the right of being the sole possessor of truth, particularly in matters related to politics and nation-building (1988, 127–128). Lamin Sanneh expresses the same phenomenon when he writes about "the state that is over-extended with the rhetoric of omnicompetence."[35]

Though they may not be familiar with the terminology, Africans know, at the practical level and by experience, what it means to be governed by a state that perceives itself to be all-competent. All Africans have dealt with either centralized bureaucracies, or single party politics, or arbitrary laws or governments refusing to be accountable to citizens they claim to serve and represent. In essence the theologian-state, in granting itself all competence, has monopolized all political power, activity, and discourse. In so doing it has prevented the general populace from active participation in politics and therefore in nation-building (see Mbembe 1988, 141). This means that civil society is absent from most aspects of nation-building in independent Africa.

Another characteristic of the post-colonial state in Africa is that of unchecked profiteering, what J. F. Bayart and Achille Mbembe graphically describe as the rule of the stomach (la politique du ventre ou la gouvernementalité du ventre). The rule of the stomach expresses itself in corruption of all kinds and the exploitation of the citizens by the state.

The authoritarian principle, the rule of the stomach and the presence of pirates or bandits in power produce one net result: institutionalized injustice. In this sense the post-colonial state in Africa has perverted the Pauline belief according to which "rulers hold no terror for those who do right, but for those who do wrong. . . . [The state] is God's servant to do you good" (Romans 13:3 and 4). The African state seems to operate by the opposite principle. The nation-state, in its present condition in Africa, has failed to provide citizens with the basic requirements, freedom and justice, for nation-building.

Given this reality one should not be surprised that Africans concluded that they should protect their own interests since the state was not going to look after the interests of its citizens. Even when majority rule is adopted as a result of political reforms, people may not see a better tomorrow because, as Gerald P. O'Driscoll, Jr. writes, "in a system of majoritarian rule with no protected rights, democracy is just two wolves and a sheep deciding what is for lunch."[36] Alas, there are instances (too many perhaps) in Africa where the Church is one of the wolves! Her participation in the integrity of mission requires that she will care for the rights of the weak, the downtrodden and exploited members of society as she embraces the fact that "it is not enough that Christian mission be redemptive; it must be prophetic as well."[37] Realistic reflection on nation-building, development, social harmony, and mission means that that no human endeavour that is worth undertaking can be accomplished in one individual's lifetime or by just one individual. This is true of nation-building; it requires the contribution of all citizens and it cannot be accomplished in a few short years.

The Church, like other organized bodies of African societies, has tended to work for the short-term, and, unfortunately, her "language and practice are not different from the tyrannies which are called governments in Africa."[38] John S. Pobee notes, "Abuse of power – the corruption of power – the sinful use of power is as much evident in Church as in politics."[39] This means that, among other things, the Church has tended to adopt the common attitude of protecting her own interests. Consequently, in many African countries the Church denounces institutionalized injustice only when her own interests are in jeopardy. This hardly counts as participation in nation-building. And such behaviour is certainly not an example of Christian mission done with integrity.

The Church's attitude is sometimes rooted in questionable theological understanding of which position the Christian should adopt vis-à-vis the state. A theology of "preaching Jesus Christ . . . [for an] appointment for the hereafter"[40] coupled with an interpretation of Romans 13 which implied blind and complete obedience to the state as a minister of God, removed Christianity from influencing the direction in which nation-building moved.[41]

The way forward is for Christians and Churches to abandon worldly foolishness. In so doing they may become hope-generating Churches. This is the third area of opportunity. Hope is necessary for nation-building because "despair does not constitute the basis for the reconstruction of our continent."[42] But how can Churches generate hope if they are not different from other institutions of society? For, as Lesslie Newbigin wrote, "the most important contribution which the Church can make to a new social order is to be itself a new social order."[43]

Notes

1 Note: This chapter is a slightly revised version of an article published in *Mission Studies*, 24, no. 2 (2007), 213–32. Used here with permission from Koninklijke Brill NV. That article was based on a Paper delivered at the 11th Quadrennial International Conference of the International Association for Mission Studies (IAMS) held in 2004 in Port Dickson, Malaysia.
2 Emil Brunner. *The Word and the World*. (Student Christian Movement Press, 1931), 108.
3 Quoted by Donald G. Miller in "Pauline Motives for the Christian Mission," in Gerald H. Anderson, ed. *The Theology of the Christian Mission*. (Nashville, New York: Abingdon Press, 1961), 79.
4 Andrew F. Walls, *The Significance of African Christianity*. Friends of St. Colm's Public Lecture, Church of Scotland St. Colm Education Centre and College, May 21, 1989. Printed by the Overseas Ministry Study Centre, New Haven, CT, 1993, 4, 5.
5 Kwame Bediako, *Christianity in Africa: The Renewal of a Non-Western Religion*. (Maryknoll: Orbis Books, 1995), 252.
6 Mission Today '96. "Regional Overview: Africa," 69.
7 Lamin Sanneh, *Whose Religion Is Christianity?: The Gospel beyond the West*. (Grand Rapids: William B. Eerdmans Publishing Company, 2003), 36.
8 J. N. K. Mugambi, "A Fresh Look at Evangelism in Africa," *International Review of Mission*, LXXXVII, no. 346 (July 1998): 357. Italics in the original.
9 John Baur, 2000 *Years of Christianity in Africa*. (Nairobi: Paulines Publications Africa, 1994), 371.
10 Arthur F. Glasser, "Missiology," in Walter A. Elwell, ed. *Evangelical Dictionary of Theology*. (Grand Rapids: Baker Book House, 1984), 726.
11 Lamin Sanneh, *Whose Religion Is Christianity?*, 37.
12 By 1956 the growth of Christianity in Africa (south of the Sahara) had so impressed Roland Oliver that he declared, "If things were to go at the same rate, there would be no pagans left in Africa after the year 1992" in *How Christian Is Africa?* (London: The Highway Press, 1956), 8. Obviously, even in 2004, there are "pagans" left in Africa!
13 See Isaac Zokoué, "The Crisis of Maturity in Africa," *Evangelical Review of Theology*, 20, no. 4 (October 1996): 354–64.
14 Sidbe Sempore, "Les églises d'Afrique entre leur passé et leur avenir," *Concilium*, no. 126 (1977): 15. In French. "Nous héritons de cette Eglise 'missionnaire' bâtie à la hâte pour nous et sans nous."
15 Klaus Fiedler, *The Story of Faith Missions*. (Oxford: Regnum Books International, 1994), 401.
16 J.N.K. Mugambi, *The Biblical Basis for Evangelization: Theological Reflections based on an African Experience*. (Nairobi: Oxford University Press, 1989), 3.
17 Klaus Fiedler, *The Story of Faith Missions*, 364.

18 Musimbi Kanyoro, "Thinking Mission in Africa," *International Review of Mission*, LXXXVII, no. 345 (April 1998): 221.
19 Musimbi Kanyoro, "Thinking Mission in Africa," 226.
20 J.N.K. Mugambi, "The Future of the Church and the Church of the Future in Africa," in Jose B. Chipenda, et al., eds. *The Church of Africa: Towards a Theology of Reconstruction.* (Nairobi: All Africa Conference of Churches, 1991), 36.
21 Robert Lyons, "Photographer's Note," *Another Africa: Photographs by Robert Lyons; Essay and Poem by Chinua Achebe.* (New York: Anchor Books/Doubleday, 1998), 118.
22 Chinua Achebe, "Africa's Tarnished Name," *Another Africa: Photographs by Robert Lyons; Essay and Poem by Chinua Achebe.* (New York: Anchor Books/Doubleday, 1998), 105.
23 Achille Mbembe, *De la postcolonie.* (Paris: Editions Karthala, 2000). 7–8, 267–75.
24 OECD Publications on Africa (Spring 2002), 1.
25 *Chicago Tribune*, June 8, 2000, Section 1, Commentary, 25.
26 I first encountered Afro-pessimism in French weekly publications in the spring of 1990 (particularly in L'Express, April 27, 1990 and other French weeklies in March and April 1990). At that time some French journalists were predicting that Africa would be wiped out in 15 to 20 years. Across the Channel, the press covered Africa in the same manner: see for example *The Economist* (September 7, 1996). Examples of Afro-pessimism in the US press are numerous. I mention the following: Robert D. Kaplan, "The Coming Anarchy," *The Atlantic Monthly* (Feburary 1994), 44–76; "Africa: The Scramble for Existence," *Time* (September 7, 1992), 40–6; Jeffrey Goldberg, "Their Africa Problem and Ours," *The New York Times Magazine* (March 2, 1997), 30–9. Afro-pessimism is also disseminated in popular and academic publications.
27 Samuel Ofori Onwona, "Africa's Prospects in the New Millennium," *Global Future* (Fourth Quarter 2000), 15.
28 Sulayman S. Nyang, "Africa: A Continent of Unending Conflicts?" *West Africa* (September 12–18, 1994), 1582.
29 Siradiou Diallo, "De la critique au mépris," *Jeune Afrique*, no. 1525 (mars 26, 1990): 33, 36, 37.
30 See in the Appendix my "Prayer for Troubled Africa." Kenneth Kaunda, the former President of Zambia did the same in 1991 when he was so burdened about Africa that he could not sleep. See his prayer in *Africa Forum*, 2, no. 1 (1992): 15–16.
31 "Nous avons dit aux Africains, il y a cinquante ans, de devenir de nations, et ils sont devenus des nations. Nous leur avons dit, il y a dix ans, de devenir des démoctrates et ils sont devenus des démocrates," *Jeune Afrique*, no. 1820 (Novembre 23–29, 1995), 9.
32 See Peter J. Schraeder and Brian Endless, "The Media and Africa: The Portrayal of Africa in *The New York Times (1955–1995)*," no. XXV1/2 (1998): 29–35.
33 Elochukwu E. Uzukwu, *A Listening Church.* (Maryknoll: Orbis Books, 1996), 8.
34 Daniel Etounga-Manguelle, "Does Africa Need a Cultural Adjustment Program," in Lawrence E. Harrison and Samuel P. Huntington, eds. *Culture Matters: How Values Shape Human Progress.* (New York: Basic Books, 2000).
35 Lamin Sanneh, "Religion and the State," *Africa Forum*, 1, no. 4 (1992): 16.
36 Gerald P. O'Driscoll, Jr. "Some Succeed, Others Resent Their Success," (A Review of Amy Chua's World On Fire) *The Wall Street Journal*, CCXL, no. 125 (December 26, 2002): D 10.
37 Arthur F. Glasser, "Missiology," in Walter A. Elwell, ed. *Evangelical Dictionary of Theology.* (Grand Rapids: Baker Book House, 1984), 726.

38 Elochukwu E. Uzukwu, *A Listening Church: Autonomy and Communion in African Churches*. (Maryknoll: Orbis Books, 1996), 121.
39 John S. Pobee, *Celebrating the Jubilee of the World Council of Churches*. (Accra: Christian Council of Ghana/Asempa Publishers, 1998), 105.
40 José B. Chipenda and André Karamaga, eds. *The Right Time for Change: What Hope for Crisis-Stricken Africa?* (Nairobi: All Africa Conference of Churches, 1991), 26.
41 Elochukwu E. Uzukwu, *A Listening Church*, 149.
42 Lesslie Newbigin, *Truth to Tell: The Gospel as Public Truth*. (Grand Rapids: William B. Eerdmans Publishing House, 1991), 85.

Bibliography

Achebe, Chinua. "Africa's Tarnished Name." In *Another Africa: Photographs by Robert Lyons; Essay and Poem by Chinua Achebe*. New York: Anchor Books, Doubleday, 1998.

Bauer, John. *2000 Years of Christianity in Africa*. Nairobi: Paulines Publications Africa, 1994.

Bediako, Kwame. *Christianity in Africa: The Renewal of a Non-Western Religion*. Maryknoll: Orbis Books, 1995.

Brunner, Emil. *The Word and the World*. Student Christian Movement Press, 1931, 108.

Chicago Tribune. *Commentary*. June 8, 2000.

Chpenda, José B., and André Karamaga., eds. *The Right Time for Change: What Hope for Crisis-Stricken Africa?* Nairobi: All Africa Conference of Churches, 1991.

Diallo, Siradiou. "De la critique au mépris." *Jeune Afrique*no. 1525 (26 mars 1990): 33, 36, 37.

Etounga-Manguelle, Daniel. "Does Africa Need a Cultural Adjustment Program." In *Culture Matters: How Values Shape Human Progress*, edited by Lawrence E. Harrison, and Samuel P. Huntington. New York: Basic Books, 2000.

Fielder, Klaus. *The Story of Faith Missions*. Oxford: Regnum Books International, 1994.

Glasser, Arthur F. "Missiology." In *Evangelical Dictionary of Theology*, edited by Walter A. Elwell. Grand Rapids: Baker Book House, 1984.

Goldberg, Jeffrey Goldberg. "Their Africa Problem and Ours." *The New York Times Magazine*. March 2, 1997, 30–9.

Kanyoro, Musimbi. "Thinking Mission in Africa." *International Review of Mission* LXXXVII, no. 345 (April 1998).

Kaplan, Robert D. "Africa: The Scramble for Existence." *Time*. September 7, 1992, 40–6.

"The Coming Anarchy." *The Atlantic Monthly*. February 1994, 44–76.

Kaunda, Kenneth. " Prayer." *Africa Forum* 2, no. 1 (1992): 15–16.

Lyons, Robert. "Photographer's Note." In *Another Africa: Photographs by Robert Lyons; Essay and Poem by Chinua Achebe*, edited by Chinua Achebe. New York: Anchor Books, Doubleday, 1998.

Mbembe, Achille. *De la postcolonie*. Paris: Editions Karthala, 2000.

Miller, Donald G. "Pauline Motives for the Christian Mission." In *The Theology of the Christian Mission*, edited by Gerald H. Anderson. Nashville, New York: Abingdon Press, 1961.

Mugambi, J.N.K. *The Biblical Basis for Evangelization: Theological Reflections based on an African Experience*. Nairobi: Oxford University Press, 1989.

———. "The Future of the Church and the Church of the Future in Africa." In *The Church of Africa: Towards a Theology of Reconstruction*, edited by Jose B. Chipenda, et al. Nairobi: All Africa Conference of Churches, 1991.

———. "A Fresh Look at Evangelism in Africa." *International Review of Mission* LXXXVII, no. 346 (July 1998).

Newbigin, Leslie. *Truth to Tell: The Gospel as Public Truth*. Grand Rapids: William B. Eerdmans Publishing House, 1991.

Nyang, Sulayman S. "Africa: A Continent of Unending Conflicts?" *West Africa*. September 12–18, 1994.

O'Driscoll, Gerald P. Jr. "Some Succeed, Others Resent their Success." (A Review of Amy Chua's *World On Fire*) *The Wall Street Journal* CCXL, no. 125 (December 26, 2002): D 10.

OECD. *Publications on Africa*. Spring 2002.

Oliver, Roland. *How Christian Is Africa?* London: The Highway Press, 1956.

Ouwona, Samuel Ofori. "Africa's Prospects in the New Millennium." *Global Future*. Fourth Quarter 2000.

Pobee, John S. *Celebrating the Jubilee of the World Council of Churches*. Accra: Christian Council of Ghana, Asempa Publishers, 1998.

Sanneh, Lamin. *Whose Religion Is Christianity?: The Gospel beyond the West*. Grand Rapids: William B. Eerdmans Publishing Company, 2003.

———. "Religion and the State." *Africa Forum* 1, no. 4 (1992): 16.

Schraeder, Peter J. and Brian Endless. "The Media and Africa: The Portrayal of Africa in *The New York Times* (1955–1995)." *Issue*, XXV1/2 (1998): 29–35.

Sempore, Sidbe. "Les églises d'Afrique entre leur passé et leur avenir." *Concilium*no. 126 (1977).

Uzukwu, Elochukwu E. *A Listening Church: Autonomy and Communion in African Churches*. Maryknoll: Orbis Books, 1996.

Walls, Andrew F. *The Significance of African Christianity*. Friends of St. Colm's Public Lecture, Church of Scotland St. Colm Education Centre and College, May 21, 1989. New Haven: Overseas Ministry Study Centre, 1993.

Zokoué, Isaac. "The Crisis of Maturity in Africa." *Evangelical Review of Theology* 20, no. 4 (October 1996): 354–64.

17 On freedom

Risking a (faithful) reinterpretation

James R. Cochrane[1]

Freedom is an idea deeply rooted in the struggles of African peoples, particularly since the Second World War, the "winds of change" that marked decolonization, and, eventually, the end of apartheid in South Africa.[2] However, in this complex and varied history of struggle and the subsequent rise of the postcolony it is not self-evident what really is meant by freedom. Clearly, the clarion call of freedom in colonial Africa rested on an insistence on being defined other than by way of the thought, norms, values, cultural resources, politics, and economics of colonizing nations. It was a call for "freedom from" determination by others, that is, for self-determination. This negative (if necessary) definition of freedom has no positive content, however. It tells us nothing about what freedom is "for," which must still be supplied, and for which it is hard to trace any consistent meaning in the postcolony. One route that we can take is well captured in an aphorism attributed to Desmond Tutu: "There is something in us that refuses to be regarded as less than human. We are created for freedom."[3] This theme – being created for freedom – shapes the argument that follows (for which the footnotes provide a crucial supplement).

Four comments situate us. First, European colonization, far from being a unified project, was messy: imperial nations acted in ways not always consistent with each other or themselves even directly competing with each other, internal resistance within their own metropoles to their policies was never absent, and local populations in the colonies they sought to subjugate were never passive in their response. The struggle for freedom from colonial rule thus took many paths according to particular constellations of forces.

Second, decolonization is equally messy, not least thanks to the enduring, deleterious legacies of slavery, widespread cheap extraction of resources for which no adequate compensation was ever paid, and arbitrary geographical delineations of territories in forming nation states, but also because of alternative views of what was to be desired in the postcolony. These were as different as the people and groups that took the lead in reshaping particular societies. Further, much that did happen gave new expression to the self-interest of ambitious new elites or groups who sought to benefit themselves.

Third, nostalgia for some "original Africa" also confuses things. Nowhere is it possible to recover any supposedly pristine African pre-history, and all face new forms of incorporation into regional, continental, and global patterns of organization and exchange. Complications arise too from the limits of national identity: nation-states that follow the arbitrary borders drawn by imperial powers often cut across the organic societies of Africa, leaving an enduring legacy for conflict, and very old patterns of human migration, encounter, and exchange out of and into Africa (for example, Ethiopian Muslims trained in Yemen served as scribes and lawyers in the first Caliphates of Malaysia a millennium ago) have had long-term impact and continue in accelerated fashion today.

Fourth, another term synonymous with freedom to shape Africa in the 20th century is liberation. Again primarily meaning "freedom from" something, it suggests that liberty is freedom, but what liberty might be varies according to one's ideological or philosophical standpoint. It has meant a national struggle, a pan-African one, a sectional one (of workers against Capital, say), one against a global power arrangement, or, more recently, one against patriarchy or discrimination on the grounds of sexual orientation, sometimes even a general human struggle.

In sum, the idea of freedom remains contested in postcolonial African societies. Problematically, when it functions as legitimation by local elites or political leaders for new patterns of domination and unjust acquisition of power and resources, it has often embodied self-interests that necessarily includes some and excludes others. A contestation for the mantle of liberator is then waged on the back of new kinds of unfreedom. A relativistic notion of freedom resting on the contingent particularities (of geography, history, and culture) is thus unhelpful, making it hard, if not impossible, to decide whose freedom is prior, whose claim trumps another's. Take your choice as to what freedom means, one could say; but then the choice is made on some other ground than freedom itself.

The possibility of a universal ground of freedom

Is there then a sense of freedom not governed by, yet capable of grounding, any particular, contingent meaning – a general or universal understanding that can help us adjudicate its particular meanings (realizing that particular needs, competing interests, and unintended consequences limit what happens in practice)? If so, what are its implications?

I believe so, and many people in different contexts act as if they do too. It also matters intellectually and practically as much now as ever in the face of new forms or expressions of domination and subjugation, not least in the new confidence of bigotry and the normalization of the lie as acceptable in public discourse, as well as the pervasive penetration of our lifeworlds by the instrumental logic of money that seeks to commodify everything, including freedom itself.

Arguing for a universal idea of freedom entails some risk, however. It appears fraught in an intellectual era that has regularly questioned (if not trashed) any "grand narratives" of history or claims for a general understanding of the human being. Dominant intellectual currents abhor all universalisms as by definition oppressive or at best ignorant of the particularities of identity and history, insisting on "located" or contingently determined readings of reality as decisive. Any and every interpretation of freedom is viewed as always a product of limited and limiting circumstances (such as gender, race, class, culture, history, or geography).

On this basis, resolving any conflict over interpretations depends on determining the credibility of a claim on the basis of its origin: who is making the claim from what social location? One then decides to what extent this circumscribes, or outright disqualifies, any particular claim. The quality of an argument is thus secondary to the determination of the "right" of its author to make any claim at all. So arises a secondary contestation – over which origins (persons or authors) are acceptable, which are not, and why. Any "universal" claim is in principle negated as untenable, as nothing more than a disguised articulation of a particular claim that must, thereby, be seen to be ideological: held in order to promote or protect particular interests. Here the heavy winds of relativism blow strong, leaving little room to secure any meaning of freedom upon which we all may depend whatever our circumstances, origin, or location.

In seeking to counter this, I take a second risk: a recovery of the thought of Immanuel Kant. Frequently rejected out of hand as a "Western" thinker who, by virtue of his social origin, is irrelevant elsewhere or, worse, positively oppressive – particularly in his purportedly racist views on other peoples[4] – Kant is often seen as an intellectual enemy. Nonetheless (and contra my own decades-long deeply negative prejudices against Kant which for good reasons I now question), I hope to show the risk is worthwhile.

Douglas McGaughey's[5] meticulous excavation of the texts (in German and English) and, to a lesser extent, Otfried Höffe's writings have helped me understand why Kant is worth recovering.[6] Both challenge a dominant, widespread reception of Kant, especially among Anglo-Americans, that assumes his thought has been thoroughly displaced by pragmatic, communicative, and relativist frameworks. Further, instead of assessing Kant's work by deciding what kind of a person he was or social context he reflected (which Höffe calls "the principle of malevolence"),[7] Höffe insists first on an "immanent" reading of the texts that analyses its arguments and consistency, only secondarily to be augmented by an historical or contextual reading. To this McGaughey adds a concern about "metaphor interference" – misunderstandings arising from anachronistic readings of key terms or concepts, unhelpful translations of the original, and intellectual prejudices transmitted by Empiricism or Rationalism.[8] Their congruent reinterpretation helps us grasp Kant's critical understanding of freedom.

The ground of freedom

Central to Kant's corpus, including his critiques of theoretical reason, practical reason, and judgement and writings on religion, is a concept of freedom. What he means by this helps illuminate and deepen what we already intuit about freedom and liberation irrespective of Kant, not least in Africa. Without inventing or discovering it – it is evident across all cultures and times – he saw something fundamental and definitive about what it means to be human that is no less relevant or important today: a non-contingent foundation for all of our contingent judgements about freedom that otherwise, because of their contingency, are ultimately arbitrary.

The crucial insight is that we possess to an extraordinary degree a causally effective *capacity of creative freedom* that allows us intentionally to transform nature and ourselves in unprecedented ways, for which reason our intentions and actions in the world, willy-nilly, acknowledged or not, carry with them an enormous moral responsibility. This is an ineradicable and inalienable capacity that marks us as specifically human and is the condition of every other kind of freedom. What kind of capacity is this, then?

It is *a capacity of spirit*[9] that, though limited by its material conditions (e.g., the physical laws of nature), can through a form of *non-material* efficient causality accomplish goals in the material world that physical causality on its own cannot accomplish. This occurs through our use of symbol systems such as language and mathematics (which must be acquired) by which we add to the phenomena we experience (natural and social) an understanding of them that enables us to go beyond what nature itself can achieve, thereby transforming nature and ourselves at the same time. This capacity allows us to escape instinct and mere needs by grasping in the actual (that which is before us) what is possible but not yet realized and finding ways to bring those new possibilities into being. Shared by other creatures to some extent, it is nonetheless a capacity that we possess *to a degree* that is patently extra-ordinary.

This is most obvious in the domain of nature. By assuming that there is a unifying causal (that is, lawful) character to nature and by attributing (that is adding) to natural phenomena concepts and theories that progressively enable us better to grasp the causes that produce the effects we experience, we are able to understand phenomena that our sensible experience denies. The most obvious but exemplary indication of this capacity are that, contrary to ordinary experience, we are able to discern that the earth circles the sun and not vice-versa, and that we stand on a planet that spins at up to 1000 miles an hour while orbiting the sun at roughly 67,000 miles per hour. Only by carefully observing all relevant phenomena and then *adding to those observations* a theory to explain what our senses otherwise deny are we able to arrive at such understandings.

The extra-ordinary power of this capacity is also evident in our ability to manipulate natural phenomena in unparalleled ways, such as controlling fire, inventing the hoe and plough, launching a huge piece of metal through the air safely carrying hundreds of people, programming a computer, undertaking genetic engineering or building nanotechnologies, or destroying the world itself and ourselves along with it should we so choose.

In short, if we are creatures of nature, we are also capable of standing "above" nature, of deliberately transcending what is given (without ever being able to ignore it) to bring into being that which did not exist before.[10] This capacity to "see things that are not there" as potential thus allows us to act teleologically, to transcend our biological needs and instinctual patterns of behaviour to initiate sequences of events that nature could never accomplish on its own. This is as momentous as it is also potentially dangerous, for our freedom above nature can be both creative and destructive.

The reminder that we possess this power and must decide how to use it is the moral law within. Our creative freedom also means that we have the capacity intentionally to "give ourselves the law," to act in a way that is not determined by any external force or law, that is, autonomously. This second, positive sense of ourselves as creatures that possess creative freedom allows us to ask how we *ought* to act in any particular moment and to act accordingly, that is, with causal effect. Only now we act not in relation to nature and its causal structures but in relation to ourselves and our relationship to other beings (and by implication, to nature itself). The moment we do so we enter the world of morality.[11] We can (and on occasion do) hold ourselves responsible for the intentions with which we act in the world. However "imperfect," we are moral creatures of spirit because, no matter the constraints of one kind or another upon us, we can determine what we intend when we act and thus take responsibility for our creative freedom.

There is an influential view that our will – our capacity intentionally to give ourselves the law by which we act, that is, to decide for ourselves – has no independent authority of the needs or desires that drive us.[12] Kant is not naïve about this: "We like to flatter ourselves by falsely attributing to ourselves a nobler motive, whereas in fact we can never, even by the most strenuous self-examination, get entirely behind our covert incentives"[13]; we "are also affected by sensibility, by incentives of a different kind [inclinations arising from need, desire and self-interest], and in whose case that which reason by itself would do is not always done."[14] Need, desire and self-interest (inescapably part of us) are always inmixed in our motives but, and this is the vital point, we are *also* capable of transcending them – of acting on the basis of something other than need, desire or self-interest.

We can now say that morality presupposes autonomous freedom above the imposed laws of nature (which we do not escape). Autonomy has nothing to do with individualism here; rather, it is our capacity intentionally to choose the principles ("laws") upon which we decide to act, something only we can do for ourselves even when shaped or influenced by others. The alternative is to adhere to some heteronomous law externally imposed upon us, either mechanically (without thought or consideration) or to "please" the external source of the law – for civic or customary law, the expectations of one's society; for theonomous law, the expectations of the deity deemed to be its author.

Clearly, we can (often do) freely decide to adhere to an external law or expectation if we believe it to be of great value. The key moral question is whether we do so for the sake of all and of the whole or, rather, for the sake of particular needs or limited interests. If we give (our choice!) ultimate authority to a limited, particular external demand or obligation, then we do so at the cost of foregoing any principle upon which one may judge the morality of the demand or obligation itself. We know that a particular code, regulation, obligation or law can be unjust or, alternatively, complied with formally but only for the sake of self-interest (of oneself, a group, a society, even a religion or faith tradition). Either we accept that we have no way of deciding what is moral other than merely pragmatically and comparatively (a widely held view), or we hold that there is a foundation that grounds justice and that is capable of providing us with a critical principle for assessing any particular code, regulation, obligation, or law. I stand for the latter.

To recognize our freedom as grounding the moral law within is to acknowledge the power of our internal creativity and our responsibility for it. Whatever the external influences upon us (positive or negative), we always possess the causal power and authority to determine the principle that governs us in each non-trivial decision. Nothing other than a destruction of our humanity can take that freedom from us. Whereas the moralizing impact of theonomy or of society is also real, it may or may not be positive. That can only be decided on other grounds, specifically, the grounds of our own dignity as autonomous beings capable of acting morally (noting, precisely because of our freedom, that we are not deterministically programmed to act morally).

That we are not automatons nor merely act according to external imperatives – that we can legitimately assume the causal capacity of our freedom – is evident from our struggles for justice. The very idea and possibility of justice depends upon an exercise of freedom that we cannot prove but out of which we nonetheless act. Freedom, in this sense, is the condition of the moral law.[15]

Human dignity, the demand of freedom, and the role of community

We are now able to ask further about human dignity, what freedom demands of us, and what the role of community is in upholding our creative freedom and fostering the moral responsibility it carries.

Creative freedom is the ground of human dignity because no one can think for someone else or act or take responsibility for another. To assume otherwise is in effect to deem others as less capable of acting and being responsible for their acts than oneself, to deny their full humanness. In history, this takes the form of the subjugation and dehumanization of myriads of people across different times and places.

To repeat, when we act intentionally in the world we express a causal agency within two systems of lawful order – nature and autonomous, creative freedom. In acting intentionally in either order, we *uncover the possible in the actual* and, so, accomplish things to a degree that no other species of which we are aware is capable. Not only are we able to transform nature (for better or worse) thereby, but we are also innovatively able to reimagine and reconstruct our social life with others.[16]

This capacity of creative freedom is not defined by any contingent aspect of our being – by gender, ethnic identity, sexual orientation, physical condition, or anything similar – nor is it the privileged possession of the clever or a genius. It is universal, intrinsic, and inalienable, defined by the very meaning of human being and becoming, and, thus, the basis of our dignity and the ground for any and all justice and virtue. Only this enables us to adjudicate between contingent freedoms or assess their achievements and failures, and this is what every particular construction of freedom ultimately depends upon.

We can take this further. As Kant notes in *Groundwork of the Metaphysics of Morals*[17] most human action gains its value by serving our needs, desires and interests, all of which are relative and not universal. But in taking them to be important for ourselves *we treat ourselves as ends*. This is the subjective principle of human action and it points directly to an objective principle: that which we expect for ourselves we are capable of attributing (hence, ought to attribute) to all other human beings. Here human dignity as intrinsic, inalienable, and possessed by all passes over into a general imperative,[18] one that arises from the fact of our creative freedom and the moral responsibility that accompanies it: "So act that you use humanity, whether in your own person or in the person of any other, always at the same time as an end, never merely as a means."[19]

This radical demand is not derivable directly from experience; it is a *condition* of our experience of being and becoming human rather than a result of it. We cannot extract it with much confidence from the vagaries of human action, so often inclined to our self-interest rather than the objective presence of other human beings. It is radical because it asks us to act intentionally beyond our needs, desires and self-interests. Its assumption – one by no means outside our experience even if rarer than we might like – is that we have the capacity so to act. When we sense that someone intentionally does act for the sake of all and of the whole rather than to gain some reward or recognition, we are generally drawn to honour them as truly moral, as worth emulating to the extent we are able.[20]

In sum, our precarious (because not determined but free) creative and moral condition allows us to think and act for ourselves, to "give ourselves the law" and take responsibility for this, and to recognize thereby an invisible, immaterial (spiritual) order that includes treating persons as ends and not merely as means. If this is true for us then it is true for every other person. In this sense we are bound together objectively (subjectively we may miss or ignore it) in a community of persons that Kant, in easy to misread language, calls a "kingdom of ends" (*Reich der Zwecke*), which he describes as "a systematic union of various rational beings through common laws."[21]

The English "common laws" (*gemeinschaftliche Gesetze*) escapes the richness of the German original. *Gemeinschaft* refers to an interdependent interaction between those who act and those who suffer (*Wechselwirkung zwischen Handelden und Leidenden*),[22] a powerful indication of the moral demand also present in Paul Ricoeur's understanding of our agency or capacity of creative freedom: "With the decrease of the power of *acting*, experienced as a decrease of the effort of *existing*, the reign of suffering, properly speaking, commences."[23]

Further, *Reich* can also be translated as "commonwealth," which better expresses the democratic thrust of Kant's thought[24] in which no human is intrinsically superior to another and morality is action for the benefit (weal) of all. The "kingdom (or commonwealth) of ends" is thus a reference to our membership in an invisible community, including the privilege and obligations that belonging to it entails. "Duty" for Kant, often hugely misunderstood, means our objective commitment to this commonwealth of ends as a member of it alongside all other members but also as "sovereign" within it, that is, as still possessing the subjective capacity to act on the basis of our creative freedom.[25]

Whereas each of us alone must ultimately assume responsibility for the self-imposed (chosen) moral principles that govern our actions, we are not alone in our precarious position. From the womb onwards, the human species is a relational species, a communal species, definitively so. Yet a parent's or community's vital role in forming us cannot erase our own moral capacity and responsibility. As the Nuremberg Trials of Nazis whose defense was that "I was just obeying orders" again made clear, an appeal to an authority outside of oneself in defense of one's immoral actions was and ought not be regarded as tenable. Not everything in whatever communal tradition or authority we live contributes to enhancing the fullness of our spiritual capacities or helps us take moral responsibility for our actions. Our very human need to gain status and prestige or acceptance and belonging from others can be a powerful contributing factor in encouraging our moral efforts, but it is no guarantee of it. It can equally result in our performing reprehensible and destructive deeds for the sake of approval, for inclusion, or in defense of one's honour.

The proper use of our autonomous freedom requires something far more. It requires a community that understands the breadth, width, and depth of spirit as the immaterial, indivisible, and ineradicable dimension of the individual and species that grounds our creative capacity. This places a high standard before every kind of human community, but it is one that is neither out of reach nor less than we ought to expect of ourselves.

Where we have arrived

Other species are capable of goal-oriented behavior that is to a degree pragmatic and caring (such as protecting another or serving the welfare of a group, African wild dogs being a great example), but their goals are instinctual and not intentional in the sense of being governed by a self-legislated moral law. So we would never seriously imagine putting a dog on trial in court, but we do create institutions like courts to hold ourselves responsible for our acts, and we do hold ourselves to some moral standard in doing so. It is this crucial difference in degree (not necessarily kind) and the nature of the causality that drives our agency that distinguishes humanity.

Autonomous freedom, then, is spirit-agency in the objective, empirical world. Its condition of possibility and its primary concern, if never free of self-interest, is the understanding, preservation, and transformation of the world to preserve and to enhance life – of the self and others. Moreover, not limited only to the effort of the individual in exercising her/his creative capacities, not just an internal, inaccessible dimension of experience, it is necessarily concerned with preserving the very conditions of possibility for exercising that creativity. Its sphere of agency thus must include the protection of the physical world, the creation of just institutions in which human creativity can flourish, and the establishment of social or political institutions that acknowledge the dignity of all. This is no less significant than it ever was given the many ways in which the dignity and integrity of persons is trivialized in consumer culture through the commodification of everything, or the far too many situations in communities and societies around the world where that dignity and integrity is ignored or impaired and persons are used as ends to a means that serves the self-interest of a few, an elite, an elect, or the purportedly righteous.

The generality of freedom and morality

One does not have to read Kant to gain insight into the vital significance of our creative freedom and its moral demand. If he has appropriately unpacked something genuinely universal, attributable to any and all human beings throughout time, then it must in some form be present to the awareness of human beings in every society or tradition. A couple of recent examples help illustrate the point.

In Frantz Fanon's penetrating analyses in *Black Skin, White Masks* and *The Wretched of the Earth*[26] of the impact upon human dignity of oppression, he unpacks the devastating effect of colonization upon the colonized in propagating a view of the latter's inferior, subhuman status. This produces guilt about one's being, engendering shame when one cannot transcend this imposed identification in the eyes of the other. Guilt, failure, and shame are obstacles to the emergence of the full humanity of the oppressed. But here they do not arise from raw self-interest or intentional wrongdoing, rather because one feels reduced as a human being through the assertion of inferiority, the assault on ones very human dignity which grounds human freedom and moral responsibility.

Without reclaiming the dignity that resides in every human being irrespective of any other differences, without rebelling against one's dehumanization, one cannot arrive at what Fanon calls the "The glowing focal point where the citizen and the individual develop and mature."[27] For Fanon this applies to every individual, not just the privileged or conquering elites but also the colonized or oppressed, to all equally. His is a universal call to the realization of our full capacities as human persons. Whatever other differences there might be, this clearly converges with Kant's understanding of human dignity and the moral (categorical) imperative.

This same theme arises again in Steve Biko's thought, perhaps in part because he drew on Fanon's work. In his aptly titled essay on "Black Consciousness and the Quest for a True Humanity," Biko writes, "Freedom is the ability to define oneself with one's possibilities held back not by the power of other people over one but only by one's relationship to God and to natural surroundings."[28] Blackness for Biko, using a Hegelian dialectic, is the antithesis of Whiteness, the thesis. Given White domination, the antithesis necessarily requires the mobilization of Black people – but as a strategic (political) and temporary necessity, not as an end in itself. There is no special privileging of one kind of human over another. The end, the synthesis, is an all-inclusive "true humanity."[29]

If Biko uses a Hegelian dialectic to articulate a temporary strategic position, he also places the notion of human dignity and its moral imperative at the heart of his call for a new confidence and certainty in being Black. Crucially, he equates Blackness neither with pigmentation nor with cultural specificity, but with a universal condition of full humanity beyond any particular racial categorizations or specific ontology. Thus our humanity, our dignity, is rooted not in any substantive identifier, any empirical or material marker; rather, it resides in a non-material capacity that we may thus call spiritual.

Unsurprisingly, surely not coincidentally, the same theme, now directly referencing Kant, arises again in South Africa in its post-apartheid 1996 constitution, which turned its back on the history of subjugation and dehumanization of specific people ("Blacks," in Biko's language) intending to create a new society open to all. In a fraught and challenging context with the pain of the past immediately present and continuing, it aimed precisely to oppose the limited self-interest and restricted understanding of human being that marked apartheid society, and colonization and segregation before it.

Laurie Ackermann, senior judge in the first post-apartheid "Mandela" Constitutional Court, articulates the founding principle upon which the Constitution is built in his *Human Dignity: Lodestar for Equality in South Africa*.[30] Human dignity is the lodestar because it enables us to navigate the complex, complicated, and contested terrain of social life by providing the guiding, foundational principle of law and jurisprudence. It functions in a way that common law or tradition-bound legal codes as "historical exercises"[31] cannot, for they are particular ways of structuring relationships between people that still require a norm capable of enabling us to adjudicate between different particulars. Referencing Kant, Ackermann notes, "A purely empirical theory of law is . . . a head, that might be beautiful, but alas! one that has no brain."[32] The empirical world of appearances can neither account for our capacity as human beings to give ourselves the law, nor ground the law in anything other than competing self-interest. What must count, instead, is intrinsic worth, which is universal.[33]

As Ackermann notes,

> The [apartheid] state did its best to deny to black South Africans that which is definitional to being human, namely, the ability to understand or at least define oneself through one's own powers and to act freely as a moral agent pursuant to this understanding or self-definition. Black people were treated as a means to an end and hardly ever as an end in themselves; an almost complete reversal of the categorically imperative concept of priceless inner worth and dignity.[34]

Human dignity is then about intrinsic worth and has no price. This intrinsic worth rests upon capacities that separate human beings "from the impersonality of nature, enables them to exercise their own judgement, to have self-awareness and a sense of self-worth, to exercise self-determination, to shape themselves and nature, to develop their personalities and to strive for self-fulfillment in their lives."[35] Human dignity is thus central to restitution, to equality or unfair discrimination, to the relationship between people and the state as well as between subjects themselves, and to the limitation of rights. It is embodied in society when each person embraces her or his autonomous, creative freedom and the moral responsibility it calls forth, and when the society within which particular persons live acknowledges, respects and enhances it as core to any other functions it plays.

A recovery of the significance of human spirit and its capacities is thus relevant not just to particular forms of oppression and dehumanization. To place human spirit (creative freedom and its moral imperative) at the centre is to place possibility above actuality and thus, faced with the question of what we will that ought to be, to open up the means for transforming the conditions of our existence. It is, in other words, at the heart of liberation or historical freedom.

Can we "listen to" a purported racist?

Racism is a denial of the human worth and dignity of particular people, and Kant is often treated as an icon of European racism whose thought should therefore ipso facto be disqualified.[36] As my argument depends on Kant and

I obviously hope to be heard, it is necessary briefly to address this issue.[37] This subjective motive has a second, objective, and in the end more important one: Kant's exploration of creative freedom, human dignity and moral responsibility still has substantial value for our ability critically to respond to the confusing moral and ethical challenges that lie before us in Africa as elsewhere.

Leaving aside whether any texts can survive ad hominem criticism, is the charge of racism against Kant well founded? If not, as I believe,[38] then it should be easier to "listen to" what he might have to offer. Kant may well have shared the widespread racist ways of thinking and being of his place and time. Though we cannot prove or disprove whether and to what extent this is so, the key texts that seem to support this are less clear than is often claimed. Two of the worst frequently attributed to Kant actually come from others: Hume in one case (cited by Kant as claiming that the difference between "Negroes" and whites "appears to be as great in regard to mental capacities as in color"); and Father Labat in the other ("this fellow was very black from head to foot, a clear proof that what he said was stupid").[39] Besides being statements made by others – we do not know if Kant agreed with them – they come from Kant's very early writings (1764), prior to his so-called "critical phase" and most important writings. That justifies nothing but it gives pause for thought, especially as what Kant says in his later writings is so different, as I shall indicate.

Another major point of attack concerns what seems to be a description by Kant of different human races that appears in Friedrich Christian Starke's edition of Kant's *Menschenkunde oder philosophische Anthropologie* from 1831. A focus of Eze's claim "that Immanuel Kant produced the most profound raciological thought of the eighteenth century,"[40] these are lecture notes taken by Starke as a student and published some quarter century after Kant's death. The offending passages, however, are in a footnote, not in the lecture notes themselves. We don't know, then, if they are Kant's words or someone else's, nor why Starke thought them worth including. It is equally possible, likely even (again, we don't know), that Kant used them in class as a negative foil to his own positive argument, as many teachers do to provoke reaction.

The footnote appears in an extended argument by Kant about morality, concerning what today we might call race classifications. In his argument he explicitly identifies such classifications as "speculation," against which he defends his own theory of monogenesis: that all human beings come from the same, single stock regardless of their "epigenetic" differences (those shaped by environment and circumstances). In an astonishing anticipation of DNA and genetics, he suggests that there are "seeds" (*Keimen*) that allow for differences between humans but that they in no way allow one to deny full humanity and a common origin to all human beings. Here and in many related discussions Kant employs theoretical reason (scientific thinking) in search of a "biological" understanding of how evident physical differences between human beings arise. In no way does he employ practical reason at this point, that is, give any "moral" account that would ground a difference in human beings in terms of their capacities or humanity per se.

This is far more consistent with much of the rest of his thought. Indeed, his entire enterprise depends upon a view of humanity – regardless of external or contingent circumstances, personal characteristics (including biological or cultural differences), physical condition, or one's age – as possessing, from the moment one is in the world and as long as one is human, the same inalienable and profound capacities of creative freedom that ground one's dignity.

To be sure, there are less flattering passages in Kant's works, so we cannot exclude the possibility of his racism. But enough has been said to suggest that this is not definitive of what we gain from him, namely, a clearer understanding of what is absolutely central to his position: his emphasis on creative freedom, its conditions of possibility, and the moral demand that accompanies it.

Back to Jesse (and others)

We do not need Kant, nor "Western" or European thought per se, to see for ourselves what is at the heart of our freedom as human beings by which we may judge any contingent, partial, or empirical claim and struggle for freedom. If it truly is universal then it requires no other basis than a consideration of our humanity in the world, something virtually every civilization or culture has sought to articulate even when, perhaps especially when, it betrays that ground.

Nonetheless, Kant helps us reinforce and extend insights that are also strongly present elsewhere, not least in the thought of Jesse Mugambi about both liberation and reconstruction. Deeply shaped by decolonization in his home country Kenya and by its charismatic first President, Jomo Kenyatta, Mugambi has both championed an African liberation theology and faced the challenge of rebuilding a damaged society in writing about reconstruction.[41] In the latter he uses the metaphor of Nehemiah who rebuilt Jerusalem rather than Moses who led the people out of slavery, seeking a new dispensation "against racism, colonial domination and ideological branding" that would remake Africa by calling upon its cultural and intellectual resources.[42]

We may think of the liberation as a form of *freedom from* unjust coercion and control. However, because this is a limited sense of freedom that tells us nothing about what it might mean to think and act in terms of *freedom for* something else, a shift to reconstruction seems logical.

Mugambi, it seems to me, drawing on the resources derived from his religious faith tradition, has never failed to advocate for freedom defined in terms of mere need and desire, or personal, communal, social, national, cultural, or even confessional self-interest. The ends of freedom and not just its means remain important, and the distinction between negative freedom

("freedom from") and positive freedom ("freedom for") is clearly hinted at in Mugambi's 1995 book on liberation and reconstruction.[43] It is this distinction that I have attempted to reflect upon further. However, one parses the relationship between liberation and reconstruction (about which there is considerable debate)[44] the idea of freedom, concretized in social, political, and economic structures and practices, is at the heart of his work. As his writings amply demonstrate, moreover, he does not restrict freedom to any narrow cultural, national, religious, or ideological interests.

Thus, in celebration of his contributions, it is more than appropriate to ask again about the kind of freedom that allows us to understand not just the thrust of liberation and an interest in reconstruction but also, more fundamentally, how it marks us as human beings capable of confronting that which damages us and of acting, together, towards that which represents the highest of which we are capable.

Notes

1 I acknowledge financial support towards this work from the National Research Foundation (Grant 103705), and the University Research Committee, University of Cape Town; opinions and conclusions expressed here are mine and no liability applies to them or any other agent. jim.cochrane@uct.ac.za

2 "Winds of Change" speech was delivered by Harold Macmillan to the South African Parliament in 1960. He said, "The wind of change is blowing through this [African] continent, and whether we like it or not, this growth of national consciousness is a political fact. We must all accept it as a fact, and our national policies must take account of it." See www.thoughtco.com/wind-of-change-speech-43748. (accessed October 4, 2017).

3 www.goodreads.com/author/quotes/5943.Desmond_Tutu?page=3. (accessed October 4, 2017).

4 Towards the end of this essay I comment briefly on the most common charges in this regard.

5 See particularly Douglas R. McGaughey, "Freedom on This and the Other Side of Kant," in n.k., ed. *Proceedings of the 12th International Kant Congress 2015* (Berlin: Walter de Gruyter, 2018). For pre-publication versions, see: http://criticalidealism.org/freedom-on-this-and-the-other-side-of-kant-2/.

6 See Otfried Höffe, *Kants Kritik der Praktischen Vernunft: Eine Philosophie der Freiheit*. (München: C. H. Beck, 2012); *Kant's Kritik die reinen Vernunft: die Grundlegung der modernen Philosophie*. (München: Verlag C. H. Beck, 2011 [2003]).

7 Höffe, *Kant's Kritik die reinen Vernunft: die Grundlegung der modernen Philosophie*, 12.

8 Problematic ways of thinking about Kant include: 1) the error, cued from the Critique of Pure Reason, of seeing his contribution primarily as epistemological when, as his second Preface makes clear, epistemology is inseparable from his metaphysics in general and view on morality or practical reason in particular; 2) the mistake of treating his metaphysics as reflecting a particular (European) ontology – a contextually conditioned theory of substances or essences – whereas it deals with the conditions of possibility for the way we experience anything at all, telling us something about ourselves rather than about any external or externalized reality; 3) the claim that Kant, like Descartes, views the human being dualistically as a "rational" being (mind) removed from "animality" (body),

whereas he insists that i) only as sensual creatures do we experience anything at all, ii) experience precedes all knowledge, and iii) reason exists for us only as embodied creatures in the world; and, 4) treating Kant as "the representative" of the Enlightenment (anything but a homogenous movement), hence, the embodiment of all that is wrong with colonial thought, when he is its first great critic – especially regarding the (human) limits to reason, knowledge, and action.

9 By "spirit" I mean all that we experience as real about ourselves that is non-material or supersensible; see Douglas R. McGaughey and James R. Cochrane, *The Human Spirit: Groundwork*. (Stellenbosch: SUN Media, 2017).

10 This does not imply that we are not part of nature, that we can do with nature as we wish without repercussions, or that there is some realm "outside" and wholly independent of nature of which we have certain knowledge (we may assume this in faith, but that is in principle neither provable nor disprovable).

11 Morality here stands above particular cultural norms, customs, mores, codes of conduct, or ethical prescriptions, though these are its necessary (but always contingent) expressions in embodied human life.

12 Jonathan Haidt, echoing earlier theories of moral sentiments (David Hume, Adam Smith, Adam Ferguson), uses the metaphor of an elephant (our "intuitions" driven by needs, desires, and self-interest and shaped by evolutionary development) as determining our actions, with the elephant's rider (the will) merely providing their post-facto legitimizations.

13 Immanuel Kant, *Groundwork of the Metaphysics of Morals*. Translated by Mary Gregor and Jens Timmerman, Second Edition. *Cambridge Texts in the History of Philosophy*. (Cambridge: Cambridge University Press, 2012), 19 (AA 4:407).

14 Ibid., 55 (AA 4:449).

15 See Immanuel Kant, *Critique of Practical Reason*. Translated by Mary Gregor, Revised edition. (Cambridge: Cambridge University Press, 2015), 3–4 (AA 5:4). As Kant elsewhere says, "Teleology [or theoretical reason, as in the sciences] considers nature as a kingdom of ends, morals [practical reason] considers a possible kingdom of ends as a kingdom of nature. In the former the kingdom of ends is a theoretical idea for explaining what exists. In the latter, it is a practical idea for the sake of bringing about, in conformity with this very idea, that which does not exist but which can become real by means of our conduct"; see Groundwork of the Metaphysics of Morals, 44 (AA 4:436). "Conduct" in the German is "Thun und Lassen," better translated as "doing and allowing," which indicates the agency we exercise at this point.

16 Because the effects of our capacity of creative freedom are so evident in the world that we must assume we have it, Kant calls this the one "fact of Reason"; see *Critique of Practical Reason*, 28 (AA 5:31), also 37–8 (AA 5:42–3). See also *The Critique of the Power of Judgement*. Translated by Paul Guyer. (Cambridge: Cambridge University Press, 2001), 337–8 (AA 5:474).

17 *Groundwork of the Metaphysics of Morals*, 36–8 (AA 4:428–9).

18 Kant calls this the categorical imperative, meaning that it is not dependent on contingent circumstances or realities (which can only produce hypothetical imperatives, recognized by an "if . . . then" structure).

19 Kant, *Groundwork of the Metaphysics of Morals*, 38 (AA 4:431).

20 Equally, when it becomes evident that someone acts out of self-interest, we generally do not give it great moral worth. For a longer discussion, see "The Incentives of Pure Practical Reason," in the *Critique of Practical Reason*, 60ff. (AA 5:71f, especially 81*).

21 *Groundwork of the Metaphysics of Morals*, 41 (AA 4:433).

22 Eisler, *Kant Dictionary*, www.textlog.de/32334.html.

23 Paul Ricoeur, *Oneself as Another*. (Chicago: University of Chicago Press, 1992), 320.

24 For Kant the human capacities to which he gives the name Reason are by definition intrinsic and held by all equally, unlike Plato who held a hierarchical view. This is far broader than Locke's view of instrumental, calculating reason which tends to dominate contemporary discourse.
25 Kant, *Groundwork of the Metaphysics of Morals*, 41 (AA 4:433).
26 Frantz Fanon, *The Wretched of the Earth*. Translated by Jean-Paul Sartre and Constance Farrington. (New York: Grove Press, 1963); *Black Skin, White Masks*. Translated by Richard Philcox. (New York: Grove Press, 1967). Whether he unsure (and irrelevant); he did read many other European philosophers, notably Hegel.
27 *The Wretched of the Earth*, 40.
28 Aelred Stubbs, ed. *I Write What I Like: Steve Biko. A Selection of His Writings*. (Oxford: Heinemann, 1987), 93. The essay first appeared in Basil Moore, ed. *Black Theology: The South African Voice*. (London: C. Hurst & Co, 1973).
29 Stubbs, 90.
30 Laurie Ackermann, *Human Dignity: Lodestar for Equality in South Africa*. (Cape Town: Juta & Co., 2012).
31 The foundational role of human dignity as a universal claim must necessarily be embodied in particular traditions, cultures, or societies. It does not negate the need for historical or contingent "exercises" in law.
32 Ackermann, 3. See Kant's *Metaphysics of Morals*. (AA 6:230).
33 Ibid., 12.
34 Ibid., 12. Ackermann quotes Kant's famous phrase here too: Sapere aude! [literally: "dare to be wise"].
35 Ibid., 23–4.
36 Prominent here is the piece by Emmanuel Chukwudi Eze, "The Color of Reason: The Idea of 'Race' in Kant's Anthropology," in Emmanuel Chukwudi Eze, ed. *Postcolonial African Philosophy: A Critical Reader*. (Oxford: Blackwell Publishers, 1997).
37 These brief comments depend heavily (and gratefully) on Douglas McGaughey's research; see "Was Kant a Racist?" at http://criticalidealism.org/was-kant-a-racist-posted-1-november-2016/. See also James R. Cochrane, "Het Verborgen Geweld Van Racisme: Verhulde Uitingen Van Het Blank Zijn," *Wereld en Sending* 4 (2002), translated from "The Epistemic Violence of Racism Hidden Transcripts of Whiteness," at www.researchgate.net/publication/237785657_The_Epistemic_Violence_of_Racism_Hidden_Transcripts_of_Whiteness).
38 See also the more recent compilation by Jon M. Mikkelsen, ed. *Kant and the Concept of Race: Late Eighteenth-Century Writings*. (New York: State University of New York Press, 2013). Mikkelsen directly addresses the influential works of Eze (see earlier footnote) and Tsenay Serequeberhan, both of whom heavily criticize Kant in this regard.
39 All citations unless otherwise specified are to McGaughey's online essay (see footnote 36 above).
40 Eze, 103.
41 Jesse N. K. Mugambi, "The Future of the Church and the Church of the Future in Africa," in Jose B. Chipenda, et al., eds. *The Church of Africa: Towards a Theology of Reconstruction*. (Nairobi: All Africa Conference of Churches, 1991).
42 *Christian Theology and Social Reconstruction*. (Nairobi: Acton, 2003), 128.
43 Mugambi, *From Liberation to Reconstruction*.
44 Much of this debate reflects a concern that discourses of reconstruction, besides sidelining a theology of liberation, might too easily pass over unreconstructed oppressions, not least racism but including patriarchy, and the negative impact of elite globalization.

References

Ackermann, Laurie. *Human Dignity: Lodestar for Equality in South Africa*. Cape Town: Juta & Co., 2012.

Alexander, Neville. *Thoughts on the New South Africa*. Johannesburg: Jacana Media, 2013.

Cochrane, James R. "Het Verborgen Geweld Van Racisme: Verhulde Uitingen Van Het Blank Zijn." *Wereld en Sending* 4 (2002): 41–50.

Eze, Emmanuel Chukwudi. "The Color of Reason: The Idea of 'Race' in Kant's Anthropology." In *Postcolonial African Philosophy: A Critical Reader*, edited by Emmanuel Chukwudi Eze, 103–40. Oxford: Blackwell Publishers, 1997.

Fanon, Frantz. *Black Skin, White Masks*. Translated by Richard Philcox. New York: Grove Press, 1967.

———. *The Wretched of the Earth*. Translated by Jean-Paul Sartre and Constance Farrington. New York: Grove Press, 1963.

Höffe, Otfried. *Kant's Kritik die reinen Vernunft: die Grundlegung der modernen Philosophie*. München: Verlag C. H. Beck, 2011.

———. *Kants Kritik der Praktischen Vernunft: Eine Philosophie der Freiheit*. München: C. H. Beck, 2012.

Kant, Immanuel. *Critique of Practical Reason*. Translated by Mary Gregor. Revised ed. Cambridge: Cambridge University Press, 2015.

———. *The Critique of the Power of Judgement*. Translated by Paul Guyer. Cambridge: Cambridge University Press, 2001.

———. *Groundwork of the Metaphysics of Morals*. Translated by Mary Gregor and Jens Timmerman. Cambridge Texts in the History of Philosophy. Second edition. Cambridge: Cambridge University Press, 2012.

Maré, Gerhard. *Declassified: Moving Beyond the Dead End of Race in South Africa*. Johannesburg: Jacana Media, 2014.

McGaughey, Douglas R. "Freedom on This and the Other Side of Kant." In *Proceedings of the 12th International Kant Congress 2015*, edited by n.k. Berlin: Walter de Gruyter, 2018.

McGaughey, Douglas R., and James R. Cochrane. *The Human Spirit: Groundwork*. Stellenbosch: SUN Media, 2017.

Mikkelsen, Jon M., ed. *Kant and the Concept of Race: Late Eighteenth-Century Writings*. New York: State University of New York Press, 2013.

Moore, Basil, ed. *Black Theology: The South African Voice*. London: C. Hurst & Co, 1973.

Mugambi, Jesse N. K. *Christian Theology and Social Reconstruction*. Nairobi: Acton, 2003.

———. "The Future of the Church and the Church of the Future in Africa." In *The Church of Africa: Towards a Theology of Reconstruction*, edited by Jose B. Chipenda, A. Karamaga, Jesse N. K. Mugambi and C. K. Omari, 29–50. Nairobi: All Africa Conference of Churches, 1991.

———. *From Liberation to Reconstruction: African Christian Theology after the Cold War*. Nairobi: East African Educational Publishers, 1995.

Ricoeur, Paul. *Oneself as Another*. Chicago: University of Chicago Press, 1992.

Stubbs, Aelred, ed. *I Write What I Like: Steve Biko. A Selection of His Writings*. Oxford: Heinemann, 1987.

18 The challenge facing the next generation of African theologians

Laurenti Magesa

Footprints in the sands of time

In recent years I have heard this remark – by some it was made half-in-jest, but others were very serious and concerned: "What will happen to African Theology when the present generation of African theologians passes on?" In whatever mood uttered, it is an observation that draws attention to the faith, hope, courage, and charity of the pioneers of African Christian Theology who, through their daring work, have left footprints on the history of the Christian faith in Africa. I am convinced that the sands of time cannot wipe them away. Among the most prominent pioneers of African Theology must be counted Professor Jesse N. K. Mugambi. His tireless effort during approximately four decades of teaching, writing, speaking, and – above all – his living out the implications of all these initiatives are familiar to any student of theology in Africa. In this regard he is accompanied by other like-minded sons and daughters of Africa as witnesses of a Christian Church planted firmly in African soil. This reflection is a tribute to him as a person and as an appreciation of his scholarship.

Determined development of African theology

Beginning in the 1950s, African and Africanist theologians embraced the task of recording and examining the history and ministry of the Church in Africa. Theirs was an undertaking not unlike St. Luke's writing of his Gospel and the book of Acts for the purpose of recording the life and ministry of Jesus Christ. They could identify with the remarks Luke made to his friend Theophilus:

> Since many have undertaken to compile a narrative of the events that have been fulfilled among us, just as those who were eyewitnesses from the beginning and ministers of the word have handed them down to us, I too have decided, after investigating everything accurately anew,

> to write it down in an orderly sequence for you, most excellent Theophilus, so that you may realise the certainty of the teachings you have received.
>
> (Lk. 1:1–4)

Such was the challenge that Luke, a non-Jew or gentile, faced at a time when the Church was still dominated by Jewish membership, outlook, and culture. It was a very similar challenge that faced the pioneering generation of African theologians more than six decades ago. At that time the Church in Africa was a missionary Church, and as such was controlled by western structures and perceptions. To "investigate everything accurately anew" and to record it "in an orderly sequence" for African believers so that they could understand "the certainty of the teachings they . . . received" was therefore a duty that they could not with a clear conscience evade. A similar duty is incumbent upon the next generation of African theologians, one that they cannot with a clear conscience avoid.

A bird's-eye-view of major challenges for the future

Throughout the history of Christianity, christology and ecclesiology have posed the major challenges to the development of theology. The challenges continue to this day. Christology and ecclesiology constitute the ever present task of inculturating the gospel. Beyond a set of teachings to be believed, faith in Jesus constitutes primarily and above all a way of life. Doctrines certainly chart a way of understanding Jesus and the Church, as the bases of the communion of believers, his instruments. Yet the ultimate goal of the teachings is to indicate a way of following Jesus, to indicate a way of constructing a community that embraces the Reign of God. Doctrines bespeak questions that can be answered only partially in the past tense. What did Jesus do? How did the Christian community organize itself and what did it expect of its members years or centuries ago? How did the Apostle Paul and the other apostles relate with the gentiles – the non-Jewish Christians – at the very beginning of the Christian movement? How did the early Christians, the Doctors of the Church, respond to critical issues of their time and locations? These are important questions; the responses they evoke cannot be easily ignored, but they do not, and cannot, provide the whole picture for contemporary faith in Jesus Christ.

Christology and other dimensions of theology, such as ecclesiology, raise questions, the responses to which must be sought in the present, in the "joys and hopes, in the griefs and anxieties of the men and women of this age, especially those who are poor or in any way afflicted," to use the apt expression of the Second Vatican Council.[1] Such may have been the inspiration of the pioneers of African Theology, working no doubt under the inspiration of the Holy Spirit. They had encountered a missionary Church that alienated Africa and African peoples and they asked themselves fundamental questions: Why must Jesus Christ and his liberating mission continue to be explained in language and symbols fundamentally alien, inaccessible and, consequently, incomprehensible to the African experience? Why should the Church be organized according to structures foreign to the people of Africa? In their attempt to address these questions, African theology emerged. These questions continue to confront and challenge contemporary African theologians and they pose a particular challenge to future generations of African theologians who will need to address them in situ. It is the challenge of ongoing inculturation, inspired by Jesus's own supreme act of incarnation, the act of God-becoming-human so as to liberate humanity. It is the process of inculturation that must be attended to unceasingly by Christian theology.

Significant history with enduring consequences

The third Christian missionary attempt to evangelize Africa took place 1800 years after the death of Jesus Christ. In terms of longevity and geographical reach in Africa, it was the most successful, encompassing virtually the entire continent and persisting to the present day. Earlier Africa had experienced two other encounters with Christianity, the first coincided roughly with the initial 500 years of its existence, but was confined to the northern regions of the continent. The North African Church, distinguished by great scholars and Churchmen such as Origen, Tertullian, Cyprian, Anthony, Athanasius, Cyril, and Augustine, was for all practical purposes obliterated by Muslim invasions in the 7th century.

The second encounter, beginning in 1500, spanned three centuries and this time included portions of the southern half of the continent.[2] Missionary penetration into the southern regions of Africa was erratic. It was in any case so closely associated with European commercial interests, including prospectors for gold, ivory, and slaves, that it floundered and disappeared from the scene when those enterprises were either no longer profitable or, in the case of slavery, grossly inhuman. As is well known, neither of these encounters prevailed. However, at the end of the 19th century, accompanying what is generally referred to as the "scramble for Africa" (when the continent was partitioned into territorial segments "owned" and ruled by European powers), Christianity re-established itself in the continent and has prevailed until the present time.

This history is so familiar to students of African Christianity that the lessons it provides to the Church in contemporary Africa tend to be overlooked or ignored. Which are among the poignant lessons relevant to the future of African Theology? From the advent of Christianity in the continent, perhaps one of the most important lessons for the present and the future is that while theology must be erudite and profound, it must not be limited to its intellectual and theoretical aspects alone, or to the "schools" or to the cities. Whatever else it is, theology must also be "popular," that is to say, it must touch the sensibilities and aspirations of the faithful, taking account of their experiences and intuitions in the context of the gospel of Christ. This means that theological reflection must deploy language and symbols with which the majority of the people can identify. The wisdom and lasting effect of theology on a given population are thus beholden to this approach.

In the context of the historical realities that shaped the Church throughout the centuries, the new generation of African theologians will obviously need to pay special attention to the events that moulded its theology and its structures during this, its third phase in the continent. Chief among these are colonialism, followed by the African struggle for political independence. The re-evaluation of these events in the light of the gospel, accompanied by new understandings and demands for dignity and identity of the African person, prompted the emergence and development of African Theology by the pioneers. These same dynamics will keep African Theology rejuvenated and dynamic. The struggle continues.

Global developments in theology

Generally it is considered that the exercise of continual theological assessment is engaged in instinctively, but in fact it is best done deliberately. Several pertinent historical factors can be recalled. First, what has been called the "Jesus question," the attempt by the continent and its peoples to understand Jesus and his role in the world from the context of Africa, was not prominent in the continent before the second half of the 20th century. This was because of the preoccupations with different practical circumstances and needs. For one thing, formal Christian theological enquiry with an African accent and agenda did not take place among Africans until the late 1950s, triggered by the publication in Paris of a collection of essays by African priests titled, *Des pretres noirs s'interrogent*. The essays were critical of the stance of contemporary Catholic theology vis-à-vis Africa.[3] But even then this critique was very cautious and tentative. Also relevant was the fact that political and economic realities at the time inhibited theological enquiry; Christian education available to very few Africans fortunate enough to attain it, was not sufficiently empowered to critique and contextualize the study of the Bible and the history of Christianity. In fact, in the Church such attempts were generally considered to be wrongheaded or, worse, blasphemous and were strictly proscribed. In that light and from the present vantage point, it must be admitted that even the hesitant questions raised by *Des pretres noirs s'interrogent* in reality represented great courage. Under the circumstances, the volume was nothing less than revolutionary.

Second, there was the cultural factor. Apart from the catechetical instructions that they were receiving, which generally discouraged biblical criticism and independent theological inquiry, African Christian leaders in training were discouraged from making informed comparisons between their own cultural experiences and those they found in the Bible. Even so, most Christian faithful made such comparisons, observing and admiring the congruence of some of their customs with those of the Bible, regarding them as "revelation." Instinctively, and in spite of all efforts to the contrary, the Bible and its contents were being contextualized on the popular level in Africa in ways different from the manner in which Christianity had been received from European missionaries.

But the inhibitions in Africa concerning relevant approaches to the Bible and the identity of Jesus were not the same as elsewhere in the Christian world. In Europe, and later in America, from the end of the 18th until the middle years of the 20th century, Christian academic institutions witnessed a surge of new approaches to the Bible and theology, particularly in the area of christology. At the time there arose among northern theologians in dogmatic and biblical studies a yearning for what was described as the "historical Jesus." Many renowned intellectuals took part in addressing the issue.[4] Theirs was an attempt to reconstruct exactly the life of Jesus as he lived on earth and to write a kind of *pure* biography of the man whom some referred to as "Jesus the Jew," uninfluenced, as they insisted, by any element of faith-inspired interpretation of his life and work. They criticized the faith elements in earlier Jesus portrayals as distortions unworthy of the scientific mind or Christian maturity which they claimed humanity had now attained. As they saw it, contemporary Christian faith required a more "rational" or "historical" approach to the reality of Jesus and his work.

This quest for the historical Jesus emerged as a result of the Enlightenment – also referred to in European historiography as the Age of Reason – a movement originating in 18th century Europe. The Enlightenment was seen as the coming of age of humanity and its liberation from ignorance and superstition, a description shared by many European philosophers, including the famous German personality, Immanuel Kant. The audacity to doubt, to question, and to seek new knowledge emerging from this philosophical stance provided the motivation for the search for the historical Jesus among contemporary European and American theologians.

The process produced some interesting and indeed some useful results in terms of understanding the social, political, and religious atmosphere of 1st century Palestinian Christianity. It helped Christian scholarship to identify the influences of the surrounding contemporary cultures on the earthly Jesus by insisting on the socio-historical hermeneutical approach to the scriptures as well as other relevant ancient documents. The process illumined the theological understanding of Jesus and his mission in the world.[5] Jesus himself and his teaching – as the content of the faith – could now be situated more intelligently within the proper context. In spite of all its achievements, this "demythologisation"[6] process proved largely inconclusive in its attempt to discover who "the real earthly Jesus was," Jesus the man as he truly walked this earth. The effort achieved for theology an important methodological insight; it made christological scholarship aware of the necessary distinction between the Jesus of history, about whom little can be known for certain, and the Christ of faith, about whom, from the perspective of belief, there is a great wealth of information from the New Testament and many other sources. This awareness facilitated the process for the inculturation of christology.

Historical portrayals of Jesus explained

Portrayals of Jesus as received and known since New Testament times are intimately linked with his role as the Christ ("the anointed one of God") and are more faith-inspired interpretations or understandings of the meaning of his life-story than strictly historical accounts. They are not an exact chronicle of names, places, and dates in Jesus's life. The point is that Christianity came into existence as a result of this interpretation of the nature and life of Jesus, pertaining to the meaning of his life to purpose of humanity. As Garry Wills explains, Christianity as a movement "arose from a recognition of Christ's divinity. Only then was his human career studied in the light of that faith."[7] Belief, therefore, preceded the narrative, so that the Gospel stories should be seen as justifications for Christian faith: "The Gospels are a product of the belief, not vice versa," Wills asserts.

> That is why attempts to create "the historical Jesus" or his "authentic sayings" begin at the wrong end. These elements were recalled, in the attempt to articulate what was adequate to the Christ of faith and to the needs of his believers.[8]

Albert Nolan articulates the same conviction. He emphasizes that the need for the pertinence of Jesus in different circumstances was paramount in the minds of the authors and editors of the Gospels and all New Testament literature. It accounts for the diverse genres and content that the New Testament contains and reveals. With reference to the Gospels, Nolan writes, "The four small books that we call the Gospels are not biographies and were never intended to be."[9] They have too many inconsistencies, even when they draw from the same sources – such as the Synoptic Gospels of Matthew Mark and Luke – to pass as such.

> Their purpose was to show how Jesus could be relevant to people who lived *outside* Palestine a generation or two after Jesus' death. This first generation of Christians obviously did not feel the need for an exact biography of Jesus' life. They wanted to know how Jesus might be relevant to them in their situation outside Palestine.[10]

And according to Wills, The only Jesus we have is the Jesus of faith. If you reject the faith, there is no reason to trust anything the Gospels say. The Jesus of the Gospels is the Jesus preached, who is the Jesus resurrected. Belief in his continuing activity in the members of his mystical body is the basis of Christian belief in the Gospels. If that is unbelievable to anyone, then why should that person bother with him?[11]

However, the primacy of faith in Christ must not be mistaken to mean that Jesus did not exist as a historical figure, as a few people now and then have alleged, nor that the faith-based interpretations included in the New Testament, for example, are not theologically "factual," or worse, that they are inventions, fabrications, or falsehoods. Neither Jesus nor faith in him is fantasy. Jesus did exist, as many historical documents contemporary with him or written shortly after his death attest. Furthermore, much of the theology about him – christology – is factual in the sense that it reflects the intention of his life and mission, much of which was founded on the evidence of eyewitnesses. Wills is impressed by the magnificence of the Jesus story. He finds "the story of Christianity more convincing precisely because it begins with a great blinding light, from which men stumble only gradually, their eyes still dazzled, toward more coherent attempts to understand what happened."[12] Initiatives in this regard have persisted for two millennia and they seem to be as fresh as when they first began.

Always imagining and imaging Jesus anew

The challenge for African theologians flows from that point of encounter. As learned from developments in the older Churches, briefly described above, the challenge lies basically in the call to always re-image Jesus, in terms of the Christ of faith. The African theologian is aware that the Church gives priority and pride of place to the New Testament's reflections and portraits of Jesus in the Christian's understanding of him. This is because the narrative contains the interpretations of those who the Church believes knew him best; they saw him face to face, heard him speak, and accompanied him during his ministry, or were otherwise close to those who had done so. Luke, as noted, gives a clue to this understanding.[13]

Luke's primary interest is not in the person of Jesus *per se* but in his teachings, as they were received. Already in Luke's time, some years after the death of Jesus, there was a tradition of a handing on of the faith. This is what Luke acknowledges as his preoccupation. In his second book, the "Acts of the Apostles," addressed to the same Theophilus, Luke logically takes up the story of Jesus from the point at which his ministry had been carried forward by his friends and followers, the apostles. What is interesting in this regard is the principle, or condition, which according to Luke was being invoked by Peter. It was for the sake of faithfulness to this task, so soon after the death of the Master, that only those who personally knew him were eligible. To select one for the position of apostleship left vacant by the death of Judas, Peter spells out the condition that "it is necessary that one of the men who accompanied us the whole time the Lord Jesus came and went among us . . . become with us a witness to his resurrection" (Acts 1:21–22). The one exception to this rule, of course, was Paul, who, though he never saw the earthy Jesus, was given a special privilege to be an apostle (Acts 9:19b-30), as he himself is at pains to explain (Gal. 1:11–2:14).

Therefore, according to Albert Nolan, "we don't need a biography, but we do need to know the historical truth about Jesus."[14] And it is important to point out that truth about any person is not merely biographical; it may include social or devotional factors as well. We do not need to emphasize this fact in today's technological era because we know how much power the media of mass communication commands; it can easily make or break the personal image and career of virtually anyone. Particularly for a religious leader such as Jesus, devotional truth was by far the more relevant element. The truth about a religious figure depends to a great extent on the believer, and such truth often relies on events that transpired a long time after the leader's earthly existence, endorsing (or refuting) the truth or meaning of his/her claims and their relevance to experienced situations and needs. It is therefore the followers of such a leader who largely establish his/her life's truth, usually against forces that may wish to instil doubt or denial. Indeed, one might contend that much of the truth that human beings live by in their political, economic, social, and psychological spheres is constructed in a similar dialectic.

Consequently, as far as is known now, images of the historical Jesus are mostly suppositions or assumptions: "Jesus *must* have been this or that" or "he *must* have done such and such." Even these are mostly based on and sifted from theological intentions and accounts of the biblical writers who themselves held theological understandings. These scriptural images are taken to be "definitive" in the sense that they are a result of "original" theological imagination proximate to Jesus. They were imagined in the service of the spiritual needs of first generation Christians, experientially very close to the Jesus of history. They are faith perspectives culturally proximate to his time and related memory. Clearly, the Jesus story has from the very beginning been "contextualized" by way of language and symbols used to actualize him through the ages. Since perceptions of Jesus are bound to be place-, time-, and culture-specific, there are also bound to be many christologies. "Some years after the death of Jesus, rational and systematic reflection began to explore the role of Jesus in the final destiny of humankind."[15] This process of reflection and mental adjustments to prevailing conditions did not stop at any given point in the history of Christianity's existence. "As Christianity spread throughout the Roman Empire . . . the reflection became even more intense and widespread; it developed in proportion to the increasing symbiosis between this new faith and the various cultures constituting the sprawling empire."[16] What has been at stake since the beginning of the Christian movement is the discernment from age to age regarding the meaning of Jesus' life and teaching – what Jesus meant to specific times and peoples.

Just as the Old Testament (the Hebrew scriptures) was the end product of a long process of realizing the identity of Israel as God's chosen people, with Yahweh at the centre of events, so also did the Christian movement evolve. For the past two millennia, the images of Jesus – its central figure – have been developing and changing. Beginning with the New Testament accounts of him, there has been a continuing process of trying to understand the implications of his message and ministry for the Christian faithful and for the world generally. Organized and structured visibly as Church, the Christian movement continues the process of incarnating Jesus in various places, times, cultures, and changing circumstances. This is the process of inculturation. For Jesus to impact the lives of peoples, inculturation is a necessity, in the absence of which death and decay in the Church sets in. For the healthy existence of the Christian movement, it is not an option to hang onto "frozen" images of Christ, however time-honoured they may be; the faces of Jesus, our impressions of him, must change as the movement itself transitions in time to new mental, social, political, economic, or geographical shores.[17] This is how it must be and how it has been from the very beginning. New generations of African theologians are consequently confronted with the same challenge.

African theologians must continually explore the characteristics or features of the face of Jesus in Africa, taking into account the African reality in situ. They can do so dynamically after considering some of the major manifestations of the process of inculturating Jesus throughout the ages. In this way, they will appreciate most deeply the necessity of the theological and social constructions of the "faces of Jesus for Africa."[18] By its very nature, this is an exercise that must continue to metamorphose as situations on the ground change. It cannot be presumed to reach a final conclusion anywhere.

Following Paul of Tarsus

The most revolutionary and far reaching development in the 2000-year history of the Christian movement was undoubtedly the shift from its existence as a minor Jewish sect, concerned only about Palestinian Jewish questions as "the chosen race" of God, to a worldwide organization, inclusive of all human beings as "children of God." The success of this shift, substantially initiated by Paul of Tarsus, was extraordinary in terms of its philosophical-theological impact and in terms of its geographical outreach. Philosophically, Paul was a synchronizer, a shrewd "creolizer," or "syncretizer" of cultures. He was an expert at taking the best of disparate ways of looking at and doing things and blending them together as one. Paul successfully integrated Greek philosophy, metaphysics, and ordinary linguistic metaphors from a predominantly Roman world and deployed them to express Jewish-Christian messianic expectations, placing Jesus Christ at the centre.

A classic example often cited by scholars of Paul's shrewd syncretism was his address on the rocky heights of the city, known as the Hill of Mars or Areopagus, opposite the Acropolis, to the curious but ever sceptical urban Athenians of his time, people accustomed to cosmopolitan ideas and many gods (Acts 17:16–34). Having heard elsewhere in the city of his discussions about the resurrection of Jesus, some Greek Epicurean and Stoic philosophers thought he was a promoter of new gods. So they brought him to the spacious Areopagus to engage him in debate: "May we learn what this new teaching is that you speak of? For you bring some strange notions to our ears; we should like to know what these things mean." Paul rose superbly to the occasion and, in his ever shrewd manner, explained the sense of God's presence (in Jesus Christ) among all peoples, even when some may not have been explicitly aware of it:

> People of Athens [Paul said in his address], I see that in every way you are very religious. For as I walked around and looked carefully at your objects of worship, I even found an altar with this inscription: to an unknown god. So you are ignorant of the very thing you worship – and this is what I am going to proclaim to you.
>
> The God who made the world and everything in it is the Lord of heaven and earth and does not live in temples built by human hands. And he is not served by human hands, as if he needed anything. Rather, he himself gives everyone life and breath and everything else. From one man he made all the nations, that they should inhabit the whole earth; and he marked out their appointed times in history and the boundaries of their lands. God did this so that they would seek him and perhaps reach out for him and find him, though he is not far from any one of us. 'For in him we live and move and have our being.' As some of your own poets have said, 'We are his offspring.'
>
> Therefore since we are God's offspring, we should not think that the divine being is like gold or silver or stone – an image made by human design and skill. In the past God overlooked such ignorance, but now he commands all people everywhere to repent. For he has set a day when he will judge the world with justice by the man he has appointed [Jesus Christ]. He has given proof of this to everyone by raising him from the dead.
>
> (Acts 17:22–31)

This is vintage discourse by the Apostle Paul. He challenged the thinking and attitudes of everyone and particularly the followers of Jesus so profoundly that he transformed Christianity in ways that few of his contemporaries thought prudent, advisable, or even possible. In the process he drastically changed prevailing perceptions of Jesus and his message. The authors or compilers of the four Gospels – assuming they had access to Paul's writings, which most scholars today agree was the case – seem to have taken a leaf from Paul's portrayal of Jesus as *the* "universal Messiah," but incarnated differently in each location.

In the footsteps of Paul, future generations of African theologians need to accompany Jesus as interpretive reporters. They will do well to jot down notes and impressions that strike them as "Christ-like" as they travel with him across the continent, just as the evangelists did in the villages and towns of Galilee 2000 years ago. They will describe as well his subsequent faith-encounters with different peoples in different countries of the African continent, rejoicing with the joyful and sympathizing with the sorrowful, eating their food and drinking their beverages, playing with their children and counselling their youth. In practical terms, the central question of this travelogue on Jesus in Africa will always be: What would Jesus do today as he encounters these various situations of the African continent, a place that must be dear to his heart because, even if only symbolically, it is where his parents hid him when as an infant his life was threatened by a murderous tyrant (Mt. 2:13)? To the African theologian, these are reference points to be revisited and reinterpreted again and again.

Conclusion: repossessing the African Church

The motivation of the pioneers of African Theology, of which Professor Jesse N. K. Mugambi was (and is) a shining example, was the struggle to claim the African Church as rightfully African. In their view of the history of Christianity in the continent, they encountered a situation of alienation, born of human prejudices against the continent and its peoples, but unwarranted by faith in Christ. Their efforts launched the process of undoing this damage. As has been emphasized throughout this tribute, however, the struggle is not over; it continues, albeit with a more constructive focus.[19]

What kind of future, then, pertains to theology for Africa? In short, it is one that seeks authentic African values from within African culture, inspired by gospel values. Some of these have been identified over the last three generations by the pioneering African theologians. They have been synthesized (in terms of Catholic Christianity, at least), among other places, by the two synods for Africa that took place in 1994 and 2009.[20] The African contribution to understanding the person and ministry of Jesus and the life of the Church in the world continues as a task that will occupy the Christian imagination of generations of African theologians for a long time to come.

Notes

1 Vatican II, *Constitution of the Church in the Modern World.* (Gaudium et Spes, GS), no. 1.
2 See John Baur, *2000 Years of Christianity in Africa: an African Church History, 62–1992* (Nairobi: Paulines Publications Africa, 1994). Also John Paul II, *Apostolic Exhortation Ecclessia in Africa*, 1995, 30–54.
3 A. Abble, et al., *Des pretres noirs s'Interrogent.* (Paris: Editions du Cerf, 1956).
4 See Thomas P. Rausch, *Who Is Jesus? An Introduction to Christology.* (Collegeville, Minnesota: Liturgical Press, 2003), 9–22.
5 See Albert Nolan, *Jesus before Christianity.* (Maryknoll, New York: Orbis Books, 1976).

6 A concept coined by Rudolf Bultmann, one of the most prominent proponents of this endeavour. For example, see his *New Testament and Mythology and Other Basic Writings*. Edited by Schubert M. Ogden. (Minneapolis, Minnesota: Fortress Publishers, 1984).
7 Gary Wills, *Why I Am a Catholic*. (New York: Houghton Mifflin Company, 2002), 318.
8 Wills, *Why I Am a Catholic*, 18.
9 Nolan, *Jesus before Christianity*, 10.
10 Ibid., 10.
11 Gary Wills, *What Jesus Meant*. (New York: Viking, 2006), xxvi.
12 Wills, *Why I Am a Catholic*, 319.
13 In his two books: the "Gospel according to Luke" and the "Acts of the Apostles."
14 Nolan, *Jesus before Christianity*, 10.
15 Laurenti Magesa, *Anatomy of Inculturation: Transforming the Church in Africa*. (Maryknoll, New York: Orbis Books, 2004), 3.
16 Magesa, 2004, 3.
17 See Geza Vermes, *The Changing Faces of Jesus*. (New York: Penguin, 2000).
18 See Robert Schreiter, ed., *Faces of Jesus in Africa*. (Maryknoll, New York: Orbis Books, 1991).
19 See Mugambi, *From Liberation to Reconstruction*. Edited by Isaac M. T. Mwase and Eunice K. Kamaara, *Theologies of Liberation and Reconstruction: Essays in Honour of Professor J.N.K. Mugambi, Ph.D*. (Nairobi: Acton Publishers, 2012), and Laurenti Magesa, "A Portrait of Professor J.N.K. Mugambi's Project of Reconstruction: A Review Article of Theologies of Liberation and Reconstruction: Essays in Honour of Professor J.N.K. Mugambi, Ph.D., edited by Isaac M.T. Mwase and Eunice K. Kamaara," *Studies in World Christianity*, 19, no. 2 (2013): 187–97.
20 See the Apostolic Exhortations Ecclesia in Africa, 1994, by Pope John Paul II and, Africae Munus, 2011 by Pope Benedict XVI respectively summarizing the gist of the relevant synod.

Bibliography

Abble, A. et al. *Des pretres noirs s'interrogent*. Paris: Editions du Cerf, 1956.

Baur, John. *2000 Years of Christianity in Africa: An African Church History*, 62–1992. Nairobi: Paulines Publications Africa, 1994.

Bultman, Rudolph. *New Testament and Mythology and Other Basic Writings*. Edited by Schubert M. Ogden. Minneapolis Fortress Publishers, 1984.

John, Paul II. *Ecclesia in Africa*. 1994.

———. "Apostolic Exhortation." *Ecclessia in Africa* no. 30–54 (1995).

Magesa, Laurenti. *Anatomy of Inculturation: Transforming the Church in Africa*. Maryknoll, New York: Orbis Books, 2004.

———. "A Portrait of Professor J.N.K. Mugambi's Project of Reconstruction: A Review Article of Theologies of Liberation and Reconstruction: Essays in Honour of Professor J.N.K. Mugambi, Ph.D., edited by Isaac M.T. Mwase and Eunice K. Kamaara." *Studies in World Christianity* 19, no. 2 (2013): 187–97.

Mugambi, J. N. K. *From Liberation to Reconstruction: African Christian Theology after the Cold War*. Nairobi: East African Educational Publishers, 1995.

Mwase, Isaac M. and Eunice K. Kamaara, ed. *Theologies of Liberation and Reconstruction: Essays in Honour of Professor J.N.K. Mugambi, Ph.D*. Nairobi: Acton Publishers, 2012.

Nolan, Albert. *Jesus before Christianity*. Maryknoll, New York: Orbis Books, 1976.
Pope Benedict XVI. *Africae Munus*. 2011.
Rausch, Thomas P. *Who Is Jesus? An Introduction to Christology*. Collegeville Liturgical Press, 2003.
Schreiter, Robert, ed. *Faces of Jesus in Africa*. Maryknoll: Orbis Books, 1991.
Vatican II. "Constitution of the Church in the Modern World." *Gaudium et Spes*, *GS*, no. 1.
Vermes, Geza. *The Changing Faces of Jesus*. New York: Penguin, 2000.
Wills, Gary. *Why I Am a Catholic*. New York: Houghton Mifflin Company, 2002.

19 Narratives of the future in African history

Advancing aspirations for liberation and reconstruction in Africa[1]

Loreen Maseno

Africa of the 21st century ought to preoccupy itself with reconstruction. This is a step after liberation, whose aim was to deliver Africa's people from oppression to achieve self-actualization. Jesse N. K. Mugambi points to the important process of liberation, and equally to the task of reconstruction which must be pursued without delay to reconstruct social institutions in Africa and rebuild broken relationships. This chapter uses the concept of aspirations to mark out the liberation and reconstruction paradigms. It advances the functioning of aspiration for the cause of social reconstruction. Further, a treatment of the aspirations of African women's theology and imagination is provided for future Africa.

The preoccupation of leaders who championed African independence in the 1960s and the 1970s was liberation. Independence and liberation looked forward to a "future" that would bring freedom to all people. Liberation, both as a concept and as a goal of the historical struggle in Africa today has taken on different emphasis in various parts of Africa. Africa has seen different systems of oppression: namely brutal colonialism, racism, and the global neglect during the Cold War, which dampened the hopes of independence. Economic challenges, conflicts, and political domination by the ruling class have led scholars to call for a new agenda, the reconstruction of African societies. In the 1970s African leaders were at the helm of the struggles for liberation in Africa. However, after two decades Jesse Mugambi suggested that it is essential to move beyond the paradigm of liberation. Scholars of religion and theology contributed essays in an edited book to discuss Mugambi's theology of Liberation and reconstruction in Africa and called for all concerned to articulate a vision of a world moving towards healing and justice.[2]

Introducing aspirations

According to Caroline Hart,

> Imagination is a creative, ethereal concept which may neither be goal-oriented nor related to the self. Individual aspiration, in contrast, is

> both goal oriented and concerns the future of the self or the agency of the self in relation to goals concerning others.[3]

In other words, aspiration is virtually non-existent without future and agency. Each aspiration is linked to a goal,[4] that of becoming something in the future and it takes an effort on the part of the individual to attain or reach out to and which may include cooperation, collaboration, competition, amiability, and inclusivity. At the same time, a distinction is to be made between the capability to aspire (the freedom and possibility of aspiring which individuals enjoy to varying degrees) and the functioning of aspiring (an active endeavor undertaken through abstract thinking, developed further through verbal, written or other forms of physical and creative expression).[5]

Self-determination theory (SDT), research on aspirations, indicates that aspirations may be intrinsic or extrinsic. Kasser and Ryan present an aspiration index in which the intrinsic aspirations have been listed to include personal growth, affiliation, community contribution, and physical health. The extrinsic categories include financial success, fame, and appealing image.[6] In general, intrinsic aspirations have a focus on personal growth and the possibility of proper integration into society. These include aspects such as meaningful relationships, personal growth, and community contributions for wholeness in life. On the other hand, extrinsic aspirations tend to focus heavily on making good impressions on others and include parameters such as wealth, fame, and image.[7]

The types of aspirations include first, revealed aspirations – these are those aspirations that an individual has shared with others; second, concealed aspirations – these have not been shared with others; third, adapted aspirations – these are in flux, subject to review and change. Individuals change the attribution of weight to different choices where these options initially seemed to have the same weight. Fourth, apparent aspirations – these are those which reflect the aspirations of significant others and not the individual though the individual could voice them. They do not reflect an individual's true aspiration, but later on they could be adapted.[8]

For both liberation and reconstruction, the aspirations of persons involved play a role in the inauguration of a new social order. Their visions and realities drove the aspiration by Africans in the colonies to live a fuller life and flourish in freedom, and this led to resistance against colonial domination. The overthrowing of colonialism and the rebuilding of societies included the various types of aspirations above mentioned at different times within the functioning of aspiring. In what follows is a treatment of Liberation and reconstruction with a pointer on how aspirations can move forward an understanding of the two paradigms for the future.

The paradigm of liberation in Africa

In Africa, the theme of Liberation is as old as the imperial legacy, entrenched in the Berlin Treaty of 1884–1885. However, the notion of Africa is as old as the Roman Empire, dating from 146 BC. It was the trans-Atlantic slave trade and colonialism which destroyed Africa and underdeveloped it.[9] In his book *How Europe underdeveloped Africa*, Dr. Walter Rodney gives a vivid picture of this African tragedy. More recently, the theme of Liberation has directly been related to the Pan-Africanist Movement, dating from 1899. The ideology of Pan-Africanism has been said to be a complex belief system that sought to unify persons of color to aspire to a calling beyond their self-interests. Through this, they were able to racially self-actualize their own experience and delivered Africa from the hands of its colonial oppressors.[10]

The Fifth Pan-Africanist Congress at Manchester in 1945 is perhaps the most important event in the history of Africa's "Liberation." Ninety-nine delegates attended including 26 from Africa. The Manchester manifesto that emerged from this meeting represented a passing of the torch of leadership from Pan-Africanists outside Africa to young generation Pan-Africanist intellectuals within Africa.[11] As a movement, Pan-Africanism began in 1776. The Manchester Congress, England, advanced Pan-Africanism and applied it to the decolonization of the African continent politically.[12] Several African leaders were involved in this, including but not limited to Kwame Nkrumah, W.E.B. du Bois, Jomo Kenyatta, and Patrice Lumumba. In general, Pan-Africanism includes the intellectual, political, and economic cooperation that should lead to the political unity of Africa. According to Nkrumah, the seizure of political power was the first step towards and the necessary prerequisite to complete social, economic, and political emancipation.[13]

The formation of OAU in 1963 was the next important event, followed by the release of Mandela in 1990 and the subsequent establishment of post-Apartheid South Africa. In 2003 the OAU was transformed into the African Union. All these events are rungs in the ladder of the Liberation of Africa. Premised on the exodus narrative, which has been thought to be inadequate on the African Scene, Moses was seen as the liberator in the exodus narrative. The first generation of African leaders in the 1960s and the 1970s was linked to liberation. Mugambi argues that the Exodus motif as the exemplary leader is unfruitful for self-actualization of a community. Similar leadership has been seen in most African countries for three decades 1960–1990 characterized by coups and counter coups.

Many theologians have widely utilized the liberation paradigm because of the historical experience of colonial and neo-colonial domination. The African leaders in transition from colonial rule have been likened to Moses, to fulfill the same role as the liberation of the Hebrew community from Egypt.[14] Liberation theology has been critical of the "Christian Heritage" that is the western historical interpretation and understanding of Christ. Traditionally, this heritage has been presented as the criterion for all other attempts to know and live out the gospel. Therefore, liberation theology is not reactionary but proactive. It entails a commitment to faith and practice, to strive against oppressive religious and civil structures.[15] However, some notable shortcomings of liberation include the presupposition of an oppressor/oppressed dichotomy. This dichotomy has to be present in a context to see to it that the praxis and possibility of liberation are realized. Second, liberation alludes to the winner/loser configuration which ordinarily discourages those who envision loser status from taking steps to enable the emancipation of the other category.

Aspirations for liberation

The process of liberation from colonial masters in various African contexts took different forms. Indeed, for the Mau Mau in Kenya, the aspirations that presented themselves included concealed aspirations. At the very start, the vision bearers of independence did not share their aspirations for fear of the reprisals that would follow.[16] Colonial masters in Kenya did not respond well to the aspirations of the Kenyan masses for independence that was championed by the Mau Mau leaders who were not intimidated by threats from the colonial masters.[17]

Once the Mau Mau revealed their aspirations, they recruited many sympathizers to join their cause and fight for the liberation of Kenya. The aspiration for fuller life and a desire for freedom played a part in the crafting and sustaining of both the concealed and revealed aspirations in the Kenyan case. The aspirations for the Mau Mau were both goal oriented and concerned the future of the country. They wanted to achieve complete independence from the British. However, freedom from colonial rule did not fulfill all the aspirations of the Kenyan people. Therefore, a new paradigm was necessary to move the Kenyan and African communities into the future.

A future vision of reconstruction in Africa

Mugambi then argued that in the 21st century Africa should focus on the reconstruction of African communities.[18] Nations, Churches, and individuals in Africa were called to respond to this main concern, to facilitate this process of reconstruction.[19] Theologians and Churches treated reconstruction as an important theme that would open space for Africans to address cultural and political issues that hindered development and socio-economic progress. In his book on the theme of reconstruction, Mugambi argued that the task of the 21st century was a reconstruction of African societies that were in ruins because the dreams of liberation were not fulfilled.[20] Reconstruction is a vital paradigm for African Christian Theology in the 21st century. The historical context of this is newly independent nations, ideological and economic conflicts produced by the cold war and the emergence of the capitalist economy.[21] During the cold war, newly independent African states saw prices of exported commodities both agricultural and mineral tumble, while the costs of industrial products and expatriate services shot up. The free market policies worked to the advantage of former colonial rulers to the detriment of new sovereign African nations. The task of Africa's social reconstruction is both multi-disciplinary, meaning that which embraces both the social and natural sciences: humanities and creative arts and is ecumenical. This paradigm, therefore, has the potential for comprehensiveness and inclusivity. Reconstruction thus requires introspection and self-criticism. Reconstruction proceeds from the foundation laid by those who struggled for liberation and builds a new consciousness.

According to Mugambi,

> My first paper on Reconstruction in February–March 1990 was sparked by my observation that Africa's preoccupation with liberation, without Reconstruction, had delayed measures that could have been undertaken much earlier with regard to various aspects of African social institutions. But it is never too late to re-construct social institutions. Looking back, it seems that my assessment was correct. Since 1990 many African nations have re-written the constitutions bequeathed to them by their respective former imperial masters. The process of constitutional reform is still in process. This is what I had in mind under the theme of Social Reconstruction. At the Theological level, I suggested that Religion provides the raison d'etre that facilitates social reconstruction. Again, my observation seems vindicated, in view of the growing importance of Religion as a rallying instrument for groups struggling for "liberation" according to their understanding of "liberation."[22]

To be more precise on how the vision and representation of reconstruction have taken place in Africa, one would have to review all aspects of culture such as economics, which include problematic distribution (or lack of distribution) of resources. Other aspects of socio-political life which call for attention under the reconstruction paradigm include reorganizing political power and social influence, rethinking ethics, including but not limited to African values, aesthetics, kinship, and religion. For Mugambi, the way of reconstruction constitutes the wisdom of Jesus, the wisdom, not of bitterness at injuries suffered, but of "befriending and winning over" the oppressor, or, in other words, "reconstruct[ing] . . . relationships." It is this approach that, for Mugambi, spells the difference between the theologies of "liberation" and those of "reconstruction." He unreservedly advocates and embraces the latter orientation as the one adequate for today.[23]

Laurenti Magesa has argued,

> The core of the 'Theology of Reconstruction', of which Mugambi is one of the originators and continuing main proponent is to be found in the spirit of 'building up'. This is very much akin to the biblical image of 'building up' or 'constructing' the Reign of God, a task to which all Christians (indeed, all people of faith and good will) are invited by divine Providence. It involves repairing broken relationships in the

> community of persons, humanity and nature, and between humanity and God. While rejecting the institutions of oppression and discrimination and the structures of sin that are all too prevalent in human society, the theology of reconstruction urges, as its foundational method, the approach of communion between perpetrators and sufferers of injustice, between oppressors and the oppressed.[24]

Mugambi's idea of reconstruction as communion indicates a move towards non-oppressive biblical hermeneutics.[25] However, there are some shortcomings to reconstruction as noted. Conradie notes that the strength of the reconstruction metaphor as elaborated by Mugambi may at the same time become problematic. To him, while the metaphor allows for a multidisciplinary approach of social engineering in which the role of the social sciences is pivotal . . . its theological content may easily become rather shallow.[26] According to Elelwani Farisani, it is important also to note that in addition to "cultural," "ecclesiastical," and "socio-political" reconstruction there is, indeed, a strong sense of "personal reconstruction" too. He further critiques the use of Nehemiah/Ezra texts which have several interwoven narratives. Reconstruction is one motif, and further critical exegesis of the biblical texts would suggest other ways of addressing the current malaise in African society.[27]

Aspiration for reconstruction

To advance reconstruction as proposed by Mugambi, a closer look at aspiration is fruitful. Effective social reconstruction will entail a continuous review of processes, paradigms, and metaphors. Mugambi notes,

> Without continuous review, there is always the risk that younger generations might continue to use old ideas, while history has already moved on. This, in my view, is what Jesus meant by the metaphor of old wine in new wineskins! New wine requires new wineskins. However, the grapes remain the same, the wine presses may not be changed, and the wine makers and drinkers may be the same. But the wineskins will have to be changed, if making of good wine is to be achieved![28]

For persons to participate in creating a new social order, it is important to consider the role of aspirations. Though social reconstruction invites all sectors of the population to take part in the inauguration of a new social order, the aspirations of the population play a role in contributing to its effectiveness. Mugambi points out that the primary goal of reconstruction is not the demise of oppressive institutions and structures as an end in itself, but the transformation of relationships toward universal communion. It is on the premise of good relationships in the universal community that justice will prevail.[29]

Since individuals enjoy the freedom and possibility of aspiring for transformations of relationships to varying degrees, it is clear that when individuals have limited opportunities to develop their aspirations, and fully function therein, their participation in repairing broken relationships or even resisting oppressive institutions becomes weakened. The optimal functioning of aspiring ought to be seen as integral to social reconstruction and should, therefore, be nurtured and encouraged. For this reason, efforts toward reconciliation remain work in progress. At the same time, reconstruction has to be done historically and critically. Critical decisions should be made on what to abandon and what should be restored. The task of reconstruction is time-consuming, but it is important to note that it never ends.[30] A constructive future that rebuilds Africa from its current socio-economic ruins should be intrinsic to the aspirations of people to promote personal growth and community development. In which case, the community of humans, nature, and the divine can flourish and be inclusive of all that entails wholesome relationships.

Liberation and reconstruction as narratives of diversity and translatability

The paradigm shift from liberation to reconstruction should be seen as a continuation rather than a break from the past.[31] Mugambi states as follows:

> In these processes individuals are involved with specific reference to their actual situations and contexts. Thus any generalization is misleading and even dangerous! Take the 1950s in Kenya, for example. Depending on the part of Kenya where one lived, Kenyans were affected differently, and they have a wide variety of narratives of what actually happened. Each narrative is correct, if it is honestly narrated. But the truth about Kenya's history in the last decade of British imperial rule, is embedded in all the narratives, not in any one of them specifically. The narratives are not ends in themselves. They are means to an end – the end is to enable people articulate what they have undergone, as means towards greater appreciation of themselves, their joys, their sorrows, their fears and their aspirations.[32]

The literature that document African modern history especially during the colonial and postcolonial period demonstrate that the African people have been robbed of their future. In the same vein, since liberation, reconstruction, and revitalization move as a carry-over, it is clear that stolen moments from that rich past remain untold and such narratives need to find their way back into the archives of many African countries. Scholars have also pointed out that human imagination and creative works in the arts, literature, and cinema can also open up critical spaces that make imagining another world possible. Looking through literature in African languages, it is possible to come across constructions of different ideas of futures. Moving into the future, the places where new liberation and reconstruction narratives should be seen are in spaces such as African Instituted Churches with their rich interpretative array of theological and ritual material, African political Movements with the recent constitutional reforms in various African countries, African art, drama, music, transformation of the African family, and the continued transformation of the African economy.

The aspirations of African women's theology for these futures

African women's theology can play a role in the future of Africa by bringing into being what has not been reflected upon before in Africa. African women's theology may take up the activity of reconstruction by employing symbols, metaphors, models, and theories. In so doing, the functioning of aspiring is developed from abstract thinking to written and oral form. Such deeper constructive theological method values pluralism, and this task by African women theologians would lead them into valuing critical approaches to theological reflection. Within African women's theology, it is necessary to be conscious of the constructive character of all human activities, including religions. To bridge the gap between practice and religious concepts, visions, dreams, and the like which are not actively studied in the academy, African women's theology would make a positive contribution. In such studies, the currency of power about God, spirits, and ancestors add to make a bridge from religious experience to theology.

African women's theology for the future should be an intermediary theology. A theology which is not closed and finished, rather of many sorts, open, hesitant, and unfinished. A recent example is that of an unbounded Christology of Jesus as articulated by widows in Africa. Such describes the emergence of variant Christologies that are fluid and concern intermediate ("in between") areas of experience. The intermediacy widow's experience creates the possibility for them to see Jesus Christ in a manner which is similarly fluid, shifting, "in between" and on the threshold thereby producing a new Christology that is unbounded and creative, through metaphoric theology.[33] In so doing, African women's theology will open up for reflections that have a component of the timeline in theology, taking into cognisance how things change and the differences therein. Such leaps in theological reflection require re-orientation and retraining to facilitate the participation of creating a new social order in Africa. The place and space for aspirations in African women's theology for Africa cannot be underestimated even though there are entangled histories from the global past in Africa. African women theologians should unwind these strands with a critical gaze to provide alternative frameworks for future Africa.

This calls for dedicated training of African women theologians. As a former undergraduate student of Prof. Mugambi, from 1998 in second year to 2001 and in fourth year at the University of Nairobi, when looking at the past, what stood out for my course mates and I were the books, often between two and four that we had to review in Prof. Mugambi's class each semester. Mugambi was the only Professor who ever made us do this. Each of the books he brought were neatly rubber stamped with his names. We students did not like it then, but now in the future, I remain indebted to Mugambi for the additional training. I also salute Mugambi for this one occasion when I almost dropped from my master's degree class in Oslo, Norway. The phone conversation in winter with Professor Mugambi sobered me up when amidst all my reasons he said, "No excuse will ever be sufficient to explain you are quitting what you started." You can be sure that winter was one reason.

Since history starts first before the history of the future, African women's theology for the future remains to come from the past. As an African woman theologian, my past is present in my present and my future. Going forward and with other women theologians, for future Africa, we may use narratives outside what is standardized truth for the future. These may include the use of orality and bodyless voices as may be found in religious domains which remove a gaze from a body and thus conflate the politics of representation.

Conclusion

Though aspirations can provide fruitful avenues to explore liberation and reconstruction further, it is also noted that for both paradigms, when self-interested or competitive aspiration frames[34] come into play, a lot is left to be desired. Self-interested aspiration frames are self-seeking and can be noted from those considered traitors who dealt major blows to quest for independence, as in the case of the Mau Mau traitors in pre-independence Kenya. Often for self-interested aspiration frames, the aspirations are held without consideration of other points of view or are advanced at the expense of another person's perspective. The reverse is the other-interested or cooperative aspiration frames which seek mutual concessions and relationships.[35]

This chapter has advanced the role of aspirations for the work by Jesse Mugambi on liberation and reconstruction paradigms in Africa. It has also pointed to the aspirations of African women's theology and imagination. Concepts of the future remain deeply bound in history, and Africa has a role in rethinking Future not limited to European categories. African women's theology can provide such a space by its use of experience in the world space. Further, since Africa's being in the world has been a unique experience of systemic peripherality, exploitation, and trauma, these and such experiences can be fore-grounded by African women's theology to engage the same for the future critically.

Notes

1 This chapter originates from research during a fellowship stay at the Bayreuth Academy of Advanced African Studies in 2013. My working Group B dubbed, multiple futures through Time sought to contribute to the sub-project, Narratives of the Future in Modern African History. Additional sources for this chapter include interviews with Prof. Jesse Mugambi and the conference "Future Africa and Beyond" – Review and Outlook, the Academy culminating conference held between June 16–17, 2016 in Bayreuth.

2 Isaac M. T. Mwase and Eunice K. Kamaara, eds. *Theologies of Liberation and Reconstruction: Essays in Honour of Professor J. N. K. Mugambi, Ph.D.* (Nairobi: Acton, 2012).

3 Caroline Sarojini Hart, *Aspirations, Education and Social Justice: Applying Sen and Bourdieu*. (London: Bloomsbury, 2013), 79.

4 Aspirations refer to people's life goals. See http://selfdeterminationtheory.org/aspirations-index/.

5 Hart, *Aspirations, Education and Social Justice*, 79.

6 See Tim Kasser and Richard Ryan, "Further Examining the American Dream: Differential Correlates of Intrinsic and Extrinsic Goals," *Personality and Social Psychology Bulletin*, 22, (1996): 280–7.

7 Jelena Hollman, Julia Gorges and Elke Wild, "You Will Attain My Goal: The Structure of Parental Goals for Children Based on an Adapted Version of the Aspirations Index," *European Journal of Psychological Assessment*, (2016), 1.

8 Hart, *Aspirations, Education and Social Justice*, 86–92.

9 Walter Rodney, *How Europe Underdeveloped Africa*. (Cape Town: Pambazuka Press, 2012).

10 Cary D. Wintz and Paul Finkelman, *Encyclopedia of the Harlem Renaissance. Vol. 1 and 2. A–Z*. (NewYork: Routledge, 2004), 952. See also Road To Panafricanism, www.panafricanperspective.com/pheko.html. (accessed July 27, 2017).

11 Adi Hakim, Marika Sherwood and George Padmore, *The 1945 Manchester Pan-African Congress Revisited*. (London: New Beacon Books, 1995).

12 William Ackah, *Pan-Africanism: Exploring the Contradictions: Politics, Identity and Development in Africa and the African Diaspora*. (Brookfield Ashgate Publishing Company, 1999). See also Road To Pan-africanism, www.panafricanperspective.com/pheko.html. (accessed July 27, 2017).

13 See Opoku Agyeman, *The Failure of Grassroots Pan-Africanism: The Case of the All-African Trade Union Federation*. (Lanham: Lexington Books, 2003), 11. See also Road To Pan-africanism, www.panafricanperspective.com/pheko.html. (accessed July 27, 2017).

14 Margaret Gecaga, "Globalisation and Churches," in Isaac M. T. Mwase and Eunice K. Kamaara, eds. *Theologies of Liberation and Reconstruction: Essays in Honour of Professor J.N.K. Mugambi*. (Nairobi Acton Press, 2012), 321–3.

15 Ibid., 322.

16 Wunyabari O. Maloba, *Mau Mau and Kenya: An Analysis of a Peasant Revolt*. (Nairobi: East African Educational Publishers, 1993).

17 Bethwel Ogot, "Mau Mau & Nationhood: The Untold Story," in Elisha Stephen Atieno-Odhiambo and John Lonsdale, eds. *Mau Mau and Nationhood: Arms, Authority and Narration*. (Oxford: James Currey, 2003), 8–36.

18 Jesse Mugambi, *From Liberation to Reconstruction: African Christian Theology after the Cold War*. (Nairobi: East African Educational Publishers, 1998). See an earlier version of this discussion from which the material here is taken from; "Narratives of the Future In Modern African History: The, www.bayreuth-academy.uni-bayreuth.de/resources/Loreen-Maseno.pdf. (accessed July 27, 2017).

19 See Isaac T. Mwase, *Southwestern Baptist Theological Seminary*, 1993; Stephen I. Munga, Lund University, 1998; Joern Henrik Olsen, Copenhagen University, 2000 and John Fischer, University of Western Cape, 2010 amongst others.
20 Jesse Mugambi,1998.
21 I.M.T. Mwase and E. K. Kamaara, "Preface," in Isaac M. T. Mwase and Eunice K. Kamaara, eds. *Theologies of Liberation and Reconstruction: Essays in Honour of Professor J. N. K. Mugambi.* (Nairobi Acton Press, 2012), 7.
22 Interview with Prof. Mugambi, at the University of Nairobi on Monday, October 14, 2013.
23 Laurenti Magesa, "A Portrait of Professor J.N.K. Mugambi's Theological Project of Reconstruction: A Review Article of Theologies of Liberation and Reconstruction: Essays in Honour of Professor J.N.K. Mugambi, Ph.D.," in Isaac M. T. Mwase and Eunice K. Kamaara, eds. *Studies in World Christianity*, 19, no. 2 (2013): 189–90.
24 Ibid.,190.
25 Ibid., 192.
26 Ernst Conradie, "African Perspectives on 'The whole household of God' (OIKOS)," in Isaac M. T. Mwase and Eunice K. Kamaara, *Theologies of Liberation and Reconstruction: Essays in Honour of Professor J. N. K. Mugambi.* (Nairobi, Kenya: Acton Press, 2012), 281–97.
27 Elelwani Farisani, "The Post-Exile Motif in Mugambi's Theology of Reconstruction," in Isaac M. T. Mwase and Eunice K. Kamaara, eds. *Theologies of Liberation and Reconstruction: Essays in Honour of Professor J. N. K. Mugambi.* (Nairobi, Kenya: Acton Press, 2012), 198–220.
28 Follow up interview with Prof. Mugambi, at the University of Nairobi on Monday October 17, 2013.
29 Feedback via email following an interview with Prof. Mugambi held at the University of Nairobi on October 17, 2013.
30 Hans-Dieter Betz, "Remarks of SNTS President 1999–2000," in Isaac M.T. Mwase and Eunice K. Kamaara, eds. *Theologies of Liberation and Reconstruction: Essays in Honour of Professor J. N. K. Mugambi.* (Nairobi, Kenya: Acton Press, 2012), 32–3.
31 Isaac Mwase, "African Religious Scholarship as the Context of Mugambi's work," in Isaac M. T. Mwase and Eunice K. Kamaara, eds. *Theologies of Liberation and Reconstruction: Essays in Honour of Professor J. N. K. Mugambi.* (Nairobi, Kenya: Acton Press, 2012), 184.
32 Interview with Prof. Mugambi, at the University of Nairobi on Monday, October 14, 2013.
33 Loreen Maseno, "Unbounded Christologies: The Case of Widows' Christology – 'Jesus Christ Is Breath'," *Scriptura*, 114, (2015): 1–12.
34 See Sarah Ogilvie on Frame Characterizations. www.sicotests.com/darticle.asp?page=16. (accessed July 12, 2017).
35 See Beyond Milgram: Expanding Research Ethics Education to, http://teachpsych.org/resources/Documents/otrp/resources/barber12.pdf. (accessed July 27, 2017).

Bibliography

Agyema, Opoku. *The Failure of Grassroots Pan-Africanism: The Case of the All-African Trade Union Federation*. New York: Lexington Books, 2003.

Ackah, William. *Pan-Africanism: Exploring the Contradictions: Politics, Identity and Development in Africa and the African Diaspora*. New York: Ashgate Publishing Company, 1999.

Betz, Hans-Dieter. "Remarks of SNTS President 1999–2000'." In *Theologies of Liberation and Reconstruction: Essays in Honour of Professor J. N. K. Mugambi*, edited by Isaac M. T. Mwase, and Eunice K. Kamaara. Nairobi: Acton Press, 2012.

Conradie, Ernst. "African Perspectives on 'The whole household of God' (OIKOS)". In *Theologies of Liberation and Reconstruction: Essays in Honour of Professor J. N. K. Mugambi*, edited by Isaac M. T. Mwase, and Eunice K. Kamaara, 281–97. Nairobi: Acton Press, 2012.

Farisani, Elelwani. "The Post-Exile Motif in Mugambi's Theology of Reconstruction." In *Theologies of Liberation and Reconstruction: Essays in Honour of Professor J.N.K. Mugambi*, edited by Isaac M. T. Mwase, and Eunice K. Kamaara, 198–220. Nairobi: Acton Press, 2012.

Gecaga, Margaret. "Globalization and Churches." In *Theologies of Liberation and Reconstruction: Essays in Honour of Professor J.N.K. Mugambi*, edited by Isaac M. T. Mwase, and Eunice K. Kamaara, 321–3. Nairobi: Acton Press, 2012.

Hart, Caroline. *Aspirations, Education and Social Justice: Applying Sen and Bourdieu*. London: Bloomsbury, 2013.

Hollman, Jelena, Gorges, J. and Elke Wild. "You Will Attain My Goal: The Structure of Parental Goals for Children Based on an Adapted Version of the Aspirations Index." *European Journal of Psychological Assessment* (2016): 1.

Kamaara, Eunice. "Gender Empowerment in Africa." In *Theologies of Liberation and Reconstruction: Essays in Honour of Professor J.N.K. Mugambi*, edited by Isaac M. T. Mwase, and Eunice K. Kamaara, 301–18. Nairobi: Acton Press, 2012.

Kasser, Tim and Richard Ryan. "Further Examining the American Dream: Differential Correlates of Intrinsic and Extrinsic Goals." *Personality and Social Psychology Bulletin* 22 (1996): 280–7.

Magesa, Laurenti. "A Portrait of Professor J.N.K. Mugambi's Theological Project of Reconstruction: A Review Article of Theologies of Liberation and Reconstruction: Essays in Honour of Professor J.N.K. Mugambi, Ph.D." In *Studies in World Christianity*, edited by Isaac M. T. Mwase, and Eunice K. Kamaara, 19, no. 2 (2013): 187–97.

Maloba, Wunyabari O. *Mau Mau and Kenya: An Analysis of a Peasant Revolt*. Nairobi: East African Educational Publishers, 1993.

Maseno, Loreen. "Unbounded Christologies: The Case of Widows' Christology – 'Jesus Christ is Breath'." *Scriptura* 114 (2015): 1–12.

Mugambi, Jesse. *From Liberation to Reconstruction: African Christian Theology after the Cold War*. Nairobi: East African Educational Publishers, 1998.

———. *Christian Theology and Social Reconstruction*. Nairobi: Acton, 2003.

Mwase, Isaac. "African Religious Scholarship as the Context of Mugambi's work." In *Theologies of Liberation and Reconstruction: Essays in Honour of Professor J. N. K. Mugambi*, edited by Isaac M. T. Mwase, and Eunice K. Kamaara, 171–191. Nairobi: Acton Press, 2012.

Mwase, Isaac, and Eunice K. Kamaara, eds. *Theologies of Liberation and Reconstruction: Essays in Honour of Professor J. N. K. Mugambi, Ph.D*. Nairobi: Acton Press, 2012.

Ogilvie, Sarah. "Frame Characterizations." www.sicotests.com/darticle.asp?page=16. Accessed July 12, 2017.

Ogot, Bethwel. "Mau Mau & Nationhood: The Untold Story." In *Mau Mau and Nationhood: Arms, Authority and Narration*, edited by Elisha Stephen Atieno-Odhiambo, and John Lonsdale, 8–36. Oxford: James Currey, 2003.

Padmore, George, Adi Hakim, and Marika Sherwood. *The 1945 Manchester Pan-African Congress Revisited*. London: New Beacon Books, 1995.
Rodney, Walter. *How Europe Underdeveloped Africa*. Cape Town: Pambazuka Press, 2012.
Vahakangas, Mika. "Church-State Relations in Theology of Reconstruction." In *Theologies of Liberation and Reconstruction: Essays in Honour of Professor J. N. K. Mugambi*, edited by Isaac M. T. Mwase, and Eunice K. Kamaara, 245–56. Nairobi: Acton Press, 2012.
Ukachukwu, Chris. *Intercultural Hermeneutics in Africa: Methods and Approaches*. Nairobi: Acton, 2003.
Wintz, Cary, and Paul Finkelman, *Encyclopedia of the Harlem Renaissance. Vol. 1 and 2. A–Z*. New York: Routledge, 2004.

20 African theology and African literature

Rediscovering a daring intellectual project

Abraham Waigi Ng'ang'a

Introduction

African arts, literature, and aesthetics, which have contributed to our understanding of Christian history and practice, invite theological reflection.[1] In this chapter, I focus on Wole Soyinka, a representative voice for those mission-educated Africans who have offered a critical perspective on Christianity.[2] J.N.K. Mugambi's *Critiques of Christianity in African Literature* discussed broadly African literature and Christianity and set the stage for theologians to consider creative literary works seriously because they address the mission, and post-mission Christianity in Africa as the African Church has established its own identity.[3] Mugambi's book was published in 1992 to promote a greater Christian engagement and reflection on the contemporary situation and the future of Africa by encouraging Christian scholars to respond to literary work that criticized African Christianity, and in doing so Mugambi followed the example of missionaries and theologians like Saint Paul, Origen, and Justin, who engaged the literature of their day in dialogue with Christianity.[4]

Christianity in light of "Thought Patterns and Cultural Awareness"

Mugambi calls followers of Christ to cultivate a critical engagement with "the relationship between Christianity and particular cultures and other religious perspectives; a task that has been "controversial issue since the beginning of the Church."[5] Since Christianity involves interaction with other people, Christians must take the concerns of others about the Christian faith seriously.[6] C. S. Lewis argued that Christians should consider the writer's originality as they may reflect "eternal Beauty and Wisdom."[7] In my view, this is important because as I have argued elsewhere, "the poetic, intellectual or theological reflections that emerge would then be congruent with their surroundings, as well as identify with the cultural sensibilities of the larger community."[8] On both accounts, Wole Soyinka appears to be in agreement, for he talks of "eternal values" that are requisite for "humanistic ends," as well as "humanistic values" that constitute the "eternal bequest" to a needy world. The logical end of this engagement appears to be resolved in the discourse of Humanity and the Transcendent.[9] This calls for a good understanding of the literary production of the continent, particularly in a time which according to Andrew Walls, "demographically, the composition of the Christian church has shifted southwards; but its *thought-processes and cultural awareness* have not yet moved proportionately with the demographic shift."[10] Andrew Walls presents Paul, Origen, and Justin as three paradigmatic figures in Christian history, noting how "the demand for scholarship occurred as soon as the gospel crossed its first cultural frontier, that between Israel and the Hellenistic world," as well as how "distortions, exaggerations, misunderstandings about Christianity abounded" and the "scholarly virtues of insight based on knowledge, patient examination and disciplined imagination"[11] were deployed by these daring scholars as they presented Christ to their respective audiences.

The fact that theology always deals with "culturally-rooted questions"[12] raised by those inside as well as outside the Church necessitates theological answers. However, there was a particular group, apart from the "ill-educated, credulous and superstitious," whose stance towards Christianity required a highly specialized approach. The "highly educated, skeptical and urbane"[13] needed Paul, the "outstandingly open, learned and culturally-sensitive Jewish missionary, who delved as deeply into the Hellenistic culture as perhaps any outsider could."[14] Concerning Paul's ability to engage Hellenistic culture, Walls writes, "He could take Hellenistic words and ideas like *mysterion* and *pleroma*, flood them with Christian meaning and daringly use them to reinterpret Christ, in Hellenistic terms."[15] Walls presents Justin Martyr and Origen as the later representative figures, like Paul, of the process of reinterpreting (incarnating) Christ into thought patterns and cultural awareness. Justin, "the converted philosopher, who having investigated all the philosophical schools, eventually chose to teach Christianity as the true philosophy," found in the Christian Scriptures a valuable teaching as well as "a means to critique his cultural past, affirming and rejecting."[16] As he followed the Christian teachings, he also discovered Christ within his Greek heritage. On his part, Origen, drawing from his dual heritage (Greek and Christian), was able to "re-conceive Greek learning so that it presented Christ and led people to God."[17] Walls notes further, "Not only did he invent, or give impetus to, new areas of scholarship – textual criticism, systematic theology, biblical commentary – he brought almost every trend of existing philosophy and science into Christian service."[18] Additionally, Walls argues that Christian scholars revived and renewed the Greek tradition and Christian scholarship strengthened scholarship all over the world.[19] Leland Ryken agrees with Dorothy Sayers' view that "the Church as a body has never made up her mind about the arts," and some do not think literature is important for the Christian faith.[20] The neglect of literature goes in the West and even more so in Africa where Kwame Bediako claims Christian formation is in crisis.[21] This perhaps explains why there has been little response from Christians to the works of writers such as Wole Soyinka, even though these works are overwhelmingly critical of Christianity and organized religion, in general.[22]

This indifference towards literature by African Christians ignores religion and especially literature whose importance has been highlighted, and Soyinka himself mentioned in the epilogue to *Ibadan at Fifty, 1948–1998: Nigeria's Premier University in Perspective* by B. A. Mojuetan,

> Education, the cultivation of the intellect, is the key to the releasing of the enormous potential embedded in the human species; and literacy is the medium, the staircase, as it were, to the exalted intellectual heights – the universe of Forms or Ideas – made possible by the edifice of education; which explains why education looms very large in the organization of the idealized state in Plato's *Republic*, so much as to elicit Rousseau's description of the book as a treatise not so much on politics as on education.[23]

It continues,

> A non-literate society lacks the mode of articulation of the intellectual development of mankind, crystallized, for instance, in the physics of Newton, Max Planck, and Einstein, in the Darwinianism of the *Origin of Species*, and in the political economy of Marx's *Das Capital*. Such flowering of collective genius as is embodied in William Shakespeare and Wole Soyinka is impossible in a non-literate culture, remaining dormant or inchoate for want of an outlet or a medium of epiphany. Literacy provides an indelible means of expression and communication, and so preserves "the records of civilization" . . . The record becomes "the general bank and capital of nations and of ages," of which future generations may "avail themselves" – in the words of Edmund Burke – to expand the cognitive awareness and the capability of mankind in the manner of capital as a self-expanding resource.[24]

While most of the scholars mentioned are Europeans, Mojuetan mentions two literary icons as exemplars of intellectuals whose work has contributed to human knowledge and one of them is Soyinka.

Overarching framework: tripartite thematic of Wole Soyinka's writings

For us, Soyinka represents the "highly educated, skeptical and urbane," and to whom Christianity is, at best, a foreign religion, and at worst, an inconvenience to his cause. The three themes, which summarize the central concerns in Soyinka's works are: "Advocacy of Indigenous Heritage," "Vision of a Greater Humanity," and "Reconstituted Transcendence."

Advocacy of indigenous heritage

Soyinka who won the Nobel Prize for Literature in 1986 and a Lifetime African Achievement Prize in 2010 for his contribution to "African Cultural and Traditional preservation" among numerous honors is a leading cultural ambassador.[25] Soyinka has stated,

> I have long been preoccupied with the process of apprehending my world in its full complexity, also through its contemporary progression and distortions – evidence of this is present both in my creative work and in one of my earliest essays, The Fourth Stage, is included in Soyinka's most intense work, *Myth, Literature and the African World*.[26]

Published in 1976, this book was arguably the long-delayed product of his Rockefeller Fellowship, awarded in 1960, for research into traditional dramatic forms.[27] It is perhaps Soyinka's most important theoretical statement on African literature and Christianity for it is "triggered," to use Soyinka's preferred term,[28] by the need for "continuing objective restatement of that self-apprehension, to call attention to it in living works of the imagination, placing them in the context of primal systems of apprehension of the race."[29] This effort is geared towards the "creation of a new cult of the self's daily apprehended reality," a reality which is in Soyinka's judgment, being "contemptuously denied or undermined by other cultic adherents." The people that Soyinka is addressing here are his compatriot, Bolaji Idowu, John Mbiti, Ogotommeli, Kagame, Willie Abrahams, Cheikh Anta Diop, and "foreign triers like Father Tempels, Pierre Verger, Herskovits," and others.[30] To him, they are "the new breed of deniers" for they apply foreign criteria in the study of Africa and Africans.

Significant in this representative charge is the conspicuous absence of engagement, by Soyinka himself, with offending works by the named pioneer African theologians and their foreign counterparts. However, an assessment of Soyinka's critique of Christianity reveals a weakness in his case. For instance, he does not show how Bolaji Idòwu's *Olódùmarè: God in Yoruba Belief* is "an otherwise excellent work," when he judges its author as a "cultural denier."[31] Soyinka's articulation of the African world is salutary and deserving of attention, even theological engagement. Vision would be required to sustain the ideals of that world about other people in other parts of the world. Similarly, a uniting principle would be essential if humanity is to transcend racial, economic and ideological barriers that threaten its harmonious survival. His advocacy of indigenous heritage is further developed in his vision of a greater humanity as well as his vision of a reconstituted transcendence.

Vision of a greater humanity

Soyinka's vision is premised on the understanding that humanity constitutes the "primary incontestable asset" without which a society falls into a dehumanized zone of existence.[32] However, to undergird humanity, justice must be the first guarantor, of the wellbeing of all the members of society. Justice is, therefore, the "existential *raison d'être*."[33] Soyinka has articulated the theme of justice in his 2004 BBC Reith Lectures, published as *Climate of Fear: The Reith Lectures*,[34] his lecture entitled "Corporate Gains and Human Deficit,"[35] and his play, *Madmen, and Specialists*.[36] Soyinka attacks in these publications the rampant dehumanization of people, in racism, global colonial repression, exploitation of labor by both foreign and domestic masters,[37] and the marginalization of humanity.[38] For Soyinka, dehumanization is a universal phenomenon in which the wealthy and powerful victimize people. His answer and remedy to this malady are an African humanism and spirituality, which would lead to an African inspired "age of Universal understanding."[39] This humanism, itself an "elusive extract" that he believes is key to African renaissance,[40] is the main subject of his recent book, *Of Africa*.

The quest for justice has been a concern of Soyinka since childhood.[41] It is understandable then, that the saying "justice is the first condition of humanity"[42] would be attributed to him. Noteworthy here is the fact that Soyinka's fight against injustice is not confined to Nigeria or Africa. He identifies views of the 19th- and 20th-century commentators on Africa, which form the backdrop of his exposition.[43] The European philosophers, Hegel, Locke, Hume, Voltaire, Levi-Strauss, and others, are identified as some of "the most revered names in European philosophy" who "were unabashed theorists of racial superiority and denigrators of the African history and being."[44] Soyinka argues that theirs was an era of "lies, distortion, and opportunism in high places, even among the holy of holies of intellectual objectivity," resulting in "the centuries of Eurocentric blasphemy that have placed the Black man, the so-called primitive man, under the categorization of some kind of semi-human creature possessing some sort of 'pre-logical mentality.' "[45] Their offspring, Soyinka reflects, "willfully remain a child, a stubborn, self-destructive child, with certain destructive powers, but a child nevertheless."[46] Thus, while speaking for "the victims of that intellectual dishonesty," he demanded the severing of the cord that has nurtured the values of the oppressive/denigrating systems.[47]

Naturally then, Soyinka locates himself outside the European intellectual climate.[48] To Soyinka, "the whole of European intellection" is Eurocentric and thus, "very inaccurate . . . and a very untruthful system of analysis and conceptualization." This is particularly so in connection with the study of human beginnings and development.[49] His compatriot since the days of Ibadan, Chinua Achebe, was himself moved to write – to give a true account of his country and his people – after reading Joseph Conrad's *Heart of Darkness*. His famous novel, *Things Fall Apart* (1958), was the result. He has since written and spoken at length on "the central question of dispossession and its consequences." [50] Until his death in 2013, Achebe's call for a "balance of stories among the world's peoples" (through "the process of 're-storing' peoples who had been knocked silent by the trauma of all kinds of dispossession") remained a central focus. Achebe believed that "an erosion of self-esteem is one of the commonest symptoms of dispossession."[51]

Soyinka's poem, *Ogun Abibiman*, even with its limited scope for a Pan-African framework can thus be taken as Soyinka's contribution towards restoring or reinforcing those broken bridges. In this poem, as in other works mentioned below, Soyinka's intention is the "apprehension of a psyche altered through the loss of human contact."[52] The export from Africa, her humanism, and spirituality would then become a vital corrective for hegemonic tendencies.

Reconstituted transcendence

Soyinka's advocacy of indigenous heritage is primarily a case for the Yoruba god, Ogun. However, he insists that Ogun is "best understood in Hellenic values." The question as to why Ogun cannot be understood in African or Christian terms/values must be raised. If he did raise it, would there be a meeting point with, say, Justin Martyr who saw in Greek heritage Christ-affirming values? It would seem to follow here that Soyinka's "paganistic leanings" (his phrase)[53] are more oriented towards the European Romantic value system, which had an impact on every sphere of life.

The poem *Ogun Abibiman* is essentially about the coronation of Ogun over the spheres of black African life. However, this very notion appears to expose Soyinka to his criticism of those who, through their missionizing effort, promote anti-terrestrials.[54] By claiming Ogun as the god of all black people, notwithstanding the fact that even in Igboland, as Achebe asserts, "every man has his *chi* and every woman has her *chi*,"[55] Soyinka is reconstituting the traditional viewpoint of other Africans. Similarly, the shattering of the original framework that upheld *Olódùmarè* (God) above all other *Orisa* (deities) betrays Soyinka's indebtedness to an alien framework of analysis. He ignores what Jacob Olupona describes as "the diversity of Africa's cultural mosaic."[56] African scholars demonstrate a resounding consensus on the reality of an African world. The descriptions differ but the essential elements, what John Mbiti describes as "African ontology"[57] remain intact. Therefore, Soyinka's secular orientation, which he articulates in *Myth, Literature and the African World*, and his idea of "secular gods," must be interrogated.[58] Standing in contradistinction also is his own experience of the "numinous," recounted in his longest memoir to date.[59] This experience has the potential to be identified as a spiritual experience when taken to its logical conclusion. Similarly, his promotion of paganist leanings is undifferentiated from the spirituality of Middle Ages paganism, which shared a common experience with the asceticism of monastic Christianity. This asceticism neither constitutes an ingredient of Soyinka's aesthetics nor bears any practical affinity with his lifestyle.

In Africa, Kwame Gyekye observes that one can do philosophy without losing religious faith.[60] The humanism that Soyinka promotes as the basis for justice is devoid of the Christian faith. This understanding is difficult for some Africans to accept. One could argue that for many Africans it may even render justice itself illusory, for it lacks a superintending function that can only derive from a transcendent reality. Aestheticism devoid of faith leads to what C.S. Lewis describes as "Pure Iconography."[61] To Soyinka, therefore, the "use" of myth is for ethical expediency and justice grounded in an African worldview rather than for the life of devotion as envisaged in the Christian tradition. The viewpoint of those who see in mythology a transcendent dimension is also important and must be placed on contrast with Soyinka's position. Bediako in light of Samuel Huntington's *Clash of Civilizations* has argued that religion remains important in the affairs of a vast majority of people.[62] This approach is contrary to Soyinka's advocacy of "secular gods,"[63] which some would contest are not original to African ontology.[64] It appears from reading Soyinka that to counter Eurocentrism one must invent a non-theistic alternative to Christianity (which regarding its origin and theological orientation, has always been a non-Western religion).[65]

In his article, "Christianity and the Logic of Nationalist Assertion in Wole Soyinka's Ìsarà," J.D.Y. Peel highlights the place of religion in the making of a nation. As a self-confessed "Africanist" and a "sociologist-cum-historian of the Yoruba,"[66] he links African nationalism with the phenomenon of Christianity. He also remarks that there is "ironic potential"[67] in Soyinka's writings. He does this having identified Soyinka's lineage, which is "replete with connections in the Anglican Church in which he grew" and "ascends to his great-great-grandfather Daniel Olubi."[68] Peel does not, however, identify those areas of ironic potential.

I followed through Peel's promptings to identify these areas to include: unity in the diversity of Africa's cultural mosaic; identification with the preaching of biblical prophets (the champions of justice); the abdication of Ogun and subsequent enthronement of Jesus (taking the "Avatar thematic"[69] to its transcendent dimension, thus, reinstating *Olódùmarè* to his rightful place); redirecting of art to religious service and worship (connection of creativity and spirituality);[70] and that *Alafia* (the epitome of Yoruba religious aspiration and cultural fulfillment) is achievable in Jesus Christ, as has been demonstrated by the conversion of many Yorubas to Christianity. Space will not allow a fuller exposition on these areas of ironic potential in Soyinka's writings. However, to conclude this section, it is worth pointing out at least two bases for the assumptions above.

Peel also shows how *Alafia*, "a term usually translated 'peace' but which has a much broader connotation, to embrace health, success, and prosperity,"[71] is indeed a pursuit of the Yoruba, just as Knowledge was for the Greeks, Glory for the Romans, and Light for the Jews (Cf. 2Cor 4:6). Like Bolaji Idowu and John Mbiti whom Soyinka single out for criticism, Kibicho of Kenya and Gabriel Setiloane of South Africa have argued for the continuity of pre-Christian African heritage into Christianity.[72] In *The Meaning of Religious Conversion in Africa*, Cyril Okorocha has debunked the notion that Christianity has nothing to do with the African world, and this invites dialogue with the themes raised by Soyinka.[73]

Conclusion

Mugambi, *Critiques of Christianity in African Literature – With Particular Reference to the East African Context*, has helped shape the framework for my reflection on literature. Like Paul, Justin, and Origen, who, as they *followed* Christ into their own cultural and intellectual world discovered that Christ had indeed preceded them and located himself among their setting, also contributed immensely to the advancement of scholarship in their respective times, we are truly indebted to the efforts of African Christian scholars. For their works show that there is indeed a "close connection between mission and scholarship."[74]

For Soyinka to arrive at an aesthetic referential avowal, as well as a social vision and activism that require the old deities to be secularized,[75] he must reconstitute the framework that supports the thought patterns that enrich cultural awareness. Soyinka subscribes to "secular gods" akin to the Olympian Greek deities.[76] It is up to Christian scholars to understand his approach and make a case for why Christianity offers a place for others to feel at home[77] and also demonstrate that Soyinka has taken a different path from his progenitors back to Aké, in Abeokuta, where they planted their first mission station in Yorubaland, where missionaries introduced as counter forces to Ogun, and all the other Orisa the Christian tradition and planted the first Church, named after the Apostle Peter.

Notes

1 Abraham Waigi Ng'ang'a, "African Literature, Arts and Aesthetics in Christian Reflection: Engaging the Thought of Wole Soyinka," *Journal of African Christian Thought*, 19, no. 1, (June 2016): 19–28.
2 See Roland Oliver, *The Missionary Factor in East Africa*, first published in 1952 (London and Harlow: Longmans, Green and Co Ltd., 1969), xiv. See also J. D. Y. Peel, *Religious Encounter in and the Making of the Yoruba*. (Bloomington and Indianapolis: Indiana University Press, 2000).
3 Roland Oliver, 1952, 29.
4 J.N.K. Mugambi, *Critiques of Christianity in African Literature – With Particular Reference to the East African Context*. (Nairobi: East African Educational Publishers Ltd., 1992), 16.
5 J.N.K. Mugambi, 1992, p. 1.
6 Ibid., 21.

7 C. S. Lewis, "Christianity and Literature," in Walter Hooper, ed. *Christian Reflections*, (London: Geoffrey Bles, 1967), 1–11 (1).
8 Ng'ang'a, "African Literature, Arts and Aesthetics in Christian Reflection: Engaging the Thought of Wole Soyinka," 21.
9 Biodun Jeyifo and Wole Soyinka, "Wole Soyinka, A Transition Interview," in *Transition* (No. 42, 1973): 62–4, (62).
10 Andrew Walls, "Christian Scholarship in the Twenty-first Century," *Journal of African Christian Thought*, 4, no. 2 (December 2001): 44–52.
11 Ibid., 44.
12 Kwame Bediako, "African Theology," in David Ford, ed. *The Modern Theologians: An Introduction of Christian Theology in the Twentieth Century*, Second Edition. (Oxford: Blackwell Publishing Ltd., 2003), 426–44 (432).
13 Op Cit., 44.
14 Walls, "Christian Scholarship in the Twenty-first Century," 44.
15 Ibid., 44.
16 Ibid., 44.
17 Ibid., 44.
18 Ibid., 44.
19 Ibid., 45.
20 Leland Ryken, "Literature in Christian Perspective," in D. A. Carson and John D. Woodbridge, eds. *God and Culture: Essays in Honour of Carl F.H. Henry*. (Grand Rapids: William Eerdmans Publishing Company and Carlisle: The Paternoster Press, 1993), 215–34 (215).
21 Kwame Bediako, "Biblical Perspectives on Christian Leadership in the Ghanaian Context," *Journal of African Christian Thought*, 17, no. 2 (December 2014): 10–15.
22 See my analysis in "African Theology and African Literature: A Theological Critique of Wole Soyinka's Aesthetic Framework for Reconstituting African Life and Thought," Unpublished PhD Thesis, submitted to Akrofi-Christaller Institute, Akropong, May 2015.
23 B. A. Mojuetan, ed. "Epilogue," in B. A. Mojuetan, ed., *Ibadan at 50 (1948–1998) Nigeria's Premier University in Perspective*. (Ibadan: Ibadan University Press, 2000), 437.
24 Ibid.
25 See "Millennium Excellence Foundation," (www.mefafrica.org/index.php/about-mef/the-foundation/overview-of-mef). (accessed December 12, 2010), 12:30 GMT. See Dapo Adelugba, ed. *Before Our Very Eyes: Tribute to Wole Soyinka, Winner of the Nobel Prize for Literature*, first published 1987 (Ibadan: Spektrum Books Limited, 2005); Wole Soyinka, *Of Africa*. (New Haven and London: Yale University Press, 2012); and Ivor Agyeman-Duah and Oguchukwu Promise, eds. *The Crucible of the Ages: Essays in Honour of Wole Soyinka at 80* (Ibadan: Bookraft, 2014).
26 Wole Soyinka, *Myth, Literature and the African World*. (Cambridge: Cambridge University Press, 1976), ix.
27 Wole Soyinka, *You Must Set Forth at Dawn*. (Ibadan: Bookraft, 2006), 53.
28 See Chima Anyadike, "Beyond Individual 'Dare': Soyinka's Fiction and the Problem of Individual Vision," in Oyin Ogunba, ed. *Soyinka: A Collection of Critical Essays*. (Ibadan: Syndicated Communications Ltd., 1994), 35–44 (36).
29 Soyinka, *Myth, Literature and the African World*, xif.
30 Ibid, x.
31 See Soyinka, *Myth, Literature and the African World*, x and 108.
32 Wole Soyinka, *Of Africa*. (New Haven and London: Yale University Press, 2012), viii.
33 Wole Soyinka, "Justice Is Never 'Siddon Look'!" www.osundefender.org/?p=129530 (italics added).

34 Wole Soyinka, *The Climate of Fear: The Reith Lectures*. (London: Profile Books Ltd., 2004).
35 See Wole Soyinka, "Corporate Gain and Human Deficit," in *Sahara Reporters* (September 17, 2012), published online: http://saharareporters.com/report/corporate-gains-human-deficit-wole-soyinka. (accessed March 9, 2013).
36 See also Swamp Dwellers, *The Lion and the Jewel, The Invention, Mandela's Earth and Other Poems as Well as Art, Outrage and Dialogue.*
37 See Bankole Olayebi, ed. *WS: A Life in Full*. (Ibadan: Bookraft, 2011), 11ff.
38 See Soyinka, *Of Africa*, 19–26.
39 Ibid, viii.
40 Soyinka, *Of Africa*, 20.
41 Soyinka, *You Must Set Forth at Dawn*, 39. See also Soyinka, *Aké: The Years of Childhood*. (London: Rex Collings, 1981 and New York, Vintage, 1983), 177–86.
42 Soyinka, *The Man Died*, 96.
43 See Gillian M. Bediako, *Primal Religion and the Bible: William Robertson Smith and His Heritage*. (Sheffield: Sheffield Academic Press, Ltd., 1997), 46–73; Basil Davidson, *The Africans: An Entry to Cultural History*. (London: Longmans, Green and Co. Ltd., 1969); Matthew Parris, "As an Atheist, I Truly Believe Africa Needs God," in *The Times* (December 27, 2008), published online: www.timesonline.co.uk/tol/comment/columnists/matthew_parris/article5400568.ece. (accessed March 24, 2009, 16:10 GMT).
44 Wole Soyinka, "Nobel Lecture 1986: This Past Must Address Its Present," *Modern Language Association* (Vol. 102, No. 5, October, 1987), 762–71, Modern Language Association: www.jstor.org/stable/462306. (accessed May 29, 2012, 09:14 GMT) p. 766. The term "devices," rather than "devises," is perhaps more suitable here.
45 Henry Louis Gates, Jr., "An Interview with Wole Soyinka," *Black World*, 24, no. 10 (1975): 30–48.
46 Soyinka, "Nobel Lecture 1986: This Past Must Address Its Present," 765.
47 Gates, Jr., "An Interview with Wole Soyinka," 53. Emphasis/clarification and italics original.
48 Ibid., 53.
49 Ibid., 53.
50 See Achebe, *Home and Exile*. (Oxford: Oxford University Press, 2000), 59, 73–105 (78 and 79 respectively).
51 Ibid., 79.
52 Wole Soyinka, *Selected Poems: Idanre, A Shuttle in the Crypt, Mandela's Earth*. (London: Methuen Publishing Ltd., 2001), 95.
53 See Wole Soyinka, *The Interpreters*. (London: Andre Deutsch, 1965 and New York: Macmillan, 1970), 17.
54 Myth Soyinka, *Literature and the African World*, 4.
55 Kalu Ogbaa, "An Interview with Chinua Achebe," in Bernth Lindfors, ed. *Conversations with Chinua Achebe*. (Jackson: University Press of Mississippi, 1997), 66. See interview in *Research in African Literature* (Vol. 12, 1981), 1–13 (67).
56 Jacob Olupona, "The Study of Yoruba Religious Tradition in Historical Perspective," *Numen* (Vol. 40, No. 4, September 1983), 240–73, 241.
57 John S. Mbiti, *African Religions and Philosophy*. (London, Ibadan, Nairobi: Heinemann Educational Books Ltd., 1969), 14ff, 59, 75f, and 78. See also John S. Mbiti, *Concepts of God in Africa*, first published in 1970 (London: SPCK, 1971): 229ff, 233 and 268.
58 Wole Soyinka, "Faiths that Preach Tolerance," *The Guardian* (Saturday 4 May, 2002), *Saturday Review*, 13.

59 Wole Soyinka, *You Must Set Forth at Dawn*. (Ibadan: Bookraft, 2006), 545f. See also Wole Soyinka, *Idanre and Other Poems*. (London: Methuen, 1967), 57.
60 Kwame Gyekye, *Tradition and Modernity – Philosophical reflections on the African Experience*. (Oxford, New York: Oxford University Press, 1997), 10.
61 Lewis, "Christianity and Literature," 2.
62 Kwame Bediako, "Africa and Christianity on the Threshold of the Third Millennium: The Religious Dimension," *African Affairs*, 99 (2000): 303–23, 303. See Samuel Huntington, "The Clash of Civilizations?" *Foreign Affairs*, 72, no. 3 (1993): 23–49, See also his *The Clash of Civilizations and the Remaking of World Order*. (New York: Simon & Schuster, 1996).
63 Soyinka advocates "the promotion of the secular gods" in his article "Faiths that Preach Tolerance."
64 "Secular gods" is a problematic phrase and oxymoron presupposing that the discourse on the gods must proceed along non-theological concerns.
65 See Bediako, *Christianity in Africa – The Renewal of a Non Western Religion*.
66 Peel, "Christianity and the Logic of Nationalist Assertion in Wole Soyinka's Ìsarà," in David Maxwell and Ingrid Lowrie, eds. *Christianity and the African Imagination: Essays in Honour of Adrian Hastings*. (Leiden, Boston and Cologne: Brill, 2002), 127–55, 129.
67 J.D.Y. Peel, "Christianity and the Logic of Nationalist Assertion," 149.
68 Peel, *Religious Encounter and the Making of the Yoruba*, 311.
69 In his poem, Mandela's Earth, as well as his memoir, *You Must Set Forth at Dawn*, Soyinka associates greater humanity with the personality and achievement of Nelson Mandela. See Soyinka, *You Must Set Forth at Dawn*, 24ff, 273, 296, 299, 304, 312 and 499.
70 See Illingworth, *Divine Immanence*, 145ff.
71 Peel, *Religious Encounter and the Making of the Yoruba*, 91.
72 See Ng'ang'a, "African Theology and African Literature: A Theological Critique of Wole Soyinka's Aesthetic Framework for Reconstituting African Life and Thought," 346–77.
73 Cyril C. Okorocha, *The Meaning of Religious Conversion in Africa – The Case of the Igbo of Nigeria*. (Aldershot: Gower Publishing Company, 1987).
74 Walls, "Christian Scholarship in Africa in the Twenty-first Century," 44.
75 Soyinka, *Myth, Literature and the African World*, 86–97, 86.
76 Soyinka, *You Must Set Forth at Dawn*, 52f and 133, (133); Anthony Appiah, "An Evening with Wole Soyinka," in Biodun Jeyifo, ed. *Conversations with Wole Soyinka*. (Jackson: University Press of Mississippi, 2001), 129–37, (134). Originally published in *Black American Literature Forum* (Vol. 22, no. 4, Winter 1988): 777–85.
77 John Mbiti, "Christianity and East African Culture and Religion," *Dini na Mila*, 3, no. 1 (May 1968), 4; Bolaji Idowu, *Towards an Indigenous Church*. (London: Oxford University Press, 1965), 11; and F. B. Welbourn and B. A. Ogot, *A Place to Feel at Home*. (London: Oxford University Press, 1966).

Bibliography

Achebe, Chinua. *Home and Exile*. Oxford: Oxford University Press, 2000.

Adelugba, Dapo, ed. *Before Our Very Eyes: Tribute to Wole Soyinka, Winner of the Nobel Prize for Literature*, first published 1987. Ibadan: Spektrum Books Limited, 2005.

Agyeman-Duah, Ivor, and Oguchukwu Promise, eds. *The Crucible of the Ages: Essays in Honour of Wole Soyinka at 80*. Ibadan: Bookcraft, 2014.

Anyadike, Chima. "Beyond Individual 'Dare': Soyinka's Fiction and the Problem of Individual Vision." In *Soyinka: A Collection of Critical Essays*, edited by Oyin Ogunba, 35–44. Ibadan: Syndicated Communications Ltd., 1994.

Appiah, Anthony Kwame. "An Evening with Wole Soyinka." In *Conversations with Wole Soyinka*, edited by Biodun Jeyifo, 129–37. Jackson: University Press of Mississippi, 2001.

Bediako, Gillian M. *Primal Religion and the Bible: William Robertson Smith and His Heritage*. Sheffield: Sheffield Academic Press, Ltd., 1997.

Bediako, Kwame. "Africa and Christianity on the Threshold of the Third Millennium: The Religious Dimension." *African Affairs* 99 (2000): 303–23.

———. "African Theology." In *The Modern Theologians: An Introduction of Christian Theology in the Twentieth Century*, edited by David Ford, Second edition, 426–44. Oxford, Malden: Blackwell Publishing Ltd., 2003.

———. "Biblical Perspectives on Christian Leadership in the Ghanaian Context." *Journal of African Christian Thought* 17, no. 2 (December 2014): 10–15.

———. *Christianity in Africa – The Renewal of a Non Western Religion.*

Davidson, Basil. *The Africans: An Entry to Cultural History*. London: Longmans, Green and Co. Ltd., 1969.

Gates, Henry Louis Jr. "An Interview with Wole Soyinka." *Black World* 24, no. 10 (1975): 30–48.

Gyekye, Kwame. *Tradition and Modernity – Philosophical Reflections on the African Experience*. New York: Oxford University Press, 1997.

Huntington, Samuel. "The Clash of Civilizations?" *Foreign Affairs* 72, no. 3 (1993): 23–49.

———. *The Clash of Civilizations and the Remaking of World Order*. New York: Simon & Schuster, 1996.

Huxley, Julian, J. Bronowski, Gerald Berry, and James Fisher, eds. *Growth of Ideas, Knowledge, Thought, Imagination*. London: Macdonald and Co. Publishers Ltd., 1965.

Idowu, E. Bolaji. *Olódùmarè: God in Yoruba Belief*. London: Longman, 1962.

———. *Towards an Indigenous Church*. London: Oxford University Press, 1965.

Illingworth, John R. *Divine Immanence*. London: Hansebooks, 2016.

Jeyifo, Biodun and Wole Soyinka. "Wole Soyinka, A Transition Interview." *Transition* no. 42 (1973): 62–4.

Lewis, C. S. "Christianity and Literature." In *Christian Reflections*, edited by Walter Hooper, 1–11, London: Geoffrey Bles, 1967.

Maxwell, David, and Ingrid Lowrie, eds. *Christianity and the African Imagination: Essays in Honour of Adrian Hastings*. Leiden: Brill, 2002.

Mbiti, John S. *African Religions and Philosophy*. London: Heinemann 1969.

———. "Christianity and East African Culture and Religion." *Dini na Mila* 3, no. 1 (May 1968).

———. *Concepts of God in Africa*. London: SPCK, 1971.

Mojuetan, B. A. "Epilogue." In *Ibadan at 50 (1948–1998) Nigeria's Premier University in Perspective*, edited by B. A. Mojuetan, 437. Ibadan: Ibadan University Press, 2000.

Mugambi, J.N.K. *Critiques of Christianity in African Literature – With Particular Reference to the East African Context*. Nairobi: East African Educational Publishers Ltd., 1992.

Ng'ang'a Abraham Waigi. "African Literature, Arts and Aesthetics in Christian Reflection: Engaging the Thought of Wole Soyinka." *Journal of African Christian Thought* 19, no. 1 (June 2016): 19–28.

———. "African Theology and African Literature: A Theological Critique of Wole Soyinka's Aesthetic Framework for Reconstituting African Life and Thought." Unpublished Ph.D. Thesis, submitted to Akrofi-Christaller Institute, Akropong, May 2015.

Ogbaa, Kalu. "An Interview with Chinua Achebe." *Research in African Literature* 12 (1981): 1–13.

Okorocha, Cyril C. *The Meaning of Religious Conversion in Africa – The Case of the Igbo of Nigeria*. Aldershot: Gower Publishing Company, 1987.

Olayebi, Bankole, ed. *WS: A Life in Full*. Ibadan: Bookcraft, 2011.

Oliver, Roland. *The Missionary Factor in East Africa*. London and Harlow: Longmans, Green and Co Ltd., 1969.

Olupona, Jacob. "The Study of Yoruba Religious Tradition in Historical Perspective." *Numen* 40, no. 4 (September 1983): 240–73.

Paris, Matthew Parris. "As an Atheist, I Truly Believe Africa Needs God." *The Times*. December 27, 2008, published online: www.timesonline.co.uk/tol/comment/columnists/matthew_parris/article5400568.ece accessed March 24, 2009, 16:10 GMT.

Peel, J. D. Y. "Christianity and the Logic of Nationalist Assertion in Wole Soyinka's Isara."In *Christianity and the African Imagination: Essays in Honour of Adrian Hastings*, edited by Maxwell, D. and Lawrie, I., 127–55. Leiden: Brill, 2003.

———. *Religious Encounter in and the Making of the Yoruba*. Bloomington & Indianapolis: Indiana University Press, 2000.

Ryken, Leland. "Literature in Christian Perspective." In *God and Culture: Essays in Honour of Carl F.H. Henry*, edited by D. A. Carson, and John D. Woodbridge, 215–34. Grand Rapids: William Eerdmans Publishing Company, 1993.

Sanneh, Lamin. *Whose Religion Is Christianity? The Gospel Beyond the West*. Grand Rapids: William B. Eerdmans Publishing Company, 2003.

Soyinka, Wole. "Corporate Gain, and Human Deficit." *Sahara Reporters*. September 17, 2012. published online: http://saharareporters.com/report/corporate-gains-human-deficit-wole-soyinka. Accessed March 9, 2013.

"Faiths that Preach Tolerance." *The Guardian*. May Saturday 4, 2002.

———. *Of Africa*. New Haven and London: Yale University Press, 2012.

———. *You Must Set Forth at Dawn*. Ibadan: Bookcraft, 2006.

———. *Aké: The Years of Childhood*. London: Rex Collings, 1981.

———. *Selected Poems: Idanre and Other Poems*. London: Methuen Publishing Ltd., 2001.

———. "Nobel Lecture 1986: This Past Must Address Its Present." *Modern Language Association* 102, no. 5 (October 1987): 762–71.

———. *Art, Dialogue, and Outrage: Essays on Literature and Culture*. New York: Pantheon Books, 1988.

———. *Myth, Literature and the African World*. Cambridge: Cambridge University Press, 1976.

———. *The Climate of Fear: The Reith Lectures*. London: Profile Books Ltd., 2004.

———. *The Interpreters*. London: Andre Deutsch, 1965.

———. *The Man Died*. London: Rex Collings, 1972.
———. *You Must Set Forth at Dawn*. Ibadan: Bookcraft, 2006.
Wa Thiongo, Ngũgi. *A Grain of Wheat*. London: Heinemann, 1968.
———. *The River Between*. London: Heinemann, 1965.
———. *Devil on the Cross*. London: Heinemann, 1987.
Walls, Andrew. "Christian Scholarship in the Twenty-first Century." *Journal of African Christian Thought* 4, no. 2 (December 2001): 44–52.
Welbourn, F. B., and B. A. Ogot. *A Place to Feel at Home*. London: Oxford University Press, 1966.

21 Theological education in Africa

Concerns and contribution of Professor Jesse N.K. Mugambi

Dickson Nkonge Kagema

Introduction

This paper offers an analysis of Jesse N. K. Mugambi's perception of, and participation in, theological education in Africa. It explores Mugambi's thinking on this theme, and some of the things he has personally done to ensure there is relevant theological education in the African Church. Professor Mugambi is an African icon who has made a significant contribution in World Christianity, African religions, Christian theology in Africa, mission, ecology, ethics, social justice, ecumenism, academic publishing, and Christian leadership.[1] He is thus a theologian with many faces. Academic papers, books, and dissertations have been written on Mugambi's works; however, many of them focus on his contribution on liberation and reconstruction theologies.[2] This is understandable because in 1970s and 1980s, when he started his theological reflection as Africa was going through the difficult period of recovering from colonial domination, a challenge that was still problematic due to the unscrupulous African leaders who had taken over power and who seriously wanted the status quo perpetuated.[3] During the 1970s Mugambi emphasized the need for the theology of Liberation in Africa. For example, his emphasis concerning the content of African Christian theology as long as African nations were struggling to liberate themselves from the shackles of colonialism was that "the objective task of the African Christian theology is liberation."[4]

In 1990 he shocked theologians and Church leaders in the whole in the world with his unexpected call for a paradigm shift from the theology of Liberation to Reconstruction theology in Africa.[5] He denoted,

> Reconstruction is the new priority for African nations in the 1990s. The churches and their theologians will need to respond to this new priority in relevant fashion, to facilitate this process of reconstruction. The process will require considerable efforts of reconciliation and confidence-building. It will also require reorientation and retraining.[6]

This new emphasis was further elaborated and clarified in his book *From Liberation to Reconstruction*, in which he urged African leaders (religious and secular) to shift from the traditional dominant theme of liberation to a new premise of reconstruction.[7] In this new paradigm, he declared that the old colonial image of Africa as the "sleeping question mark" has to be replaced by a new one, of Africa as the "waking answer."[8] This new theological paradigm that Mugambi proposed was accepted by some theologians and critiqued by others – as illustrated in an anthology of essays titled *Theologies of Liberation and Reconstruction*.[9] Some of the scholars such as Julius Gathogo acknowledge Mugambi as the father of the theology of reconstruction in Africa.[10] Some theologians such as Tinyiko Maluleke expressed caution over Mugambi's Theology of Reconstruction in view of the challenges that lay ahead.[11]

Thus Mugambi's name features prominently in the discourse on theologies of liberation and reconstruction in Africa, but there are other themes of African Christian theology on which he has made considerable contribution. For instance, I met Prof. Mugambi in the year 2002 when I joined the University of Nairobi for my post-graduate studies. Since then, I have interacted with him in many instances as his student and friend. For the many times we have talked he has always emphasized the importance of equipping Church leaders (clergy and laity) in the African Church through theological education as a dire necessity. He is so concerned with theological education in Africa that even when he devised the famous theology of reconstruction, he did not fail to explicate the significant role that theology plays in the mission of the Church.[12] In other words, social reconstruction is impossible without theologically sound theologians and Church leaders to be charged with the tasks of articulation and implementation of this vital theological model.[13] It is therefore imperative to appreciate Prof. Mugambi's concern for, and contribution towards, theological education for the Church in Africa as one of the core elements in his theological output.

The influence of Jesse Mugambi's background

In his inaugural lecture published in 1996, Mugambi listed upbringing and socialization as the main pointers to religious adherence.[14] These "pointers" are broadly illustrative and applicable to him – a scholar who has maintained his religious ideals – as John Mbiti attests.[15] Mugambi grew up in a Christian home. His parents were staunch Christians. His father Timothy Kanyua was a dedicated Church leader at Emmanuel Church Kigari, a great missioner and a "contextual theologian," while his mother, Jemimah Kori, was a devoted adherent of the East African Revival Movement. Mr. Kanyua together with Canon Daudi Petro pioneered the Anglican mission work in Meru region. In 1962 he, together with a few colleagues, helped in the establishment of St. Matthew's ACK Kiangima Church. I also refer to him as a "contextual theologian" because when he together with four other Church elders from Kigari went to Meru in February 1969 to survey the area where they would plant a Church, they found that the Ameru had prepared for them a local brew called *Marwa*, which culturally was the best drink for respected visitors. The Anglican Church basically taught against this brew and while they were contemplating on what to do, Timothy Kanyua advised them to take a mild response rather than condemning the Ameru. Because of this approach, they were highly welcomed and even given a piece of land to construct a Church building.[16]

Such influence is vital because relating the gospel with culture requires people who have the knowledge and skills on how it can be effectively done. He asserts, "When a theologian tries to answer questions which are not relevant amongst whom he or she lives, the theology thus articulated is deemed irrelevant and no one bothers or cares about the concerns of such a theologian."[17] But how can the Church in Africa nurture theologians who can effectively articulate such issues of ultimate and contextual concern as gospel and culture? Mugambi's answer to this question is that the Church in Africa needs relevant theological education, with a curriculum sensitive to the needs of the communities the trainees will serve after graduation.[18] He emphasizes, "The effective consolidation of Christianity in Africa will depend directly on the effectiveness of authentically African theological articulation."[19] This articulation should be cultivated and followed up in the theological institutions.[20]

The situation of the Church in Africa

Mugambi discusses the situation of the Church in Africa in the 21st century in *The Biblical Basis for Evangelization: Theological Reflection Based on an Africa Experience*.[21] Mugambi echoed Roland Oliver's serious concerns about the East African Church and its leadership, about which no satisfying solution could be offered in the 1950s: the utter failure of the Church since 1920s to attract into the Christian ministry even a handful of the best educated East Africans.[22] This shortcoming was in contrast with the first three decades of the colonial period (until 1940) during which African elites became either chiefs or churchmen. With the development of colonial secondary education, and with the widening of secular opportunities, the Churches began to be outpaced in the competition for the elite. With the introduction of colonial higher education, the situation became even more serious.[23] Oliver expressed concern that in the early 1950s, when the first lot of students graduated from the University College of East Africa there was still not a single ordained minister in any of the Churches who had received even the beginnings of higher education in any of the non-Church institutions of higher learning.[24] In view of this shortcoming, Oliver remarked, "A Church led by peasant priests may start to disintegrate at the centre while expanding at the circumference."[25] Mugambi observes that this shortcoming continues unabated, at a time when the numerical growth of

Churches is unprecedented. A recent study by Dickson Nkonge on training needs in the Anglican Church of Kenya confirms that this challenge is real and worrying. Tremendous numerical growth is worth celebrating, but if it is not matched with well trained leaders, its future is doubtable.[26] In view of this alarming concerrn, Mugambi raises pertinent questions regarding the personnel needs for the Church in Africa in the 21st century, in comparison and contrast with the 1950s: Is the situation different? Has it improved? Is it worse? What can be done?[32] Mugambi proposes that this is a challenge with which the Church in Africa must continually and inescapably wrestle, now and in future.[27]

Mugambi's other quote[28] is from John S. Mbiti's book titled, *New Testament Eschatology in an African Background*, published in 1971.[29] In this book, Mbiti assessed the general situation of the Church in Africa in the 1960s. He concluded that the Church in East Africa and Africa as a whole "has come to existence and has grown evangelistically but not theologically."[30] Mbiti's conclusion was very similar to the trend Oliver had observed concerning the Church in Africa in 1950s. According to Mbiti, this "evangelical growth" also concerned "numerical growth." The Church had grown remarkably in terms of numbers of members, sponsored schools, clinics and dispensaries, and other physical facilities. Sadly, however, although the Church that had contributed significantly toward the training and support of a majority of "secular" African leaders and thinkers, it had itself hardly any theologians. The African pastor had remained the least educated person among the local elite in contrast with the early centuries of Christianity in Africa when the churchman was the most educated person in society.[31] Mbiti was stunned by the fact that by 1971 African Churches could not count more than half a dozen African theologians engaged in theological output, teaching, preaching, and writing.[32]

Mugambi observes with concern that the situation has not changed at the beginning of the 21st century. He raises two concerns that ought to be of priority today: "What is the situation now?" "Is the Church beginning to grow theologically in order to match its numerical outreach and growth?" These two concerns constitute the main challenge on which the Church in Africa needs to focus.[33] While concurring with both Roland Oliver and John Mbiti, and while confirming that the situation today is not very different from what it was in the 1950s and 1970s, Mugambi observes, "In terms of the physical outreach, the Church has grown tremendously. But as far as theological growth is concerned, it appears that the Church has not yet grown significantly."[34]

While the success of the Church depends entirely on the availability of trained leaders, the Churches, particularly the non-Catholic denominations, lack adequately trained personnel to cope relevantly with the needs of the Churches in Africa. The problem is aggravated by the fact that it affects theological training itself, such problems as: lack of sufficient resources, westernized conceptual tools, problems of analysis and synthesis, irrelevance of training itself, and un-contextualized curriculum. These challenges continue to negatively affect the training of the Church leaders in Africa.[35]

Mugambi's diagnosis is confirmed in the findings of a doctoral research on ministerial formation, which he supervised between 2006 and 2010, authored by Dickson Nkonge. It focused on the Anglican Church of Kenya (ACK) as the case study. Nkonge found that the ACK was a tremendously growing denomination at a rate of 6.7 percent per annum. By 2010 the ACK had a membership of about 3,711,890, yet it was served by only 1,555 ordained pastors, translating to a clergy per Christians ratio of 1:2,387.[36] This implies that on average, in the ACK, one pastor caters for about 2,400 Christians. Nkonge asks a pertinent question worth our reflection: "Is it practically possible for one clergy to effectively nurture 2,400 Christians spiritually?"[37] Moreover, even the few available clergy are not well trained. For example, out of 1,555 clergy serving in the ACK, only 16 percent have first theological degrees and above qualifications. The remaining 84 percent have diplomas, certificates, and short courses in theology.[38]

As confirmed by Mugambi, this scenario gives the general picture of the Church in Tropical Africa.[39] It is growing numerically, but without sufficient and well equipped Church leaders to effectively run it. One can say that it is "an expanding flock without enough and qualified shepherds." In view of this constraint, Mugambi observes that although theological training should be a life-long vocation, and although clergy and lay leaders are expected to know more than ordinary believers, many pastors and lay leaders in the Protestant Churches in Africa have little or no theological training. Mugambi then goes on to ask a challenging question worth reflection by all Church leaders in Africa today: "If African church leaders cannot provide theological and doctrinal leadership . . . how can African Christianity be sustained?"[40]

With regard to the curriculum design and content of Theological Education in Africa, Mugambi observes with concern,

> One of the shortcomings of the present process of theological formation is that much of what students study at college is neither relevant nor applicable to the situations in parishes and institutions where they go to work after completing their training.[41]

Theological education in Africa continues to encounter challenges due to lack of contextualized curricula. Bible colleges continue using syllabi that were designed in the West and brought to Africa by the missionaries who knew little or nothing about the dynamics of the African cultural and religious heritage. The result has been that the curricula currently used in the Church training institutions in Africa have been overloaded with cultural values from Europe and North America at the expense of the African cultural and religious heritage.[42] Western cultural values are not necessarily "Christian"! Definitely, such curricula cannot produce relevant, responsive, and effective leaders for the African Church and society. Over all, such curricula lead to the loss of what Mugambi calls "denominational identity," as there are no role models for the learners to emulate.[43] Dickson Nkonge, on the basis of his research concurs with Mugambi, that the curriculum of any institution is very important as it determines the kind of the products produced by that institution. If the curriculum is haphazardly done, the people produced by it are haphazard and their work is haphazard.[44]

What is the way forward for the Church in Africa according to Mugambi?

Watson Omulokoli, in an article titled "The Challenge of Leadership Training for Churches," concurs with Mugambi that the African Church is in a real crisis that requires urgent measures to rectify, if the long term future of the Church is to be secured in the short term.[45] Mugambi's insights about the Church in Africa today and its future are summarized in his moving and inspiring words, articulated during his address to the General Committee of All Africa Conference of Churches (AACC), in Nairobi on March 30, 1990. He had been invited to reflect on "The Future of the Church and the Church of the Future in Africa":

> In Africa today we are in great need of hope. Despite all the very demoralizing and frustrating propaganda, we need to affirm that tomorrow need not to be like yesterday. Today, in faith we can commit ourselves to work for a better tomorrow, knowing that with God nothing is impossible. . . . We dare affirm that since the God we worship is the creator and director of all human history, tomorrow need not to be like yesterday.[46]

Mugambi shares the same concern highlights challenges facing theological education in Africa, such as lack of contextualized curriculum; high cost of residential training; imported cultural and religious values with little regard to the African cultural and religious heritage; lack of denominational identity; lack of enough adequately trained theologians, and many others. In the same paper he emphasizes that this crisis does not signal the end of theological education in Africa.[47] Theological education is the backbone of any Church, as it determines the route the Church will take and ought therefore not to be taken lightly.[48] Mugambi, aware of this caution, does not conclude that either the Church in Africa or its system of theological education has no future. Instead he suggests possible ways of stabilizing theological education by enhancing the sustainability of the Church in Africa. He emphasizes, "The long term sustainability of churches greatly depends on the effectiveness of pastoral and lay training."[49]

Possible ways of improving theological education in Africa

Mugambi suggests various methods which he believes that if adopted by the Church in Africa can make theological education relevant, viable, and effective. Some of these include:

i) Utilization of public tertiary institutions

He advises Churches to provide ordination courses for graduates from public universities. This option would considerably reduce the recurrent cost of theological training and ministerial formation. The main cost would then be carried by the public sector. The implication is that Dioceses, Synods, or Presbyteries will have to keep track of their brilliant members during their undergraduate training, and involve them in lay activities in anticipation of ministerial formation on completion of the course. Another implication is that the remuneration of graduate clergy should, at least, be commensurate with the public salary scales. There are many advantages in this option. Most of the older Protestant Churches in Africa have well trained lay people in many professions. This option makes it possible for the Church to make use of this expertise in a formal and structured way, without the necessity to invest heavily to train its own specialists. Mugambi feels that this is the way of the future.[50]

ii) Consolidation and amalgamation of existing institutions

Mugambi advises that rationalization of theological education will require, to the extent possible, the eradication of duplication and competition, and the enhancement of mutual support and complementation. For this option to work, all those involved, including Church leaders and donors, will have to be willing to take a rational, rather than political approach to theological education and ministerial formation. The option may require consolidation and amalgamation of the existing theological institutions which can be done across provinces or even across continents. He sees it as irresponsible to continue doing things separately, as many Churches in Africa are doing, what can be achieved much more efficiently and effectively, through joint and united initiatives.[51]

iii) Ecumenical co-operation in theological education

He elucidates that during the 1950s and 1960s there were established in Africa what came to be called "United Theological Colleges." This model did not last long due dissatisfaction of participating denominations loss of confidence that emanated from the way these united theological colleges were managed, whereby partner Churches established their own training institutes in competition with the ecumenical ones. Mugambi recommends that this is still an ideal approach for the African Church today. Unity of the Church (both locally and globally) cannot be manifested in a model of theological and ministerial formation that is divisive and competitive. Jesus urged his followers to evangelize in unity and cooperation – that the world may believe. Competition and rivalry are counter to this cardinal principle of effective and sustainable evangelization.[52]

iv) Theological training through para-Church institutions

Mugambi proposes that theological education can also be enhanced through institutions owned by trusts independent from dioceses and provinces, but maintaining the ethos of the Church. He cites an example of Carlile College in Nairobi, owned by Church Army in Eastern Africa (Anglican), which has been used by the Anglican Church of Kenya to train its clergy, lay leaders, and evangelists for a long time. He considers this initiative to hold great promise, because it makes it possible for such institutions to meet the national and international standards in tertiary education, while at the same time serving the needs of the Church with regard to human resources development.[53]

v) Use of relevant modes of delivering theological education

Mugambi affirms that theological education in Africa has conventionally been conducted through the lecture method, but there is need to consider other methods as the world is changing. Communication Technology has advanced greatly since the 1960s. Today it is possible to deliver efficiently and effectively full examinable courses without direct physical contact between lecturers and their students. It is important for the African Church to consider new and more efficient ways of delivering high quality theological education. In addition to the conventional lecture method, theological education educators can use delivery through electronic mail; audio visual media; teaching guides; travelling seminars and field workshops; and interdisciplinary, multi-campus, and multi-media delivery.[54]

vi) Use of a relevant curriculum in the institutions

Mugambi is emphatic that for a successful and sustainable theological education system in Africa, the institutions must provide a relevant curriculum for the learners, not for the teachers.[55] To meet such criteria, theological education in Africa will need to be organized in accordance with the most up-to-date educational principles. He thus proposes that the development of the theological education will need to be done through the "involvement of professional educators who are familiar with and sympathetic to, the needs of the Churches."[56] A broad-based curriculum will be essential, including such courses as philosophy, comparative study of religion, sociology, and psychology of religion would be useful courses to prepare theological students for the ministry which awaits them on completion of their studies.[57]

Mugambi's participation in theological education in Africa[58]

In this section, I want to give a brief participation of Mugambi in theological education. Mugambi has physically participated extensively in theological education in Africa and in the international community. In research and publication, Mugambi has published widely in the area of theology, philosophy, and religious studies. He is among the leading African theologians in research and publications. His most theological impact has been in the theology of reconstruction. Mugambi has balanced his research and teaching with engagement in social activism and policy making. Mugambi has been involved in numerous policy making bodies in Africa, especially those dealing with theological education. For example, he is the resource person in theology and religion at the Kenya Commission for University Education, the resource person in the Anglican Church of Kenya on matters of theological education and training, representative of the World Council Churches working group on climate change (ecology has become a concern for theological reflection in Africa today), the resource person with All Africa Conference of Churches, director of Kenya Literature Bureau, and many others. Previously, he served as a senior consultant on development and research in All Africa Conference of Churches and also in religious education panel of Christian Churches Educational Association.

Conclusion

In the past decade the scholarship and theology of Mugambi has shaped theological discourse in Africa. He has served as a model scholar for many African theologians and theologians around the world interested in addressing the many issues facing Africa. Mugambi has contributed significantly to theological education in Africa and called on the ecclesial community remain relevant to the people of Africa in addressing their felt needs.

Notes

1 University of Nairobi staff Profile, 2016. https://profiles.uonbi.ac.ke. (accessed September 15, 2016).
2 Ibid.
3 Zablon Nthamburi. *The African Church at the Crossroads: A Strategy for Indigenization*. (Nairobi: Uzima, 1991), 5.
4 J.N.K. Mugambi, *African Christian Theology: An Introduction*. (Nairobi: EAEP, 1989), 12.
5 J.N.K. Mugambi, "The Future of the Church and the Church of the Future in Africa," in J. B. Chipenda, et al., eds. *The Church in Africa: Towards a Theology of Reconstruction*. (Nairobi: AACC, 1991), 25–50.
6 Ibid., 36.

7 Mugambi, *From Liberation to Reconstruction.*
8 Ibid., 49.
9 I.T.M. Mwase and E. K. Kamaara, eds. *Theologies of Liberation and Reconstruction.* (Nairobi: Acton, 2012).
10 J. Gathogo, "Jesse Mugambi's Pedigree: Formative Factors," uir.unisa.ac.za. (accessed September 15, 2016).
11 T. Maluleke, "Mugambi, J.N.K. From Liberation to Reconstruction: African Christian Theology after the Cold War," *Missonalia*, 24, no.1 (2006), 3–19.
12 See Mugambi, "The Future of the Church and the Church of the Future in Africa," Op.Cit, 40–1 and *From Liberation to Reconstruction*, Op.Cit, 21–32.
13 Mugambi, *From Liberation to Reconstruction*, 26.
14 J.N.K. Mugambi, *Religion and Social Construction of Reality.* (Nairobi: UoN Press, 1996), 12.
15 J. S. Mbiti, "Forward," in I.M.T. Mwase and E. K. Kamaara, Op.Cit, 2–3.
16 Interview with Canon J. P. Mutiria, The first Anglican Priest in Meru, now retired, at Kiriribu on 14/9/2016.
17 Mugambi, *From Liberation to Reconstruction*, 20.
18 Ibid., 27.
19 J.N.K. Mugambi, "The Future of the Church and the Church of the Future in Africa," Op. Cit, 41.
20 D. K. Nkonge, "Theological Institutions in Kenya and the Future of the Church," *Journal of Adult Theological Education*, 10, no. 2 (2013): 147–61.
21 J.N.K. Mugambi, *The Biblical Basis for Evangelization: Theological Reflections Based on an African Experience.* (Nairobi: Oxford University Press, 1989).
22 Roland Oliver, *The Missionary Factor in East Africa.* (London: Longman, 2nd edition, 1970).
23 Ibid., x–xi.
24 Ibid.
25 R. Oliver, Op.cit, 292. Mugambi refers to this quote many times when he is talking about the African Church today.
26 D. K. Nkonge, "Theological Institutions in Kenya and the Future of the Church," Op.cit.
27 J.N.K. Mugambi, *The Biblical Basis for Evangelization*, 2.
28 Ibid.
29 J. S. Mbiti, *New Testament Eschatology in an African Background.* (London: Oxford University Press, 1971).
30 Ibid., 177. See also J. N. K. Mugambi, *The Biblical Basis for Evangelization*, 3.
31 J. S. Mbiti, *New Testament Eschatology in an African Background*, 177.
32 Ibid.
33 J.N.K. Mugambi, *The Biblical Basis for Evangelization*, 3.
34 Ibid.
35 Ibid., 70–6.
36 D. K. Nkonge, "Leadership Training for Mission in the Anglican Church of Kenya," Unpublished Doctoral Thesis, Pretoria: UNISA, 2008, 58.
37 Ibid., 63.
38 Ibid., 66.
39 Oral discussion with Prof. Mugambi on 22/1/2016.
40 J.N.K. Mugambi, "The Future of Theological Education in Africa and the Challenges It faces," in I. A. Phiri and D.Werner, eds. *Handbook of Theological Education in Africa.* (Oxford: Regnum, 2013).
41 J.N.K. Mugambi, *The Biblical Basis for Evangelization*, 74.
42 J.N.K. Mugambi, "The Future of Theological Education in Africa and the Challenges It faces," Op.Cit, 117.
43 Ibid.

44 D. K. Nkonge, "Leadership Training for Mission in the Anglican Church of Kenya," 156.
45 W. Omulokoli, "The Challenge of Leadership Training for Churches," *Evangelical Journal of Contemporary Mission and Research in Africa*, no. 1 (2002), 46–8.
46 J.N.K. Mugambi, "The Future of the Church and the Church of the Future in Africa," 30.
47 J.N.K. Mugambi, "The Future of Theological Education in Africa and the Challenges It Faces," Op.cit, 117–25. See also his "Theological Education in Africa," which Mugambi had published in the Cambridge Dictionary of Christianity. (New York: Cambridge University Press, 2010).
48 D. K. Nkonge, "Leadership Training for Mission in the Anglican Church of Kenya," Op.Cit.
49 J.N.K. Mugambi, "The Future of Theological Education in Africa and the Challenges It Faces," 122–3.
50 Ibid.
51 Ibid.
52 Ibid.
53 J.N.K.Mugambi, 1993, 20–7.
54 J.N.K. Mugambi, *The Biblical Basis for Evangelization*, 75.
55 J.N.K. Mugambi, 1993, Op. Cit.
56 Ibid.
57 Ibid.
58 Most of the information from this section was gotten from Mugambi's Curriculum Vitae, available at https://profiles.uonbi.ac.ke.

Bibliography

Chipenda, J. B. et. al., eds. *The Church in Africa: Towards a Theology of Reconstruction*. Nairobi: All Africa Conference of Churches, 1991.

Gathogo, J. "Jesse Mugambi's Pedigree: Formative Factors." 2006, uir.unisa.ac.za. Accessed September 15, 2016.

———. "Post-liberation Theology: A Critical Appreciation." In *Theologies of Liberation and Reconstruction*, edited by I. M. T. Mwase, and E. K. Kamaara, 55–94. Nairobi: Acton, 2012.

Maluleke, T. "Mugambi, J.N.K. From Liberation to Reconstruction: African Christian Theology after the Cold War." *Missonalia* 24, no. 1 (2006): 3–19.

Mbiti, J. S. *New Testament Eschatology in an African Background*. London: Oxford University Press, 1971.

Mugambi, J. N. K. *African Christian Theology: An Introduction*. Nairobi: EAEP, 1989.

———. *The Biblical Basis for Evangelization: Theological Reflections Based on an African Experience*. Nairobi: Oxford University Press, 1989.

———. *From Liberation to Reconstruction: African Christian Theology after the Cold War*. Nairobi: EAEP, 1995.

———. *Religion and Social Construction of Reality*. Nairobi: UoN press 1996.

———. "The Future of the Church and the Church of the Future in Africa." In *The Church in Africa: Towards a Theology of Reconstruction*, edited by J. B. Chipenda, et. al., 25–50, Nairobi: All Africa Conference of Churches, 1991.

———. "The Future of Theological Education in Africa and the Challenges it Faces." In *Handbook of Theological Education in Africa*, edited by I. A. Phiri, and D. Werner. Oxford: Regnum, 2013.

Mwase, I. T. M., and E. K. Kamaara, eds. *Theologies of Liberation and Reconstruction*. Nairobi: Acton, 2012.

Nthamburi, Zablon. *The African Church at the Crossroads: A Strategy for Indigenization*. Nairobi: Uzima, 1991.

Nkonge, D. K. "A Study of the Anglican Church in Meru, 1969–2004: Challenges Encountered in Evangelization." Unpublished MA Thesis, Nairobi: University of Nairobi, 2004.

———. "Leadership Training for Mission in the Anglican Church of Kenya." Unpublished Doctoral Thesis, Pretoria: UNISA, 2008.

———. "Theological Institutions in Kenya and the Future of the Church." *Journal of Adult Theological Education* 10, no. 2 (2013): 147–161.

Oliver, Roland. *The Missionary Factor in East Africa*. London: Longman, 1952.

Omulokoli, Watson. "The Challenge of Leadership Training for Churches." *Evangelical Journal of Contemporary Mission and Research in Africa* 1, (2002): 46–8.

Rabai to Mumias. *A Short History of the Church of the Province of Kenya, 1844–1994*. Nairobi: Uzima, 1994.

University of Nairobi Staff Profile. 2016. https://profiles.uonbi.ac.ke. Accessed September 14, 2016.

22 Missions and money revisited[1]

Jonathan Bonk

I first met Jesse Mugambi, a dedicated ecumenist at an international conference hosted by the Faculty of Theology, University of Helsinki in April 2014. At this face to face meeting I became aware that we were kindred spirits, separated by continents but linked by overlapping intellectual, ethical, and faith concerns. The conference had been organized by the International Association for Mission Studies, Europe, with a view to exploring the implications of global economic inequities for faithful Christian mission. As someone who had published to the point of tedium on the subject of missions and money – like some kind of one-stringed-drone instrument – I had been invited to present the plenary paper on "Economic Development and Christian Mission" from a historical perspective.[2] Not surprisingly, the first person to raise his hand after my presentation was Prof. Mugambi. It was clear from his questions that not only had he listened attentively to my lecture, but that he was familiar with other things that I had written elsewhere. Before we went our separate ways, we agreed to trade publications. He did me great honor by requesting multiple copies of my book, *Missions and Money*, to distribute among some of his friends and colleagues.[3] It is appropriate, then, that I return to that theme in this chapter.

Mugambi is a man whose intellectual gifts have not prevented him from being deeply and effectively engaged with "grass roots" peoples, contexts, and issues. A seminal thinker among African Christian theologians, an active churchman, and a deeply committed Christian, Prof. Mugambi has been and still is a profound and steady influence on students, scholars, and Churches across the broad African ecclesiastical spectrum. I am personally in his debt because of the service he renders as an active and valued member of the senior Advisory Council of the *Dictionary of African Christian Biography*, an enterprise that has been dear to my heart since 1995.[4]

My interest in the relational dynamics of material and social disparity in close social proximity – with particular attention to its Christian missionary dimensions – was probably inevitable. As a child of missionary parents, my most formative years were spent in Ethiopia, where, until I reached my later teens, I unconsciously absorbed the values and assumed the entitlements of material and social privilege. Reminiscent of the privileged children who were among the subjects of Robert Coles' famous *Children of Crisis* series, I early confronted the burden of my own privilege, subconsciously at first, and later consciously.

The boarding school that I attended was unapologetically a bastion of privilege. Ethiopians were permanently relegated to kitchen, laundry, garden, and custodial duties. Tinkle the small bell on the dining room head table, and a bare-footed servant would patter in from the kitchen, apron scarcely concealing his own threadbare clothing. The school was surrounded by a chain-link fence, intended to keep us in and Ethiopians out. Aware that we were members of a privileged superior class, we accepted, expected, and sometimes demanded the obsequious deference shown to us by Ethiopians. In our play and discussion, Ethiopians were subjects of curiosity, sometimes the butt of ridicule, and on occasion even admired for their incorrigible bravery in the face of persecution; but they were seldom friends, and never social peers.

Returning to Canada to complete my education, it would be 14 years (1974) before I would return to Ethiopia – this time as a missionary with the Sudan Interior Mission. My wife and I were assigned to work in Tigre Province, leading a multi-national relief and development team trying to help the survivors of the terrible famine that precipitated the collapse of Ethiopia's ancient monarchy, and the murder of its venerable last emperor, Haile Selassie. By now a convinced egalitarian, thanks to my natural instincts, my Mennonite orientation, and my somewhat critical view of the modus operandi of traditional mission societies, I ensured that each member of the team – an eclectic mix of medical doctors and nurses, hydrologists and water engineers, agriculturalists and mechanics, drivers and cooks, evangelists and interpreters – received an equal portion of the financial pot. We worked and lived together both in the field and at the home base. I regret to recall that my not-always-subliminal attitude vis-à-vis other missionaries bordered on that of the infamous Pharisee in our Lord's parable whose self-consciously conspicuous piety compared so unfavorably with that of the wretched tax collector who prayed nearby (Luke 18:9–14).

With the deposition of the emperor came a palpable shift in the way that foreigners were portrayed in the public media. The country was in a state of hope-suffused euphoria, as its military junta (the *Derg*) proceeded to move the country from oppressive feudalism to enlightened socialism. For the first time in several millennia, peasant farmers could contemplate the prospect of owning and reaping 100 percent of what they sowed, since absentee landlords were a thing of the past. Millions faced the happy possibility of learning to read and write as the country's students poured into the countryside to teach literacy and socialism. Students, in turn, would learn to respect the peasantry and hard manual labor.

Completing our stint in Tigre province in northern Ethiopia, my wife and I were relocated to Kaffa province in the south, the birthplace of coffee. Here we worked with established congregations scattered across the province. Our primary role was to lend support to the work of evangelists sent by the Kale Heywet Church. The Church, seeing in the emerging stress on literacy an ideal opportunity, commissioned Christian teachers and their families to assist in congregational and community literacy in the hinterlands of the province. Impoverished rural communities were encouraged to construct simple single-room schools for which the mission agency agreed to provide roofing tin and a blackboard, while the Kale Heywet (Word of Life) Church would provide the teachers.

As the presumably neutral foreigner, residing not far from a small town that boasted a post office and a telephone, I was to serve as communications and finance conduit between the Kale Heywet Church and their employees, the literacy teachers. The monthly stipend for each family was roughly equivalent to US $20 while mine as a white foreigner was 60 times that amount – US $1200. To this was added such benefits as medical insurance, a semi-furnished house, travel funds, and educational opportunities for my children. None of this was available to my Ethiopian colleagues.

I felt a certain smugly self-righteous satisfaction from what I imagined to be my ability to work in a fraternal, non-patronizing way with these dedicated teachers. Our home was as open to them as theirs was to me when I would visit them each month, delivering their meager monthly wages and their mail. Although I was vaguely disquieted by the conspicuous material inequities that marked our lives, I did not give any serious thought to what might be done about it. An unwritten code among foreign missionaries obliged one to toe the line on wages and other forms of fiscal reward. Being overly generous with our Ethiopian colleagues would set a dangerous precedent, "spoiling" employees so that they would no longer be satisfied to work for standard parsimonious compensation.

Following the departure of our senior missionary colleagues in 1975, government school teachers across the country went on strike. Although Kale Heywet teachers did not join them, several of our teachers were detained by the police on suspicion of complicity in the national strike. They were required to show proof that they were legitimately employed by a recognized organization, and not – as suspected – illegally striking government teachers. Since this was an emergency, and the Kale Heywet Church headquarters was hundreds of miles away, where its leaders were dealing with myriad Marxist-revolution-related challenges of their own, I provided the teachers with temporary identification cards on which was clearly marked the name of the mission society that employed me. To add emphasis to the fact that they were in good standing as teachers, I also provided them with receipts indicating the amount and dates of their monthly reimbursement. The receipts, like the ID cards, bore the imprimatur of the foreign mission agency.

Three weeks later the bailiff served me with a 23-point indictment, signed by the seven Ethiopian colleagues for whom I had provided verification of their good standing. Charging that I was a "running dog capitalist and exploiter of the people," the document went on to enumerate misdemeanors typical of privileged foreigners, reaching its climax by accusing me of consistently defrauding them of fully half of their contracted wages. When I protested that the teachers were not in fact employed by me, but by their denomination, they declared flatly that I was a liar, presenting their ID cards and pay receipts as proof. On these documents was the name of the mission society by whom I was employed.

When I told officials of the individual contracts that each of the teachers had with the Kale Heywet Church, and which were kept in a filing cabinet in the central office of the elementary school, they responded that there were no contracts, and that I was lying. An inspection of the filing cabinets revealed that they were right – the contents of the file drawers had disappeared.

Mission society policy clearly stipulated that Ethiopian employees be reimbursed a minimum of US $40 per month, yet according to the SIM receipts signed by me, these men had been receiving only half of that amount. It was all too evident that I was guilty as charged. The only recourse open to me was to compensate them for their back-pay and damages.

This painful experience opened my eyes. I became acutely self-aware of the gross material inequities dividing me from my colleagues – jarring inequities that I had until then passively tolerated or ignored. The standard self-justifying clichés downplaying the social consequences and theological implications of gross economic and social inequity in close social proximity were exposed for the empty rationalizations that they were.

I understood as never before why the rich try to live their lives apart from the poor. And why, when circumstances force them to live in close physical proximity, the rich must protect themselves and their possessions with walls, bars, dogs, armed guards, and – if necessary – lethal violence or even war.

This experience provided me with an opportunity to view myself from the vantage point of the poor among whom I lived and worked, and the more closely I looked, the less I liked what I saw. My thinking eventually resulted in the book, *Missions and Money: Affluence as a Missionary Problem*, drafted during a 1987–1988 sabbatical, and published by Orbis in 1991. After 11 printings, a revised and expanded edition of the book, now in its third printing, was published in 2006.[5]

In my writing over the years I attempted to show how both the *effectiveness* and the *integrity* of decent, well-meaning missionaries and mission organizations is compromised when theories and practices are demonstrably at odds with those of the Lord they proclaim. My argument may be summarized as follows:

- Western missionaries tend to be materially wealthy, relative to most people in the so-called "mission fields" in which most of them serve, and this affluence is largely due to historical factors which cannot be replicated by the poor today;

- It follows that what the Bible says *to* and *about* the rich, it says *to* and *about* western missionaries. *Wealth* and *poverty* are among the most frequently recurring themes in our Christian scriptures.[6] While gross economic inequity in close social proximity poses profound relational, communicatory, and strategic challenges for Christian missionaries, more serious are questions about the ethical integrity of wealthy followers of Jesus in contexts of profound poverty;
- Since neither missionary training nor on-field orientation adequately prepare aspiring missionaries to acknowledge or address the ethical compromises characterizing those who – in St. Paul's words – "*peddle the word of God for profit*" (II Corinthians 2:17) in contexts of poverty, it is vital that the institutions and agencies responsible for training missionaries and facilitating mission work address the issues directly, deliberately, persistently, and biblically through training, mentoring, and policy.

Western missionary affluence

Western missionaries tend to be materially wealthy, relative to most people in their so-called "mission fields," and this affluence is largely due to factors that cannot be replicated by the poor today. While the statistical data informing any book quickly goes out of date, the integrity of my book's central argument has been reinforced since it first appeared in 1991. In an earlier article published in the *International Bulletin of Missionary Research*, I noted that throughout the period often referred to as the "William Carey Era" of modern missions, the per capita gross national products of the developed and underdeveloped worlds widened from a factor of less than two to one in 1792, to three to one by 1913, and seven to one by 1970. Since then, the situation has deteriorated for more than 20 percent of the world's population. The best estimates indicate that more than three billion people live on less than US $2.50 per day, and that at least 80 percent of humanity lives on less than US $10 per day.[7]

Missionaries from western lands, on the other hand, reflecting the culturally-prescribed material entitlements of aggressively consumer cultures, grow ever richer by the standards of most of the world's population. As long ago as August 17, 2005, the "basic support" of a missionary family – good friends of mine who were heading to South Africa with a well-known mission agency – was pegged at US $4,344 per month, supplemented by an additional US $600 in monthly "ministry funds" and topped up by "outgoing funds" in excess of US $19,000.[8] However inadequate US $60,000 per annum might be for sustaining a North American family at levels of minimal social and material entitlement in a bi-cultural, intercontinental ministry, such an amount guarantees them a place among the privileged in the social hierarchy of South Africa. How easily accustomed we become to our escalating scale of material entitlements, with one generation's luxuries mutating into another generation's needs. Peter C. Whybrow observes, "As America's commercial hegemony has increased and our social networks have eroded, we have lost any meaningful reference as to how rich we really are, especially in comparison to other nations."[9]

Libraries of books have been written explaining how this fortunate state of economic affairs arose, and how – with assiduous attention to the proper economic ideology – increasing levels of consumption can continue not only forever but for everyone. In fact, western affluence, with its attendant continental "discoveries," conquests, mass human enslavements, relocations, and sweeping genocides is not likely to be replicated by the poor any time soon. In a more innocent age, it was possible for western missionaries to believe that their relatively comfortable way of life was the inevitable outcome of a national social life organized in a Christian way, and that, given enough time and sufficient conversions, the poorer peoples of the world could one day likewise enjoy the good life.

Sixteen years into the 20th century, with "civilized" nations in the throes of one of the most savage and pointless struggles in the pathetically war-strewn record of humankind, it was still bravely asserted,

> The civilisation which is called western is the slowly developed product of religion . . . [and has] surged forward to its present high water by means of the internal pressure of its inner Christian élan . . . an impulse which is but the expression of a Christian principle of life moving within.[10]

Many Americans, imagining their nation to be the apex of western civilization and avatar of universal progress, unapologetically pursue their "manifest destiny" of political, cultural, economic, and military hegemony. But to those who look more closely at the why and how of this ascendancy, both Christendom and neo-Christendom – born and sustained through violence – have been resoundingly demystified. Obscured by the noble ideals and economic ideology to which we attribute a way of life that is the envy of the world lies a more sinister, well-documented history that includes centuries of brutal slavery that emptied Africa of an estimated 60 million of its inhabitants; genocidal conquest of three continents that issued in the obliteration of an estimated 90 percent of their incumbent populations; a two-ocean moat and a century of relatively cheap national defense; maintenance of a privileged position through both the actual and threatened use of nuclear and chemical weapons of mass destruction; such instruments of development are not available to the poor today.[11]

While factors such as these may not mitigate the economic and social advantages of a way of life based on law and the protection of private property, they should at the very least induce a profound humility in those of us who consciously serve as exemplars of Christianity or development among the "underdeveloped" populations of our world. It is difficult to imagine what the lands of old Christendom would be like today if virtually the entire populations of the Americas, Australia, and New Zealand – together with large segments of South Africa and Israel – were packed into what is today known as greater Europe.

Furthermore, there are now distressingly incontrovertible proofs that for most human beings there neither *is* nor *can be* any possible road to the West's vision of the ideal life, with its visions of ever increasing levels of comfort and consumption. The stark truth is that the natural resources of our planet are sufficient to support "developed" life for only a tiny fraction of its human population. Accordingly, emissaries of the western Churches must be prepared to test the truthfulness of their assertion that "Christ is the answer" in contexts of acute material deprivation.

While the siren allure of manifest destiny in all of its self-congratulating and self-serving permutations is the natural fuel of the idolatry known as nationalism, even the most patriotic Christian, when confronted with the gulf between God's kingdom standards and his or her nation's self-serving agenda, admits to the impossibility of spanning the chasm. The truth is, no nation will ever be Christ-like. No nation will lay down its life for its enemies. No nation will love those who wish it ill, in the self-sacrificing spirit of our Lord. Even the best nation is, in the end, inexorably self-serving and self-promoting, rather than Christ-serving and self-denying.[12]

2 The relative affluence of western missionaries has serious strategic implications, both positive and negative. On the negative side:

   (a) Western mission strategies, beginning with the support of missionary personnel, are money intensive. Without ample supplies of money missionary efforts from the west would be severely truncated. Indeed, it is safe to conjecture; they would virtually cease.
   (b) Possession of wealth virtually ensures missionary insulation. A primary advantage of wealth is its capacity to provide those who possess it with goods and services which serve to cushion them from the harsh realities of life.

The word "insulate" is thought to have derived from the Latin *insulatus* – meaning to make into an island. In its contemporary usage, the verb "to insulate" means "to prevent or reduce the transmission of electricity, heat, or sound to or from a body, device, or region by surrounding with a non-conducting material."[13] Both the etymology and the definition of this word are instructive in the context of the present discussion, since to a remarkable degree western missionaries, because of their affluence, inhabit an island in a sea of poverty. Their affluence constitutes quite literally the "non-conducting material" which protects them from the "heat" and "sound" of the poverty in which the majority of the globe's inhabitants live and move and have their being. Since biblical faith is above all a *relational* faith, it is not only sad, but sinful, when personal possessions and privileges prevent, distort, or destroy the relationships of Christ's followers with the poor.

Economic gulfs make genuine fraternal friendship so awkward as to be virtually impossible.

A friend is an intimate . . . someone with whom one generally has much in common. In their friendships, people naturally gravitate to those with whom they are not only temperamentally but socially and economically compatible. It is humanly almost impossible for a wealthy family to share a deeply fraternal relationship with a family whose material and economic resources are a pathetic fraction of their own; who cannot afford an education for their beloved children beyond minimal literacy, while the children of the wealthy family anticipates as a matter of course opportunity and money for education up to the very highest levels; whose house is a tiny one-room shack (made of straw or cardboard) with no amenities, while the wealthy family resides in a western-style bungalow, complete with kitchen, bathroom, private bedrooms for each member of the family, carpeted floors, stuffed furniture, closets and bureaus filled with clothes, and personal servants; who must rely solely upon leg power to get anywhere, while the wealthy family has access to car, jeep, power-boat, or airplane; for whom the concept of vacation doesn't even exist, while the wealthy family spends one month of each year traveling and sightseeing, or simply taking it easy in a resort far away from the grind of every-day work. The poor in such situations are mere spectators, not participants.

(c) The staggeringly high relational price which western missionaries must pay for their affluence could perhaps be overlooked, or at least endured, were it not for its insidious effects upon the communication process. For medium and message are both significantly affected by the relationship of the missionary to the convert or would-be convert. If the message of the cross consisted simply of a series of theologically correct propositions about God, man, and salvation, then the obligation to preach the gospel could be fulfilled by means of public announcements over the radio. But the Word must always be made flesh, and dwell among people. A missionary is not simply a voice box, but a way-shower, whose life converts must be able to imitate.

Rich, poor, and mammon in the Bible

When within a given social environment we are rich, it follows that what the Bible says *to* and *about* the rich, it says *to* and *about* us. Missionaries are not an exception to this rule. *Wealth* and *poverty* are among the most frequently recurring themes in our Christian scriptures. While gross material inequity in close social proximity raises profound ethical questions that challenge any wealthy follower of Jesus serving in contexts of profound poverty. As those who make their living by speaking *for* God and *about* God, Christian missionaries are acutely aware of the need for consistency between what they say and how they live.

In both the Old and the New Testaments, there is a modest stream of teaching that is of comfort to the rich: the sanctity of private property, the association of wealth with happiness, prosperity as a reward for righteousness, and the frequent link between personal behavior and poverty. Such teaching is of no small comfort to those who, by whatever means, find themselves in the happy state of relative comfort and affluence.

A brief survey of Biblical teaching shows any self-justification to which the materially blessed might appeal is more than anticipated by the less flattering portrayal of the rich that is woven into the warp and woof of God's directives about what is good and appropriate for His people. Here's why:

(a) Rights associated with acquiring, using, or disposing of personal wealth are – for the people of God – subordinated to an obligation to care for the poorer, weaker members of society. The divinely sanctioned guidelines were to be followed literally, and were intended to prevent a fragmentation of society into those who enjoyed perpetual economic advantage over those who suffered perpetual economic hardship. Included in the Mosaic guidelines were provisions for: (1) **recurring years of jubilee,** when all land was to revert to its original owners – Leviticus 25:8–28; (2) a regular **sabbatical year** when debts were to be forgiven – Deuteronomy 15:1–6; II Chronicles 36:15–21; (3) **tithing** every year, with the poor as primary beneficiaries every third year – Deuteronomy 14:22–29; (4) **strict guidelines, favoring the borrower, on loans, interest, and loan collateral** – Leviticus 25:35–38; Deuteronomy 23:19–20; 24:6, 10–13, 17–18; (5) **gleaning regulations strictly for the benefit of the poor** – Deuteronomy 24:19–20; (6) **debt repayment guidelines, favoring the poor** – Deuteronomy 15:1–11; (7) **stipulations regarding treatment of employees by employers, favoring employees** – Deuteronomy 24:14–15; and (8) strict **limitations on the wealth of kings** – Deuteronomy 17:14–17; (cf. I Kings 6–7; 11:1–6). The divine intention is clear: not only were the poor to be protected from exploitation; the law was designed to ensure that they were its chief beneficiaries.

(b) Wealth and prosperity are inherently dangerous, frequently associated with fatally destructive personal and national orientations. (1) **The prosperous tend to marginalize God** – Deuteronomy 8:10–20; (2) **Wealth is the natural culture in which pride and a self-deluding sense of security and self-congratulations [self-made man or nation] seem inevitably to flourish, at both personal and national levels** – Ezekiel 28:4–5; Jeremiah 6:13–15; Jeremiah 12:1–4; 17:11; I Timothy 6:6–19; (3) **Wealth is almost inevitably associated with overindulgence, gluttony and greed, which is idolatry** – I Kings 6–7; 10:14–29; 11:1–6; I Corinthians 5:9–11; Colossians 3:5 [Greed is the insistence on more than enough in contexts where your neighbors have less than enough];

(4) **The wealthy frequently abuse personal power by mistreatment of the weak and contempt for the poor** – I Kings 10:14–29; cf. I Kings 12:1–24; Jeremiah 22:13–17; Ezekiel 16:49; 22:25–29; Job 12:5; (5) **The priorities and orientations of the rich seem almost inevitably to be fatally misguided** – Isaiah 5:7–8, 20–23; (6) **Personal overindulgence and craven respect for the wealthy compromise the integrity of those who claim to speak for God** – Jeremiah 6:13–15; 8:10–11; Micah 2:6–11; 3:5, 10–11. Religious leaders and missionaries in the early days of the Church who "loved money" warranted especially harsh criticism – Matthew 23:23–26; Luke 11:39–42; Cf. Matt. 7:21–27; Luke 6:46; 11:28; II Corinthians 2:17; (7) **Christ pronounced woes on the rich and made it clear that it was almost impossible for a rich man to inherit eternal life**, and that to be a "wealthy disciple" comes close to being an oxymoron – Matthew 19:16–24; James 5:1–6; (h) **Preoccupation with self, money, and pleasure are signs of a doomed "last days" way of life** – II Timothy 3:1–5; (8) **Personal wealth demands absorption in mammon, deadening a person's or a nation's sense of their spiritual destitution** – Matthew 13:22; 22:5; Luke 12:13–21; Rev. 3:14–21 (The Laodicean Church, apparently surfeited with mammon, lacked the most elementary Christian essential, Christ himself!); (9) **Wealth never satisfies, but breeds covetousness and greed . . . a continual desire for more** – Ephesians 4:17–19; 5:3–11. Our Lord's description of those whose hearts are weighed down with "dissipation" – unrestrained indulgence in the pursuit of pleasure – is an apt description of consumers and consumerism (Luke 21:34–36); such teaching should give sober pause to Christians living as aliens and strangers in a culture in which the pursuit of happiness is a constitutionally guaranteed right of every citizen. When this orientation to life is on conspicuous display in contexts of poverty, certain consequences are inevitable.

(c) **Wealth and prosperity do not signal righteousness, but are in fact often signs of greed-driven exploitation of the poor** – Proverbs 13:23; Isaiah 32:7; Job 21:7–16; (1) **Faithfulness to God is no guarantee of personal prosperity or security** – Jeremiah 44:15–18; (2) **Not only is it possible to have too little, it is possible to have too much** – Proverbs 30:8–9; (3) **Not just active oppression, but complacent neglect of the poor leads inexorably to judgment** – Deuteronomy 8:19–20; 28:15; II Chronicles 36:15–21; (4) **Religious orthodoxy without practical concern for the poor is a hollow sham** – Isaiah 1:10–23.

(d) **God not only actively identifies with the poor and the oppressed, but He resists the rich who oppress or simply ignore them** – Exodus 22:21–27. (1) **The promised Messiah would identify with the poor and the oppressed**, coming for them and as one of them – Psalm 22; Isaiah 53; Jesus was born in a stable, and, judging from the nature of their offering, his parents were far from rich – Luke 1:46–56; 2:1–20, 21–24; cf. Leviticus 12:8. His first recorded public words related to the poor – Luke 4:18–30; Matthew 15:31–46. (2) **God's children are marked by their proactive concern for the poor** and the oppressed – Job 30:24–25; 31:16–28; Amos 5:4–24; 6:4–7; 8:4–7; (3) **God meets the needs of the poor through the actions and interventions of His obedient people.** This was the intent of the laws dealing with the treatment of the poor by the rich – Nehemiah 5:1–13. (4) **Christ's true followers proactively identify with the poor in practical, costly ways** – Matthew 23:1–39; 25:31–46.

(e) **Economic repentance is costly, and therefore very rare.** The powerful and wealthy customarily deal with prophetic preaching by dismissing or destroying the preacher, and engaging the services of those willing to offer a more sanguine interpretation of their greedy self-indulgence (Isaiah 30:9–11). A rare Old Testament account of repentance is found in Nehemiah 5:1–12, while in the New Testament Zacchaeus serves as a rare example in Luke 19:1–9. In the early days of the Church, **rich Christians were commanded "*not to be arrogant nor to put their hope in wealth . . . to do good, to be rich in good deeds, and to be generous and willing to share*"** (I Timothy 6:17–19).

(f) **Genuine spiritual revival is closely associated with economic reformation and justice.** Repentance without the fruit of repentance is meaningless (Micah 6:6–16).

For those of us who enjoy access to the material entitlements thought to be minimally to a western lifestyle, biblical teaching on wealth and poverty is vaguely disquieting. We are aware that this world is home to vast numbers of impoverished and destitute peoples, and that some of these live nearby. But qualms of conscience are easily quelled. There is nothing that we can do about it. Our detachment serves as a kind of sedative, dulling the reality of what we are seeing, and relieving us of any responsibility. But when a "spiritual leader" is caught up in consumer materialism, biblical teaching becomes more difficult to explain, let alone model. This is the western missionary credibility conundrum.

In summary: (1) Western missionaries are often relatively wealthy relative to their ministry contexts; (2) When this is so, what the Bible says *to* and *about* the wealthy it says to and about the missionaries themselves; (3) Since the Christian faith is lived out in social and cultural contexts, the proclaimed gospel is contradicted by the gospel on display in the missionary's lifestyle; and (4) While this contradiction has a profound impact on communications, strategies, and personal relationships, it raises fundamental questions about the missionary's belief in the gospel itself.

Missionaries typically respond to this conundrum by: (1) associating primarily with those of equal social and economic privilege; (2) assuming an artificially simple lifestyle that thinly masks their privilege, while maintaining entitlements to medical care, transportation, education of children, and retirement; (3) shifting the debate from its moral/ethical dimensions to questions of dependence or interdependence; and, finally, (4) adopting a radically incarnational lifestyle, giving up privilege and living as those among whom they minister. But could there be a fifth approach?

A theology of the "Righteous Rich"

The modern world is, if possible, even more economically polarized than it was when I wrote my book, *Missions and Money*, 25 years ago. The United States, Korea, and other consumer driven countries are increasingly characterized by profound and growing internal inequities that threaten the harmony and even the viability of these societies.[14]

Each person in any society is defined by a series of statuses, acknowledged and recognized by other members of that society. It is understood that each status carries with it certain roles and their associated behavioral expectations, which vary with the social context. Human identities and relationships are shaped by the complex interplay of recognized statuses, roles, and self-images that comprise the society. For a missionary's communication of the Gospel to be effective, teaching must be accompanied by behavior that is consistent with what is being taught. Role sincerity is crucial to integrity.[15]

I would like to propose that Christians generally, including missionaries – whenever they either anticipate or discover that their way of life and its entitlements make them rich by the standards of those around them – embrace the status of "*righteous rich*" and learn to play its associated roles in ways that are both culturally appropriate and biblically informed.

The Christian scriptures draw a sharp distinction between (1) the righteous who are prosperous and (2) the rich who are unrighteous. The distinction between the two is determined primarily by the way they relate to the poor. In his suggestive summary of Old Testament teaching on the righteous rich, Christopher Wright notes, "God may choose (but is not obliged) to make a righteous person rich."[16] He goes on to observe that the righteous rich are those who:

- Remember the source of their riches – namely the grace and gift of God himself, and are therefore not boastingly inclined to take the credit for achieving them through their own skill, strength, or effort (even if these things have been legitimately deployed) (Deut. 8:17–18; I Chron. 29:11–12; Jer. 9:23–24);
- Do not idolize their wealth by putting inordinate trust in it, nor get anxious about losing it. For ultimately it is one's relationship with God that matters more and can survive (and even be deepened by) the absence or loss of wealth (Job 31:24–25);
- Recognize that wealth is thus secondary to many things, including wisdom, but especially personal integrity, humility, and righteousness (I Chron. 29:17; Prov. 8:10–11; I Kings 3; Prov. 16:8, 28:6);

- Set their wealth in the context of God's blessing, recognizing that being blessed is not a privilege but a responsibility – the Abrahamic responsibility of being a blessing to others (Gen. 12:1–3). Wealth in righteous hands is thus a servant of that mission that flows from God's commitment to bless the nations through the seed of Abraham;
- Use their wealth with justice; this includes refusing to extract personal benefit by using wealth for corrupt ends (e.g., through bribery), and ensuring that all one's financial dealings are non-exploitative of the needs of others (e.g., through interest) (Ps. 15:5; Ezek. 18:7–8);
- Make their wealth available to the wider community through responsible lending that is both practical (Lev. 25) and respectful for the dignity of the debtor (Deut. 24:6, 10–13);
- See wealth as an opportunity for generosity – even when it is risky, and even when it hurts, thereby both blessing the poor and needy, and at the same time reflecting the character of God (Deut. 15; Ps. 112:3; Prov. 14:31; 19:17; Ruth);
- Use wealth in the service of God, whether by contributing to the practical needs that are involved in corporate worship of God (I Chron. 28–9), or by providing for God's servants who particularly need material support (II Chron. 31; Ruth);
- Set an example by limiting personal consumption and declining to maximize private gain from public office that affords access to wealth and resources (Neh. 5:14–19).

It is because such a righteous rich person is marked by genuine, life-transforming fear of the Lord that the blessings he or she enjoys are not tainted with wickedness, the whiff of oppression, or selfishness that hardens the heart against the call of human need.

Job is probably the best known and most ancient biblical character to be characterized as both *rich* and *righteous*. It is fitting that this article be concluded with his characterization of a righteous rich person – in this case, himself. It should be the goal of any modern righteous person of means – whether missionary or business tycoon – to sincerely and truthfully repeat Job's words to God, and having said them, to hear an echoing "Amen" from the poor among whom they reside.

A careful reading of Job 29:11–17 and 31:16–28 makes it clear that Job understood himself obligated by God to active and generous involvement in the material well-being of poor people in his orbit. For those of us who are wealthy, it is sobering to find in the scriptures scarcely any record of repentance on the part of the rich. Nehemiah provides one heartening instance, a reminder that no matter how complicated the issues or how deeply entrenched and personally vested the self-interests, it is possible to repent. What would repentance look like from the vantage point of powerful mission organizations in contexts of poverty? That is difficult to say, since the righteous rich missionary or mission agency, while informed biblically, must be defined contextually.

A missiology of the righteous rich is, at its core, no more than a willingness to be useful in terms defined by the local contexts and people. For this there can be no better exemplar than our Lord himself. With a mandate more sweeping in magnitude than those of even the most daring mission strategists, his commission was to save the world. Oddly, by the standards of western missions, Jesus spent his life as a laughably parochial figure, never venturing in his ministry beyond the borders of his own foreign-occupied country. His short-lived mission on earth seemed to be defined by the concrete physical and emotional needs of those who intercepted him with their tales of woe.

Almost everything written in the Gospel accounts of his life relates directly or indirectly to the wrenching, but strategically petty, personal agendas of the ordinary men and women who pressed in on him from all sides during the few short years of his ministry. The Creator God incarnate, bent on saving the whole world, allowed himself to be interrupted by the sick, the lame, the blind, the withered, the bereaved, the outcasts, the pariahs, the deaf, the demon possessed, the grieving. Whatever he may have been doing at the time, he seemed never too busy or tired to stop and pay close attention to their agendas.

How understandable it would have been for Jesus to turn away the ordinary people who constantly sought his attention, reminding them that as Creator of their planet, now charged with redeeming it, he simply did not have time to attend to the personal details of their everyday lives. But instead, he demonstrated that any proclamation of the Good News that does not intersect with the actual needs of ordinary people is not good news, but mere religious propaganda. On this he was at distinct odds with the religious conventions of his day, as his followers today should likewise be. In this way he turned the world upside down.

Notes

1 Much of the material in this paper has appeared in a variety of journals and books. The materials used here have been edited and updated.

2 "Economic Development and Christian Mission: A Perspective from History of Mission," in Mari-Anna Auginen-Pöntinen and Jonas Adelin Jørgensen, eds. *Mission and Money: Christian Mission in the Context of Global Inequalities*, (Leiden: Brill, 2016), 145–70.

3 Jonathan J. Bonk, *Missions and Money: Affluence as a Missionary Problem . . . Revisited*. Revised and Expanded Edition. (Maryknoll, NY: Orbis, 2006).

4 www.dacb.org

5 Jonathan J. Bonk, *Missions and Money: Affluence as a Missionary Problem . . . Revisited*. Revised and Expanded Edition. (Maryknoll: Orbis Books, 2006).

6 See the appended article by Jim Wallis, "A Bible Full of Holes," appearing in *The Mennonite* (November 21, 2000), 6–7.

7 www.globalissues.org/article/26/poverty-facts-and-stats.

8 In an email dated August 17, 2005. This amount would cover salary, administration, health care, and pension.
9 Peter C. Whybrow, *American Mania: When More Is Not Enough*. (New York: W. W. Norton, 2005), 38–9.
10 Allan John MacDonald, *Trade, Politics and Christianity in Africa and the East*. (London: Longmans, Green and Co., 1916), 54. A less flattering assessment of the impact of monotheistic belief can be found in Sam Harris, *The End of Faith: Religion, Terror, and the Future of Reason*. (New York: W. W. Norton, 2004).
11 See, for example, David E. Stannard, *American Holocaust: Columbus and the Conquest of the New World*. (New York: Oxford University Press, 1992). Or Benjamin Madley's *An American Genocide: The United States and the California Indian Catastrophe, 1846–1873* (New Haven: Yale University Press, 2016).
12 See Reinhold Niebuhr, *Moral Man and Immoral Society: A Study in Ethics and Politics*. (New York: Charles Scribner's Sons, 1932, 1960).
13 Collins English Dictionary of the English Language (1979).
14 See Richard Wilkinson and Kate Pickett, *The Spirit Level: Why Greater Equality Makes Societies Stronger*. (New York: Bloomsbury Press, 2009). This book is the distillation of 30 years of research showing the connection, and multiple levels, between economic inequity and social dysfunction.
15 Jacob A. Loewen and Anne Loewen, "Role, Self-Image and Missionary Communication," 426–7, passim.
16 Christopher J. H. Wright, "The Righteous Rich in the Old Testament," in Jonathan J. Bonk, ed. *Missions and Money: Affluence as a Missionary Problem . . . Revisited*. (Maryknoll, NY: Orbis 2006), 199–200.

Bibliography

Bonk, Jonathan. *Missions and Money: Affluence as a Missionary Problem . . . Revisited*. Maryknoll: Orbis Books, 2006.

———. *Missions and Money: Affluence as a Western Missionary Problem*. Maryknoll: Orbis, 1991.

Coles, Robert. *Children of Crisis: A Study of Courage and Fear; The South Goes North; Migrants, Sharecroppers, Mountaineers; Eskimos, Chicanos, Indians; and Privileged Ones: The Well-off and the Rich in America*. Boston: Brown, 1977.

———. *Privileged Ones: The Well-Off and Rich in America, Vol 5. Children in Crisis*. Boston: Atlantic-Little, Brown Books, 1977.

East, David Jonathan. *Western Africa: Its Condition, and Christianity the Means of Its Recovery*. London: Houlston & Stoneman, 1844.

Easterly, William. *The White Man's Burden: Why the West's Efforts to Aid the Rest Have Done So Much Ill and So Little Good*. New York: Penguin Books, 2006.

Harris, Sam. *The End of Faith: Religion, Terror, and the Future of Reason*. New York: W. W. Norton, 2004.

Hobsbawm, E. J. *The Age of Empire, 1875–1914*. New York: Pantheon Books, 1987.

Loewen, Jacob A. "Missions and the Problems of Cultural Background." In *The Church in Mission: A Sixtieth Anniversary Tribute to J. B. Toews*, edited by A. J. Klassen, 286–318. Fresno: Mennonite Brethren Church, 1967.

Loewen, Jacob A. "Missions and the Problems of Cultural Background."

Loewen, Jacob A., and Anne Loewen. "Role, Self-Image and Missionary Communication." *Culture and Human Values: Christian Intervention in Anthropological*

Perspective. Selections from the Writings of Jacob A. Loewen, 426–7. Pasadena: William Carey Library, 1975.

Loewen, Jacob A., and Anne Loewen. "Role, Self-Image and Missionary Communication." and "The 'Missionary' Role." In *Culture and Human Values: Christian Intervention in Anthropological Perspective*. Selections from the Writings of Jacob A. Loewen, 412–27. Pasadena: William Carey Library, 1975.

MacDonald, Allan John. *Trade, Politics and Christianity in Africa and the East*. London: Longmans, Green and Co., 1916.

Madley, Benjamin. *An American Genocide: The United States and the California Indian Catastrophe, 1846–1873*. New Haven: Yale University Press 2016.

Niebuhr, Rienhold. *Moral Man and Immoral Society: A Study in Ethids and Politics*. New York: Charles Scribner's Sons, 1960.

Packer, George. "When Here Sees There." *New York Times Magazine*, April 21, 2002.

Pöntinen, Mari-Anna, and Jonas Adelin Jørgensen, eds. *Mission and Money: Christian Mission in the Context of Global Inequalities*. Leiden: Brill, 2016).

Russel, W. E. *Sydney Smith*. London: MacMillan & Co., 1905.

Smith, Stephen C. *Ending Global Poverty: A Guide to What Works*. New York: Palgrave Macmillan, 2005.

Stannard, David E. *American Holocaust: Columbus and the Conquest of the New World*. New York: Oxford University Press, 1992.

Stark, Rodney. *For the Glory of God: How Monotheism Led to Reformations, Science, Witch-Hunts, and the End of Slavery*. Princeton: Princeton University Press, 2003.

———. *The Victory of Reason: How Christianity Led to Freedom, Capitalism, and Western Success*. Random House, 2005.

Wallis, Jim. "A Bible Full of Holes." *The Mennonite*. November 21, 2000, 6–7.

Weber, Linda. *Mission Handbook: U.S. and Canadian Protestant Ministries Overseas*, 21st Edition. Edited by Linda J. Weber. Wheaton: Evangelical Missions Information Service, 2010.

Whybrow, Peter C. *American Mania: When More Is Not Enough*. New York: W. W. Norton, 2005.

Wilkinson, Richard, and Kate Pickett. *The Spirit Level: Why Greater Equality Makes Societies Stronger*. New York: Bloomsbury Press, 2009.

Wright, Christopher J. H. "The Righteous Rich in the Old Testament." In *Missions and Money: Affluence as a Missionary Problem . . . Revisited*, edited by Jonathan J. Bonk, 199–200. Orbis, 2006.

23 Managing religious diversity in Tanzania

Islamic revivalism and modes of governance

Frans Wijsen

Introduction

In 2006 the then president of the United Republic of Tanzania Jakaya Kikwete gave a speech at the University of Boston to demonstrate how his country had managed ethnic and religious diversity by following in the footsteps of the Father of the Nation, Julius Nyerere.[1] However, when looking at contemporary Tanzania, where Muslims and Christians have an equal share of 40 percent of the nations' population of 50 million people, it seems that there are "seeds of conflict" between Muslims and Christians.[2] It is noted that "things are getting out of control" and that the "authoritarian techniques of the single party era" to deal with citizens' legally accepted democratic rights no longer work.[3]

Former president Kiwkete may have been aware of this when he said,

> I would like to conclude by cautioning that managing religious diversity is perhaps one of the greatest challenges we face now, nationally and internationally. We have no choice but to work harder to promote inter and intra-religious tolerance and understanding as we deal with religious-motivated terrorism and political violence.[4]

In this paper I look at some of these issues, which are well-documented in various sources, from a governance perspective. In harmony with the waning of welfare states in the neoliberal age, "governance" as a concept has replaced "government" in many publications on public administration.[5] Bakari and Ndumbaro gave a quantitative account of religion and governance issues in Tanzania.[6] This chapter aims at a qualitative, in-depth investigation of some of the Muslim voices in this debate. It is based on a correlation of a review of literature and an analysis of interviews. The interviews were conducted in the framework of a research project on Islamic Revivalism and Modes of Governance at the University of Dar es Salaam.[7] The review and the analysis make use of insights taken from critical discourse analysis.[8]

Muslims are rediscovering their history

In his book *The Life and Times of Abdulwahid Sykes (1924–1968)*, Mohamed Said studies the role of Muslims in Tanzania's independence struggle.[9] According to Said, Muslims played a major role in the struggle for independence by TANU (Tanganyika National Union). Muslims supported Julius Nyerere as the leader of TANU because he had studied in Britain and he knew how to deal with the British people. However, when Nyerere took this position he marginalized Muslims. According to Said, this struggle started when EAMWS (East African Muslim Welfare Society) president, Tewa Said, and EAMWS vice-president, Bibi Titi Mohamed, who were both cabinet ministers, lost their parliamentary seats in the 1965 general elections.[10] The government was afraid that the two were building a new political power base through EAMWS. The EAMWS was perceived as a threat to TANU and had to be banned.[11] This materialized in 1968, and Said states that "the history of the country is being erased," that "more research by independent scholars needs to be done," and that "Muslims are at present in the process of rediscovering themselves and their rich history."[12] This is what the Islamic Revivalism is all about. As one interviewee said,

> Looking at history, it is seen that . . . Muslims were leading this country [Tanzania], they had control, though that control did not directly extend to mainland Tanganyika. History shows that Islamic rule extended from Mozambique through Kilwa till Somalia. Later, that rule was overthrown [by Belgians]. Then the Belgian rule was overthrown by the Germans. Then the British came, then came independence. But the problem is that Muslims have been deprived of some of their development activities since the German rule, British rule, even this independence rule. This is the legacy they passed over to each other against Islam.

The over-wording of "leading," "rule," "control" shows strong preoccupation of the interviewee with the issue.[13]

The union between mainland and the Islands

One of the topics that appears through most of the other topics is the Union between Tanganyika and Zanzibar in 1964. Among others it was put on the political agenda by Aboud Jumbe (1994) who served as Vice-President. It remains unclear what the exact reason was for the Union and who was responsible for it. Some say that it was the United States of America. The Revolution in Zanzibar took place just after the Cuba Crisis. It was the United States of America which forced Nyerere to establish the Union because it did not want a Communist stronghold in East Africa, comparable to Cuba. Others claim that it was the Roman Catholic Church which forced Nyerere to do so. The Roman Catholic Church was not only afraid of communism but also of Islam.

However, this may have been, by questioning the Union Vice-president Jumbe was said to endanger national unity. In 1984 he had to resign. Shivji holds that the Union is what remained of Nyerere's dream of pan-Africanism. Nyerere strongly believed in an African Union, or at least an East African community.[14] When it turned out that the presidents of Kenya and Uganda did not share his dream, what then remained was the Union with Zanzibar. Nyerere saw the Union as a first step to the East African Community. One interviewee said that it was none of these reasons. It was an issue of security. It was not Nyerere who pushed for a Union but Abeid Karume, the first president of independent Zanzibar, who feared a counter-revolution, overthrowing the newly established revolutionary government. According to one interviewee, Karume wanted a one-tier government. But it was Nyerere who convinced him to have a two-tier government.

Whatever the reasons may have been, and it is possible that there was a multiplicity of reasons which may have had contradictory effects, fear for a Muslim stronghold along the East African Coast is one of the reasons behind the push to maintain the two-tier government, even if it is against the peoples' draft constitution (see later). Knowing the growing Islamic revivalism, from the bombing of the US embassy in Dar es Salaam in 1998, over the Mwembechai killings in 1998, and the Zanzibar riots in 2000 till the enduring threat of Al Shabaab, which is more or less successfully fought in Kenya and now seeks refuge in Tanzania, very few people want Muslims to have stronghold in Zanzibar. This is also true for a majority of Muslims which are liberal or even secular. After the 2015 elections there was again a "Zanzibar Crisis." According to one interviewee it was a national security issue. We come back to this later.

The BAKWATA controversy

The abandoning of the EAMWS came back on the political agenda, among others, by public speeches by sheik Ponda issa Ponda, the general secretary of BARAZA KUU (Baraza Kuu la Jumuiya na Taasisi za Kiislamu Tanzania), who was sent to jail because he illegally entered a plot in Chang'ombe. According to Ponda issa Ponda the plot belonged to EAMWS. It was given to BAKWATA (Baraza Kuu la Waislamu Tanzania) after abandoning EAMWS. EAMWS planned to build a Muslim University on the plot. But BAKWATA members gradually sold parts of the plot for private purposes.[15] The Chang'ombe controversy draws on an unresolved issue in history. In 1968 the EAMWS was banned and BAKWATA was put in its place. The reasons why this happened are not clear. Some say it was an internal EAMWS conflict. The power base within EAMWS was with Asian Shia Muslims. Soon after independence, some patriots within EAMWS stated that EAMWS had to split into three national chapters, and that its secretary-general had to be an African Sunni Muslim. Thus it was a conflict between Asian Shia and African Sunni Muslims, and the government had nothing to do with it.

Others claim that it was a conflict between the state and a religious organization. As was shown before, the EAMWS president and the secretary were former cabinet ministers who lost their posts after the 1965 elections. However, they remained popular within EAMWS and TANU leadership feared that the two would create their own power base through this religious organization. Thus EAMWS was perceived as a threat to TANU and had to disappear. Again others say that it was a national unity issue. The Arusha Declaration of 1967 promoted socialism and nationalization of private property. The power base within EAMWS was with Asian businessmen who did not like their businesses to be nationalized. So they were said not to be loyal to the socialist policy. This was the reason to abandon EAMWS.

Whatever intentions Nyerere may have had, many Muslims complain that BAKWATA is just an extension of the government. It was not established for religious purposes but for political reasons; and BAKWATA leaders were not interested in promoting Islam. As one interviewee said, "Their Islamic consciousness was not a priority. . . . They were longing to be accepted and trusted by the government and be liked by government leaders." Various interviewees argue that EAMWS was promoting the development of Muslims, and by abandoning EAMWS, the Father of the Nation has contributed to their backwardness. Another interviewee said,

> Maybe the First President did not want Islam to develop. He tried to do so many things, for example arresting sheikhs and lock them up, one of them being Sheikh Takdir [who] wanted [to do] so much [to help Muslims develop].

Again another interviewee said,

> He [Nyerere] did not like Muslims' development. And for that matter, he wanted it [the Muslim community] to be a society of lower class, a class which is merely ruled. This means, [a class] of little ability, a lower class, not a class that is powerful. It should not be a class with economic power, it should not be a class with political power, meaning that it also has a voice in politics, and so on. Nobody knows what reasons he may have had. This is the general view of Mwalimu [Nyerere].

The same interviewee continued,

> And this [being a lower class] was not by bad luck. We [Muslims] believe that he [Nyerere] had been doing it purposely wanting Muslims to remain backward, meaning to oppress them. In the society that he envisaged they [Muslims] should not have leadership positions. They should just remain as they were. That is why the government itself had

> no efforts to develop Muslims. Whenever Muslims tried to develop themselves, you see very openly that *Mwalimu* [Nyerere] went there to stop them from doing this.

Muslims' complaints about BAKWATA are many, not only from outside but also from inside BAKWATA. As one interviewee said, "I am a BAKWATA member, but I am a critical one." Complaints vary from violating Muslims' rights to selling Muslims' properties for personal benefits. According to one interviewee, "Selfishness is the root of all evils."

It is no surprise that some Muslims disliked BAKWATA and came up with alternative Muslim organizations such as BALUKTA (Baraza la Kueneza Kurani Tanzania), which was later banned, and the earlier mentioned BARAZA KUU. One interviewee said,

> Many Muslims in this country fear BAKWATA; it has not been a catalyst to assist them in different matters. Therefore, BAKWATA has got a serious challenge from the Muslims of this Country because it does not look as if it provides a solution to them. . . . People see that BAKWATA is like a certain nightmare to oppress Muslims.

Asked if BAKWATA could reform itself to gain the trust of Muslims again, another interviewee said,

> I do not think they can. . . . The things they have done are many. People are fed up with them. They are fed up with BAKWATA. If you talk about BAKWATA, people are fed up with it and others vomit on them. Do you hear? So leave BAKWATA there to stay. Only the Almighty God knows where will he take its leaders or what will he do those who will be able, that is all.

President Mwinyi, successor of Nyerere, is liked because he allowed new religious organizations to register, but BAKWATA remains the "supreme" organization for the Muslims.

> Other Muslim voices are not pleased with BAKWATA's supremacy and advocate for reforms. One interviewee when referring to the mandate given to BAKWATA to recommend registration of other Muslim faith-based organizations said, "Whenever you want to register any [Muslim] organisation, you are asked a letter from BAKWATA, meaning, you are requested to bring a reference letter from BAKWATA . . . Even with knowledgeable people like us, you have to argue, you must stand very firmly, and if they don't see it as problematic, you are given it [registration]. But that lags the development process behind. Many would like to do so [to register Muslim organizations] but are discouraged because of reasons like this. You see. Now that is a problem which is there."

Sheikh Ponda issa Ponda, who put the Chang'ombe issue on the political agenda was released from jail because according to the Court, he did nothing illegal.

Abandoning OIC membership

The OIC membership has been featured in public discourses since 1993.[16] In January 1993 it became known that Zanzibar had become member of the OIC (Organization of Islamic Conference) in 1992. Fierce debates followed between the Zanzibar Government and the Union Government. The Union Government demanded the Zanzibar Government to withdraw from OIC, because Zanzibar is not an independent state.[17] Through mediation of the Father of the Nation the issue was settled, at least temporarily. In August 1993 the Zanzibar government decided to withdraw OIC membership. The official reason given was that Tanzania was a secular state and it could not be a member of a religious organization such as OIC.

Various interviewees ask themselves why so many other secular countries, who have a lower percentage of Muslim population, are members of the OIC. And if Tanzania could not have official relations with religious bodies, why does Tanzania have diplomatic relations with the Vatican, and why does it have a Vatican ambassador who performs both political and religious functions? In 2008, the then Minister of Foreign Affairs, Bernard Membe, said that he had no objection against Tanzania's OIC membership. Christian umbrella organizations immediately reacted stating that this could and should not happen. Membe was sidelined during the 2015 election campaign. According to Said it is clear that "the government of Tanzania does not want to join OIC because it is its desire to weaken Muslims."[18]

Nationalizing and returning religious schools

Crucial in the whole debate is the issue of education.[19] When the Germans ruled the country, coastal people were preferred employees because many of them knew how to read and write, and they happened to be Muslims. When the British abandoned Arabic script and introduced Roman script Coastal Muslims who were employed by the German colonial Government became illiterates from one day to the next. The introduction of Roman script caused the number of Christian schools, which used this script, to grow much faster than the Muslim schools. Consequently there was a growing gap between Muslims and Christians in terms of education, and gradually Muslims became marginalized and second-class citizens in their own country.

Nyerere nationalized schools in 1969. This point is often used as an argument against the Muslim complaints about their marginalization.[20] However, Nyerere did not nationalize the Christian seminaries, and the majority of those who left the seminaries did not opt for the priesthood but instead took leadership positions in society, as well as in the government. After referring to the marginalization of Muslims during the colonial era, one interviewee said, "After independence, our independent government continued the problem of making us second class citizens when the government nationalized all schools. This was not so the case [for the Christians]. But it did nationalize all Muslim schools."

Since the liberalization era schools were given back, but more schools were given back to Christian organizations than to Muslim organizations. Various interviewees ask themselves, why this is so. The official reason is that Muslim organizations do not meet the conditions to run those schools properly. And the latter is confirmed by an interviewee in relation to his critique on BAKWATA: "Even today, if the government decides to return Zamzam to BAKWATA, it [BAKWATA] cannot manage it [Zamzam], in the way it [BAKWATA] is organized now."

Other interviewees perceive the government's reluctance to return the schools back to Muslims in the same pace as they were returned to Christians as a continuation of the government's oppression of Muslims, and as clear evidence that the government measures by double standards in dealing with religious affairs.

Several Muslim interviewees said that they were discriminated against because they were not able to receive funds from Middle Eastern countries, whereas Christian organizations receive funds from Western countries. As one of them says,

> This is what gives us a challenge and becomes an obstacle. You may get somebody from Saudi Arabia, you may get somebody from Pakistan, from . . . Indonesia, you reach agreement. But he [the donor] says sending this money is difficult. If he sends it, you often find that this money is retained without reaching the school. It does not reach the intended institution for no basic reason.

The interviewee continues,

> These are challenges we face. Therefore you find that we do not get donations. . . . Even we who are ready to receive those donations we fail to know how to follow them up. If you get the money, let's say, you have got one billion from outside, you are questioned about who sent the money, for what purpose, on what grounds, and as a result they are confiscated, and things like that. Let's say there is that element of saying these Muslim organizations are not clean.

When professor Kighoma Ali Malima became the Minister of Education in 1987 this was a break-through because this position had been held by Christians since independence. But, when he wanted to address the imbalance between Muslims and Christians in education, he was given another post.[21]

University enrolment and positions in government

Closely related to the issue of education is the issue of university enrolment and representation in the government. Prof. Malima had calculated that more than half of the students in primary schools were Muslim, but in secondary schools Muslim students were few. And less than one-fifth (18 percent) of the 1988–1989 and 1989–1990 student enrolment at the University of Dar es Salaam were Muslim. In the Ministry of Education, between 1961 and 1989 there were 31 Christian directors versus 6 Muslim directors, and 7 Christian commissioners versus 1 Muslim commissioner.[22]

Jumbe alleges that when it comes to primary school enrolment, 40 percent of all enrolments are Christians and 40 percent Muslims. But, Christians constitute 64 percent of secondary school enrolments and 86.1 percent of university enrolments, whereas for Muslims these figures are 35.6 percent and 13.9 percent, respectively.[23] This was confirmed by an interviewee who accused Nyerere of sabotage:

> Those were, what we [Muslims] are saying, tactics which he used because he tried to promote one [group] other and harm the other. Look for example at school results. When hundred pupils sit for exams, about ten pupils [Muslims] will continue [for further studies], but Christians will raise up perhaps to ninety or something. Now, a situation like this was showing us the selection; the way selection was done for the promotion [of Christians].

According to Jumbe Christians have been favored by the government not only in education, but also in receiving leadership positions. Quoting 1993 figures, he says that there were only 8 Muslims in the union government compared to 16 Christians; 8 district commissioners were Muslims compared to 113 Christians.[24] The same imbalance applies to leading positions in the Bank of Tanzania, the National Bank of Commerce, Postal and Telephone Services.

Some interviewees say that Kikwete restored the balance by bringing in Muslims while others say that he brought in "his friends" who happened to be Muslims. The same argument is used for Nyerere. Nyerere did not favor Christians. He surrounded himself with people who were loyal to him, many of whom happened to be Christian Catholics. According to another interviewee people are doubtful, even under the present one-year-old government of President John Magufuli, when it comes to the representation of Muslims and Christians in various government positions. The interviewee said,

> During the [2015 general] election, as I have observed, a mixture of people campaigned. It were Muslims and Christians in the campaign. That is how it was, the Tanzanian society as it is. When you see people doing

> campaign, all parties, also CCM [Chama Cha Mapinduzi], include Muslims and Christians. This is how it was. But after the election, the government that the president has formed is not seen to be representative of the image which we used to see during the campaign.

The interviewee continued,

> For example, if [there are] 8 Muslims out of 34 ministers, it means this government is not representative [of the society]. [In the newspaper] I saw the regional commissioners he [Magufuli] appointed recently. I think 5 out of 26 are Muslims; this is not representative. When you start providing that image of not being representative. . . . The society itself is a mixed one. [It exists] of Muslims and Christians and they are the ones we saw in the campaigns, and they are the ones who gave mandate to political parties. When by luck your party has won, but you have been forming a government which is not representative of the society, of the citizens, this means that the feedback to the citizens is not correct. That is one among other things that causes big doubt. Furthermore, when you look at the permanent secretaries, I have forgotten that data, it is also not well. It is not representative of that society itself. This is what I can say about this short time [of the incumbent government]. . . . It is something that can make us doubtful.[25]

The repetition (over-wording) of "not representative" shows strong preoccupation of the interviewee with the issue.[26]

One interviewee, who commented on this, argued that the imbalance would be best explained by the president himself by making public the criteria he used in selecting them. The interviewee said,

> Maybe the President would say that the big problem that causes this situation [few Muslim presidential appointees in the government] is that by very bad luck, there are no [Muslim] people who have the level of education we need in that post of minister. And if they are there, tell me who they are. . . . But this issue is difficult to explain because we do not believe that this is how it is, that in the Muslim society there are [only] people with very low capability.

Laws on blasphemy and terrorism

In the same vein, Muslims complain that comparatively there are far more Muslims in jail than Christians. Is this because Muslims are more criminal than Christians, or is it because of the prejudice against Muslims and of the unfair treatment by the policy and in court?[27] Muslims claim that the juridical system is a Christian system (Mfumo Kristo). It is easier to organize a

Crusade for Christ than a Muslim open air preaching, and when you say that "Jesus is not the Son of God" you are sent to jail but when you say that "Mohamed is not a prophet" you are not.[28]

Njozi starts his book with the Dibagula Case in which a Muslim called Hamisi Dibagula was sent to jail for 18 months because he had stated, "Jesus is not the son of God." According to the magistrate's court Dibagula deliberately intended "to wound the religious feelings" of Christians. In Dar es Salaam and other parts of the country Muslims openly protested on the streets.[29] Demonstrators were severely beaten by the police, and several of them were injured. The High Court summoned the case for review. It released Dibagula from jail because the sentence given was too high. Dibagula proceeded to the Court of Appeal which released him arguing that he was merely repeating what the Quran states.[30] Nevertheless, Muslims' suspicion against the juridical system was enforced. There are similar blasphemy cases against Christians, making fun of the Quran or the prophet Mohamed, but cases against Muslims are far more than those against Christians.

Muslims' detention in Tanzania and the Prevention of Terrorism Act 2000 have become a hot issues since Muslim advocates opened case no P/:29/2014 in High Court against the Tanzania Attorney General. Their main complaint is that 23 arrested Muslims, including four very respected sheikhs, namely Farid Had Ahmed, Msellem Aly Msellem, Nasoro Hamad Abdallah, and Abdallah Said Ally, are remanded in custody at Segerea for three years now on terrorist claims under the above mentioned Act, without trial. One interview states that law enforcement has double standards when it comes to the treatment of the religious leaders of Muslims and the Christians. He queries the arrest of Muslim leaders saying,

> Today Muslims are being arrested . . . Sheikhs . . . are sodomised! Honestly, is it possible for a bishop to be arrested, sodomized in prison, and we remain in peace in this country? . . . What I know is that they too have the right to be respected just as priests. . . . Our sheikhs are being mistreated.

The right to have Kadhi courts

The right of Muslims to have Kadhi courts became an issue during the 2005 general election campaign. Muslims threatened that they would vote for the opposition parties if their demand to be allowed to have Kadhi courts was not taken seriously by the CCM leadership. The ruling CCM Party promised Muslims that it would settle the issue if they were re-elected. At independence, the Tanzania Government honored the agreement between the Sultan of Zanzibar and the British Government which had given the Muslim community the right to have Kadhi Courts.[31] After the Union between Tanganyika and Zanzibar it was agreed that Zanzibar and a mainland coastal strip of ten miles were allowed to have Khadi courts. After the Arusha declaration this decision was reversed, except for civil cases between Muslim parties, because it was thought to endanger national unity.

The right to have Kadhi courts has become one of the main topics in the Islamic Revivalism and Muslims' complaints against the government. When this issue came up recently during the Constitution Review process, Christian umbrella organizations protested loudly, arguing that Tanzania is a secular country. Muslims from their side argue that Catholics have their religious courts. The Government's official reply is that Catholic tribunals are purely an internal religious affair, that they are not facilitated by the Government in any way, and that these courts remain within the national legislation.

In 2008 the then Minister of Finance, Mustaf Mkulo, included Kadhi courts in the national budget. But the parliament did not allow it, nor were Kadhi courts included in the proposal for a new constitution. Muslims were allowed to have Kadhi courts but they had to pay for these courts themselves. Some of our interviewees argued that Kadhi courts settle various disputes between the Muslim people and that they offer social services so they must be paid for by the Government.

The constitution review process

Apart from the powers allocated to the President, and to a much lesser extent the right for Muslims to have Kadhi courts, the Union became a major stumbling block in the constitution review process. The second draft, also called the "citizen's draft," proposed a three-tier government, after reviewing the input of the people's panels to the first draft.

The Constitution Review Act, whose terms of reference were debated a lot during the first rounds in 2011, said that after the second draft, which included the peoples' panels to the first draft, a Constituent Assembly (CA) would be set up as the official organ for debating and passing the Final Drafty Constitution, to be voted for in a Referendum.[32] However, the Constitution Review Act gave the President the power to appoint the members of the Constituent Assembly.

After chaotic deliberations the Constituent Assembly came up with the "Final Draft of the Proposed new Constitution," in which the three-tier government was abandoned and the two-tier government would remain in place. Many people saw in this the manipulative power of the CCM. The four main opposition parties decided to quit the process, and to unite as UKAWA (Umoja wa Katiba ya Wananchi) coalition. The wording is noteworthy here. The first draft, which was based on a collection of "raw," "untempered" opinions of the citizens, is commonly known as the "draft with the citizens views" (rasimu ya maoni ya wananchi). The second draft, with the opinions of the Commission on the citizens' views, is called the "Warioba draft" (rasimu ya Warioba) or "Citizen's draft" (rasimu ya Wananchi) by UKAWA.[33] The final draft, proposed by CCM, is commonly known as the "proposed draft" (rasimu pendekezwa).

The Referendum to vote for the "Final Draft" was to be held on April 25, exactly six months before the general elections, but was postponed until after the election. In his speech to mark the first year of his presidency which was on November 5, 2016, president Magufuli said that his government has taken over the remaining portion of the constitution review process and promised Tanzanians that he would continue with the draft issue. But, whereas he has been very active in making other electoral promises come true, it is still unclear how he is going to solve this issue.

The 2015 general election campaign

Implicitly the constitution review process that ended up with UKAWA quitting the process became an issue in the 2015 election campaign. Whereas the CCM sidelined candidates who had been critical of it and came up with a relatively unknown candidate, Dr. John Magufuli, UKAWA remained undecided. They announced that they would come up with a candidate the day after the CCM did, but it was officially postponed till July 25 because the chapter of CUF (Civic United Front), one of the opposition parties and UKAWA members, said that its General Assembly had to decide on the candidate.

The competition within UKAWA was between Dr. Willibrord Slaa of CHADEMA (Chama cha Demokrasia na Maendeleo) and Prof. Ibrahim Lipumba of CUF. Although united in their struggle for the "citizen's draft" and against the "proposed draft," they had quite different interests. Prof. Lipumba is a Muslim from Zanzibar. And although CUF formed a coalition with CCM in the Zanzibar government, they favored the three-tier government, officially not for religious but for socio-economic reasons. Dr. Slaa is a Catholic from the mainland, an ex-priest and previously secretary-general of TEC (Tanzania Episcopal Conference).

Interestingly, the two candidates that were most likely to compete, Dr. John Magufuli, and Dr. Willibrord Slaa were both Catholics from the mainland. However, Dr. Slaa resigned and UKAWA came up with one of the sidelined CCM candidates, Edward Lowassa. The rumor has it that Dr. Slaa resigned after his pastor told him he would never win the elections because he was divorced and his ex-wife had spread rumors about him. The reason Dr. Slaa gave himself was that he disagreed with the procedure that was used to allow Lowassa to become CHADEMA member and UKAWA presidential candidate, and that he was against Lowassa's candidacy because of his reputation of being corrupt. He could never accept Lowassa worthy of being a presidential candidate and therefore decided to leave the party.

Unofficial sources say that Dr. Slaa had won the 2005 general elections and conquered both Kikwete and Lipumba. The National Electoral Committee (NEC), whose chairperson is the president and CCM member, stopped counting the votes and declared Kikwete to be the new president. It is said that Dr. Slaa wanted to combat this decision but the Roman Catholic Church advised him against it in order to maintain harmony and peace in the country.

The Zanzibar crisis

In 2015, the Zanzibar Electoral Committee refused announcing the outcome of the election in Zanzibar due to observed "irregularities," and ordered a do-over. CUF rejected to participate in this, which brought the CCM candidate back to office with more than 91 percent of the votes. National and international observers said that the initial election was free and fair. Some of our interviewees claim that CUF, the main opposition party in Zanzibar, had won the election and that the ruling party, CCM, tried to compromise with them.

The same had happened in 2010. In that year, CCM and CUF formed a Government of National Unity, after a dispute about election results. In 2000 controversies over the Zanzibar elections caused "Tanzania's bloodiest political tragedy in recent history."[34] Thirty-one people were killed. For some of our interviewees the Zanzibar autonomy has become symbolic for the right of Muslims to decide for themselves.

With respect to the 2015 elections the official statement was that the Union Government had no say because elections are an internal Zanzibar affair. But it is common knowledge that behind the scenes the Government and the Party are involved, and that the issue has an international flavor to it. Because of the threat of Al Shabaab, described earlier, the Zanzibar Crisis was labeled as a "national security issue."

Summarizing the Muslim complaints given above, one interviewee says,

> The government does not listen to Muslims and is not ready to sit down with them to listen to their grievances. Muslims feel that they are being oppressed, that they are being denied their rights by the government. One of the main violations of rights is the government's refusal to sit down with Muslims, so as to listen to their demands. This has not happened thus far. That is the most important problem that has contributed to the government's relationship with the Muslim community to continue being stagnant.

To be more precise, this interviewee refers to the complaint that the Government only listens to the official or, in their own view, "supreme" Muslim umbrella organization, which are closely related to the ruling party, and not to the other Muslim organizations which are considered to be deviant.

Conclusions and discussion

From the above evidence that was given it is safe to conclude that the Tanzanian Government has tried to maintain unity and avoid conflict by silencing deviant and peripheral voices. Vice-President Aboud Jumbe and Finance

Minister Kighoma Ali Malima were fired. Decisions over OIC membership and Kadhi courts were reversed, Muslim activists such as Ponda issa Ponda were sent to jail and Hamza Njozi's book about the *Mwembechai Killings* (2000) was banned.[35] These strategies may have worked in the socialist era but no longer do so in the neoliberal era (Maghimbi 1992). Whereas the Tanzanian Government has adjusted to more freedom in the economic field it still has to address the issue of freedom in the political field. The demand for more autonomy and self-determination cannot be addressed without a change in the present governance climate.[36]

From a governance perspective, the neoliberal era is characterized by decentralized societies and absence of universally accepted values. Whereas the philosophy of national unity in Tanzania is still very strong, which may explain its relative stability during the past decades,[37] there are "seeds of conflict" which need to be addressed properly, otherwise national unity will be at risk.[38] However, unity is not the same as uniformity. The government has to accept that there are huge diversities within the country, and it has to accommodate these in its concept of unity. "Balancing" divisions is to be understood in terms of regulating, not controlling.

During the socialist era the government was the main producer of knowledge and it controlled the dissemination of knowledge through state controlled media. This is no longer the case. There is an abundance of civil society organizations and independent research institutes, and a variety of printed and digital media. But, the director of one of the anti-corruption websites, JamiiForums, was recently arrested because he did not want to release the names of people who reported corruption on the website. With respect to the issue of Islamic revivalism argued in favor of secularism.[39] However, the issue is not secularism or strict separation of religion and state, but neutrality, or the impartiality of the state towards religions. It is unrealistic to ask religious organizations to play a part in building a nation on the one hand, and not give them a voice in political affairs on the other. Public – private partnership (United Republic of Tanzania 1999) does not only assume that civil society organizations are instrumental in implementing decisions, but they are also involved in the process of decision-making itself.

The principle of separation of Church and state signifies that the state is neutral regarding religious issues, not that the state does not interfere in religion or that citizens may not organize themselves politically according to their religious backgrounds.[40] Interestingly, one of the complaints of Muslims is that the state is not neutral. According to them, the state favors Christians. Moreover, by abandoning EAMWS and putting BAKWATA in place, the Tanzanian Government was directly involved in religions affairs. It not only collaborated with a religious organization but moreover established one. Unlike the CCT (Christian Council of Tanzania), which is an independent and bottom up umbrella organization, BAKWATA is a state dependent and top-down organization. There are three modes of governance they are the mono-centric, the multi-centric, and the poly-centric one.[41] The Tanzania government thus far sticks to the mono-centric one. Although the Tanzania state abolished one-party politics, the ruling party CCM rules as if it is the only one. It has yet to include the principle of democratization of democracy which is not to rule by majority vote, but to include peripheral voices of minorities in the decision-making process. It may be questioned if one can rule a country whose population is overwhelmingly religious according to secular principles and if accepting for example Kadhi courts and OIC membership will endanger the neutrality of the state. Experiences in neighbouring countries show that it does not.[42] Political liberalism starts from the assumption that the secular view is universal, but it is as particular as any other view. In this sense, the neoliberal era is also a post-secular era.[43]

Notes

1 J. Kikwete, "Managing religious diversity in a democratic environment: the Tanzanian experience," Speech September 25 at Boston University, US (2006). Retrieved from http://ajabutv.com/tzpresident'sspeech.html
2 F. Wijsen and B. Mfumbusa, "Seeds of Conflict. Muslim-Christian Relations in Tanzania," in J. Gort, H. Jansen and H. Vroom, eds., *Religion, Conflict and Reconciliation. Multifaith Ideals and Realities.* (New York: Rodopi, 2002), 316–26. In 2001 I conducted a survey in Mwanza. I found that 58.9 percent of my respondents had witnessed religious tensions and that 77.6 percent thought that there would be more tensions in the future. See F. Wijsen, "Religionismin Tanzania," in A, Borsboom, F. Jespers, eds. *Identity and Religion.* (Saarbrücken: Verlag für Entwicklungspolitik, 2003), 121–37.
3 J. Ndaluka, S. Nyanto and F. Wijsen, "Things Are Getting Out of Control," "An Analysis of Muslim Revivalism Discourses in Tanzania," in T. Ndaluka, F. Wijsen, eds. *Religion and State in Tanzania Revisited.* (Münster: LIT Verlag, 2014), 61–80; M. Bakari and L. Ndumbaro, "Religion and Governance in Tanzania. The Post – Liberalisation Era," in R. Mukandala, S. Othman, S. Mushi and L. Ndumbaro, eds. *Justice Rights and Worship: Religion and Politics in Tanzania.* (Dar es Salaam: E&D Limited, 2006), 334–59.
4 J. Kikwete, 2006.
5 T. Martikainen and F. Gauthier, eds. *Religion in the Neoliberal Age: Political Economy and Modes of Governance.* (Farnham: Ashgate, 2013).
6 M. Bakari and L. Ndumbaro, 2006.
7 The interviews were conducted by Peter Mosha, lecturer in de Department of Philosophy and Religious Studies at the University of Dar es Salaam. I am grateful to him for allowing me to use the interviews and for reviewing the first draft of this paper.
8 N. Fairclough, *Discourse and Social Change.* (Cambridge: Polity Press, 1992).
9 M. Said, *The Life and Times of Abdulwahid Sykes (1924–1968). The Untold Story of the Muslim Struggle Against British Colonialism in Tanganyika.* (London: Minerva Press, 1998).
10 M. Said, 1998, 286.
11 Not only Said accuses Nyerere of silencing his opponents. Mwijage (1994, 63) writes, "The detention of government critics was order of the day under Nyerere."
12 M. Said, 1998, 307, 339, 315.
13 N. Fairclaugh, 1992, 193.

14 I. Shivji, *Pan-Africanism or Pragmatism. Lessons of the Tanganyika-Zanzibar Union.* (Dar es Salaam: Mkuki na Nyota Publishers, 2008).
15 J. Ndaluka, S. Nyanto and F. Wijsen, 2004, 72.
16 Said, M., 1998b, *Islamic Movement and Christian Hegemony. The Rise of Muslim Militancy in Tazania. Tanga.* www.asclibrary.nl/docs/337985022.pdf. (retrieved 15.10.16); H. Njozi, *Muslims and the State in Tanzania.* (Dar es Salaam: Dar es Salaam University Muslims Trusteeship, 2003).
17 Zanzibar is a semi-autonomous part of Tanzania. The two countries merged in 1964 as was explained before.
18 M. Said, "Islamic Movement and Christian Hegemony," 1998, 61.
19 M. Said, 1998, 72–80.
20 L. Mbogoni, *The Cross Versus the Crescent: Religion and Politics in Tanzania from the 1888s Top the 1990s.* (Dar es Salaam: Mkuki na Nyota Publishers, 2004).
21 M. Said, 1998, 76.
22 Ibid., 75.
23 A. Jumbe, *The Partnership. Tanganyika–Zanzibar Union. 30 Turbulent Years.* (Dar es Salaam: Amana Publisher, 1994), 22.
24 A. Jumbe, 1994, 123.
25 The figures are confirmed by Khalifa Khamis in Mizan newspaper, November 11, 2016, Pg 11, ISSN 0856–3241/No. 222. Khamis calculated that out of a total number of 726 presidential appointments in 2015–2016, 582 (80.2 percent) Christians were appointed and 144 (19.8 percent) Muslims.
26 Fairclaough, 1992, 193.
27 H. Njozi, *Mwembechai Killings and the Political Future of Tanzania.* (Ottawa: Globalink communications, 2000), 59–60.
28 H. Njozi, 2000, 78–85; A. Aziz, (1998). Submission to the Attorney General of Tanzania on the Mishandling of the issue of Muslim Preaching by the CCM Government, Dar es Salaam, May 15, 1998, (reprinted in Njozi 2000, 146–227).
29 H. Njozi, *Muslims and the State in Tanzania.* (Dar es Salaam: Dar es Salaam University Muslims Trusteeship, 2003).
30 M. Bakari and L. Ndumbaro, 2006, 348–9; R. Makaramba, "Religion, Rule of Law and Justice in Tanzania," in R. Mukandala, S. Othman, S. Mushi, and L. Ndumbaro, eds. *Justice Rights and Worship: Religion and Politics in Tanzania.* (Dar es Salaam: E&D Limited, 2006), 360–92.
31 R. Makaramba, 2006.
32 T. Maliyamkono, H. Mason andB. Rutinwa, eds. *A 100 Academics Search for Katiba Bora Tanzania.* (Dar es Salaam: Eastern and Southern African Universities Research Programme, 2014).
33 The draft was called after the chairman of the Commission, the former Prime Minister Joseph Warioba.
34 H. Njozi, 2003, 94.
35 H. Njozi, 2000.
36 M. Bakari and L. Ndumbaro, 2006, 347.
37 F. Wijsen and T. Ndulaka, 2012; T. Ndaluka, "Social Cohesion and Religious Intolerance in Tanzania," in R. Mukandala, ed. *The Political Economy of Change in Tanzania. Contestations Over Identity, Constitution and Resources.* (Dar es Salaam: Dar es Salaam University Press, 2015), 35–54.
38 F. Wijsen and B. Mfumbusa, 2002.
39 S. Maghimbi, "Secularisation and the Rise of Religious Fundamentalism in Tanzania," in T. Ndaluka, F. Wijsen, eds. *Religion and State in Tanzania Revisited.* (Münster: LIT Verlag, 2014), 181–96.
40 P. Norris and R. Inglehart *Sacred and Secular: Religions and Politics Worldwide.* (New York: Cambridge University Press, 2011).

41 T. Martikainen and F. Gauthier, eds. 2013.
42 D. Westerlund and C. Hallencreutz, *Questioning the Secular State: The World-wide Resurgence of Religion in Politics*. (London: Hurts and Company, 1996); M. Bakari and L. Ndumbaro, 2006), 348.
43 A. Molendijk, J. Beaumont and C. Jedan, eds. *Exploring the Postsecular*. (Leiden: Brill, 2010).

References

Aziz, A. (1998). Submission to the Attorney General of Tanzania on the Mishandling of the issue of Muslim Preaching by the CCM Government, Dar es Salaam, 15 May (reprinted in Njozi 2000, 146–227).

Bakari, M., and L. Ndumbaro. "Religion and Governance in Tanzania: The Post–Liberalisation Era." In *Justice Rights and Worship: Religion and Politics in Tanzania*, edited by R. Mukandala, S. Othman, S. Mushi, and L. Ndumbaro, 334–59. Dar es Salaam: E&D Limited, 2006.

Fairclough, N. *Discourse and Social Change*. Cambridge: Polity Press, 1992.

Jumbe, A. *The Partnership. Tanganyika–Zanzibar Union. 30 Turbulent Years*. Dar es Salaam: Amana Publisher, 1994.

Kikwete, J. Managing Religious Diversity in a Democratic Environment: The Tanzanian Experience, 2006. Speech September 25 at Boston University, USA. Retrieved from http://ajabutv.com/tzpresident'sspeech.html.

Maghimbi, S. "One-Party Aggrandisement and the Problems of Reorganising a Monolithic Political System: The Case of Tanzania." In *Multi-Party Democracy, Civil Society and Economic Transformation in Southern Africa*, edited by J. Hunter, and C. Lombard, 113–30. Windhoek: SAUSSC, 1992.

———. "Secularisation and the Rise of Religious Fundamentalism in Tanzania." In *Religion and State in Tanzania Revisited*, edited by T. Ndaluka, F. Wijsen, 181–196. Zürich–Münster: LIT Verlag, 2014.

Makaramba, R. "Religion, Rule of Law and Justice in Tanzania." In *Justice Rights and Worship: Religion and Politics in Tanzania*, edited by R. Mukandala, S. Othman, S. Mushi, and L. Ndumbaro, 360–92. Dar es Salaam: E&D Limited, 2006.

Maliyamkono, T., H. Mason, and B. Rutinwa, eds. *A 100 Academics Search for Katiba Bora Tanzania*. Dar es Salaam: Eastern and Southern African Universities Research Programme, 2014.

Martikainen, T., and F. Gauthier, eds. *Religion in the Neoliberal Age: Political Economy and Modes of Governance*. Farnham: Ashgate, 2013.

Mbogoni, L. *The Cross Versus the Crescent. Religion and Politics in Tanzania from the 1888s Top the 1990s*. Dar es Salaam: Mkuki na Nyota Publishers, 2004.

Molendijk, A., J. Beaumont, and C. Jedan, eds. *Exploring the Postsecular*. Leiden, Boston: Brill, 2010.

Mwijage, L. *The Dark Side of Nyerere's Legacy*. London: The Addelphi Press, 1994.

Ndaluka, J., S. Nyanto, and F. Wijsen. "'Things Are Getting Out of Control'. An Analysis of Muslim Revivalism Discourses in Tanzania." In *Religion and State in Tanzania Revisited*, edited by T. Ndaluka, and F. Wijsen, 61–80. Zürich, Münster: LIT Verlag, 2004.

Ndaluka, T. "Social Cohesion and Religious Intolerance in Tanzania." In *The political Economy of Change in Tanzania: Contestations Over Identity, Constitution and Resources*, edited by R. Mukandala, 35–54. Dar es Salaam: Dar es Slaaam University Press, 2015.

Njozi, H. *Mwembechai Killings and the Political Future of Tanzania*. Ottawa: Globalink Communications, 2000.

———. *Muslims and the State in Tanzania*. Dar es Salaam: Dar es Salaam University Muslims Trusteeship, 2003.

Norris, P., and R. Inglehart. *Sacred and Secular: Religions and Politics Worldwide*. New York: Cambridge University Press, 2011.

Said, M. *The Life and Times of Abdulwahid Sykes (1924–1968): The Untold Story of the Muslim Struggle against British Colonialism in Tanganyika*. London: Minerva Press, 1998a.

———. *Islamic Movement and Christian Hegemony. The Rise of Muslim Militancy in Tazania. Tanga*. (1998b). www.asclibrary.nl/docs/337985022.pdf (retrieved 15.10.16).

Shivji, I. *Pan-Africanism or Pragmatism. Lesseons of the Tanganyika-Zanzibar Union*. Dar es Salaam: Mkuki na Nyota Publishers, 2008.

United Republic of Tanzania. *The National Framework on Good Governance. President's Office, Good Governance Coordination Unit (GGCU)* (Dar es Salaam: Government Printer, 1999).

Westerlund, D., and C. Hallencreutz. *Questioning the Secular State: The Worldwide Resurgence of Religion in Politics*. London: Hurts and Company, 1996.

Wijsen, F. "Religionismin Tanzania." In *Identity and Religion*, edited by A. Borsboom, and F. Jespers, 121–37. Saarbrücken: Verlag für Entwicklungspolitik, 2003.

Wijsen, F., and B. Mfumbusa. "Seeds of Conflict: Muslim-Christian Relations in Tanzania." In *Religion, Conflict and Reconciliation: Multifaith Ideals and Realities*, edited by J. Gort, H. Jansen, and H. Vroom, 316–26. Amsterdam, New York: Editions Rodopi, 2002.

Wijsen, F., and T. Ndaluka. "Ujamaa Is Still Alive: A Sign of Hope for Africa?" In *Africa Is Not Destined to Die: Signs of Hope and Renewal*, edited by A. Bwangatto, 240–53. Nairobi: Paulines Publications, 2012.

Index